BOMBERS OVER BERLIN

BOMBERS
OVER
BERLIN

THE RAF OFFENSIVE
NOVEMBER 1943 - MARCH 1944

ALAN W. COOPER

Pen & Sword
AVIATION

First published in Great Britain in 1985 by
William Kimber & Co. Limited, 100 Jermyn Street, London, SW1Y 6EE
Published in paperback format in 2003
by Airlife Publishing Ltd, Shrewsbury

Re-printed in this format 2013 by
PEN & SWORD AVIATION
An imprint of
Pen & Sword Books Ltd
47 Church Street
Barnsley
South Yorkshire
S70 2AS

ISBN 978 1 78159 065 2

The r_____ ·hor
of this   with

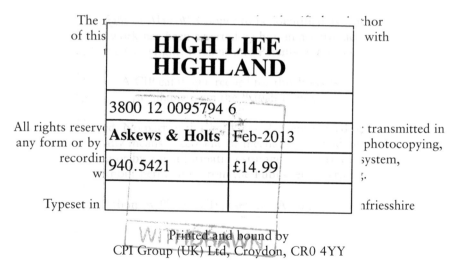

**HIGH LIFE
HIGHLAND**

3800 12 0095794 6

Askews & Holts	Feb-2013
940.5421	£14.99

All rights reserv___   · transmitted in
any form or by   photocopying,
recordin___   system,
w___

Typeset in   ifriesshire

Printed and bound by
CPI Group (UK) Ltd, Croydon, CR0 4YY

Pen & Sword Books Ltd incorporates the Imprints of Pen & Sword Aviation,
Pen & Sword Family History, Pen & Sword Maritime, Pen & Sword Military,
Pen & Sword Discovery, Pen & Sword Politics, Pen & Sword Archaeology,
Pen & Sword Atlas, Wharncliffe Local History, Wharncliffe True Crime,
Wharncliffe Transport, Pen & Sword Select, Pen & Sword Military Classics,
Leo Cooper, The Praetorian Press, Claymore Press, Remember When,
Seaforth Publishing and Frontline Publishing

For a complete list of Pen & Sword titles please contact
PEN & SWORD BOOKS LIMITED
47 Church Street, Barnsley, South Yorkshire, S70 2AS, England
E-mail: enquiries@pen-and-sword.co.uk
Website: www.pen-and-sword.co.uk

Contents

List of Illustrations

Line Illustrations

The diagrams are reproduced with permission from documents held at the Public Record Office.

Acknowledgements

To enable me to write this book, I have had to rely on many people and organisations, and to the following I offer my grateful thanks:

M.J. Allen, Ralph Barker, Len Barnes, Les Bartlett DFM, Ken Bate, T. Beckett, Marshal of the Royal Air Force Sir Michael Beetham GCB, CBE, DFC, AFC, Air Marshal D.C.T. Bennett CB, CBE, DSO, Steve Bethell, Robert Boots, O. Brooks DFC, C. Bryant, Alan Bryett, W/C G. Cairns, E. Cole, A. Cordon, H. Coverley, A. Crowley-Smith, Hal Croxson, Ernie Cummings DFM, Reg Davey, Jim Davis, Albert Dicken DFC, Norman Digwell, John Douglas, B. Downs, B.S. Downs, Eddie Edmunds DFC, Eddy Edwards, M.M. Emery, John Evans (for his great help with photographs), Chris Evett, G. Fairless, Jimmy Flynn, John Flynn, Alan Forsdike, Michael Foster DFC, R. Gardner, John Grett, Fred Hall, Jack Hambling DFC, Roland Hammersley DFM, Marshal of the Royal Air Force Sir Arthur Harris Bt GCB, OBE, AFC, LLD, R. Hartley DFC, Albert Hepworth, Bill Howarth DFM, A. Hughes, Mrs. Olivia Hughes (Pathfinder Association), Jimmy Hughes DFM, C. Hutchinson, Ron James, Dan Kelsh, Mrs. Noreen King, Nick Knilans DSO, DFC, Arthur Lee, Basil Leigh DFC, Norman Ling, Alf Lorimer, H. Mackinnon, Group Captain Hamish Mahaddie DSO, DFC, AFC, Ken Maun, John McDougall, J. McQuillan DFC, Martin Middlebrook, Bernard Moorcroft DSO, DFC, Reg Moore DFM, Peter Moran, E. Mulholland, Eric Nelson DFC, J.E. Nicholas, W. Ogilvie, William Parker DFC, Harry Pitcher DFM and Mrs Pitcher, Harry Prendergast, Alf Price, Syd Proctor, John Remmington, Gordon Ritchie DFC, Owen Roberts MBE, Bill Rust, A.J. Smith, J.R. Spark DFM, Norman Storey DFM, Arthur Tindall, Derek Tulloch DFC, DFM, John Tyler, Danny Walker DFC*, Syd Waller, Donald Westerman, W/C Stephen Whetham DSO, DFC, Ian Willsher, H.D. Wood.

Last, but not least, my thanks to Horst Muller for all his great support, Norman Franks for his help in the presentation of this book and to all the members of the staff of William Kimber & Co.

CHAPTER ONE

Target Berlin

Berlin. The Big City. 'Big B.' Whatever the Royal Air Force or American Air Force called it during the Second World War, it was an awe-inspiring target. In their minds the mere mention of Berlin conjured up a myriad of thoughts and fears. Some targets did that. Hamburg, the Ruhr Valley, Frankfurt, Hannover – Berlin …

For one thing, it was a long way away, deep inside Germany. So deep that to reach it and get back while it was still dark, attacks could only really be mounted during the winter when the nights were long. The RAF bombers knew from experience for they had been there before. It was the German capital, the very heart of the Nazi Germany they were fighting. As such it was well protected: flak, searchlights, and enemy night-fighters defended it tooth and nail. It was no 'Milk Run', no easy trip to add to one's tour of operations. To have flown to Berlin, and more importantly, to have got back, meant something. Something to tell the folks at home, perhaps to feel good about, it looked impressive in the log book, nice to drop into the conversation with a girl friend. Once done, the tour could continue with other targets, perhaps no less dangerous, but certainly less heart-stopping when the curtain that covered the map of Germany in the briefing room was pulled aside.

Yet in the winter of 1943-44, RAF Bomber Command went to Berlin on no less than sixteen occasions. Between November 1943 and March 1944, the curtains were swept back to reveal the red ribbon reaching out from home base to Berlin sixteen times. Many bomber crews who were just starting, were mid-way, or even nearing the end of their tours had to add Berlin to their log books almost repeatedly. Many others did not. They did not get home. They 'failed to return', were 'missing from air operations over Germany' or just 'missing' – which could mean they were dead, prisoners of war and even wounded, or bobbing about in a rubber dinghy in the deadly cold North Sea awaiting rescue or chilling death.

There were other targets too, of course. It was not Berlin night after night, but it was on sixteen nights. This is the story of those nights when the heart stopped a beat – for it was: *Target Berlin*.

*

Berlin was a large target, 339 square miles. Including its suburbs it was 883 square miles. It was the seat of the German government as well as an important industrial city. In 1924, fifteen years before the war, it already had nearly 300,000 business concerns, employing over 700,000 people. Of these 60% were located in the six central districts of Berlin. Nine years later, with a population of 4,242,500, its built-up administration area covered 221,000 acres. Houses, factories and yards covered 43,600 acres, streets and railways another 25,000 acres, while open spaces, gardens, cemeteries and parks accounted for a further 10,500 acres.

It was a sprawling city with wide streets. A chain of lakes with the River Spree running through the city centre helped the flow of industrial output and brought raw materials to the factories, as Hitler's new regime brought life and work to a Germany crushed by World War One. The largest lake was the Wannsee – a landmark for future air raiders – and this, with the others, was formed by the Havel River on the western outskirts. By the end of the 1930s Berlin had one of the finest subway systems in Europe, consisting of 92 stations and 46.6 miles of track.

Its industries were, in the main, textiles, iron and steelworks, rail cars, sewing machines, chemicals, china, breweries and machine works. After the war began, and Berlin went into top gear, its factories were producing one tenth of the Luftwaffe's aero engines and precision instruments; one third of Germany's electrical output, one quarter of the army's tanks and one half of its field artillery. Berlin was a political target, but nevertheless, an important industrial one too.

Its importance was evident by 1938 when thoughts of a future war were in the air. Wing Commander R.V. Goddard at the Air Ministry, asked the Air Attaché at the British Embassy in Berlin, what the reaction might be of the German people to an air bombardment in the event of war. Unfortunately the answers were not very conclusive but this shows the mode of thinking at that time – that a future air bombardment might be an eventuality.

The two largest concerns were Siemens (they still make a very good radio) and the AEG Company, producing electric cables and submarine motors. Another concern, Lorenz, made vital wireless transmitter equipment, while Alkett was the largest single tank factory in Germany. There were famous aircraft factories too, BMW, Dornier, Heinkel and Focke Wulf. Rheinmetal Borsig produced guns, Argus made aero engines, Deutsche Solvay Werke its chemicals. Most of these were in the outer part of the city, outside the Ringbahn, along the water and railway routes.

Another important target was the communications and traffic. Berlin, like all great cities, imported food stuffs and raw materials and also exported valuable manufacturing goods. This amounted to an annual average of about 30 million tons, of which 80% was inward traffic (coal, lignite, manures and chemicals). Of this two-thirds went by rail, one-third by water on the inward journey, four-fifths rail, one-fifth water on the outward routes.

In addition to its industrial might, Berlin was the entire centre of administrative and economic life. The German Air Ministry, built in 1935-6, was bounded on the north by Leipzigerstrasse and on the east by Wilhelmstrasse and the south by Prinz-Albrecht Strasse. On the western side was the building of the former Prussian House of Representatives, but by 1943 this housed the Aero Club. The site of the ministry covered 400,000 square feet, 250,000 of which was the building itself. It had, 2,800 rooms and offices, 4,000 staff and had extensive bomb and gas proofing.

Four other important buildings were those of the German Foreign Office, the Ministry of Propaganda, The Reich Presidential Chancellory, and the Headquarters building of the Gestapo.

The city's suburban area lay far outside Berlin, built up between 1923 snd 1943, and was not unlike London's suburbs. There were villas, single family houses either detached, semi-detached or in terraced rows. Like many large cities, blocks of flats were common, either two or three storied, and separated from each other by great areas of forests and lakes.

*

When war came in 1939, the British and the Germans were very careful not to bomb each other's towns and cities, although the Germans had no such qualms about Warsaw and other Polish cities. Hermann Göring, commander of the Luftwaffe, even boasted that no enemy aeroplanes would fly over Reich territory – an unfortunate prediction in the light of future history. The RAF were not only over Germany but over Berlin very early in the war. The first RAF squadron over the city was No 10 Squadron in September and October 1939, though they carried nothing more deadly than propaganda leaflets. Only three of the four that set off actually reached Berlin; the fourth dropped its load over Denmark and then failed to return to base.

Up to August 1940, Berliners suffered many air raid warnings but no bombs were ever dropped. At this time, the German defences were limited, but reserves were being drafted in, including 29 heavy, 14 medium and some light AA batteries, as well as four railway flak units, plus two night fighter staffels.

Finally, on 23/24th August 1940, during the Battle of Britain, Luftwaffe bombs fell on London. After a day of fighting, Luftwaffe aircraft flew a night raid towards the oil storage tanks at Thameshaven – which they missed – but bombs fell in the East End of London. It was nothing of great import but the gauntlet had been thrown down and Churchill took up the challenge. A retaliatory raid was arranged for the night of 24/25th August, but because of cloud, to say nothing of Bomber Command's lack of sophisticated navigational aids, of the 96 aircraft from 3, 4 and 5 Groups despatched, only 81 got off, and of these only 29 reached Berlin. Of the others, 21 turned back being unable to find Berlin, but eighteen of these bombed secondary targets. In all six aircraft failed to return, three ditched in the sea and two were damaged. The force was all made up of twin-engined aircraft (the later four-engined bombers were still in the design stages) such as Wellington, Whitley and Hampden bombers. It had been a 580 mile trip to Berlin, and in the 20 mph cross wind encountered, a bomber could be thrown off course by as much as 66 miles.

A total of 22 tons of bombs had been dropped, a number of bombs having delay time fuses, and a large part of the German business area and private houses was affected. On their return, the bomber crews reported heavy defences over Berlin, and a need to avoid flak and searchlights.

As the war escalated, further raids took place in September against both London and Berlin, which changed the whole course of the war. Hitler, angry at the bombing of Berlin, ordered a change of emphasis in the air war against England, ordering Göring to bomb London and not RAF Fighter Command's airfields. In so doing he lost the Battle of Britain. On 7th September the Luftwaffe sent 272 bombers against London. On the 15th, now known as Battle of Britain Day, four RAF bombers, two each from 58 and 77 Squadrons, were over Berlin – but at night. As the Battle of Britain ended and the Blitz began, Londoners began to learn how to 'take it' and other cities further north and in the south and south-west were bombed, such as Portsmouth, Exeter and of course Coventry in November.

The RAF raided Berlin 30 times in 1940 but only seventeen raids were sent in 1941. One of the latter, in March, occurred when the Japanese Minister of Foreign Affairs was visiting Berlin. It was known that he had taken the growing might of the RAF with a grain of salt, so Bomber Command was happy to show him just how strong, hoping the raid would, for him, prove salutary. The Chief of the Air Staff, Air Chief Marshal Sir Charles Portal, gave the instructions for the raid to be laid on during the Minister's visit, which took place on the night of 23/24th March. Sixty-three bombers of 1, 3, and 4 Groups took part.

In October, the American Air Attaché in Berlin sent back reports of the raids on the German capital. Damage had so far been light, casualties amounted to about 1,200, but the bombing had not been indiscriminate. Boldness, courage and determination of the RAF crews had been praised by the population, and the crews were obviously continuing to look for their specific targets and were not letting flak deter them.

In 1942, Air Marshal A.T. Harris, took command of Bomber Command, a post he was to retain until the end of the war. In the autumn of that year, Harris was urged to attack Berlin in strength, but having only 70 to 80 of the relatively new four-engined Avro Lancasters in his command, the task was impossible.

On 17th August, Winston Churchill sent a letter to the Secretary of State for Air, Sir Archibald Sinclair, stating that the Russian leader, Stalin, attached special importance to the bombing of Berlin. Stalin had said that they themselves were going to start bombing the city shortly – they had bombed it twice previously, on 7th and 8th of August 1941, six weeks after the German invasion of Russia.

In reply to Churchill, the Secretary of State said:

… during the next moon period, attacks could be made but our maximum strength of aircraft [of all types – Author] was 250 and that we consider the minimum number to be 500, necessary to saturate the defences and give a chance of effective damage and an acceptable rate of casualties of about 50 with such a force. If we started a bombing campaign on Berlin with less than 500, and suffered an anticipated rate of casualties of 50, our bombing effort would be crippled for a month. We are of course keen to meet the wishes of the Soviet Government in this project, but unless reasons of major policy necessitate early attacks regardless of cost, we would propose to wait until a larger force can be used.

Churchill replied:

... 250 far exceeds weight and numbers of any previous attacks on Berlin. What date will 500 be possible? ... I had always understood darkness was the limiting factor, not numbers. Certainly no attack should be made regardless of cost, but Harris mentioned an attack in the August moon period. Can you do it in September?

To this Portal, as CAS, replied on the 20th:

... number of aircraft and not hours of darkness is the limiting factor. In September we could have 300 aircraft, but neither Harris or myself is in favour of an attack in September.

On the 29th, Harris sent a letter to the CAS in which he said:

... I'm as keen as anybody to bomb Berlin, but I am certain when we do this, we must make a good job of it. The facts are as follows:
1. Numerous reports indicate that Berlin is well defended by flak and searchlights and there is also in existence a very elaborate system of decoys.
2. Berlin is a city of four million inhabitants, which is five times as big as Cologne, and 1,000 heavy bombers would not be too many (the number which in fact attacked Cologne in 1942) if we are to inflict serious and impressive damage on it.
3. The attack should be sustained. One isolated attack would do more harm than good and would, like Dieppe, play into the hands of enemy propaganda.

*

It was not, therefore, following this exchange, until 16th January 1943 that another attack was mounted on the Big City. It is of interest that this was the first time a war correspondent went on a bombing raid with the RAF. The correspondent was Richard

Dimbleby, his pilot Wing Commander Guy Gibson DSO DFC, then CO of 106 Squadron. (Gibson was later to win the Victoria Cross leading 617 Squadron on their famous Dams Raid in May 1943.) Another future VC winner who flew on this Berlin raid was Wing Commander Leonard Cheshire DSO DFC, who had flown on six previous Berlin raids. On the 16th he found it easier, reporting:

> ... instead of the customary wall of anti-aircraft fire we saw only one small searchlight and flak was negligible. Identification was made difficult by cloud all the way across Germany, but clear patches over the city allowed the moon to combine with the flares in lighting up the place.

The attack lasted about an hour and 8,000 lb bombs were among the bombs dropped. Large fires were seen after the raid and only one aircraft was lost. The attack was resumed the following night, again with large bombs and good results were seen. However, losses were considerably more, 22 in all, but of course, this is the up and down nature of night bombing. It seemed that many more night fighters were to be seen and the flak was much heavier. Many guns seemed to have been rushed in following the previous night's attack.

Berlin had woken up to the fact that they could be attacked and that the British had not given up. If you awaken a lion it may take a while for him fully to come to, but when he is, take warning – his attack can be formidable!

*

Following the Casablanca Conference in January 1943, a directive was issued to Harris instructing him that his primary objective should be 'the progressive destruction and dislocation of the German military, industrial and economic system, and the undermining of the morale of the German people to a point where their capacity for armed resistance is fatally weakened. Accordingly in order of importance the targets should be German submarine construction yards, the aircraft industry, transportation, oil plants, other targets in war industry.' With his eyes set firmly on bombing of German cities, this would not have been in accord with Harris's own thinking, but the directive went on to add 'moreover other objectives of great importance either from the political or military point of view must be attacked. Examples of this are ...' And the second example was Berlin 'which should be attacked when conditions are suitable for the attainment of specially valuable results unfavourable to the morale of the enemy or favourable to that of Russia.'

By January 1943, Germany had 4,491 heavy AA guns, 6,456 medium and light guns, 3,330 searchlights and 1,680 balloons, to meet the challenge of the RAF night raids and the growing might of the American 8th Air Force in England flying daylight raids.

Before the next Main Force attack on Berlin was executed, Mosquito aircraft made their first daylight raid on the city. This was on 30th January, and was as much a propaganda effort as anything else, the date being the tenth anniversary of Hitler's assumption of power as German Chancellor. Also it warned Berliners that they were now no longer safe from daylight attacks.

The Mosquitos returned to Berlin that same afternoon. It was also Luftwaffe Day in Berlin. On the morning raid, three Mosquitos of 105 Squadron from 2 Group, led by Squadron Leader R.W. Reynolds with his navigator Pilot Officer E.B. Sismore, hit Berlin at exactly 11 am just as Göring was about to speak on the radio. They dropped two tons of bombs in a long stick to the north-east and west of the city, and as a result, the speech was delayed by one hour, the radio announcer having to make excuses for the delay. The 'Mossies' met no opposition from the AA defences; either their arrival was too much of a surprise or the gunners had been stood down for the celebrations.

At 4 pm Doctor Goebbels, the Propaganda Minister, was about to speak on the radio when three Mosquitos of 139 Squadron, led by Squadron Leader D. Darling, dropped three tons of bombs about a mile south of the city centre. However, the defences were alert this time and Donald Darling, who came from London, aged 24, was shot down and killed.

*

On 16th February 1943, Arthur Harris received a message from the CAS which read: 'Recent events on the Russian front have made it most desirable, in the opinion of the Cabinet, that we should rub in the Russian victory by further attacks on Berlin.' Harris was asked to 'act accordingly'.

It was, however, two weeks before the next attack could be arranged – 1st March – and was the first time the new H_2S (a radar navigation and blind-bombing aid) was used against Berlin. The H_2S operators reported that the responses from the built-up areas entirely filled the radar screen, making it impossible to recognise the aiming points. Most of the bombing was centred on the south eastern outskirts, where heavy damage to industrial plants, business and residential properties was revealed by photo reconnaissance.

Wing Commander Hamish Mahaddie DSO DFC AFC, of 7 Squadron, recalled: 'It was an excellent trip; the marking undershot but despite this, Berlin was suffering a heavy attack.' In his log book he noted a signal that Harris had sent to all crews:

Tonight you go to the Big City. You have an opportunity to light a fire in the belly of the enemy and burn his Black Heart out.

Mahaddie, soon to be promoted to group captain, became the recruiting officer for the Path Finder Force.

On 3rd March, Stalin sent a message by personal telegram to Churchill:

I welcome the British Air Force, which yesterday so successfully bombed Berlin. I regret that the Soviet Air Force, absorbed in the struggle against the Germans at the front, is not yet in a position to take part in the bombing of Berlin.

In the event, and despite earlier promises to join in, the Russians never did join a campaign against the German capital.

Two further attacks were carried out in March, on the 27th and 29th. On the latter, the H$_2$S aircraft of the Pathfinders achieved a remarkably good grouping around the aiming point. During these March attacks the crews had to contend with hail, rain, electric storms and the dreaded icing, in addition to searchlights, flak, and on the 29th, night fighters. Weather over northern Europe is traditionally bad in the winter months, and often high winds caused major problems. Prior to March 1943, the upper winds were estimated by the London Met Office, given to Bomber Command HQ and passed to each Group HQ.

In the early part of 1943, it was decided that it would be better for all crews to be given the same wind information even if it had an appreciable error, than for some to receive one wind from their group while other groups issued other wind strengths to their squadrons. It was felt better for all aircraft to arrive together, rather than some to arrive at the exact zero hour while others arrived later.

✻

As 1943 progressed, Bomber Command became stronger, and techniques of navigation and target marking were improving all the time. Hamburg was attacked on four occasions by Bomber Command between 24th July and 3rd August, plus two daylight raids by the Americans. The city was virtually destroyed and in one night alone 40,000 people were killed in a terrible firestorm. It was as great a success as the Command was to achieve, and naturally put fear into the hearts of the German leaders, that if it could happen to Hamburg, it could happen to any of their major cities.

By mid-August, Harris was being pressed for a date on which he thought heavy attacks could begin on Berlin, on the lines of the Hamburg raids. Harris's reply was that he intended to initiate operations as soon as possible, and when the present moon had waned. He estimated a total of 40,000 tons of bombs would be required if the Hamburg scale of attack was to be applied, but that the operation would be of a long term nature since it would be necessary to shift attacks intermittently to other major targets, so as to prevent an undue concentration of enemy defences around Berlin.

As a result of the attack in the spring against the Ruhr, the Luftwaffe defences were being reviewed. The night fighter zone in the west was to be increased in depth and extended to Denmark in the north and to eastern France in the south. Operational control was to be developed whereby two or more night fighters could be brought into action in any one night fighter area at the same time. Also, bombers would have to be attacked over the target which up till now was usually left to the flak gunners. The flak has to be consolidated into large batteries near the targets and concentrated at the most important of these targets. Above all, its accuracy had to be raised by the introduction of a large number of radar range finders. As a result of a suggestion by Major Hajo Herrmann – a former bomber pilot – single-engined day fighters were beginning to be used over Germany. First tried in July, their success in attacking RAF bombers was such that Herrmann was given the task of organising these operations on a larger scale. Termed *Helle Nachtjagd* at first, it later became more famous under its later name of *Wilde Sau* – Wild Sow. It all called for close co-operation by the night fighters and the flak over the target and a dependable control of single-engined fighters over a wide area. For this purpose the flak, in co-operation with the night-fighters, was limited in its range height. Co-operation was achieved by visual signals and by radio. A sort of aerial flarepath to guide the fighters and a system of radio beacons were also established, around which night fighters could orbit until given a radar contact to follow from ground controllers. Once near the RAF bomber, the twin-engined night fighter radar crew member would be able to pick up the raider on his own airborne radar set and guide his pilot to it.

The flak in the Ruhr Valley was approximately doubled by bringing in all the reserves including all railway flak guns. They were consolidated into *grossen Batterien* (large batteries) – two or three single batteries joined together, which was later increased to six and eventually to eight. In order to nullify the RAF's flare and marker dropping by the Pathfinders, lighting media (flare rockets) were developed and used in conjunction with searchlights and dummy fires and other decoys were set up on the ground.

The first attack in August on Berlin was on the 23rd and it was by far the biggest assault – 1,700 tons being dropped in 50 minutes. Smoke belched up, sometimes obscuring the fires, then shifted away to reveal burning streets and buildings.

On the arrival of the bombers, German fighters were sent up, which in turn limited the range of the flak to 5,000 metres, above which the fighters operated. In consequence the guns around Berlin seemed comparatively quiet and the defence left mainly to the fighters. The Germans used their new flare rockets, fired off by the gun batteries. The Luftwaffe pilots could see the silhouettes of the bombers moving across the sky. Field Marshal Erhard Milch, State Secretary of the German Air Ministry and Armaments Chief of the Luftwaffe, described it as in these terms: 'It is like a fly on a tablecloth.'

Of the 720 bombers despatched, 625 bombed Berlin, but 56 failed to return, a high loss ratio of 9.1%, too high to be sustained for long.

One pilot remembers that night: an American, Flying Officer Bill Day, flying R-Robert of 90 Squadron. It was the crew's thirteenth trip and they were happy that cloud most of the way limited the Germans' defences against them. Then about 60 miles from Berlin it started to ice up. Day took it down to 7,000 feet and just before they reached the city the sky became completely clear and they were welcomed by hundreds of searchlights but no flak – a sure sign fighters were up.

They made their way to the aiming point, dropped their incendiaries on the Target Indicators (TI's) dropped by the

Pathfinders, then put the nose down and headed for home. Just then a master searchlight hit them spot on. Within seconds they were coned by 50 others. Bill Day did his utmost to escape but it was impossible, and if the flak had been used they would not have survived. Suddenly they got a 'Boozer' warning – which was a light in the aircraft which came on to warn the crew that a fighter was near them, set off by radar. Moments later a Focke Wulf 190 attacked from the rear, opened fire from about 500 yards, closing in to 100. By this time, Day had corkscrewed the aircraft, a defensive manoeuvre whereby the pilot went into a steep diving turn, and at the bottom of the dive he pulled up vertically. It was very unpleasant but in the main very effective.

Sergeant Mitchinson, the rear gunner, got in a good burst at the fighter which exploded, but then two more 190s were spotted, one on the port and another on the starboard quarter. The bomber was obviously 'the fly on the tablecloth!' The fighter on the port side was slightly below them and the mid-upper gunner, Sergeant Jimmy James, was unable to bring his guns to bear. The German pilot then came in very close and fired into the bomber's port wing, knocking out the inner engine, which put the upper turret out of action, its power coming from that engine.

They were now in a steep dive and a strong smell of burning was coming from the fuselage. To Jimmy James it seemed like the end. His life was flashing before him, he thought of his mother and girlfriend, then suddenly it was as if he had passed through a barrier, his mind floating away from his body. He thought, if this is death, how wonderful.

Eventually Bill Day managed to pull the aircraft out of the dive, flying now low over the outskirts of Berlin, heading for the Baltic. He checked the crew but only the wireless operator, Jimmy Fenn, had stopped a few cannon fragments in his leg, though he was not badly hurt. The aircraft was in a sorry state. Besides the port inner engine and upper turret, most of the cockpit instruments were useless, the bombing compartment was smashed; there were holes in the airframe and fuel several inches deep swilled about in the fuselage. They were lucky they had not caught fire.

By careful economy of the remaining fuel they made landfall in England. Putting out a May-Day call they were told to make for base but knew they could not make it. Just then they saw a row of lights in front of them which turned out to be Bodney, Norfolk, the home of an American Thunderbolt unit who had only moved in that day.

The control tower was being manned by a Private First Class, who did not know the system so switched on everything he could find, hence the row of lights Day saw.

His landing was a bad one and the rear gunner Mitchinson was knocked out. Day had got down, however, and by coincidence the first American that he saw on climbing down from the aircraft was a friend he had last seen before leaving Canada to join the RAF; his friend had joined the USAAF and was now flying P47s. Bill Day received an immediate award of the DFC, Mitchinson the DFM. Luck remained with the crew, for they all finished their tour, and five went on to complete a second tour. Two of them, Jimmy James and Don Beaton, the bomb aimer, volunteered for a third tour but were turned down and given ground jobs. It was deemed they had done enough.

One Lancaster bomber on that 23rd August raid was attacked by six Messerschmitt 109s in the space of three minutes, during which it was damaged quite badly; but despite loss of fuel, they managed to get back to base, landing with just 80 gallons left. The only real grouse from the crew was that Jerry had upset and ruined their bombing point photograph!

A further raid on Berlin was made on the 25th and again on the 31st. On this, the flarepath type of defensive measure was introduced. It was a great surprise to the bomber crews to find their tracks illuminated by flares. They were described as bright white lights, which slowly descended as if on parachutes. They were dropped in lines of about a dozen and made lanes of light which the bombers had to go through.

On 3rd September came the last attack before what was later called the Battle of Berlin began. The weather on this occasion was on the side of Bomber Command, with cloud up to 21,000 feet which gave uninterrupted cover, dampened the flak and hampered the fighters. On the fringe of the city, the cloud broke up, leaving a clear space and as if arranged, as the attack concluded, the cloud drifted back over the city. Some aircraft had combats with fighters, and one was seen going down in flames with its rear gunner still blazing away.

On this operation, history was being recorded in Lancaster ED586 'F' of 207 Squadron, piloted by Flight Lieutenant Letford. On board was Wynford Vaughan-Thomas, the famous broadcaster and now war correspondent for the BBC. He, with the help of Mr Pidsley, also of the BBC, made a recording of the flight, covering the complete operation from take off to landing. They were engaged by a night fighter too, but the gunners, Warrant Officer Fieldhouse and Sergeant Devenish, shot it down.

The disc made of the sortie was rushed to London and broadcast the same day on the ten o'clock news. In all it was broadcast nine times in English and on numerous European and foreign programmes as well as the American network. It was described as 'the outstanding broadcast of the war'. Forty years later when Vaughan-Thomas was asked for his most vivid memory of the war while being a correspondent, he said it was this raid on Berlin that he remembered most.

*

On 3rd November, Arthur Harris sent a memorandum to the Prime Minister saying that the highest priority should be given to Berlin:

> ... But I would not propose to wait for ever, or for long if the opportunity serves. We can wreck Berlin from end to end if the USA will come in on it. It will cost between us 400-500 aircraft. It will cost Germany the war.

However, he was not given full support by the Americans – they had just been severely mauled in their second assault on Schweinfurt on 14th October, losing 60 four-engined bombers. (They had lost 60 on the first Schweinfurt-Regensburg raid in August.) Nor was Harris supported by his immediate superiors. The final conclusion, approved by the CAS, was that Harris should, when he saw fit and when suitable occasions when weather and other tactical conditions gave the most favourable chance, attack Berlin. He should not plan for a sustained and costly series of assault, or rely on assistance from the 8th Air Force.

On the same 3rd November, Harris also reacted strongly against any information being given to the Russians as to when his bombers had taken off to attack Berlin. His reasons were strictly ones for security as to be successful in any sustained attack, tactics of feints and diversions would have to be made, and any transmissions to the Russians by simple codes, might well imperil the security of subsequent missions.

(*Right*) Flight Lieutenant Letford

(*Below*) Air Chief Marshal Sir Arthur Harris and Lady Harris

CHAPTER TWO

The Battle Begins

The Battle of Berlin officially began on Thursday, 18th November 1943, although some former aircrew members feel it had begun in September. Either way it matters little. Over the next four months the all-out attacks on the Big City were to be a fierce and bitterly fought campaign.

The First Raid

Raid number one was to be a two-target operation. A force of 440 Lancasters and four Mosquitos were detailed to take part, while at the same time 395 aircraft, mostly Halifaxes and Stirlings, were to bomb Mannheim. In addition, Mosquitos were to make harassing attacks on Essen, Frankfurt and Aachen. Over the latter target, route markers were also dropped for the two Main bomber streams making for Berlin and Mannheim.

At part of the plan and to try and keep the enemy fighters busy, a force of seven Wellingtons would drop leaflets over Northern France, a duty shared by a small force of American Flying Fortresses. Meanwhile, under the cover of the bomber streams, 32 sea mines would be dropped off the Dutch coast and French Atlantic ports by sixteen Wellington aircraft.

At the time of this first raid, Bomber Command had some 513 Lancasters, 271 Halifaxes, 137 Stirlings, 23 Wellingtons, and 46 Mosquitos available. The force for this raid comprised:

1 Group	–	153 Lancasters
3 Group	–	12 Lancasters
5 Group	–	182 Lancasters
6 Group	–	29 Lancasters
8 Group	–	64 Lancasters and four Mosquitos.

440

That day at the various airfields all over Lincolnshire and Yorkshire, crews were hanging around flight offices to see if ops were on that night, and if so (and more important) if they themselves were on the Order of Battle. This, of course, depended on the weather, not only in England but equally, over the course and target. It was also important to know the predictions in the weather for returning aircraft, lighter in load, possibly damaged, with men tense and tired, seeking the safety of their home bases – or any 'friendly' airfield!

Whenever a crew was on for that night, the captain of each aircraft would come back from the ops room to tell the rest of his crew they were operating and an air of tension and of apprehension set in. For each member of the crew now there was a strict routine which had to be adhered to, a routine that could mean the difference between them returning or not returning safely.

For the pilot it meant a night flying test (NFT) or practice bombing exercise perhaps, combined with the NFT. The procedure for abandoning the aircraft and ditching in the sea was reviewed. Many a crew were saved after ditching because the captain had done his homework or practised regularly the procedure when landing in the sea. Flying on three or even two engines was carried out by some pilots, to experience for his own benefit and that of the others, flying with this loss of power and stability. Some pilots let their flight engineers take over the controls for a time in case the pilot was hit and could not fly the aircraft; other pilots were against this and allowed nobody in their seats. The oxygen system had to be checked as was the intercom, both the responsibility of the pilot, for both systems were vital on ops.

The flight engineer was responsible for the well-being and performance of the engines, the fuel and oil, and any repairs that were asked to be attended to by him or the pilot previously. He generally checked the aircraft over before start-up time, ensured that the chocks were under the wheels, that the fuel required had been taken aboard and that the take-off weight was checked with the pilot. Inside the aircraft he checked that the first aid kits, fire extinguishers and portable oxygen sets were all in place. Before take-off he checked all four engines before flight run-up, checking the magnetos and boost. This would be done as quickly as possible to save wear and tear on the engines.

As the pilot and engineer attended to their pre-flight checks so the other crew members had their individual tasks. The bomb-aimer was responsible for the bombs they carried, although until the

(*Left*) Flight Engineer–Lancaster Bomber

(*Below*) Dingy Drill

briefing (along with the rest of the crew) he did not know the target, only details of the bomb load carried; for example one 4,000 lb, four to six 1,000 lb bombs and cans of incendiaries or any extra items such as propaganda news sheets printed in German, or 'Window' – narrow metallic strips carried in bundles which were pushed out in order to block the German radar. In the NFT, which usually lasted about half an hour, he had to check the bomb sight and bombing computer, plus all the electronics in his bombing compartment. He was also responsible for the rotation of the front turret and the elevation of the guns, its sight and, last but certainly not least, that the escape hatch in the floor of his front compartment opened easily in case of an emergency. Also, he must check that it was correctly locked in flight – very important as far as he was concerned, if for no other reason than his own safety. When on the bombing run he had to lie full length across the hatch door!

The air gunners did a daily inspection of their guns and turrets, which usually took about 25 minutes but on many occasions a gunner would find the armourer had checked it for him. The perspex of the turret had to be spotlessly cleaned. The slightest speck of grit or even a dead fly could, in flight at night, look like a fighter coming into attack. The middle perspex panel of the turret was usually devoid of perspex, many gunners preferring sore and red eyes and the blast of cold air rather than risk not returning because of a night fighter attack which they hadn't spotted quickly enough.

The Pathfinder squadrons also had to check their H_2S sets – the Plan Position Indicator (or PPI as the main cathode ray tube was called) which gave a map-like representation of the ground beneath the aircraft. In H_2S the centimetre wireless waves were generated by a transmitter in the aircraft, and then concentrated into a beam by the scanner which revolved in a cupola under the aircraft's fuselage. The scanner alternately sent the beam out and picked up the echoes returning from the ground. This sequence of transmission and reception took place 670 times during one rotation of the scanner, so there were 670 transmission and 670 sets of echoes received during a rotation of 360°. Thus there were that many sets of echoes which showed up as bright red spots or responses, on the radial line of the PPI, and the tube display during a complete revolution of the PPI recorded a map image of these responses. To identify such responses, the operator had to know three things: its identity, its range and its bearing from the aircraft.

The nature of a landmark may afterwards be decided by the shape

Bomber Command HQ Operation Room

'Window Dropping'

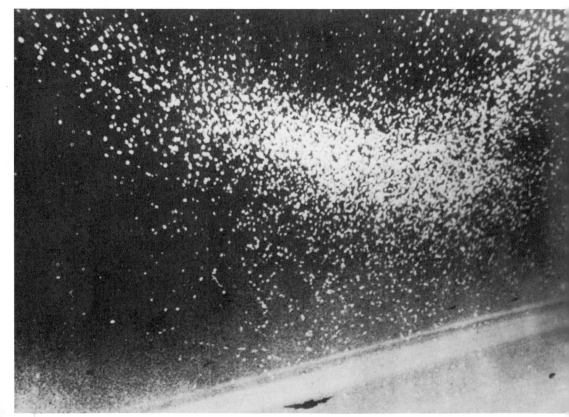

and brightness of the response. Built-up areas gave strong echoes, water weak ones, hills, forests or open fields (generally known as ground returns) fell between the two.

With all the engine and aircraft checks completed, the next stage was the planning and briefing for the operation that night. It was customary for the navigators to be called for their briefing an hour or so before the main briefing, which allowed them to work out their flight plan, using the Met winds that were forecast. This done, the navigators were ready to take part in the main crew briefing. This usually took place in a large room or hut with tables and chairs set in rows in the front of a stage. A heavy curtain covered the large wall map of Europe. The main topic of conversation quite naturally was where tonight's target was. Until the moment this was revealed, everything else was unimportant.

When the Commanding Officer arrived, along with the flight commanders and perhaps the Station Commander, plus the various specialists such as the Met and Intelligence officers, the conversation stopped and crews were called to attention. The CO might begin: 'Good afternoon, gentlemen. Please be seated,' after which one could hear a pin drop. Everyone was awaiting for the curtain to be drawn aside, nothing else mattered. The target, once revealed, would bring gasps, cheers or sighs of relief, or occasionally cries of incredulity. On 18th November, the silence was broken: 'Berlin!' All eyes followed the tape that stretched out across the map to the target, and the low murmur of voices began – 'The Big City', or for those who had been before, 'Berlin again!'

There were mixed feelings about the route. The experienced crews thought it maybe too straight, or too far north or too far south. To the new, or sprog, crews it was perhaps just a hell of a long way, the fear of the unknown, 'big league stuff', to other crews perhaps no reaction at all – they had heard and seen it all before.

The squadron commander then gave a general run down on the operation. The route was to be long, returning south instead of the well-known northern path. He also gave an outline of the Pathfinder marking over the target. Tonight it was to be marked on the outward journey by 156 Squadron, maintained by 'backers-up' of 97 and 156, plus 'blind markers' of 83 and 405 Squadrons. The supporters were from 7 and 405 Squadrons.

The method of attack was to use blind markers who were to mark the aiming point, or AP, with red target indicators by means of H_2S, after a carefully timed run from Brandenburg. Mosquitos of 139 and 105 Squadrons were to drop white spoof flares to the centre of the target with TIs. Window would be dropped at the rate of one bundle every two minutes en route, two bundles every minute within twenty miles of the target and one bundle per minute on the return route.

Next the Met Officer gave reports of expected weather at take-off, en route and over Berlin, and finally the weather expected when they returned to their bases. Not being an exact science, the weather men's information was usually greeted with a few choice expressions from the floor of the hall, all taken in good part, all part of the daily ritual on bomber stations.

Yet the weather men had help with their predictions. On this day No 1409 Met Flight had sent out two Mosquitos to examine the weather over Germany, Flying Officer W. Talbot (in LR309) and Flying Officer L.L.H. Dennis (ML903) examined the cloud along the route and found it to be 10/10ths at 18,000 feet.

The Armament Officer was next, telling them of their bomb loads, then the Gunnery Leader for the make-up of the gunner's ammunition. Wireless operators were given written call signs and identification letters, including the colour of the day for their return over England if they were challenged or fired on by their own side. It was not always successful or foolproof – occasionally a bomber was shot down by a 'friendly' night fighter or gun battery.

Then the Intelligence Officer gave details of enemy fighter airfields in close proximity to their routes and the expected flak areas to be avoided. He also gave them details of other aircraft types and numbers also operating. At this date, Berlin had 147 guns defending the city. Following the disaster at Hamburg, the German night fighter tactics underwent a massive re-organisation, as related earlier. In addition to *Wilde Sau*, there was 'Tame Boars', used by the Fighter Divisional HQ on the ground. A controller would broadcast a running commentary on the location and position of the main bomber stream, together with orders to the fighters to make for certain radio beacons in the path of the raiders; here they would circle and await directions.

Unlike the single-engined Wild Boars, the larger, twin-engined fighters carried their own radar, SN/2 Naxos, used to home in on the new H_2S sets, and Flensburg, which homed in on British 'Monica' transmissions, which was an early warning system fitted to bombers in 1943, which warned the crew of approaching enemy aircraft. These were both new developments to the basic radar,

Mid Upper Gunner

Briefing Berlin – November 1943 – 460 Sqdn

developed in the race to win the night war over Germany. For each such development or innovation, the other side had quickly to introduce a counter measure, once they discovered what the other side was using.

In the briefing rooms now, the only final thing to do was to synchronise watches by the navigation officer's watch. Perhaps a few words of encouragement from the Station Commander, and a final, 'Good luck, chaps.'

With the briefing over, the next two or three hours were spent in trying to relax and having the traditional pre-op meal of egg and bacon. One ritual in 50 Squadron was to listen to the Andrew Sisters record of 'The Shrine of St Cecilia' on the Mess gramophone. If you were a superstitious type it was a must. Not to have done so was considered unlucky, and if the rest of the crew found you hadn't listened to it, then heaven help you!

Other last minute details obviously differed from man to man. One pilot always shaved an hour or so before take-off. Others may have done this for a stubble inside the rubber oxygen mask could be irritating and leave a rash. Flasks of coffee, tea, were collected as well as sandwiches and glucose sweets. Some men kept their sweets in case they were shot down into the sea and had to spend time in a dinghy. All pockets had to be emptied before take-off, so that nothing helpful to the enemy could be found, either if you were taken prisoner – or your body was found! Long-Johns, extra thick stockings, flying boots and extra top clothing, such as a roll-neck sweater, were worn in the air to combat the low temperatures at operational height – anything up to 40° below. One bomb-aimer carried a leather school satchel, in which he carried his target maps, escape kit, gloves, razor and blades, toothbrush and paste, comb, sticking plasters, cigarettes, string – anything which might help him evade capture if he had to bale out.

The wireless operators collected two pigeons in metal containers which were secured to the rest bed in the aircraft for use as a further means of communication in the event of the aircraft ditching. (This was later discontinued owing to very few cases being recorded of it being of any use. When one's aircraft is sinking, it is dark and one is scared stiff – collecting the pigeons was not always uppermost in the mind!)

There was time for writing the 'last' letter before take-off (others had given the Adj or the padre a letter long before this raid, to be posted in the event ...). Then perhaps a little sleep until it was time

A meal before the operation

Crew room

to go to the crew room to get dressed for the operation. Besides the warm clothing there was the flying kit, an electrically heated suit for the rear gunner, the important whistle worn on the lapel to be used to establish contact if down in the sea in the dark.

The final collecting of parachutes, which had been diligently packed by the WAAFs – there were 10,000 prisoners of war from Bomber Command alone, many of whom had been grateful for the carefulness of the WAAF's packing. Then came the 'Mae West' life-jacket which would keep you afloat in the sea – long enough, hopefully, to give you time to get into the aircraft's dinghy. This was essential in winter – one didn't last long in an icy sea without a dinghy.

The only thing then was to wait for the transport out to the aircraft which could be anything up to two miles away on a big station. The journey was conducted in high spirits by the crews – most were little more than boys, many under 21, and many more only in their early twenties. It helped relieve the pressure and tension. Tonight might be their last night on this earth.

Many men carried their own good luck charms, mascots or had their own lucky routines. One pilot put a little of his girlfriend's perfume on his battledress blouse cuff and each of his crew would have a sniff. A bomb aimer had lucky charms around the bomb sight – rabbit's foot, a Cornish Pixie, a silver threepenny bit and a lady's suspender. His final routine, like that of many, many others, was a final pee over the tail wheel of the aircraft. Great for morale, but not appreciated by the ground crews who had later to cope with corroded metal.

Checks were again carried out as in the morning. The bomb aimer had a look at the bomb bay as the bomb doors were still open at this stage. They were closed when the engines were started up. The crew might write a little message on a bomb – 'To Hitler, with love' etc:

On this night one crew of 50 Squadron had a very hurried time. They found their aircraft unserviceable (U/S) and as 467 Squadron, at Waddington, had more aircraft than crews on the 18th, they were sent from their base at nearby Skellingthorpe, to borrow one. They arrived rather late, being able to do very little other than climb aboard and take off. It was a brand-new Lancaster and in the words of the rear gunner, John Flynn; 'It was as sluggish as riding a cow in the Derby.' The pilot, Len Durham, taxied the bomber out to the runway.

All over Lincolnshire and Yorkshire, crews began to climb into their bombers, each to his position. All went forward except the rear

Waiting for the off

Lancaster waiting for off signal

gunner who went into his rear turret. The mid-upper pulled himself into his turret while the others climbed over the huge main spar, which was about five foot high, and took their various seats, the flight engineer next to the pilot to assist in take-off. They both ran through the pre-take-off checks, then began to start up the engines in sequence. Once running the instruments checked for fuel, oil, temperatures, magneto, brake pressures, and all the others. Then they went through the following drill:

a   Ground to flight switch to 'flight'.
b   Navigation light to 'on'.
c   Main auto control switch to 'off'.
d   Mixer box switch to I/C position.
e   DR compass switched 'on' and to setting.
f   Set altimeter (allowing for lag).
g   Check undercarriage warning light, change switch over.
h   Magneto switches locked 'on'.
i   Switch oxygen test.
j   Check brake reservoir pressure 300 lb pressure per square inch

The trolley accumulator that had been wheeled into position to start up the engines, was pulled away as the engines were throttled back. Then a green flare was fired, giving the OK to taxi out. The skipper checked the crew over the intercom – 'OK rear gunner?' Reply: 'OK Skipper,' – and so on. The chocks were pulled away by the ground crew and the aircraft began to roll forward. All the bombers were queueing up at the end of the runway, each waiting its turn to take off. Some pilots were doing another check with the engineer on pressures and temperatures, and having been given the first course by the navigator, they waited.

At last, he was given the green light from the airfield caravan, and cheered off by groundcrews, WAAF's and anyone else who cared to do so; the aircraft moved onto the runway and with throttles eased forward to zero boost against the brakes, the brakes were released, the throttles pushed fully forward and they began to roll down the runway. The flight engineer followed up, holding the throttles forward so the pilot had both hands free for the control column, then he tightened the lock nut on the throttle quadrant. Owing to the heavy bomb load, the take-off speed had to be increased and therefore a longer run had to be made if the take -off speed of 110 mph were to be obtained. The boost read 3,000 revs, per minute, the bumps ceased and the aircraft, with seven men, 10,000 lbs of high explosives, oil and (for Berlin), 2,154 gallons of petrol, giving an all-up weight of around 65,000 lbs, was airborne.

Once airborne, the undercarriage was raised, then the flaps. The engineer loosened the lock nut on the throttles, and the skipper set his controls to climb to the operational height. They were on their way.

CHAPTER THREE

Going to the Big City

The sky was full of Lancasters forming up in the dark or darkening sky to create the main bombing force for Berlin. The start of a battle which was set to last for four months had begun. For many, this target was to become familiar over these months, for others it would be a one-way trip. They would never again see the green fields of England.

Len Durham and his crew, who had made the hurried journey to borrow the 467 Squadron Lancaster, were late in taking off, to such an extent that they were told that if they did not reach the Dutch coast by a certain time, they were to abort as they would be classed as a straggler. However, having never returned early from a trip yet, they didn't intend to start now, so they pressed on.

Once airborne the gunners cocked their guns, switched the guns from 'safe' to 'fire' and then adjusted the gun-sight light for brightness. The mid-upper guns could fire at a rate of 2,300 rounds per minute and accurately up to 400 yards. The rear gunner, with four guns rather than the upper's two, had a rate of fire of 4,600 rounds. The mid-upper only had 2,000 rounds but the rear man had 11,000 rounds – quite an arsenal. When over the North Sea, they would receive permission to test-fire their guns.

The two gunners had to settle down quickly to searching the sky and to being the eyes of the aircraft. The experienced crews never flew straight and level, but always weaved about which didn't give the fighters or flak gunners a firm sight of them. Below them the English coast slipped away – they were over the sea.

It was difficult flying weather on the night of the 18th. The temperature was down to minus 41 centigrade. Ice quickly coated the windows and turrets, inside and out. At least one member of a crew spent a lot of his time scraping off the ice. Vapour trails astern from the hot engines began to confuse the pilot. The wind was changing frequently and causing navigators many problems. Inside the aircraft all available space in the fuselage was taken up with bundles of large brown paper parcels containing Window which were opened and ready to be dropped out twenty miles from the target, and to twenty miles on the return trip.

The wireless operator never used his morse key except in an emergency, as the enemy could plot his position from the signals and alert the fighters. He maintained a listening watch only with Group, who would broadcast every 30 minutes. If there was no message, a number from one to nine was transmitted and this was entered in the log to verify the broadcast had been received. 'Tinselling' was the code name given to jamming German broadcasts from the enemy controller to his fighters. Each wireless operator had a small area of waveband to search on his receiver and any talking he heard was jammed by his pressing the morse key linked to a generator motor which effectively drowned any conversation.

He had another piece of equipment known as 'Lulu', which was a visual system of showing up other aircraft in the vicinity. It consisted of two small screens on his table, one with a vertical line to define port and starboard, the other a horizontal line to indicate above or below. Blips on the screen showed where other aircraft were in relation to his own. Those that held a steady course were usually other RAF aircraft in the stream, but a fast moving, fast closing blip was deemed to be an enemy fighter. On seeing this the WOP would give rapid directions to the gunners and then tell the pilot to corkscrew to the left or right.

His duties took him off the intercom for periods, so that he might be unaware of events taking place, and if the aircraft was suddenly buffeted he had no idea if it was flak, slipstream, or fighter attack. When approaching the target, and over it, he provided another useful extra pair of eyes to watch out for converging aircraft or perhaps another coming in above them with bomb doors open!

*

The bombers met little cloud over England but it gradually increased over the North Sea. Over the Continent there was still cloud, but with some breaks. Above the cloud visibility was moderate but very poor below. Over Berlin the crews found 10/10th cloud with tops at 10,000-12,000 feet, and below this another layer of cloud with tops of about 5,000 feet, with poor visibility and no moon. The wind strength over the city was 10 mph at 8-18,000 feet, 15 mph at 28,000 feet.

Of the groups attacking, 5 Group, for example, had planned to attack between 9 and 9.12 pm, with 177 aircraft, assisted by 43

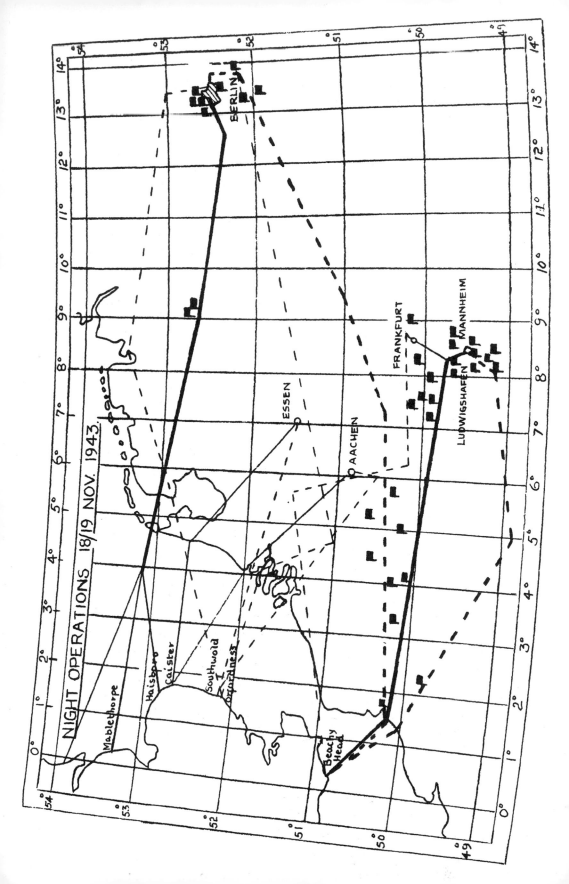

NIGHT OPERATIONS 18/19 NOV. 1943.

BERLIN

MANNHEIM

FRANKFURT

LUDWIGSHAFEN

ESSEN

AACHEN

Mablethorpe

Haisboro
Caister

Southwold
Orfordness

Beachy
Head

aircraft from 8 Group's Path Finder aircraft. The flight plan called for an outward flight at 16,000 feet to 20,000 feet, and the return at 23-25,000 feet. All crews reported 10/10ths cloud and as the expected winds were incorrect, it led to a lot of aircraft straying.

A good many crews later reported seeing the air space above Berlin bursting with flak and forests of weaving searchlight beams. The force had to rely on the H_2S aircraft to mark the target as the weather was so bad; but of the 30 5 Group aircraft so equipped, only six identified the target at the time of bombing.

Thus of the 27 blind markers detailed to drop red TIs only four dropped their markers, the remainder retaining them due to unserviceability or unreliability of their H_2S sets. The four loads of markers dropped were somewhat scattered but on time. The 'Backer-Up' markers of which there were thirteen, were detailed to drop Green TIs plus Yellow TIs and one red spot fire. Eight of these dropped their greens, achieving a nice continuity at 9.01 to 9.20 pm. Roughly two-thirds of the Main Force aimed at the greens and a quarter at the reds.

One special blind marker, Pilot Officer Britton DFM of 83 Squadron, was detailed to mark the exact aiming point with red TIs and a yellow in salvo. However, his H_2S Mark III was useless and his gunner's electric suit failed, so he brought his bombs back and dropped them on Texel instead. Of the 98 aircraft of Main Force carrying H_2S, only 45 found their equipment working over the target.

Over the city, the bomb aimers were lying prone in the nose of their aircraft, feeling very vulnerable with little between them and the bursting flak shells. The run into the target had to be straight and level. Bomb aimer's directions to his pilot were given in the following manner: 'Left, left 10 degrees, left ...' In addition they would try to give the pilot an indication of the distance from the aiming point, and then they would say, 'Steady, steady, left a litle, steady ... Bombs gone! Bomb doors closed.'

All hell then seemed to let loose. Flashes from the photo flares, dull red explosions from the 'Cookies' and patches of fire from the incendiaries over a large area. The surrounding sky became so bright that night vision became impaired. Cones of searchlights were weaving back and forth. One flight engineer recalled: 'We saw one big explosion that came up through the clouds. This was the explosions of our 4,000 lb bombs. It lasted for about twenty seconds.'

At the end of the attack, four Mosquitos of 139 Squadron dropped dummy fighter flares in lanes to the north of the city to draw off the night fighters, while the bombers turned and headed out to the south. For the air gunners now was the time not to lose concentration and start thinking about home and a warm bed – very easy to do when it's minus 40° outside. As they flew off it was the rear gunners who could see the burning target and it was equally easy to look with awe at what they had done. Before take-off they had taken caffeine tablets – 'Wakey-wakey' pills – to help them stay awake and alert, but their effects did not last forever. The area of the sky to watch closely was the dark part, from where the fighters, if they had a choice, would attack. Once again the more experienced crews did not fly the same course for too long, which would make it easier for radar-controlled fighters to be directed onto them.

Long before UK landfall, each wireless operator would tune into his own base to learn of any possible diversion or barometric pressures etc; with the airways crammed with frequencies it was sometimes difficult to get a good reception.

The number of enemy fighters encountered on this raid was considerably less than might have been expected. This was, maybe, because some twin-engined units of the Luftwaffe had been moved up to Norway during the 18th which tied up with the USAAF's attack on Oslo in which they lost nine aircraft. Also, owing to fog, fighters at Berlin were being ordered to land before the attack had begun. It also appears that the diversionary raid on Mannheim by 3, 4, 6 and 8 Groups took the majority of the fighters, as their losses were 23, of which ten were attributed to night fighters, whereas the nine lost on Berlin – a 2% loss rate – were all attributed to flak.

Nevertheless, some combats were recorded, two in the area of the Steinhude Meer. Most encounters were experienced shortly after leaving the target area; types seen were Ju88s, Me210s and three Focke Wulf 190s. A Junkers 88 was seen dropping fighter flares over Berlin from 19,000 feet.

Flying Officer Wilson of 50 Squadron saw a FW190 on the homeward journey and his rear gunner, Sergeant Bateman, ordered Wilson to corkscrew as he fired one short burst, but only one gun fired, the others being frozen. Enemy fighter pilots considered the RAF corkscrew as a most effective evasive manoeuvre; a corkscrewing Halifax was an easier target to follow than a Lancaster, but the Lancaster caught fire easier when hit. Major Heinz-Wolfgang Schnaufer of NJG/4 once described the corkscrew: 'It

FW 190 German Fighter

started with a steep dive and turn, and was usually most successful as the night fighter hadn't the speed to follow.' As Schnaufer ended the war as the top night fighter ace with 121 kills, he knew all about fighting the RAF bombers.

The aircraft in which Pilot Officer Noel Lloyd of 44 Squadron was a gunner was attacked four times by twin-engined aircraft. Each time he fired upon the fighter he skilfully directed his pilot in such a way that not a single shot hit their Lancaster. Sergeant Jimmy Flynn had the horrible experience of going through the target area with his turret and guns out of action. The oil pipe that fed the power to his turret burst, spraying hydraulic fluid into his face. He then had to contend with the nauseating smell of oil all the way back to base.

Because of the large numbers of aircraft operating over any target, the risk of mid-air collision was very great. Former aircrew still relate how other aircraft crossing their path just a few feet above or below them were so close sometimes that they could hear their engines. Another hazard was parachute flares, which were fired from the ground up to a height of the bomber stream where they hung seemingly motionless until they burnt out. They gave off a brilliant white light, which helped the fighters pick them out. Crews always knew when fighters were around, because the flak ceased. Flares were also dropped by the fighters, mainly by the experienced night fighters to assist the less experienced find the bomber stream and its direction.

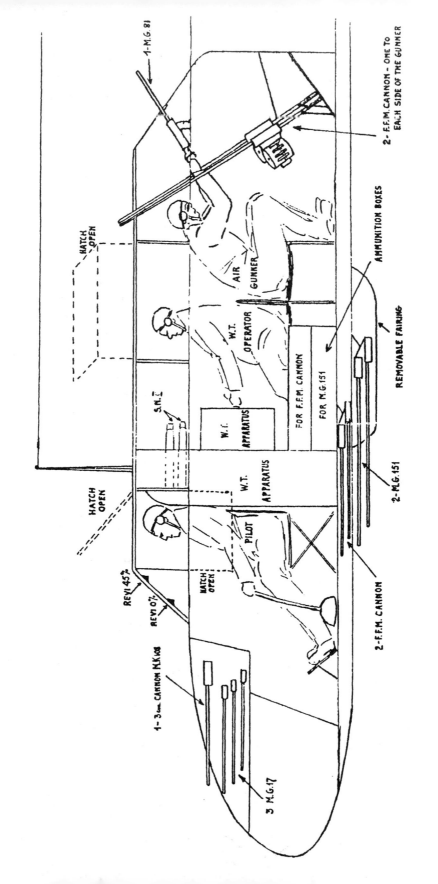

Me 110 Nightfighter

Many a crew who survived being shot down were under the impression that they had been downed by flak, having been hit from below. Yet in many of these cases they had been shot down by a new type of armament in Messerschmitt 110 fighters. These were fitted with upwards firing cannon known as *Schräge Musik* by the Germans – the translation meaning Jazz or Oblique Music. These aircraft, with a crew of three, in the original model, had a large extra fuel tank in the aft part of the cabin. In the newer model Messerschmitt, this was removed and a pair of 20 mm cannon mounted in the fuselage, firing upwards at an angle of 10 to 20 degrees. The pilot had an extra reflector sight mounted above his head, and as the guns carried non-tracer ammunition, these attacks from below were not discovered for many months by the RAF. The gunner in the 110 was responsible for the cannons working satisfactorily and for replacing ammunition drums which normally carried 50 rounds, although a later type contained 90 rounds. Besides these guns the 110 had a rear machine gun fired by the gunner and a single forward firing cannon and two cannons below the fuselage.

One German pilot had attacked twenty to thirty RAF bombers with this method of attack from a range of about 80 yards. He claimed to have shot down three while the bombers were actually corkscrewing. He would usually aim to hit the bomber between the two engine nacelles on either of the wings, or if the rear gunner became troublesome, he would aim at him. Although such attacks came from such a surprise area that few gunners saw the attacker and thus believed they'd been hit by flak. It was obviously not a good tactic for the German pilot to fire up towards the bomber's bomb bay, and the wing shot would smash engines, fuel tanks and aileron control.

The uppermost thought of the crews after dropping their bombs was to get away quickly. However, on this night, for one crew of 619 Squadron, and especially the rear gunner, Sergeant Cairns, leaving the target was anything but normal. Just after leaving the target area his oxygen mask became frozen. The spare helmet and mask was too small and in trying to fit it he became anoxic. The skipper quickly dived the aircraft to 7,000 feet, at which level Cairns's original mask defrosted and on coming to, he was able to use it although by this time his ears had been frostbitten. On arrival back at Conningsby he was admitted to hospital. There were also reports of some gunners in 83 Squadron suffering frostbite.

The role of 101 Squadron based at Ludford Magna, Lincs, was

Squadron Leader Marshall's crew – 101 Sqdn

101 Squadron ABC Aircraft dropping leaflets

slightly different to other squadrons. Their Lancasters were distributed among the bomber stream each carrying a special operator, who stayed in a special cabin between the rest bed and mid-upper turret. He operated three special transmitters and tuned into German radio and jammed instructions being given to the night fighter pilots. The official title for this was 'Airborne Cigar' known as ABC. It was so hush-hush that even the remainder of the crew knew little about it. Ken Maun, wireless operator with Squadron Leader Johnny Marshall, A Flight commander, remembers that whenever any member of the crew passed the special operator he would turn off his sets. He was cut off from the rest of the crew on the intercom while he was working and relied on the call light if he was required to listen in.

Whenever Flying Officer 'Tug' Wilson flew with Marshall he always gave the remainder of the crew an address of a 'safe house' on each leg of the trip in case they were shot down. Of course, they had to memorise it. The other requirement of the operator was that he was able to speak German fluently.

The idea of a VHF jammer, given the name 'Jostle', was considered a requirement of Bomber Command from April 1943. The immediate plan was that 100 special transmitters and 30 special receivers should be manufactured. The first batch was to be fitted into Lancasters of 100 Squadron and the equipment per aircraft was to consist of:

1. Special Receiver with panoramic display.
2. Three transmitters each of 600 watts input.
3. Three special aerials actually seven foot span.
4. The necessary power supply.

To accommodate this equipment meant sacrificing 1,000 pounds of bomb load. However, 100 Squadron were due at that time to be fitted with H_2S. and as 101 Squadron (also of 1 Group), were lowest in the H_2S fitting programme, they were chosen as the Jostle Squadron. It was decided that the Cigar leader should be a flight lieutenant and his operators should be picked from the whole of Bomber Command.

Training began with 30 operators in July 1943 and the course was due to be completed by the end of August. The first operation using Jostle was on 7/8th October on Stuttgart. It proved quite successful

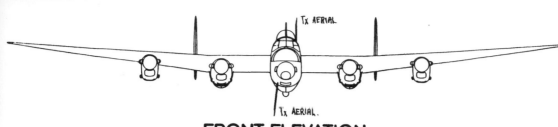

Tx AERIAL

Tx AERIAL.

FRONT ELEVATION

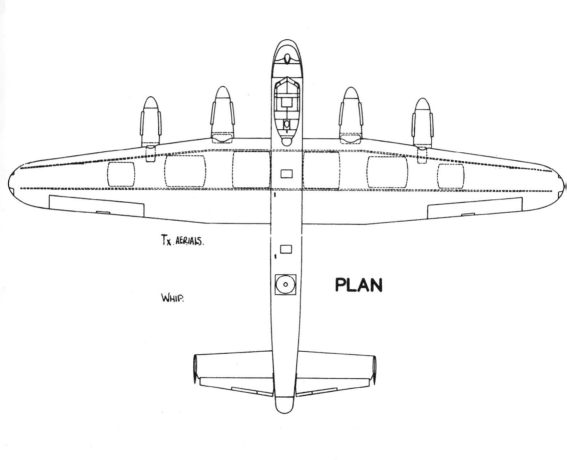

Tx. AERIALS.

WHIP.

PLAN

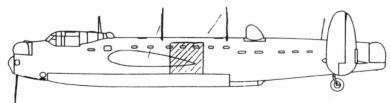

ABC AERIALS.
(TRANSMIT)

PORT

WHIP AERIAL
ABC. RECEIVE)

POSITION OF
ABC APPARATUS
(PORT SIDE)

Lancaster Mk I

for out of the eight operational frequencies; only one was readable after jamming. The Germans called the system as *Dudelsac*.

*

Having crossed the Dutch coast on the return journey, the crews would relax a little and sample the Mess coffee. The usual opinion of the coffee served in Messes was horrible, but after six and a half hours of tense flying, it tasted excellent.

Once over English soil again, the crew could not completely relax as there were a lot of aircraft around and the risk of mid-air collision was very real – there might also be German intruder aircraft about; they occasionally made their way over in the returning bomber stream, picking off the odd bomber here and there, even in the airfield landing pattern.

Once down, the crews immediately went to de-briefing where they were interviewed by Intelligence Officers who asked them for every detail of the operation. The route they had flown, fighters, flak spots – anything that could be useful to them when planning future operations. The padre was usually in attendance at the debriefing, handing out cigarettes or a comforting word when and where it was needed. The WAAFs were there handing out mugs of tea laced with rum, a very welcome drink for crews who had been flying in sub-zero temperatures.

Some crews were returning short of petrol or damaged on the 19th (a not unusual occurrence) and had to land away from their home bases. For instance, four aircraft from 100 Squadron landed away from their base. Flight Lieutenant Major, having deen damaged by flak, landed at Bossum, Pilot Officer Stow landed at Stomer, Squadron Leader Grant-Dalton at Boxted. Sergeant Crabtree landed at Bradwell Bay. His rear gunner had his oxygen pipe break and he was unconscious for two hours, suffering from frostbite.

Flying Officer Parker and his crew had their bomber run out of fuel at 4,000 feet over England and baled out, the aircraft crashing at Horsham in Sussex. They all suffered minor injuries except the navigator who received serious injuries and was dangerously ill.

From this raid, returning aircraft had, on average, 185 gallons left in their fuel tanks, which compared somewhat badly with the recent average of 235 gallons for long distance raids. The number of aircraft arriving at their bases with less than 100 gallons was 7.2%, and a number of these aircraft landed away from base.

One now famous aircraft, also damaged by flak over Bonn on this

Lancaster 'S' for sugar

raid, was R5868 'S' for Sugar, of 467 Squadron, which on this occasion was flown by Pilot Officer McClelland. This Lancaster now resides in the Bomber Command Museum at Hendon, North London. It eventually completed over 100 operations during the war, including six ops to Berlin during the battle.

Nine aircraft were missing from this first Berlin trip. One was from 156 Squadron (JB363) and flown by the Commanding Officer, Wing Commander John White, aged 28 from Weybridge, Surrey. His aircraft crashed in the Berlin area. Flying Officer Charles McManus, aged 25, and his crew, crashed at Schoonebeek in Holland, was from 101 Squadron. This aircraft was found by the Germans and the ABC equipment captured. It was sent to Telefunken for examination. On 30th November, Colonel Schwenke reported the find to Field Marshal Milch who was also told that there were eight in the crew rather than the usual seven, and that the set was called 'T.3160' – the Airborne Cigar designation.

Pilot Officer Raymond Peate of 115 Squadron hailed from Australia and was only twenty years old. He and his crew came down at

Oupeye in Belgium. Flight Sergeant Doughty of 100 Squadron and his crew were all taken prisoner after baling out. Pilot Officer Gordon Graham, a Canadian, and his 9 Squadron crew were all killed when their aircraft crashed at Burgwurben in Germany. Flight Lieutenant Gobbie and his crew of 57 Squadron were hit over Germany. Two of his crew were killed while the other, including Gobbie, were taken prisoner. Flight Sergeant James Gibson, aged 27, from Australia, and his crew of 460 RAAF Squadron were all killed after their Lancaster crashed at Zornigall, Germany.

Flight Sergeant Johnson of 97 Squadron was killed when his aircraft crashed in Belgium. Two of his crew baled out, however, and taken prisoner, while the other four who baled out all evaded capture and reached England in March 1944. They had taken off from their base at Bourne at 5.30 pm, and their H_2S set seemed in order but after crossing the English coast the navigator decided it had gone U/S. He left his seat to see if, when it had warmed up a bit, the set would be working but it did not.

At the same time, the bomb aimer reported one of the front guns was out of action. The omens began to increase when over Hanover, the mid-upper reported that his turret had gone U/S, so Johnson ordered him to the front turret. The bomb aimer was throwing out Window from the nose and Johnson ordered the WOP into the astrodome to look out for fighters. The navigator set a straight course for Berlin and on arrival they dropped their bombs, not on the TIs, but on salvo, making use of the red markers. The navigator then worked out the wind speed and direction and they set off on the return route.

Near Aachen they were shot up by flak which hit one of the port engines although it did not catch fire. Johnson put the aircraft into a dive and went down to 10,000 feet, but it was still being hit by gunfire for perhaps four to five minutes, shrapnel clattering against the wings and fuselage. The rear gunner was injured in the hand, being attended to by the WOP; in addition his oxygen supply was cut and he partially lost consciousness. As the WOP was about to take his place in the rear turret, the Lancaster was hit again and another engine had to be shut down and feathered. With this Johnson ordered the crew to prepare to abandon the aircraft. He continued to fly it until they reached Liège when the flak opened up again and the mid-upper was wounded in the knee and the bomb aimer grazed by shell fragments.

Still losing height, Johnson finally ordered the crew out. All got away except Johnson who was last seen with his parachute clipped on but was later killed when baling out. The navigator, Flight Lieutenant Pepper, bomb aimer Pilot Officer Williams, mid-upper Flight Sergeant Hesselden, despite being wounded, and the rear gunner, Flight Sergeant Billows, who was also wounded, all evaded capture and returned to England via Spain and Gibraltar. Pepper was on his 38th trip, Williams his 37th, Hesselden his 28th and Billows his 29th. Flight Sergeant Johnson was on his 23rd op, but was not the crew's regular pilot.

The WOP, Flight Sergeant John Sansam, landed safely and was helped by some Belgium people until captured. During his captivity he made one escape attempt but was re-captured, being finally liberated by the Russians in April 1945. Flight Sergeant Jackson, the engineer, was also captured and in a camp with Sansam.

The aircraft flown by Pilot Officer Lees of 9 Squadron, a peacetime policeman from Manchester, was in collision with a Lancaster of 207 Squadron (DV361 'V') about fifteen to thirty miles from the target. His aircraft was badly damaged while the 207 machine, piloted by Pilot Officer Bill Baker, had a badly damaged nose section, losing his bomb aimer who fell from the smashed front end. Baker managed to fly the aircraft back to base but lost fingers on both hands through frost bite. Before returning to base he went onto the target but found the bomb release gear was not working. On his return he was recommended for an immediate award of the DFC.

In the meantime, Pilot Officer Lees of 9 Squadron, with his rudder damaged, could not maintain height so he ordered his crew to abandon the aircraft. It crashed at Bornicke, Germany, and Sergeant Hand in the rear turret was killed. The remainder were taken prisoner. Flight Sergeant Fisher, from Huddersfield, and the navigator walked for five days before being picked up by a German policeman. While in a PoW camp, Fisher and Sergeant Alex Cordon exchanged identities with two army privates and both made an escape attempt but were later recaptured. However, on 14th April 1945, now on his third attempt, Fisher broke away from a march and ran into a wood. This time, he and two army privates got away and met up with a tank battalion of the US Army.

The story of the collision was brought to light when the flight engineer of Baker's aircraft ended up in the same camp as Cordon and Fisher. Baker is now a civil engineer in Canada – he has never flown again.

*

After the raid, some conclusions were made:

1. Lack of photographic evidence made it impossible to assess bombing results.
2. Owing to 10/10ths cloud, bombing was thought to be somewhat scattered.
3. Navigational errors due to unpredictable wind changes caused many flak defences to be brought into action.
4. Fighter activity was sub-normal due to the diversionary attack on Mannheim, and to the other counter measure operations.

The Times reported the raid on the 20th, stating that in 30 minutes 350 x 4,000 lb bombs had been dropped and that the temperature on the bombers' route was 40° below.

The tonnage of bombs dropped by the 412 aircraft which attacked Berlin was 1,595.6, broken down to 798.2 tons of high explosives and 795 tons of incendiaries. This worked out at an average of 177 tons for each missing aircraft. A further breakdown showed that 8,969 lbs was dropped per Lancaster. The raid brought the total tonnage dropped on Berlin since the start of the war to 15,626 tons.

207 Squadron Lancaster on return from Berlin

The serviceability of the H_2S sets was very low. Of the 26 blind market aircraft despatched, only five reached the target with their sets working.

A good proportion of the population of Berlin had been evacuated by Doctor Goebbels in August 1943, but by November many had returned. After this raid, plans were once again introduced to evacuate and only people whose presence was necessary were encouraged to stay. The weight of this raid had fallen in the south, north and north-west suburbs and considerable damage was caused by fire. The ARP and Fire Brigades, however, managed to prevent these fires spreading over a wider area with just a few exceptions.

The Chief of Police in Berlin reported 154 people killed and 443 others injured, and some 7,500 made homeless. His report included an estimate of the bombs dropped between 8.11 to 10.23 pm – 11 mines, 75 high explosives, 1,600 incendiaries, 940 phosphorus bombs and 36 flares.

The German European Telegraph Service reported:

The heavy terror attack caused a great deal of damage and losses among the population and numerous disruptions of the working class generally. Reports have been received of the destruction of irreplaceable works of art and historical buildings.

CHAPTER FOUR

No Respite

The Second Raid

The assault on Berlin was to continue. The largest force of bombers yet despatched to the Big City was sent just four nights later, 22/23rd November – a total of 764 bombers, all heavies except for twelve Mosquitos. Once again the weather proved poor, 10/10th cloud over the target.

Nevertheless, the good news was that with this type of weather the crews had high hopes of meeting little fighter opposition. The first wave of six Mosquitos would drop white drip flares over the aiming point but the Pathfinders were once again going to have to rely on H_2S because of the cloud cover. The weather was also to prove ideal as far as searchlight activity was concerned, but flak turned out to be heavy and accurate despite this.

The air raid warning sounded in Berlin at about 7.30 pm, at which time Doctor Albert Speer, the German Armaments Minister, was holding a conference in his private office in the City. He was informed that a large force of bombers was heading towards the city when they had reached the Potsdam area. He went to a flak tower nearby, intending to watch the raid, but he had to take cover in a shelter as heavy bomb hits were shaking the tower's concrete walls. After about twenty minutes he came out of the shelter and saw his ministry building on fire. He immediately went over to try and save the files in his office, but where they were kept was just one big bomb crater.

The Pathfinders marked the target at 8 pm with red and green TIs, which was followed by an enormous explosion which lit up the sky for about ten to fifteen seconds. One Pathfinder aircraft was seen to blow up just before reaching the target area, and was presumed to have received a direct flak hit in the bomb bay.

On the ground, Speer saw that the fires were spreading to the Army Ordnance Office, and everybody was trying to save the valuable special telephones. Speer joined in, ripping them from their wires, then piling them up at a safe place in a basement. On the

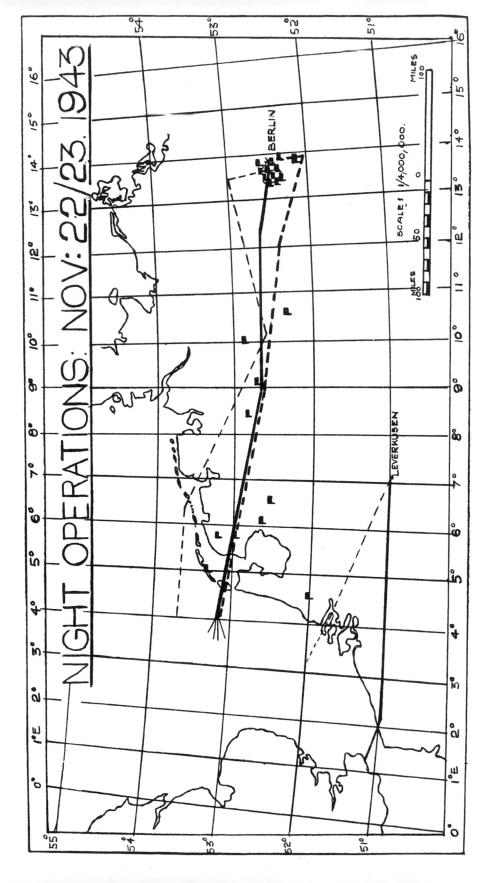

NIGHT OPERATIONS: NOV: 22/23. 1943

BERLIN

LEVERKUSEN

SCALE: 1/4,000,000.

MILES   0   50   100   MILES

morning of the 23rd, General Leeb, the Chief of the Army Ordnance, visited Speer and said, 'The fire in my building was extinguished in the early morning hours but unfortunately we can't do any work now, as somebody has ripped all the telephones from the walls!'

To Speer, from his early vantage point of the flak tower, the raid on Berlin was an unforgettable sight with illuminating parachute flares, which the Berliners called 'Christmas Trees' floating in the night sky, followed by flashes from explosions which were caught and reflected by the clouds of smoke. Hitler was told of these raids but he did not want to listen, avoiding the subject each time it was brought up.

This is perhaps the moment to mention 'scarecrows' which were reported from time to time by bomber crews. They would talk of, 'An explosion releasing a quantity of smoke, coloured stars and flaming debris, resembling an aircraft which had been hit and destroyed.' It was suggested or even believed by some aircrews that this was some form of German morale-destroying weapon, but flak gunners who were asked about this after the war denied any knowledge of such a weapon or system. It is now felt with some certainty that it was indeed bombers exploding in mid-air.

For Flight Lieutenant Wilfred Riches and his crew from 97 Squadron, this raid on Berlin became a nightmare. It was his 23rd operation, and four of these 23 had already been on Berlin. On this night he was detailed for a leading role within the Pathfinder Force. On the approach to the target his aircraft was repeatedly hit by flak with the result that the port inner engine caught fire and had to be feathered. Despite this, Riches persisted in pressing on with his attack and continued to drop his bombs and markers accurately, and to fulfil the task assigned to him.

On the return flight, after flying on three engines for about two hours, and when about to cross the Dutch coast, the starboard outer engine failed. At this time Riches was at 14,000 feet but despite this he managed to get back across the North Sea to his base and make a safe landing. He was immediately recommended for the DFC. On a previous occasion his aircraft was attacked by an enemy fighter and the damage inflicted was severe and his rear gunner killed, but Riches avoided further attacks and made it home to base.

It was the first operation on Berlin for Flying Officer Mike Beetham (later Chief of the Air Staff Sir Michael Beetham and Marshal of the RAF), and his crew of 50 Squadron. His bomb aimer,

Stirling being bombed up

F/O Beetham and crew 50 Sqdn

P/O McClelland and crew 467 Sqdn

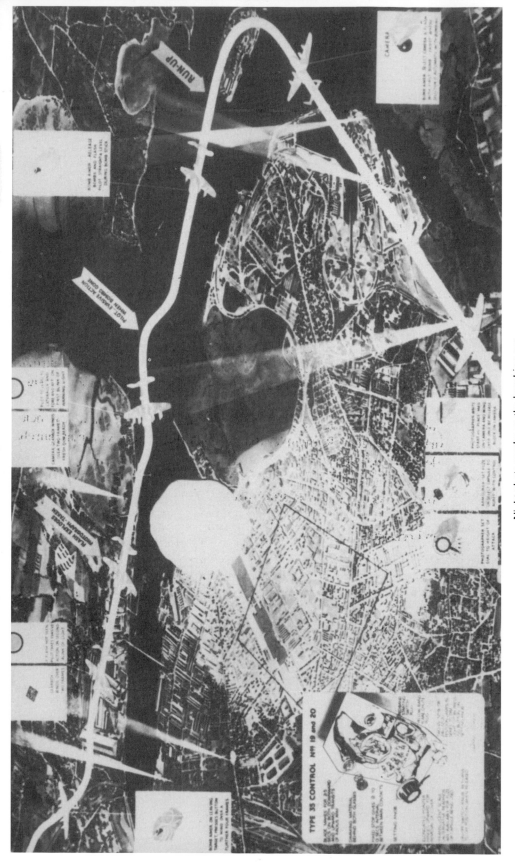

Night photography on the bombing run

Flight Sergeant Les Bartlett, was making final adjustments on his bombing panel. It was fifteen minutes to zero hour. Then the first TIs went down, yellow ones, followed by reds, cascading into greens, which gradually descended into the clouds, which were the ones they were to bomb on.

The first wave started their bombing at the same time as a line of fighter flares went down in brilliant white parallels to their track. It was about two miles away, but it had been laid by the Mosquito boys as a decoy.

In the final turn, Les Bartlett was straining to try and see everything at once, trying to decide which of the TIs were most accurate. He then gave the necessary corrections to Beetham so as to get to the chosen TIs. He ordered bomb doors open, but then way down below he saw a Halifax bomber. Mike Beetham made a quick weave, ending up on a parallel course and with a final, 'Left, left, steady …' Les pressed the 'tit' and the aircraft lurched as 4,000 lbs of bombs left the aircraft. He quickly threw the jettison bars across to ensure that there were no hang-ups in the bomb bay. Beetham kept the aircraft straight and level for about 30 seconds, which seemed like 30 minutes, while the camera photographed the aiming point of their bombs. He then yelled, 'OK, camera operated, bomb doors closed.'

The clouds themselves were insufficient to hide the destruction going on. Everywhere for miles around seemed to be burning, throwing up a pink and scarlet haze through the cloud. It was so light one could read in the bombing compartment. The flak was moderate but falling short, bursting some 3,000 feet below them.

On their port bow, Beetham's crew saw an aircraft out of control falling earthwards with smoke pouring from it but no fire as far as could be seen. In this case the crew had a fair chance of baling out. Beetham set course out of the target area. Everything ahead looked black and very uninviting from a crew's point of view. This was the danger area where fighters would be waiting. They could see red Very lights used by the fighters to attract each other's attention in the air all around them. To avoid being jumped, Mike Beetham did a steady weave for about five minutes. With over 600 miles to go there was no need to get too anxious.

Things began to quieten down, but to be on the safe side they would make a banking search occasionally, mainly to avoid being attacked from below. At 8,000 feet they were able to release their oxygen masks and breathe freely again, which was always a great relief after having had them clamped on their faces for several hours. Flasks of hot coffee were passed around and Beetham allowed a little conversation. They began to see other aircraft around them as the English coast was reached. All around was a great armada, as hundreds of red, green and white navigation lights could be seen. A message was sent to base: 'Hello Black Swan, This is Pilgrim D for Dog. May I pancake, please, over.' This was acknowledged and a glow of relief felt throughout the crew.

*

Flying in Lancaster ED974, with Pilot Officer King DFC, was Wing Commander John MacGowan, Senior Medical Officer in 8 Group. He had been a fighter pilot in France in World War One and in 1922 completed medical studies to become a doctor. There were many problems medically for aircrew; one that Doc MacGowan was keen to solve was night vision and how to cope with the dazzle and glare from flares and target markers. Other problems involved the cold, adequate oxygen supply and frostbite, which could be caused by anything metal touching the bare skin, to frozen skin and poor circulation. Another was air sickness. Wing Commander MacGowan was to go on and complete some 52 operations in his pursuit of information, for which he was awarded a very well-earned DFC.

Although the heavy bombers had finished their attack, the raid was not entirely over. A third wave of Mosquitos went to Berlin over an hour after the main raid, sending the Berliners scurrying back to the shelters. This was a planned attack of three waves – the first had dropped white flares, the second bombed after the heavies had done their work, followed by this third attack more than an hour later.

The London *Times* reported that 2,300 tons of bombs had been dropped on Berlin and among the damage had been Hitler's residence, which had been set on fire, Von Ribbentrop's palace destroyed, Speer's ministry destroyed except the ground floor. Other buildings destroyed were the Foreign Office and the Italian and Swedish legation buildings.

Berlin was described as a 'Hell's Kitchen'. A German report of the raid stated that 130 mines, 900 high explosive, 200,000 incendiaries and 20,000 phosphorus bombs had been dropped as well as 60 flares. The casualty roll was 1,757 dead, 6,923 injured with some 180,000 people made homeless, for in the attack some 2,791 homes were destroyed with another 2,300 damaged. Industries and waterways had been destroyed or damaged, including the electrical firms of Osram and Telefunken. The Albrecht Armaments works was severely damaged in addition.

There was an understandable amount of panic in Berlin after the raid. Looting became widespread, and to add to the confusion, there were, for instance, over four million ration books destroyed, causing added disruption to everyday life. Almost any raid on a town caused this type of problem which, although only disruptive, was equally damaging. On the morning of the 23rd, a press conference was held by Doctor Schmidt, the Head of the Press Bureau in the General Foreign Office, at which many foreign correspondents were present. He talked about the British terror raids but the full significance of the conference can only be gauged when it is remembered that for the past few months the German Government had been making strenuous efforts to prevent foreign and neutral press observers visiting the scene of heavy Allied air raids – that is, before the debris had been cleared away. And the streets on the 23rd were impassable. Debris and especially the entanglement of tramway wires made passage impossible. Fires were still burning in many areas and gas mains had burst in several places. Fire fighting seemed to be becoming less and less effective. The reaction from the ARP services was: 'What can one do?' Berliners wouldn't do anything unless it was their own house or flat that was in danger.

RAF casualties were 25 aircraft missing – eleven Lancasters, ten Halifaxes and four Stirlings. Three others had crashed on return to England, two of which had collided at Pocklington, both crews being killed. Ten of the losses were credited as follows: five to flak in the target area, three to controlled fighters over Berlin and two to controlled fighters in the Deelan area on the return route. Eighty aircraft were damaged by flak and one by fighter attack. Falling incendiaries had damaged another five, two more by collision and seven to other causes.

One Stirling aircraft of 214 Squadron (EF445 'J') flown by Flight Sergeant George Atkinson, aged twenty from Co. Durham, bombed Berlin at 8.06 pm from 12,000 feet. On the return flight, when twenty miles east of Hanover, the aircraft was hit by flak which damaged the intercom and wounded the rear gunner, Flight Sergeant Wilfred Sweeney, in the right leg. Then the port outer engine failed and to add to their problems, icing forced Atkinson to reduce height to between 1,500 and 2,000 feet.

They continued to fly at this height across Germany and Holland. The mid-upper and rear gunner, despite his wounds, returned the fire of several flak guns and they reckoned they damaged between fifteen and twenty searchlights! Then they were attacked by a FW190 which Sweeney managed to shoot down over the Zyder Zee.

At 10.31 pm they sent out an SOS to say they were running short of petrol; their problems increased when the starboard outer engine began to overheat and had to be shut down. They struggled on for another hour and a half, now well out over the North Sea, when at 25 minutes into the morning, the port inner engine cut as the petrol gave out. Atkinson had little choice now but to ditch. They hit the water at 00.34 am, in a choppy sea, on a dark night with no moon. The sea at the time had a 60-foot crest with waves across the swell at angles of 90° The tail hit a crest and broke off $1\frac{1}{2}$ feet behind the mid-upper turret and the aircraft nosed in. Water rushed into the nose section via the pilot's escape hatch, while the tail section disappeared, taking the wounded 20-year-old Canadian gunner, Sweeney, with it. The front section too went down quickly, taking George Atkinson down with it, but the others struggled free. The bomb aimer and engineer could not inflate the dinghy in the darkness and the mid-upper, Sergeant Boutell, having inflated his Mae West in the aircraft, had some anxious moments getting out of the escape hatch until helped by the others.

Attempts to inflate the dinghy all failed, and they spent the rest of the night supported by their life jackets. Luckily they were spotted by a rescue plane early next morning. A Lindholme lifeboat was dropped but it drifted past, for they were too weak to swim to it. But rescue was on the way and later they were picked up by an Air Sea Rescue launch – No 184 – from Yarmouth. Sergeant H. Friend, the bomb aimer, and navigator Sergeant D. Edwards, were cut and bruised. Sergeant J. Wilson, wireless operator, Sergeant Boutell, mid-upper, and Sergeant D. Hughes, the flight engineer, were all uninjured. Wilson gave credit to the others for his rescue, having been busy at his radio right to the end, enabling the rescue to come within twelve hours, although immersion in a winter sea for so long was far from pleasant.

An aircraft of 97 Squadron (JB238 'A') flown by Pilot Officer MacEgan, was hit by flak over Berlin and the return was made on two engines. They were hit again over Osnabrück and MacEgan gave the order to bale out when they were at 18,000 feet. Pilot Officer Adrian Spencer made his way towards the front of the aircraft and found the pilot's seat empty. He and the bomb aimer, Flying Officer Tyler, tried to keep the aircraft on a reasonable

Crashed Halifax

Crashed Lancaster

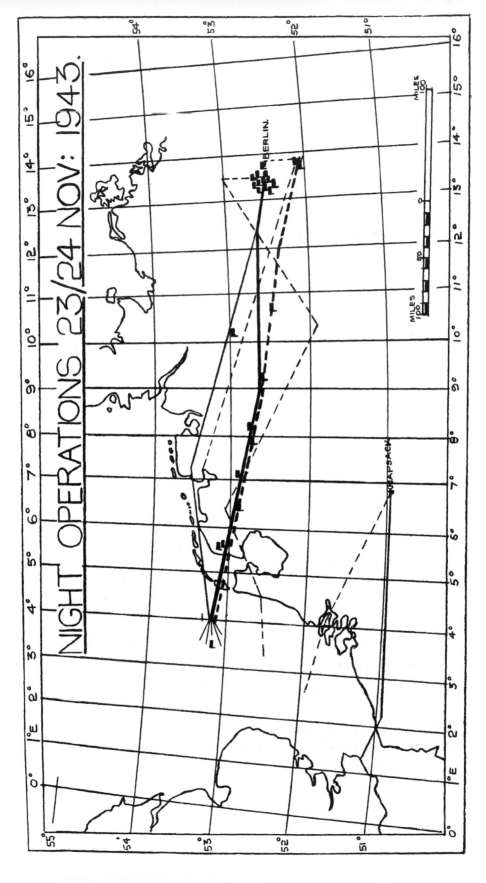

NIGHT OPERATIONS 23/24 NOV: 1943.

BERLIN.

KNAPSACK

MILES
100   50   0   MILES
100

straight and level flight-path, and found that the WOP and mid-upper had baled out.

MacEgan had in fact collapsed over the front hatch and Tyler tried to help him but by this time the aircraft was down to 200 feet. Seconds later it struck the ground, ploughing into a farmyard six miles from Osnabrück aerodrome. Spencer, Sergeant Johnson, Sergeant Gibb and wireless operator, Warrant Officer Burke, all survived. Spencer was dazed by the crash and as he crawled out of the wreckage was captured by men of the German Home Guard. He was later taken to Frankfurt for interrogation and later to Stalag Luft 1 at Barth. He remained a prisoner until liberated by Russian troops in May 1945.

Over England, Pilot Officer Hughes of 102 Squadron in Lancaster LW333 'K', was in a mid-air collision with a Lancaster of 77 Squadron killing both crews.

For many of the crews who had returned in the early hours of the morning of Sunday, 23rd November, there was to be no let up. A few hours' sleep and the call came for a morning attendance at the crew rooms to find out that they were flying again that night. The target again was Berlin.

*

The Third Raid

For this attack, 383 Lancasters, ten Halifaxes and six Mosquitos were on the line. The route would take them over the North Sea to Holland, then into Germany – 'Searchlight Alley' the men called it. They would have searchlights and guns on either side of them all the way to the Big City.

The method of attack for the Pathfinders was, first, primary blind markers, which would mark the aiming point with red TIs, and release one bundle of flares each – red with green stars – blindly on H_2S. Special blind markers were to mark the exact aiming point with reds and yellows in salvo, also dropping four bundles of flares. Secondary blind markers were to drop green TIs and release one bundle of flares. Early backers-up were to aim greens at the salvoes of reds and yellows, that is, if the target was visible, otherwise at the centre of the reds with a two second overshoot.

The Main Force aircraft were to bomb on the centre of all visible greens with a two second overshoot, or in difficult conditions, to adopt the method prescribed for the supporters, which were to bomb on H_2S unless of course, the sets were out of action, in which case they were to aim at the centre of the release point flares.

One member of 100 Squadron, Jimmy Flynn, awoke on the morning of the 23rd, having got to bed at 12.30 am, to hear the news that it was 'ops again' that night, but at the time he did not know the target. This he would discover at briefing later. He awoke with the sound of Merlin engines in his head from the night before and a taste in his mouth which he described as like a Christmas Tree, caused by the caffeine tablets taken the night before.

He had cause to remember this operation, too, as yet again his turret failed. It was very cold and he had to ensure that the saliva which ran down the oxygen mask and tube did not freeze up the flexible pipe which ran down into the main supply fitting. It was the policy to keep squeezing the tube to break up the small particles of ice which formed inside the tube. On this occasion it did not appear to work and he lapsed into unconsciousness. The last order he remembered was 'Bomb doors open' when coming up to the target. When he regained consciousness he was hanging inside the fuselage through the open turret doors, and could see the target burning behind him.

The wireless operator, Johnny MacAnaney, had somehow managed to extract him from the turret, not an easy job considering the amount of flying kit he was wearing. In doing so he would have had to disconnect the oxygen mask from the bayonet fitting and also from the intercom, and then slide him over the bulkhead into the fuselage while only wearing a small emergency oxygen bottle. He was later told by the mid-upper that while he was out a Ju88 was seen just above them, but luckily its pilot failed to see them.

The recollection of Jack Hamblin, also of 100 Squadron, was of seeing many miles ahead a large, ominous red glow in the sky. To the amazement of many crews, this turned out to be from the night before – fires still burning in the city. Then through a break in the clouds could be seen the outline of streets in the light of the fires. This break was probably caused by rising heat from the still burning city, which also threw the aircraft about like feathers over an updraught.

Over the city, Jack Hamblin was coned by numerous searchlights and his aircraft hit on the port side of the fuselage by a burst of heavy flak. Hamblin was trying to hold the aircraft steady as it bucked like a bronco at a rodeo. There was a heavy smell of cordite and a lot of noise from exploding AA shells.

The Goebbels' diaries made mention of this raid:

I just can't understand how the English are able to do so much

Jimmy Flynn

damage to the Reich's capital during one air raid. The picture that greeted my eye in the Wilhelmplatz was one of utter desolation, blazing fires everywhere.*

Fire engines were requisitioned from nearby towns and from as far away as Hamburg, while the Army had to supply two and a half divisions, some 50,000 men, whose sole job was to clear the main streets so that transport and food supplies could be resumed.

Another aircraft hit over Berlin, after releasing its bombs, was that flown by Flight Lieutenant Peter Williams of 7 Pathfinder Squadron. It was struck by a heavy burst of flak which severed the elevator controls. Williams immediately ordered the crew to don their parachutes in readiness to abandon the aircraft, but he found that by judicious handling of the engines and tail trimmers he was able to control the aircraft to a limited extent. He managed to gain height and set course for home. He eventually arrived over home base at 10,000 feet, but believing a safe landing was out of the question, he ordered the crew to bale out, though the navigator stayed with him. He then steered due north for some twenty miles and then both men baled out. For his efforts, he was recommended for an immediate DFC. It was his fifteenth trip.

*

The previous raid had been remarkable for the absence of fighters and for the accuracy and intensity of flak. On this night, the flak defences were about the same but the fighters made a greater effort. Ground controlled fighters could be heard along the route from the north of Holland to as far east as Quackenbruck, but they made no claims.

The running commentator directed freelance fighters from 6.12 pm, sending them towards Berlin at 7.30, and then concentrated them over Brandenburg at about eight o'clock – zero hour. From here they were directed to Berlin. The main body of fighters, it would appear, arrived over the city at about 8.08 pm. Two Lancasters of 50 Squadron were attacked here around about this time: Pilot Officer Dobbyn was attacked by a Ju88 which closed in from the port quarter and fired two bursts then broke away underneath. They reported a number of fighters over the target area. Flight Sergeant Loader was attacked by a Me110 and his mid-upper, Sergeant Tupman, opened up with a very long burst.

---

* Hamish Hamilton, 1948.

The fighter replied with a short burst of cannon fire and broke away to port. The navigator, Flying Officer Candy, then saw a Ju88 overhead. Once again Tupman opened fire with a long burst. The German moved to the starboard side and Tupman fired again. The rear gunner, Sergeant Coulson, was unable to fire as his guns had frozen up. Tupman claimed the Me110 as damaged in the crew's report.

A Lancaster of 100 Squadron (JB564), piloted by Warrant Officer Leman, was attacked on the way to Berlin by a fighter and the crew forced to bale out. Flight Lieutenant James Lake, the navigator, who had joined the army in 1940 and transferred to the RAF in 1941, landed in a field and after hiding his parachute and Mae West in a hollow tree, walked for some miles and met the bomb aimer, Flight Sergeant Jefferies. He had injured his back when landing and was too badly hurt to walk so they gave themselves up to a farmer; he sent for the army who came along to collect them. They were taken to a military barracks where they met Leman. After interrogation they were taken to a main camp and for the rest of the war remained PoWs. Sergeant Daniels, the engineer, was also captured but sadly the rear gunner, Sergeant Fuller, was lost and never found, and Sergeants Lloyd and Chandler also died.

Another Lancaster (JA865 'A') of 166 Squadron, flown by Warrant Officer Eric Grove, was attacked on its bombing run, being hit from below by an upward firing fighter, and the aircraft was set on fire. Attempts to put the fire out failed and so the order to bale out was given. The crew went out at 4,000 feet and five of them later became PoWs, but the two gunners were lost.

No German fighters were claimed destroyed, but observations suggest that two fighters were in fact brought down over Berlin. The missing RAF aircraft totalled 21, with 27 others damaged – 14 to flak, four to fighters and nine to other causes. On the way to Berlin, four aircraft were seen to crash between the Dutch coast and Leeuwarden. The causes of the losses were obscure, as no fighter claims were heard on the air. Four more were shot down by fighters between Groningen and Hannover, and one to guns at Texel. Over Berlin three aircraft were destroyed by flak in the first fifteen minutes of the attack and five by fighters, one in the early stages, two towards the end, and two shortly after turning for home. Of the damaged aircraft, six were beyond repair, one from flak, the others as a result of landing accidents.

A personal report by Major John Mullock of the Royal Artillery, attached to the Pathfinder Force as flak liaison officer, was made after this, his first, trip to Berlin. He flew in a Mosquito of 139 Squadron, flown by Group Captain L.C. Slee DSO DFC. They took off at 6.12 pm from RAF Wyton, carrying twelve white drip flares – 'Spoofs'. They were to release them at twenty-second intervals while over the centre of Berlin. Major Mullock was kept busy dropping Window. One bundle of this represented one aircraft echo on enemy radar screens. It did not jam, but confused and 'cluttered-up' the screens. Mullock was also trying to rub ice off the inside of the perspex in the nose of the aircraft, which he found exhausting; it was 47° outside and very warm inside resulting in heavy condensation.

They dropped their white flares at 8.12, from a height of 32,000 feet. He saw them ignite and thought how they compared with the ones the Germans used. They were in fact similar to those used by the Germans in their night fighters. Mullock later reported:

> After the attack had been going for four to five minutes the flak was entirely barrage, spread over a vast area and wildly dispersed in height. No bursts were seen above an approx height of 23,000 feet. There seemed to be no attempt to fire a barrage over any one part of the city as might have been expected. The rate of fire of most of the guns would appear to have been something in the region of five to six rounds per minute.
>
> Several of the blind markers were undoubtedly shot down in the early stages by predictor control (unseen fire). This was due to the fact that the backers-up were late and thus did not provide any cover. When the attack on Berlin had developed concentration and window cover obviously precluded the use of radar. The impression gained was that the defences were in a state of utter confusion and were firing blindly and wildly.

Major Mullock was destined to go to Berlin on two further occasions during the battle, and eventually made five visits to the Big City out of his 22 ops. He was recommended for the DFC in August 1944.

The radio counter-measure known as 'Corona' was once again used and caused considerably annoyance to the German commentators. They were forced to prefix many messages with code numbers. They also tried using a woman as a mouthpiece, but were immediately countered by a German-speaking female Corona operator in England who passed messages, including warnings such as fog at base and ordering German pilots to land as quickly as possible.

This system was first used in October 1943. It was introduced to counter the enemy's use of high power running commentary broadcasts known as 'Rapid Reporting Frequency'. The technique often involved using as many as three controllers on different frequencies. A system had to be found to confuse the enemy night fighter pilots by working on the same frequency as his own controllers. If these two signals were received by the fighters approximately equal in strength the frequency originated by the British could be modulated in such a way as to confuse and distract the enemy pilots by the transmission of conflicting instructions.

This was done by suitably placed transmitters in England of adequate power and relying on skywave propagation. The enemy pilot, when airborne, could be made to receive a very strong radio transmission signal comparable with the direct ray reception from his own ground station. The operators were fluent German-speaking, trained for the purpose and were told what to say to the enemy pilots. The controller at HQ Bomber Command would pass, by scrambler, to the controller at Kingsdown in Kent, the bombers' route out and back, about an hour before take-off time, and also the times of main and diversionary attacks, the target, diversionary target and any feint raids.

If the German controllers seemed to choose the feint or the wrong target, or re-directed fighters away from the correct target, the Kingsdown operator would take no action. If doubt were shown as to the bombers' target, or the Germans seemed confused in his orders, Kingsdown would reinforce the incorrect conclusions. If the enemy selected the right target and directed their fighters towards it in time to intercept the bombers, then incorrect information would immediately be broadcast regarding position and direction of the bombers.

*

One Lancaster of 9 Squadron (ED656 'V') flown by Pilot Officer N.J. Robinson crashed in England on its return from Berlin at approximately 11.45 am, fog having set in the area of the crash. Villagers at Belchford, near Ludford Magna, heard the four-engined aircraft circling low in the fog. They saw a brief glimpse of it as it clipped the top of a row of trees close to the village church before it reared up, stalled and then crashed nose-down into a nearby field. Six of the crew were killed instantly, but the two gunners, Sergeant Casey and Flight Sergeant Mitchell, were thrown clear. Casey went to the assistant of Mitchell despite having facial burns, to find Mitchell with a fractured leg and burns to his face and hands. He had dragged himself clear before the aircraft went up in flames. Villagers gave them first aid before they went off to RAF Hospital, Rauceby.

The site of the crash is now owned by a farmer, himself a former pilot with 101 Squadron. Parts of the aircraft have been found in the area recently.

Another aircraft of 9 Squadron (DV327), flown by Pilot Officer C. Ward, crashed on making a turn to port on his second approach to land. It went into a shallow dive to starboard, did not respond to the controls and crashed, but luckily the crew escaped unhurt.

The Germans reported the raid as starting at 7.26 pm and estimated that 120 mines, 850 high explosive, 20,000 phosphorus bombs, 250,000 incendiaries, and 70 flares had been dropped. Some 1,989 houses were destroyed and 2,442 others severely and 20,000 slightly damaged. One military installation was destroyed and 21 damaged, 15 severely. Eight industrial targets were destroyed, with 22 more severely and 22 slightly damaged. In addition the power station at Spandau was destroyed. Casualties were 13,005 killed, 6,383 injured while 300,000 people were made homeless.

On the morning of the 24th, the bombed parts of Berlin looked ghastly. Prisoners of war were put to work excavating blocked cellars but the only people who seemed to be working well were German troops – infantry, Waffen SS and men of the Luftwaffe.

The Times reported that bomber crews having said they could see a glow from 100 miles of Berlin. The weight of bombs dropped per aircraft was: Halifaxes 26,623 pounds, and Lancasters 9,639 pounds. Bomber Command lost 5.49% of the raiding force – all Lancasters, the weight of bombs dropped per missing aircraft was 66.1 tons.

A signal was sent by the Secretary of State for Air, to the C in C Bomber Command, Sir Arthur Harris:

My warmest congratulations to you and all ranks serving under your command on two crushing attacks upon the Nazi citadel. Berlin is not only the home of Nazi militarism and the capital of

De-briefing after Berlin raid

A 78 Squadron crew

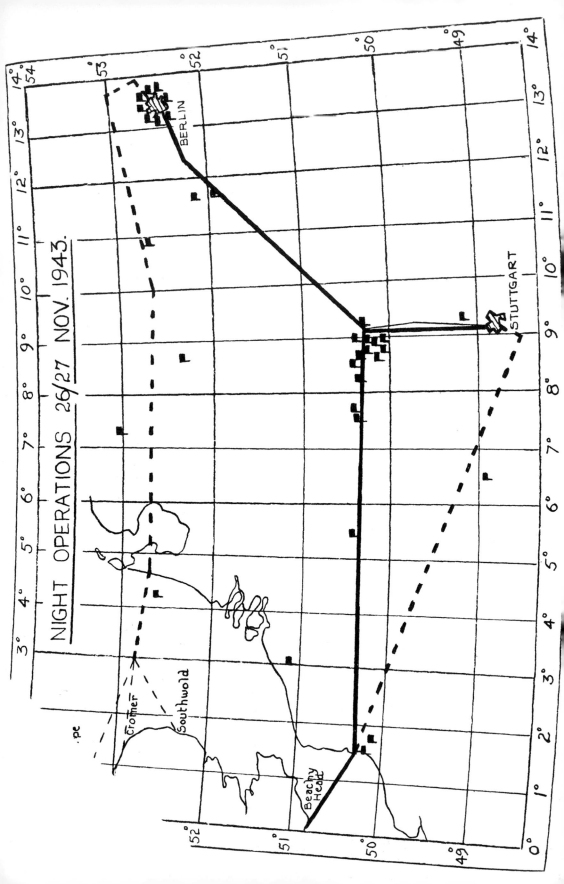

NIGHT OPERATIONS 26/27 NOV. 1943.

BERLIN

STUTTGART

Cromer

Southwold

Beachy Head

Nazi Government but is also the greatest single centre of war industry in Germany. Often before your squadrons have struck it hard. The most convincing measure of their success has been the huge deployment of the enemy's resources for its defence. Nevertheless, your attacks these last two nights have reached a new level of power and concentration and have proved that however much he may marshal his guns, searchlights and fighters, the enemy cannot match your skill and resource or the valour and determination of your crews.

*

The Fourth Raid

Another attack on the Big City was planned for 25th November but was scrubbed through bad weather. Instead the next raid was arranged for the following night. One man, Ernie Cummings, a flight engineer with 83 Squadron – Pathfinders – awoke from a deep sleep feeling warm and snug between warm linen sheets – a great luxury in the services in WW2. It was 6.45 am and dawn was just breaking. He shared a large room at RAF Wyton, near Huntingdon, with thirteen other men. Because of the op being scrubbed the night before, he had spent the evening in the local haunt for aircrew, The George, in Huntingdon itself.

After breakfast he joined his pilot, Alec Shipway, and the rest of the crew and they went to their various crew rooms. Here Ernie met fellow engineers and they discussed the problems and modification of their aircraft. Later he was to learn they were flying that night, but there was a good deal to do before dark. An air test on their new H_2S set – known as H_2S-X (Mk III), hurriedly fitted to two aircraft of 83 Squadron being virtually hand-built. One was used by Flying Officer Bernard Moorcroft and the second by Flight Lieutenant Wilson – ex-83 but now a blind bombing staff officer at HQ 8 Group.

They had not been ready for the first Berlin operation on the 18th; in fact it was not until the 19th that they were even ready for trial testing over London, the nearest conditions to Berlin itself.

It was first used on the operation of the 22nd but at 10.50 pm near the Dutch coast Moorcroft had to enter in his log: 'Y burnt out.' They had to abort so as not to risk being shot down and the new set being captured. If it was, it might in turn be used by the Germans in a night raid on London. Obviously the crew were not happy at missing the chance to add another op to their eventual Pathfinder total of 45 missions. The set again went U/S on the 23rd over Texel so once again they had to return. In fact, of ten ops to Berlin in which Moorcroft took part, three were aborted because of the set not working.

The Mark III had a three-centimetre, instead of the usual ten, waveband. By narrowing the waveband a clearer picture of the ground, and target area was given. The question of who was to get these greatly sought-after sets had been discussed earlier that month – was it to be Coastal or Bomber Command? Finally Bomber Command won and the Pathfinders were the first to receive them, for they had already begun to prove their worth in the earlier Berlin raids.

The flight Ernie Cummings and crew were to undertake to test the set was planned for over London and the aiming point was to be Fenchurch St. Railway Station. They took off at 10.35 am (in JB352) and were due over London at 11.15. Moorcroft directed them to the AP (aiming point) with his new set, as he had a complete map of the ground below the aircraft on the screen. He could clearly make out the River Thames and all the bridges and parks in London. He was asked by one of the crew if he could see the Windmill Theatre and to tell them what was showing at the time!

They made their 'bombing run' from Fenchurch Street and cameras were set and fixed to check their aiming point over two runs. The run-ups were carried out as if it were the real thing, right down to the opening of the bomb doors. Ernie wondered what people in the streets below made of this. As they were leaving London, 'Jock' Denoun, the mid-upper, sighted the Spitfire which was to make mock attacks on them. Only the gunners were allowed to speak over the intercom. The rear gunner, Flight Sergeant Phil Lewis, shouted: 'Fighter passing on starboard quarter!', then, 'Dive, dive, dive.' Alex Shipway immediately pushed the stick forward and turned very tightly; then they literally were falling out of the sky, their stomachs up in their chests. This was repeated for about twenty minutes, and all this right over London.

They arrived back at base at mid-day after an hour and 45 minutes' flying. Briefing for that night's op was at two o'clock, so little time was left for anything but lunch.

At briefing, the crews were told of their set-up. The Pathfinder blind markers would drop a bundle of release point flares (red with green stars) and mark with red TIs, while operating on H_2S special blind markers – carrying the new H_2S – would mark the exact

Lancaster bombing up with 4,000 cookie and incendiaries

Ernie Cummings' scarf

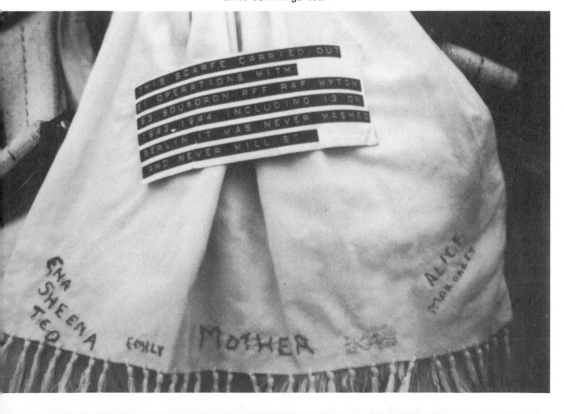

aiming points with red and yellows in salvos and drop bundles of close point flares, once again on H₂S. Secondary blind markers would bomb at regular intervals throughout the attack, keeping the AP illuminated with greens and release point flares, dropped blindly.

Early backers-up would drop greens at the salvos of reds and yellows if still visible otherwise at the centre of each with two second overshoots. Later backers-up would aim greens at the centre of all greens already dropped, once again with a small overshoot. Window of course would again be used.

Three Mosquitos of 139 Squadron were to attack the target before the Main Force began, at zero, minus six minutes, also dropping bundles of Window. Four other Mossies of 139 would proceed to the target, then turn on a track of 145° and fly for 3½ minutes on this track, then release spoof fighter flares at 20-second intervals. Three more Mosquitos would attack after the Main Force, at zero plus 120 minutes.

*

Flight Lieutenant Alex Shipway DFC 83 Squadron and his crew were to have a hectic start to the operation after their trip over London. While at dispersal, Flying Officer Hyde's aircraft blew up, killing several of its ground crew. It also damaged Flight Lieutenant Sambridge's aircraft, forcing him to cancel. The glare from the explosion was taken full in the face by Shipway's rear gunner, Phil Lewis, and so affected his night vision that he was replaced by Sergeant Adams.

Nevertheless, at exactly 5.39 pm, Shipway, from Bristol, with his engineer, Ernie Cummings, taxied out to the runway, turned the aircraft into the wind and took off. He reached the English coast at 6.10, having climbed to 14,000 feet, and was still climbing; all the crew had their oxygen masks firmly clipped in position. Looking down they were able to see the waves of the North Sea as it was not very dark; it looked like a solid mass of grease.

They reached 22,000 feet and levelled out, then reset the throttles and the propellers to cruising speed and pitch. At 6.35 came the first turning point. The navigator was checking the course to give to Shipway, so the bomb doors were opened just long enough for a white sky flare to be dropped. All the crew, on reaching the enemy coast, were checked by Shipway, the engines and controls were given a final once over, for from now on everything had to be tip-top. Shipway began to weave; no straight and level flying for him or any experienced crew. While weaving they would also drop down a few feet or so, then climb up again, giving less chance of being picked up by fighters. Another ploy to insure against being surprised from below was occasionally to turn the Lancaster over onto its wing tip and let the mid-upper get a view of the sky below.

Their next turning point was Brandenburg. From here they could go to any part of Germany, so as there was a diversionary raid on Stuttgart, the Germans would have some difficulty in deciding where the raid was to take place. To the left was Bremen and slightly ahead Hannover, both heavily defended, with searchlights already probing the sky for them. If they got a hold on an aircraft it became a cat and mouse game. The pilot would turn into them which made them pass by, then immediately swing back. The aircraft then turned again into the glare and once more it would miss.

Suddenly the wireless operator came on the intercom: 'There's a fighter close by!'

Shipway started to corkscrew and the radio signal showed they had shaken it off. The gunners saw behind and to their left an aircraft blow up and another caught in the cone of a searchlight. Things were hotting up. It was all for real from now on.

The next turning point was passed and the bomb doors opened momentarily for a white flare to be dropped. A new course was given, putting the Lancaster on its last leg towards Berlin. This was what they had come for. The navigator estimated ETA in ten minutes. Run-up checks were carried out. They were to drop TIs and bomb with the new H_2S set. All about them the flak became very intense. 'ETA four minutes.' The bomb doors were again opened. Shipway kept the aircraft straight and level for the bombing run. Searchlights were everywhere and the ride a little bumpy. Then they were coned by searchlights which followed them from west to south-east making it impossible for the operator to use his H_2S screen to bomb. It was therefore decided to drop the 4,000 lb 'Cookie' on the next run and retain the TIs and flares. Letting go the Cookie, Shipway opened the throttles to the full and went into a dive, corkscrewing all the time. The speed reached 350 mph which was the recommended limit for a dive. Beyond this and it would take some pulling out, but the speed went up to 400 mph and it took the combined strength of both the pilot and Ernie Cummings to pull the aircraft out. To them it seemed like hours but in fact it had only taken eight minutes. Gradually a height of 22,000 feet and the correct course was reached.

In ED859 'V' of 619 Squadron, the crew were also having an eventful night. They had been briefed to fly towards Frankfurt, south of the Ruhr. Lieutenant Nick Knilans, an American with Bomber Command (later to fly with the famous 617 Dambuster Squadron), saw the TIs cascading down in the red, yellow and green streams as he flew north of Berlin. He then received a message on the intercom from the mid-upper, Flight Sergeant Robinson:

'My turret is U/S!'

'Okay, keep a sharp look out where you can,' Knilans replied.

The wireless op was receiving signals and called: 'Bandit at 6 o'clock at 600 yards!' Both gunners were asked if they could see anything:

'Not yet,' came the replies.

With that a bright stream of tracer shells shot over the port wing and the rear gunner yelled: 'Corkscrew Port!' and opened fire with his four machine guns as the pilot dived and climbed in a corkscrew motion. One of the gunners shouted that it was a Ju88. The engineer, Ken Ryall, then said;

'I'm feathering the port engine.'

Everybody was looking for fighters, the WOP from the astrodome above his head, the engineer to port. In came the Ju88 again for another bite at the apple. Once again Knilans put the Lancaster into a dive and a side slip to port. The 88 flew a few feet over the fuselage with all its guns firing. It circled the Lancaster and the rear gunner was heard firing and the fighter seen to go down in flames.

As the German fighter tactics sometimes was to operate in pairs, one to draw the fire from the bomber, the other to use the exchange as an aiming point, they all kept a sharp look out. No sooner had the 88 gone down than a dark shape came hurtling towards them.

Knilans put the aircraft into a dive at the same time shouted: 'Shoot straight up, Roy,' to the rear gunner. Roy Learmouth's guns immediately chattered. The shape passed over them and the mid-upper yelled:

'It's a Me109.'

The attacks had put out the port inner engine and damaged the elevators in the tail assembly. Although he was still 240 miles from Berlin, Knilans decided to carry on. They eventually reached the city, dropped their bombs from 13,000 feet, and turned for home. The light from searchlights, explosions and fires below rocked the Lancaster and blinded Knilans so much that he had to lower his seat and fly on instruments. They then set a course for home though

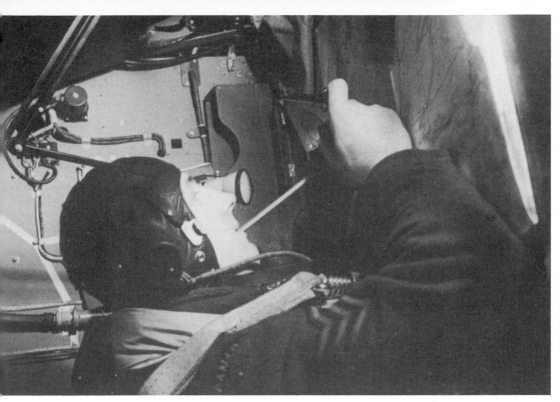

Navigator at work

619 Squadron crew

they were beginning to lose height. Whilst trying to keep up with the Main Force, by the time they were at the Dutch coast they were down to 2,000 feet.

On arrival at Woodall Spa, 619's base (later the home of 617 Squadron) they found the aerodrome shrouded in fog and were told by ground control to fly to Scotland. In their state this was impossible and so they made for nearby Spilsby and successfully landed there on three engines. From there they travelled to Woodall in a van but the journey was slow because of the fog and it needed a man walking in the front with a flashlight. By the time they arrived they had been away for over twelve hours. The problems did not always end when one had landed back in England! For his actions this time, Nick Knilans was awarded the DSO, the first awarded to 619 Squadron since its formation, and Roy Learmouth was awarded an immediate DFM.

The bad weather had kept the German fighter groups in the Berlin area grounded but when the bomber force was seen coming from the north-east, Fighter Group NJG/5 were ordered up by Command Centre Operational HQ, regardless of cost or losses, as were the day fighters of JG/3. Time, however, had been lost and the bombers had already bombed. Only the later waves were attacked and in all 27 bombers were lost and fourteen arrived back at base only fit for the scrap heap.

An aircraft of 50 Squadron, flown by Pilot Officer Weatherstone, was attacked by a Ju88 on the inward journey. The rear gunner, Sergeant Collingwood, opened fire only to find one out of his four guns working, the other three being frozen. However, he did manage to get a shot in and claimed the 88 as damaged.

Lancaster LL632 'G' of 432 Squadron, piloted by Flight Sergeant Dervine of the RCAF, was attacked by three Me210s while on the outskirts of Frankfurt and flying at 19,000 feet. A flare path had been laid down by fighters just after the 210s attacked. During the short period of four to five minutes, the fighters made three attacks. The rear gunner, Sergeant Quesnel, found his guns frozen and the mid-upper Sergeant Riding, had a stoppage in his left gun but managed to fire about 100 rounds. The Lancaster suffered about fifteen bullet holes.

Wing Commander Frederick Hilton AFC, of 7 Squadron, took off from Oakington at 5.30 pm. On the way to Berlin he was attacked by a fighter and the aircraft set on fire. Hilton gave the order to bale out and all got out except Pilot Officer Leonard who was killed.

Hilton was later taken to Stalag Luft 1 at Barth and became Senior British Officer of the camp on and off till May 1945.

Bomb aimer Jack Hamblin of 100 Squadron was lying in his bomb aiming compartment watching the bombing area, directing his pilot when they were caught fair and square by a searchlight and held. His night vision went and for a moment he was blinded. Then came a fearful flash and explosion and the aircraft was lifted by an enormous blast. His perspex window was holed but within a few seconds his sight returned and he went on to bomb the target. He remembers stuffing the holes with paper and rags.

Pilot Officer John Pryor (LM366 'H') of 207 Squadron was also attacked by a fighter in the Frankfurt area. The Monica in the aircraft (the device that let you know when another aircraft was nearby) had gone U/S and its pipping sound kept up all the way across the North Sea and continued as the WOP was instructed to use it at all times and never be put off by the rest of the crew complaining about the noise. He was finally ordered by Pryor to shut the thing off. Only ten minutes later came a terrific crack and a smell of acrid smoke. John Pryor immediately went into a corkscrew and the WOP – Albert Hepworth – turned on the Monica set and again it started pipping. By now smoke was entering the aircraft. On removing the covers over the bomb bay, sparks and flame came up and it became obvious that some of the incendiaries were on fire.

Common sense then prevailed and the bomb load jettisoned by Pilot Officer Pesme, the bomb aimer. The Monica continued to pip all the way back to the coast and just beyond when it suddenly stopped. They landed safely at Woodbridge.

The famous Lancaster S for Sugar (R5868) of 467 Squadron had a narrow squeak over Berlin. Its pilot, Jack Colpus, was flying straight and level, having completed the bombing run, allowing time for the photograph, when another Lancaster, taking evasive action from a fighter, corkscrewed into them. It hit Sugar on the starboard wing, bending but not breaking it, some twelve feet from the wing tip. The effect, however, was an uncontrollable descent from about 28,000 feet to 10,000, where Colpus finally managed to regain control. He flew it back to a safe landing at Tholthorpe in Yorkshire, not its own base at Waddington. The other aircraft, from 61 Squadron (DV311) flown by Pilot Officer J.W. Einarson, also got back and apologies were tended to Sugar's crew.

Sugar had to undergo major surgery, having to have a new wing. by this time she had flown some 80 ops. The 61 Squadron Lanc too had to have repairs but flew again in the new year.

One aircraft of 460 Squadron was also in trouble over the target. It had just pulled away when it began to fill with smoke. The windows were opened and emergency oxygen used. The cause was found to be the two electric convertors associated with GEE and the radio system position, under the navigator's table. After the electric power had been closed down the smoke subsided and later it was discovered that the damage had occurred by shrapnel while the bomb doors were open.

Once again Group Captain Slee of 139 Squadron flew in a Mosquito (DZ601) and again with Major Mullock as his observer. As before, Mullock made a full report. They had taken off at 6.55 pm from Wyton and over Cologne they saw several aircraft coned and surrounded by intense flak. As they neared Koblenz, searchlights could be observed as far as the eye could see. Just south of Koblenz, some twenty searchlights made a determined effort to illuminate them and many fighters were seen around Frankfurt.

They approached Berlin from the west and could see the defences of Brunswick and Magdeburg in action with the vast amount of searchlights. One in particular – the master beam with its bright blue extra wide light – could be seen in a dense and wide belt all around Berlin. Some 31 beams were counted ahead of them, it seemed as light as day in the aircraft.

They had arranged to communicate with a Mosquito flight commander over Berlin, but when they were coned, they called: 'Hello Junior, Junior, do you see that poor fellow cornered up there, well that's us!' After they had dropped their spoof fighter flares they then dropped twelve bundles of Window.

On his return, Mullock remarked on their being coned over the city and concluded:

> Considering the heavy bombers were beneath the Mosquito, it was most remarkable that the searchlights were able to select targets above. It would appear Radar could only operate successfully against aircraft considerably above the Main Force and out of the Window cover. The initial pick-up must have been accomplished by means of Radar after which it would appear that the control was visual. Condensation trials were a great help to searchlights. One pilot was coned at 28,000 feet over Berlin, escaping from the beams almost immediately after losing sufficient height to ensure that condensation trails did not occur.

It was an old trick of the Germans to leave a gun blacked out until an unsuspecting aircraft was well within range of the majority of defences; many pilots were caught by this ruse.

The aircraft returning to base were up against foggy conditions and many were diverted to other fields. The weather had in fact worsened by 1 am in England, except in the West Midlands and South Coast areas. Many aircraft returning were peppered with light flak holes.

Most of the bomb damage appeared to be in the Remchendorf-Tegal area where there were a group of extremely important industries, including armaments and engineering factories. The Pathfinder reports showed eleven of the twelve primary blind marking points attacked; the twelfth aircraft was shot down. The German fighter controller seemed to have been misled into thinking the attack was on Frankfurt. Over Berlin some 40 fighters were seen and nine combats took place but later many came after bombers straying off course on their way home. These were picked up by controlled fighters operating between Bremen and the Ruhr. In the main these were Ju88s, also FW200s seen near Frankfurt and Berlin.

The RAF lost 27 aircraft with 79 more damaged, 40 to flak and 11 to fighters. Three suffered collision damage, the other 25 due to other causes. Of the 27 lost, nine went down over Berlin (seven to flak, two to fighters) and four to controlled fighters in the area between Bremen and the Ruhr. Nine went down on the outward route, three to flak between the Dutch coast and Coblenz, with two more down between Bremen and Hanover.

The weather was the cause of some of the crashes in England. Flying Officer Mike Beetham and his crew were directed to Pocklington because their base at Skellingthorpe was fogbound, but at a height of 5,000 feet the aircraft started to ice up, so they went lower to where the aircraft began to thaw out. At a height of 1,000 feet they crossed the coast near the Humber. Visibility was bad at Pocklington. The flarepath was visible but on calling up Pocklington, Beetham was told to go onto Melbourne to land. By now they were nearly out of fuel but they managed it and made a safe landing. They were the first of 50 Squadron's returning aircraft to land here.

Pilot Officer R. Neil in a Lancaster (ED873) of 106 Squadron, returned early with one starboard engine surging, and he was unable to maintain height. He jettisoned his bomb load and approached Methringham on three engines but overshot and crashed in a nearby field. The rear gunner was the only casualty, suffering a broken arm.

Pilot Officer Yell, an Australian flying a Lancaster (JB354 'O') of 12 Squadron, crash-landed near Binbrook (he was one of three 12 Squadron aircraft to crash land). Sergeant A. Twitchett (JB464) and Sergeant J. Jones (JB668 'T') both had their aircraft damaged by flak. Both crews were unharmed, but sadly Twitchett and Yell were to be lost on the next operation.

Lancaster LM378 'J', piloted by Flying Officer R. Foote, landed at Woodbridge on their return at 1.05 am. Their return was far from smooth. They had been shot up by flak, had no hydraulics, were very low on fuel as their tanks had been hit and leaking petrol. In code, they broke radio silence to request emergency landing permission and were ordered to Woodbridge in Suffolk. The landing was hairy, to say the least. They straddled three runways before they came to a halt and later the aircraft was written off.

The crew, happily uninjured, had to stay the night – or what was left of it – at Woodbridge. The next morning at 8 am they were on Ipswich railway station, still in their flying kit and carrying parachutes. A dear old lady seeing the mid-upper struggling with his kit, offered to help him and grabbed his parachute by the release handle, at which the 'chute promptly spilled out, and she went careering down the platform with it billowing out as the breeze caught it. It certainly gave the Ipswich commuters something to smile at that morning. This crew later transferred to the Path Finder Force and took part in a further seven trips to Berlin during the battle.

Flight Sergeant R. Lloyd, flying Lancaster DS712 'G' of 408 Squadron, had a very difficult outward trip. Just before reaching Berlin their starboard outer engine failed, causing the aircraft to lose height, but from 18,000 feet they still managed to bomb at 12.16 pm. The bombs, however, were seen to fall some distance short of the aiming point. The engine then magically restarted but then the intercom to the mid-upper went U/S. Near Magdeburg they were hit by flak and the mid-upper, Sergeant Roberts, wounded in the foot. This was not the end of their troubles: to complete their night they were attacked by a Ju88 night fighter and the aircraft hit in the mid-upper turret. The engine pressure to the starboard inner engine fell and was feathered.

They set course for Stradishall but on reaching it safely, they decided to go on to Fiskerton. On arrival the starboard outer engine cut and the rudder trim packed up, sending the aircraft into a shallow spiral dive from 5,000 feet. The crew were ordered out, but this was countermanded as the escape hatch proved difficult to open, and it was decided to crash-land. A call of 'Darky' and 'May Day' on the radio, received no acknowledgment but they managed to pick up another aircraft and received some directions from them. They finally made a belly landing in a sewage disposal ground 1½ miles south east of Lincoln.

This was the first operation of 463 Australian Squadron since its formation on 25th November, under its new CO, Wing Commander Rollo Kingsford-Smith, nephew of the late Air Commodore Sir Charles Kingsford Smith – the first man to fly across the Pacific from the USA to Australia. At 24, the Wing Commander was the youngest squadron commander in Bomber Command. He had good support from two flight commanders, Squadron Leader H.B. Locke DFC, with 26 ops to his name, and Squadron Leader Brill DFC, who had completed a tour on Wellingtons.

*

The Germans recorded the following for the night of 26/27th November raid: Berlin was attacked between 8.52 and 10.30 pm and some 60 mines, 650 HE bombs, 10,000 phosphorus and 100 incendiary bombs, plus 100 flares, were dropped. 470 people died, 2,099 more injured and 25,000 made homeless. Eleven industrial firms were destroyed and 37 severely plus 42 slightly damaged. The official figure for HE bombs dropped was 859 plus 717 incendiaries.

Dr Goebbels in his diary recorded that this time it was the suburbs that were mainly hit, particularly the large munition plants in Reinickendorf. The Alekett factory, the most important German maker of field artillery, producing half of the entire output, was set on fire and despite attempts to put it out it was destroyed. The great Berlin Assembly Hall was burnt to the ground. The diary recorded:

That is a heavy blow. The Führer too is very much depressed. The situation has become even more alarming since one industrial plant after another has been set on fire.*

The central telephone exchange was destroyed but Hitler could still be reached by a still intact direct line, and this was when he ordered

* Hamish Hamilton 1948.

the fire departments in Berlin to the burning tank plant. When Albert Speer arrived at the plant the main workshop was mainly burnt out.

It was after this raid that regular troops of the Berlin garrison were taken off salvage and replaced by sapper units. Large numbers had been brought into Berlin and they worked magnificently in dousing still smouldering fires and in blowing up houses too badly damaged to be repaired, which had become dangerous. Confusion was beginning to set in among the people. For instance, the Ministry of Foreign Affairs had been evacuated from the Wilhelmstrasse and nobody seemed to know where it had gone. The Military Postal Censorship Centre was completely wiped out which meant that about three-quarters of all foreign mail would lie in bags until it was finally destroyed, as mail uncollected for two weeks was simply burned. The problem of the administration of such a large city was that the evacuation of many Government organisations was out of the question. The furniture and staff, of course, could be evacuated, but once out of Berlin the departments concerned could not function effectively.

Berlin was being damaged despite bad weather. This same weather was also stopping the required photographic evidence needed by Bomber Command. Almost continual cloud cover prevented the recce aircraft from seeing the ground. Bomber Command believed it was hitting hard, but just how hard they could not tell.

CHAPTER FIVE

Over Berlin

On 29th November the Chief of the Air Staff wrote to Lord Salisbury:

> There is no change in the Government's bombing policy. Our aim is to dislocate and destroy the German military, industrial and economic system. I have never pretended that this is possible to pursue without inflicting terrible casualties on the population of Germany. But neither I nor any responsible speaker on behalf of the Government have ever gloated over the destruction of German homes.
>
> A reprisal policy we have resisted despite pressure from the Poles to do so. Also the Czechs after the destruction of Lidice. We refused and stuck to the policy of military targets. Harris said – 'The heart of Germany must cease to beat.' He meant the residential heart, but he is an airman and thinks of Germany in terms of war. He thinks Berlin is the heart of the German War Organisation. Berlin is the greatest single centre of German War Industry, plus the principal centre of the canal system in Germany, also the centre of German Administration.

*

The Fifth Raid

The onslaught on Berlin continued into December. On the night of 2/3rd December, 440 Lancasters, fifteen Halifaxes of 35 Squadron and eighteen Mosquitos of 139 Squadron were detailed. The weather forecast promised low cloud and a 40 mph wind at base, with 60 mph winds over Holland, but down to 30 mph over north-west Germany and even promised lower over Berlin itself – 20 to 25 mph.

The plan of attack was much the same as the previous raids where cloudy conditions prevailed. Four Mosquitos were detailed to drop flares to the south of the city as feint attacks. Four others would drop

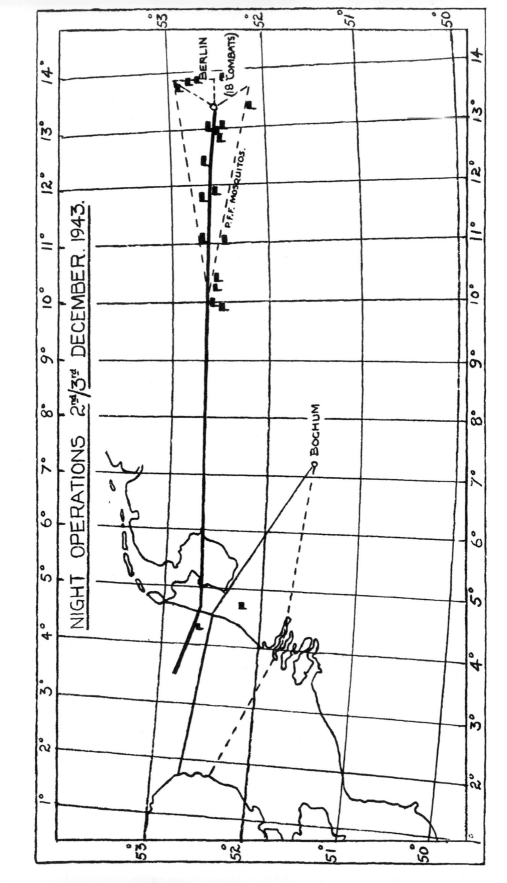

NIGHT OPERATIONS 2nd/3rd DECEMBER. 1943.

BERLIN

(18 COMBATS)

P.F.F. MOSQUITOS.

BOCHUM

Window and bombs while four more would bomb the centre of the fires. The PFF plans were for primary blind markers using H_2S while secondary blind markers were to drop red TIs, either blindly or visually. The primary blind markers were to drop red TIs on the aiming point and release one bundle of sky-markers guided by Oboe – code-named 'Wanganui', – red with green stars. Thirty primary blind markers were despatched, including four equipped with H_2S Mark III. These would not carry TIs of a distinctive colour as on previous operations. Of these aircraft, 24 attacked, three bombed alternative targets, one returned early and two failed to return. Over Berlin these markers dropped sixteen salvos of reds and fifteen bundles of 'Wanganui' flares. All seventeen secondary blind markers which set out attacked, ten dropping greens, but only seven used H_2S as six of the sets went U/S. The latter, therefore, had to act as backers-up.

Despite the forecast winds, those actually found differed considerably. Once over the Dutch coast the winds veered sharply to the north between the Dutch and German borders and over Berlin. Most crews failed to notice this change and based their flight calculations on a southerly instead of northerly wind and were blown many miles south of track, consequently arriving late at the target. Some 'Y' aircraft (H_2S) found their own winds from their H_2S fixes on route, but those differed so much from those forecast that the latter was used in preference. Few of the blind markers successfully identified the starting point for their DR runs, while others, attempting to map read on H_2S, probably mistook the towns of Genthin-Brandenburg-Potsdam, for the parallel series, Stendal-Rathenow-Nauen, thus coming into the target on a track fifteen miles south of that which was intended. Many made an attempt on a DR run but tried to home directly on the built-up area of Berlin. As a result of these errors in navigation the Red TIs were scattered. The winds in fact experienced were 50 mph over bases, 20-30 mph over Berlin.

The aircraft were spread over a period of seventeen minutes. The red TIs, while scattered, made a resemblance of a concentration five to eight miles south-east of the aiming point which was then backed up by green TIs. These attracted about two-thirds of the Main Force aircraft and a moderately concentrated attack developed over an area of fifteen square miles, centred seven miles SSE of the AP on outlying suburbs. The remaining one-third of the Force was probably scattered over a wide area, but ground sources indicated that the raid completely disorganised the administrative machinery in the city.

At Naucn the Germans had the largest decoy fire site in the Berlin region. It was fifteen miles west of the city and extended for nine miles. Decoy TIs were dropped into the decoy fire site which then attracted the searchlights and flak guns, which took some of the heat off the bombers over Berlin. The ground defences at the beginning of the attack consisted of heavy flak fired in loose barrage up to 22,000 feet, around the marker flares, and was predicted at 'seen' targets through gaps in the cloud. A continuous belt of searchlights were reported between Hannover and Emden and flak was encountered from these towns as well as from Bremen, Münster, Magdeburg, Osnabrück, Texel and Amsterdam.

Fighters were almost entirely confined to the target area and the last part of the outward journey beyond Hannover – Ju88s predominated. Many illuminated targets were provided for the fighters over the capital. Corona was warning fighters of fog and telling them to land, which angered the German fighter commentators greatly. Four enemy fighters were claimed as destroyed in the air battles, two Ju88s by 1 Group aircraft, while 5 Group claimed a FW190 and a Me109.

One Lancaster (DS707 'P') of 426 Squadron, flown by Flight Sergeant Colombe, was attacked by a Ju88 at 19,000 feet and the corkscrew order given by the mid-upper gunner, Sergeant MacKenzie, with which the fighter broke away. Two more attacks were spotted by the observant MacKenzie, followed by two more. On the last attack, MacKenzie saw his bullets richochet off the belly of the Junkers and it was last seen in a steep dive.

The Lancaster had been damaged in the attack, with wings, engines and hydraulics all hit and the R/T was knocked out. The rear gunner, Flight Sergeant Jankun, had been blinded by a blue master searchlight. During the attacks a Me109 was seen sitting off at 1,000 yards dropping white fighter flares. Despite their damage they got home safely. Flight Sergeant Colombe was soon commissioned after this action and received the DFC.

While returning from Berlin, Flying Officer Wales, in a Lancaster (DS251 'D') of 432 RCAF Squadron, encountered an unidentified four-engined aircraft which was first spotted by the rear gunner, Sergeant Dickinson. It was flying astern and slightly below them. Dickinson instructed the pilot to corkscrew at which time the other aircraft opened up with a long burst of cannon and machine gun fire from a range of 600 yards. Dickinson returned the fire with interest. The Lancaster was hit on the side of its fuselage, severing the pressure line and rendering the mid-upper turret U/S.

The unidentified aircraft followed two diving turns, opening fire at the start of each. On the third turn the mid-upper, Flight Lieutenant Ramville, instructed the pilot to alter course to port as the aircraft was closing in from that quarter, but it was not seen again.

Some five minutes later a searchlight found them and fighter flares were dropped close to them. Shortly afterwards an enemy fighter was sighted by the rear gunner and corkscrewing began again, but thankfully they lost it quickly. The bomber was severely damaged and on landing the Lancaster overshot the runway as its hydraulics were gone, and ended up in a field at Eastmoor.

An aircraft of 50 Squadron was also involved in combats with fighters. Flown by Pilot Officer Lundy, P-Peter tangled with a Ju88 and the rear gunner ordered a corkscrew as he opened fire. The fighter returned the fire and then both rear and mid-upper gunners exchanged gunfire with the attacker. On the second pass by the Ju88 it made an attack from the starboard quarter, closed to 250 yards, pulled up into an apparent stall dead astern, which gave the gunners a belly shot at it. The 88 dropped out of sight, seemingly out of control and was claimed as probably destroyed.

For Pilot Officer Garth Hughes, an Australian in 514 Squadron, flying a Lancaster (DS783 'B'), the night of 2/3rd December was probably the one he would remember for the rest of his life. At 8.30 pm flying at a height of 20,000 feet he had just completed his bombing run when he was attacked by a Me210. Its one and only burst of fire killed his rear gunner (Sergeant Wilson) and put the mid-upper turret out of action, as well as setting fire to the fuselage and bomb racks, and lasted for about 30 seconds. The mid-upper, Sergeant Moorhouse, had his clothing set alight, which compelled him to leave his turret. The fighter made a second attack, but Hughes made an effective corkscrew to starboard on instruction from the WOP, who was keeping watch in the astrodome, and lost the fighter.

Attempts were made to extricate the dead rear gunner, but the turret was jammed with the guns pointing to starboard. About five minutes later a Ju88 was reported to be diving from the starboard side. Its fire hit the port inner engine and it had to be feathered, as well as smashing the hydraulics that controlled the bomb doors which dropped open. Ten minutes later the boost pressure on the outer starboard engine fell to minus four pounds per square inch. The aircraft became difficult to control but Hughes brought the damaged bomber back home where he executed a magnificent landing with a flat port tyre. He received an immediate DFC.

Fighters were not the only problems. Flight Sergeant Elmer Trotter, a Canadian flying a Lancaster of 101 Squadron on his fourth operational sortie; three of them had been to Berlin. The Lanc was hit by AA fire after releasing its bombs and thrown completely out of control and into a dive. Trotter ordered the crew to put on their parachutes while he struggled to regain control. With great skill he managed to do this, only to find he had scarcely any aileron control and no trimmers. His starboard main plane had been shot to pieces aft of the rear spa and there were three large holes inboard, between the two starboard engines. To add to this, his mid-upper turret and compass were U/S.

His troubles were not over. As he left the target and tried to gain height, they were attacked by a fighter which Trotter evaded, though not before the port outer engine was damaged. On their way back to base they again ran into flak but avoided being hit and eventually made a safe landing. He too received an immediate DFC.

During the initial bombing run, Warrant Officer Edward Ellis of 625 Squadron, who was initiating a new crew on their first operation, had his aircraft hit in the rear turret, wounding the gunner, Sergeant D. Wightman, and knocking out his turret. The bomb run was continued, and bombs released in a long stick on target, but as they went down a fighter attacked from below, raking the aircraft from stem to stern. The rear gunner was wounded again as well as the mid-upper, Sergeant W. Jones. Still Ellis carried on the run, the delay between the HEs and the incendiary bombs being carefully timed as briefed, despite another pass by the fighter. Only then did Ellis take evasive action.

After leaving the target the crew took stock of the damage. The intercom was not working, the bomb doors would not close, the gun turrets were U/S and the mainplane and fuselage damaged. The hydraulics were U/S and, as they discovered later, the main wheel tyres were punctured. The oxygen began to run short so height was lost on the return journey. Just before crossing the Dutch coast the aircraft was again hit by flak. As fuel was also running low a landing was made at RAF Bardney, using the emergency method of lowering the undercarriage. Without flaps and with flat tyres, the aircraft nosed over on landing but then tipped back again. The crew were uninjured in the landing, but both wounded gunners were taken off to hospital. For his actions and cool courage, Ellis received the CGM – Conspicuous Gallantry Medal – the rarest award in the RAF for operational flying.

Flight Lieutenant Riches of 97 Squadron flying Lancaster JA857 'G' was hit by heavy flak and was knocked out, but managed to come to and pull the aircraft out of a vertical dive.

Not all the aircrew who were shot down on this night, or who were reported missing, were killed; there were quite a few who were made prisoners. One was Sergeant Owen Roberts who was flying in a Lancaster (JB372) of 49 Squadron, as mid-upper gunner. The rear gunner reported to the pilot, Warrant Officer R.W. Petty, when they were about half way to Berlin, that his rear guns had gone U/S, but Petty decided to press on. Within sight of Berlin they were attacked by a Me110 from the starboard quarter. Sergeant Roberts waited until it was in range, then opened fire. The fighter then opened up, Roberts continuing his fire although one of his guns then jammed, and the 110 broke away with one engine on fire.

They returned to their bombing run and the bomb aimer lined the aircraft up on the markers, when Roberts spotted another 110 about 50 feet below. He aimed and fired, or attempted to fire, as his second gun ran out of ammunition. The bomb aimer was now concentrating on the bomb run, then they were gone and he began to count the seconds before he took the bombing photograph – always the worst part of an attack, the pilot having to keep straight and level over the heart of a target. His count got to seven when they were hit by flak and the starboard inner burst into flames, and within moments, Petty gave the order to bale out.

Sergeant Roberts grabbed his parachute and made his way to the rear door, where the rear gunner was already waiting. He opened the door and baled out over the centre of Berlin right into the flak, fires, bombs and bomber stream, fully expecting a stream of machine gun bullets to come up the beam to met him, but it didn't.

When he reached the ground he landed in a tree and injured himself dropping 40 feet to the ground. It was freezing, with snow on the ground. He lay here for sixteen hours before a German civilian, who himself had been a POW in the first war, found him. He was sympathetic to his plight and called the army. Roberts was taken to the Hermann Göring Luftwaffe Hospital where he was given medical treatment and treated well by the staff. He was still there when the next Berlin raid came on 16th December and a German warrant officer took great delight in reminding him that the boot was now on the other foot!

Meanwhile, other aircraft were meeting problems in the Berlin sky. The Navigation Officer of 514 Squadron, Flying Officer Emery, flying in a Lancaster (DS738 'J') was also shot down by a fighter. Having lost their port outer engine they had to bale out, to become the first POWs from 514 Squadron, and so were subjected to many questions at the Dulag Luft Interrogation Centre. Here Emery was taken into a room on which the walls were covered with his own navigation charts and maps, all showing some partial burning.

The trip for a crew of 35 Squadron was, in the words of Flight Sergeant McDougall 'a fiasco and should have been cancelled.' Due to the Met conditions several aircraft had been taken off the rota and so the number of squadron aircraft was considerably less than first planned. However, his pilot, Lieutenant Hoverstad, a Norwegian, was detailed to mark the target, so they were not stood down. Their Halifax (HX167 'C') had a Zeiss JKN Camera on a special stand mounted in front of the H$_2$S set with which to certify the aiming point. On the way to Berlin they were hit by flak near Osnabrück. The bomb doors jammed, preventing the release or even the jettisoning of the bombs and markers. The aircraft was now on fire and Hoverstad gave the order to bale out. Everyone managed to get away except the Norwegian, who was killed when the aircraft crashed. He was one of two Norwegians in 35 Squadron at this time; the other was his engineer, Flight Sergeant Arne Storme. He and the others were all taken prisoner, remaining so until their release by the Russians in 1945.

John McDougall had an eventful war. He was shot down on his twentieth operation, having been with 76 Squadron, where he had been wounded in the chest after tangling with a night fighter in June 1943.

*

On this night of 2nd December, the task of 627 Squadron, flying Mosquitos, was to bomb Berlin after the Main Force, to add more disruption in the German capital. These nuisance raids were usually made after the 'all clear' had been sounded. Six Mossies were sent on this occasion to undertake this task, one of which was DX479, flown by Flight Sergeant L. Simpson and his navigator, Sergeant Peter Walker. One hundred miles west of Berlin they were hit by flak but continued on their way to the target on one engine and minus their navigational aids. On the return journey Walker could not obtain any pin-points to help his navigation so they continued flying until their petrol ran out, then baled out, landing near La Bény Bocage. After some months of being passed from one escape organisation to another, Sergeant Walker finally reached Berne, Switzerland, in February 1944. He finally escaped into southern France, joined up with the Maquis, and later still American troops. He arrived back at his squadron in September 1944.

By the end of November 1943, war correspondents were becoming more interested in the Berlin raids and asked permission to be allowed to go on actual raids to the German capital. Permission was given by Harris to fly on the next raid. They were Captain Nordhal Greig, Mr Norman Stockton, of the Australian Associated News, and Ed Morrow of the American News, and another American named Lowell Bennett. Greig flew with an Australian, Flying Officer A. Mitchell, Stockton with Pilot Officer James English, another Australian – both of 460 Squadron at Binbrook. Ed Morrow flew with Wing Commander Jock Abercrombie while Bennett went with Flight Lieutenant Ian Bolton, a Scot – both pilots with 50 Squadron.

Abercrombie's aircraft was coned over Berlin, but a dive shook them off. Later Morrow recorded: 'The incendiaries were going down like a fist full of rice on black velvet, and the cookies were burning below like sunflowers.' When over the target Morrow saw another Lancaster whip straight under their aircraft. 'Berlin was like an orchestral Hell,' he continued, 'a terrible symphony of light and flares. An unpleasant form of warfare, but to the men, just a job.'

Ian Bolton took off from Skellingthorpe at 5.45 pm. On route they were attacked by two fighters and his aircraft set on fire and he ordered everyone out. Both he and Lowell Bennett were taken prisoner and ended up at Stalag Luft 1 in Barth, where they remained until May 1945, when they were liberated by Russian troops. Some while after they were taken prisoner a message came to the *Daily Express* Office, which read: 'Inside Nazi Europe', by Bennett. How it was transmitted is not known, but in the *Express*, for whom Bennett worked, there appeared an article under the title of 'I was in a Lancaster'. He reported that as they approached Berlin an enemy fighter was seen climbing towards them from the right. The pilot swung the heavily laden bomber first one way then the other, but in a tightly packed stream of bombers the night fighter could hardly miss them. The world seemed to burst into an inferno of flames as cannon shells ripped into the two starboard engines which burst into flames. After feathering was to no avail, Bolton called, 'Okay, boys, bale out, Sorry.' As they put on their parachutes, Bolton said again, 'Hurry up, boys – can't hold it much longer.' As Lowell Bennett floated down in his 'chute, he recalled shouting to himself, 'You wanted a big story, well here it is!' When he hit the ground, he sank waist deep into a muddy river bank and struggle as he might he could not get free. As panic set in he yelled to himself, 'Your wife and baby are waiting, fight to get out of this.' Then two men appeared in a rowing boat and helped him out. Later taken to a camp near Berlin, he met up with Bolton, and Sergeant McCall the wireless operator. Bolton later received the DFC, having flown 25 ops, including three on Hamburg.

*

Out of 458 aircraft despatched, 361 (78.8%) attacked the primary target while 14 (3.1%) attacked alternative targets. Thirty-one aircraft had to abort because of technical defects or other problems. Another six returned because of icing, four by crew sickness and two late in taking-off – total 43 (9.4%).

The casualties were 40 aircraft missing (8.7%) and 79 damaged (53 to flak and eight to fighters, three to both flak and fighters and fifteen to non-enemy action). 1,685.6 tons of bombs were dropped which averaged 5,652 pounds for each Halifax attacking, 9,889 pounds for each Lancaster.

The old enemy, the unexpected force of the wind, caused aircraft to stray from the route allotted. Cloud gaps over the target enabled searchlights to illuminate the bombers and enemy fighters were in action over the target area as soon as the attack began. For their part, the Luftwaffe lost just three aircraft.

Following the raid, all attempts to photograph Berlin by 542 PRU Squadron, were thwarted by cloud, but reports from reliable sources on the four raids prior to this latest one indicated that most of the attacks had hit the central, western and north-western districts of the city. All embassies and legations with the exception of the Spanish, the Ministry of Foreign Affairs, Home Office, Propaganda Ministry and several other Government Departments, were either damaged or had been destroyed. Potsdam Station was burnt out and five other stations damaged. In addition electricity and gas had been cut off.

The London *Times* Newspaper reported on the 4th, that 1,500 tons of bombs had fallen on Berlin in 30 minutes and that 41 aircraft were missing, including the ones in which Norman Stockton and Lowell Bennett had been flying.

The German reports of the raid makes interesting reading. They noted that the raid commenced at 9.21 pm, although the alarm sirens began to wail at 7.27. The raid was made by some 150 to 200 bombers, which dropped 30 mines, 200 HE and 20,000 incendiary bombs, 2,000 phosphorus bombs plus 50 flares. 107 people had died, 201 injured and 826 missing, from this and the two previous raids.

*

The Sixth Raid

There was a gap of nearly two weeks before Harris mounted the next raid on Berlin, which came on 16/17th December. He sent 418 Lancasters and nine Mosquitos on a blind bombing attack through 10/10ths cloud.

The weather forecast for this night was for the cloud to break up near the hostile coast, becoming patchy over the continent but then much low cloud over southern Berlin. The weather the flyers actually found was 10/10th cloud over Berlin with tops at 3-4,000 feet but good visibility above. The wind averaged 15 mph.

Five Mosquitos attacked the target before the Main Force arrived, and four attacked at five minute intervals after the raid. The target was marked by Wanganui flares and red and green TIs. Even before briefing, the target could often be guessed at by the crews when they found out the amount of petrol being put in the aircraft. 1,250 gallons for a Ruhr trip, or 1,750 for Berlin. With the briefings concluded and the other rituals over, the men climbed aboard their four-engined bombers for the Big City – for some it was their fifth trip there in a row.

On take-off the cloud was solid from 2,000 to 18,000 feet, so the crews were hoping the cloud would be too full for icing conditions or for fighters to climb through or for even searchlights to pierce.

The outward route crossed the Dutch coast at Ijmuiden and apart from a slight right hand turn after Stendal, it led directly to the target. An unusual amount of fighter opposition was met on the way resulting in at least eighteen encounters, including seven attacks. The route of the bombers was accurately plotted by the running commentator, who ordered fighters to Osnabrück by 6.10 pm and

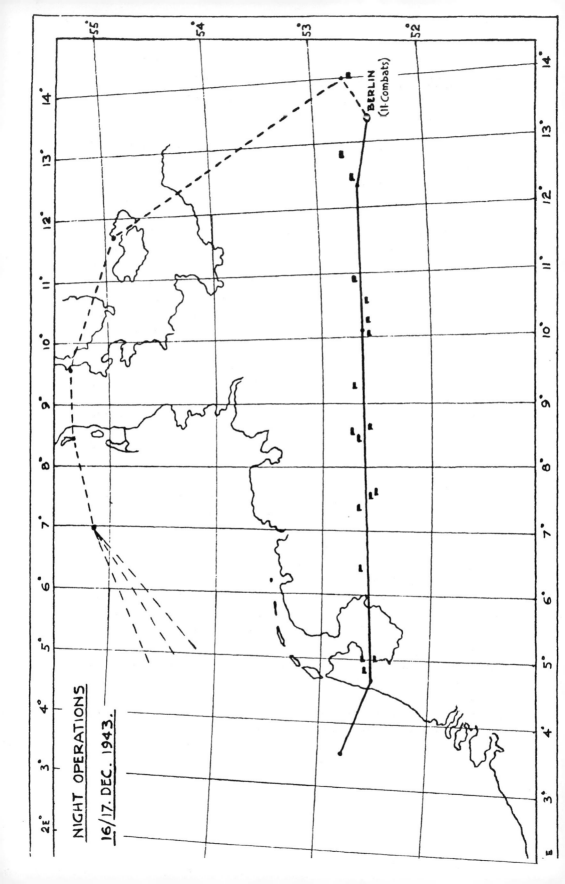

NIGHT OPERATIONS

16/17. DEC. 1943.

BERLIN
(II. Combats)

then to Oldenburg at 6.40, then to Hanover at 7.14.

At 7.55 pm, five minutes before the RAF's zero hour, all the fighters were in the Brandenburg area – just a few minutes' flying time from the German capital. Some ten attacks were recorded over the city itself. In all five Lancaster gunners claimed to have destroyed enemy aircraft, one FW190, a Ju88 and two Messerschmitt 109s, plus an unidentified twin-engined aircraft on the way from Berlin.

Corona and Airborne Cigar were used to hamper enemy communications and a new counter measure, called 'Light-up' – later known as Dartboard – was employed for the first time. This consisted of a jamming transmission, made on the frequency of the Stuttgart transmitter. From the Germans' strenuous efforts to overcome this obstacle, it would appear to have been successful, but returning crews reported that the original transmission could be heard through the jamming. Hundreds of flares were dropped by the fighters illuminating the sky over Berlin in a very few minutes, one crewman reporting that he had never seen so many before.

Flight Sergeant Crombie of 514 Squadron – Lancaster LL820 'R' – was told by his rear gunner, Sergeant Hill, that a FW190 was flying on their starboard quarter, so he immediately went into a corkscrew as the gunner opened fire. The 190 was able to follow, closing to 140 yards before it too opened up. Both rear and mid-upper gunners fired at it, scored hits and claimed it as damaged. Sergeant Hill fired 250 rounds, Sergeant James in the upper turret 150.

Flight Lieutenant Greenacre of 460 Squadron was attacked by a Ju88 and saw his rear gunner returning the fire of the German as it broke off the attack. The Lancaster was hit in several places but made it back. A Lanc of 97 Squadron (JB908) flown by Flight Sergeant William Coates, had a problem other than fighters. While over Berlin at 19,500 feet, incendiaries fell on him from an aircraft above. They hit the port wing, front turret and amidships, setting the aircraft on fire. The crew was ordered to put on their parachutes as Coates put the aircraft into a dive in an attempt to dislodge the burning incendiaries. This action toppled the DR compass, upsetting all the instruments connected to it. However, the fires were extinguished and they climbed back up to 21,000 feet. Some while later it was hit by flak which damaged the propeller tips of the starboard inner engine. One of the tips went through the fuselage cutting the hydraulic pipe lines and another piece damaged the tailplane. The starboard outer engine was also hit and with power lost in both motors on the starboard side, they had to be closed down. When twenty miles from the Danish coast, and losing height, the captain ordered everyone to take up ditching positions while the WOP sent out an SOS.

This call was eventually cancelled as he found he could maintain height at 5,000 feet. On arriving in the vicinity of base, he found weather conditions that made it impossible to land so he was diverted to Marham. They in turn sent him to Downham Market where the cloud base was down to 400 feet and visibility bad. Nevertheless, he made a perfect landing using the emergency air system for lowering the wheels. For his devotion to duty and superb captaincy, Flight Sergeant Coates was awarded the DFM.

As the bombers arrived over Berlin the Germans began putting up a box barrage, reaching to 21,000 feet, concentrating around the marker flares. Some of the crews thought that only parts of the defences were active in an attempt to conceal the full extent of the target area.

Pilot Officer Davies, flying a Lancaster of 426 Squadron, also had his own problems. The rear doors blew open on take-off due to a faulty lock and the mid-upper, Sergeant George, slipped getting out of his turret to close it, hurting his leg but told Davies he was all right. The aircraft was caught in the anti-aircraft defences north of Osnabrück and evasive action was taken, but the rear turret was hit and remained jammed for the rest of the flight. The electric system shorted and the rear gunner's electrically heated suit was made useless.

Near Berlin the aircraft was hit again and petrol lost from the main port tank. The other tanks could not be used as the cocks could not be turned and the flight engineer calculated that there was only enough left for perhaps 1½ hours to two hours flying. It was decided to try for Sweden. They reached the German coast but the port outer was spluttering and showering sparks behind them, so it was shut down. On reaching Sweden, Davies ordered the crew to jump but with the rear gunner's doors jammed, the mid-upper had to go back with an axe to release him. This took several minutes so Davies circled a small town. With the rear gunner finally released they were all ready to jump but Pilot Officer Garrick, the navigator, looking for incendiary device to put on his table (to ensure the aircraft's destruction) could not locate it, and as he searched the aircraft banked over, so he decided to forget it. The floor of his compartment was covered with bits of his torn-up maps and charts. With the order to jump given, the men tumbled out into the darkness, the bomb aimer, Sergeant Ginson having smashed the bomb sight with the axe as well as the Gee apparatus. The mid-upper was the only casualty with a broken leg, but this in fact was thought to have happened when he slipped soon after take-off.

Flying Officer F.W. Rush, in his 7 Squadron Lancaster (JB656 'D', did not get any farther than the Dutch coast when he was engaged by a night fighter. The bomber was set on fire and went into a dive. The engineer, Sergeant Ogg, baled out but on landing could not find any of the others; he was found by a farmer who took him to Broek where he was given civilian clothes and a Dutch identity card. Remaining at Broek until after Christmas he was sent to Amsterdam in the New Year but an unsuccessful attempt to put him on his way to Lisbon resulted in him remaining where he was for a whole year. In March 1945 he went to Swiendrecht in order to cross the Bies Bose into Brabant; however some airmen had been captured just the night before so it was cancelled. He remained in Rotterdam until the liberation and only after his return to England did he learn why he had found none of his crew mates. They had all died that night seventeen months earlier.

*

The RAF missing list totalled 25: 5.1% of the attacking force. 427 of the 490 actually attacked the target, ten going for alternate ones. 31 had aborted, one failed to get off with another delayed so long their op was cancelled. 17 returned damaged by flak, five with fighter damage, while 31 crashed on their return. Five collided with other aircraft, four were damaged by falling incendiaries and two damaged by other causes. Of the 25 lost, ten were known to have been shot down by fighters on the outward route (two as they reached the Dutch coast, two more on the east coast of the Zyder Zee, and six before reaching Hannover) and three to flak. Over Berlin itself, one was shot down by flak, another by a fighter, while two were seen to collide and fall in flames. Another collision involving the destruction of both aircraft was seen on the way home. Of the six, there was no news.

For each missing RAF aircraft, 73 tons of bombs had been dropped. In addition to the aircraft lost, some 34 either crashed in England or the crews had to abandon their aircraft over the countryside. This resulted in 131 casualties, most caused by aircraft hitting the ground or from loss of control when low flying under cloud. Because of the large number lost in this way, an enquiry was set up, which blamed the weather conditions. Bad weather was expected when the aircraft returned, but not as bad as it turned out. The expected conditions were approximately 10/10th cloud over base up to 1,500 feet with visibility around 2,000 yards or better. The actual conditions were cloud down to 900 feet with visibility between 1,500 and 3,000 yards, but in most places it was the latter.

The policy towards crews abandoning aircraft when short of fuel was that they were more valuable than the aircraft, and so captains were encouraged to abandon, if there was little real hope of making a safe landing. The decision to bale out was at all times left to him, although he might be advised from the ground. The conclusion of Bomber Command was that in the circumstances the losses were unavoidable. Flying Control and safety organisations could do little to help in such adverse weather conditions. In fact, that night, the only airfields not affected by weather were in either Scotland or Cornwall.

As many as 283 diversions to other fields was expected but few in fact were diverted – only 39. FIDO (Fog Disposal Installation) – burning petrol that through heat dispersed fog over an airfield – was not used as the trouble was low cloud and not horizontal visibility.

One Lancaster of 57 Squadron (JB373) had the misfortune to ditch in the North Sea; all of the crew except one were either killed or drowned, including the pilot, Sergeant John Hinde. Another crew of the same squadron thought they had reached home base at East Kirby, the pilot calling for assistance to reach their dispersal area. They were told it was waiting for them at the end of the runway, but none of the crew could see it. They followed a light which turned out to be a small van with direction lights. Eventually the penny dropped – they had landed at Spilsby, a satellite station. They were taken home the next morning and later asked: 'Please can we have our kite back?'

The German report of this raid, recorded that it had started at 9.04 pm, and that some 60 mines, 700 HE bombs, 15,000 incendiaries and 6,000 phosphorus bombs had been dropped on the city. Four industries were destroyed, twelve severely damaged with four more having medium damage, sixteen slight damage. The casualties were 545 people killed, 796 injured and 160 missing.

Daylight reconnaissance photos of Berlin were at last obtained on 20/21st December. They were obtained by a Spitfire of 541 PRU Squadron from RAF Benson. Warrant Officer K.G. Campbell DFC, an Australian from Sydney, (in EB149) made four runs over the city on the 21st, and Flying Officer A. Glover (BS499) had taken photographs the day before.

These photographs showed large areas of devastation covering some eight square miles, resulting almost entirely from fire. Besides the legations and embassies, the Great War Office building was partially demolished, the wing used by the Secret Service HQ of the armed forces was burnt out as well as the main income tax office. In addition several civil administrative buildings had been gutted. Altogether 1,250 acres of business and residential property in the fully built-up areas were affected. Five to six barracks, several military stores and depots and the military academy and artillery school in the north Tiergarten, were heavily damaged. In 25 hutted encampments, a total of 236 of 483 huts were destroyed.

It was later learned that the Foreign Department (Fremdenamt) of the Berlin Police, including the Jewish Section of the Gestapo, was hit, including a building which contained hundreds of tons of documents which burnt like a torch. All the files concerning foreigners in Germany, which the Gestapo had compiled over many years were destroyed. Many of Himmler's high ranking officials were buried and killed when the shelter in the Police HQ collapsed.

On the 22nd, Dr Goebbels, as Gauleiter of the City, received and addressed members of the Nazi Party Organisation, police, municipal authorities, and the ARP workers, to thank them after the heavy recent terror attacks, and for the excellent services they had rendered. He also expressed the Führer's appreciation. He also stressed that there would undoubtedly be further attacks in the future. From an informant in Berlin during the time of the battle, came the following information. The people were passive after the recent big raids and of stunned stupefaction. The general feeling against the Nazi Party had been strongly accentuated by the attacks. On no occasion during these weeks did the source of this information, find a single expression of specific hatred against the British. On the contrary, the general attitude of people, people who had lost friends, relatives and property, was to hold the German Government responsible. After the 22nd November raid, production in the city came practically to a halt and in December it was still down to an absolute minimum. There was also an extraordinary lack of mutual co-operation and people just moved on when asked to help in ARP or fire fighting work. Men of the Gestapo mixed with the people listening for any signs of derogatory talk against the

Control tower Waddington awaiting returning aircraft

JU 88 German Fighter

Party and if any was heard, those talking were arrested.

*

The Seventh Raid

The next attack was mounted just before Christmas – on the night of 23/24th December – the seventh raid in five weeks. 379 aircraft were despatched: 326 Avro Lancasters, six Halifaxes and six Mosquitos.

The weather in England was variable with amounts of layer cloud and moderate visibility. North-west England, Scotland, Cornwall and Devon would remain clear but for 1, 5 and 8 Groups, with bases in eastern and north-eastern areas there was every chance the poor weather would force many returning bombers to divert after midnight. Over Germany they should meet little cloud in central and southern areas while over Berlin there was good chance of broken cloud. The winds would probably vary between 30 and 55 mph between England and Berlin.

Little flak was experienced on route, although the defences of Ijmuiden, Frankfurt, Leipzig and Osnabrück were notably active. The running commentator plotted the bomber force accurately almost from the time it crossed the enemy coast but successfully mistook Frankfurt, Leipzig, Weimar or Auerbach as the main objectives. They were confused mainly by the feint attack on Leipzig by seven Mosquitos and Berlin was not recognised as the target until zero minus two minutes.

The most intense fighter opposition were met in three areas, the mouth of the River Scheldt, between Aachen and the north of Frankfurt, and then over Berlin itself. Although Luftwaffe night fighters did not reach the target in strength until the raid was well underway, they appeared to be experiencing severe trouble from the weather conditions too.

One fighter was destroyed by an aircraft of 5 Group. A Lancaster (LL625 'C'), flown by Flying Officer Kingswell of 514 Squadron, encountered a Ju88 approaching almost head-on. As the aircraft passed over the rear gunner, Warrant Officer Fidge, warned of its position, opened fire with a short burst as it passed over at 100 yards range. The 88 rapidly disappeared, but it was the first of three encounters this crew was to suffer. About eleven minutes later the bomb aimer reported another, or the same, Ju88 on the port bow. He yelled for Kingswell to corkscrew as the fighter opened fire. It passed overhead, followed by fire from the mid-upper, Sergeant

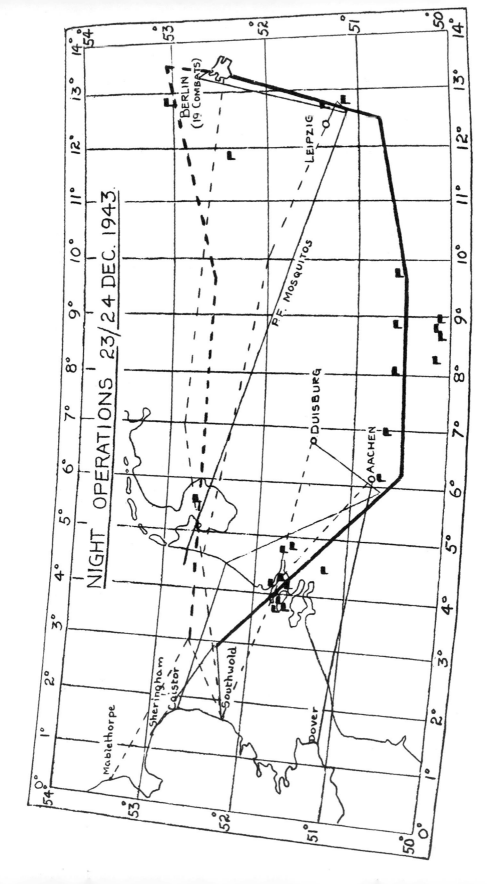

NIGHT OPERATIONS 23/24 DEC. 1943

Taylor. The third encounter came just four minutes later. This time a FW190 came in and Taylor opened up as he ordered the corkscrew to starboard. This fighter too was lost to view.

A Lancaster of 50 Squadron flown by Pilot Officer Toovey, tangled with two twin-engined aircraft flying in formation. The rear gunner, Sergeant Rodgers, ordered a corkscrew to port and both he and the mid-upper, Sergeant Melbrick, opened fire. Tracer appeared to enter one of the fighters and it was claimed as probably damaged. Another crew from 50 Squadron, captained by Pilot Officer Smith, was attacked, the rear gunner, Sergeant Brown, saw tracer coming from the darkness then a fighter appeared. He and the mid-upper, Flight Sergeant Humphrey, beat off the fighter with their return fire.

A third 50 Squadron crew engaged was that of Flight Lieutenant Short. His rear gunner, Pilot Officer Beale, saw a twin-engined aircraft and told Short to corkscrew as he opened fire. It broke off without opening fire and disappeared.

A Lancaster of 166 Squadron (W4996) piloted by Pilot Officer Peedall, had been attacked by a Ju88 on the outward route, but it was hit by the rear gunner, Sergeant Harris. They were attacked again over Berlin, but this time Harris had fallen unconscious through lack of oxygen. Evasive tactics were ordered by the mid-upper, Sergeant Brown, and the fighter was shaken off. The bomber then lost an engine, but they made Coltishall for an emergency landing with fuel running short.

Squadron Leader C.A.W. Dery, a member of the Pathfinder Force, in Lancaster 'T for Tommy' of 97 Squadron, was attacked by a Ju88, not on one occasion but eight times – and with all guns in the aircraft frozen. One engine was knocked out, the aircraft damaged, and the squadron leader himself lucky when a bullet hit the heel of his flying boot. 'Tommy' excelled itself and probably reached twice its normal speed when in a final effort to shake off the fighter the pilot dived it from 18,000 to below 6,000 feet before heading for home. Soon afterwards a second engine began to show signs of stress and had to be shut down.

They returned on two engines and on nearing base asked for an emergency landing, but their approach was as normal as could be expected in the circumstances. Unknown to them, the starboard tyre had been punctured, though they soon realised it when they touched down. Although the pilot was able to keep the aircraft straight, it pulled to the right eventually and they finished up off the runway. It was obvious that Tommy would not fly again. Following de-briefing it was between nine and ten o'clock before the crew got to bed, only to be awoken because it was Christmas Eve. With their groundcrew they went into Cambridge for a drink – in fact many drinks!

For Squadron Leader Joseph Marshall AFC of 101 Squadron, the trip was one he would remember. Shortly after he was airborne, one of his navigational aids caught fire, causing clouds of smoke inside the aircraft. He gave instruction to deal with the fire and ordered all windows to be slid open, hopefully to get rid of the smoke. The fire was put out and they decided to carry on.

Two aircraft of 550 Squadron (LM319 'G2') collided, flown by Sergeant H. Woods and Flight Sergeant W.R. Cooper (JB604 'K'). Both aircraft fell to the ground at Fulstow shortly after taking off from Waltham, near Grimsby, and everyone was killed.

A member of one crew of 100 Squadron, Jimmy Flynn, remembers taking off at 12.48 – Christmas Eve and a very cold morning. They had quite a journey to the target but as they dropped their bombs they were hit by flak although it did little damage. Jimmy could hear the flak hitting the aircraft behind his turret in which he was sitting. His pilot, Bill Brooke, threw the aircraft across the sky and out into the comparative comfort of the darkness. The trip home was equally quiet until they went off track and flew directly over Emden. Without any warning the searchlights coned the aircraft and the guns opened up with a box barrage. Bill Brooke, known to his crew as Wilf, threw the Lancaster into turns and dives in ways that Jimmy had not thought possible. Despite this the aircraft was held in the beams so Brooke then put the bomber into a screaming dive from 21,000 feet down to 4,000. Then he yelled to Vic Condell, the flight engineer and oldest member of the crew, from Dublin, to use the trimmer as he was unable to pull out. Condell spun the trimmer back sharply, a little too sharply as it nearly pulled the wings off, but they managed to leave the area with the searchlights left still probing hopefully the piece of sky they had been in. Inspecting the aircraft after landing, they counted 40 holes through its wings and fuselage. It was 8.30 am – they had been out for over eight hours.

The attack was generally scattered owing to the failure of many of the H$_2$S sets. In fact of the 23 primary blind markers sent by the PFF squadrons, only eleven sets remained operable. Of the secondary markers, six sets worked but three failed. The timing of the blind markers was good but owing to the high rate of unserviceability of H$_2$S, there was a scarcity of TIs and flares throughout most of the raid.

Losses were down for this raid, just fifteen failing to return – all Lancasters, a percentage loss of 4%. Of these, four aircraft fell in combat on the way out – one over the mouth of the Scheldt and three north of Frankfurt. Three more went down over Berlin, and two on the way home at Lingen and Egmond. Flak losses were observed over Aachen (one), Berlin (two) and Egmond (two). Another 32 aircraft were damaged; sixteen to flak, five to fighters, four to damage by falling incendiaries, two to collision and five to other causes. The weight of bombs dropped per missing aircraft was 1,287.9 pounds, a total of 85.41 tons.

Two days after Christmas, German industrial munition workers were told: 'Be brave, keep up your ideals, let your ideals be sacred to you. Germany firmly believes in Adolf Hitler, the Führer."

*

The Eighth Raid
Five days after the seventh raid came number eight on 29th/30th December. 457 Lancasters, 252 Halifaxes and three Mosquitos attacked the city, dropping 1,099.1 tons of HE 1,215.4 tons of incendiaries and 124 flares. This took the total tonnage dropped so far on Berlin during the battle to 14,074. In these eight raids, 4,081 aircraft had been despatched of which 3,646 had made Berlin their primary target.

On this December night the weather forecast at base was for 10/10th cloud with light rain or drizzle, with cloud tops at 12,000 feet. Visibility was only moderate to good. Conditions over Berlin were expected to be similar except that the cloud tops should not be above 4,000 feet with poor visibility. The winds over England were 60 mph at 10,000 feet, increasing to 85 mph at 30,000. Over Berlin the wind was expected to be between 50 to 75 mph.

A diversionary attack on Magdeburg and Leipzig was made by 8 Group Mosquitos who succeeded in holding the main German night fighter force back from the Berlin raiders until the attack was almost over. It must have been most frustrating for the German controllers, always aware that Berlin might be the target, but thinking too that with so many recent raids on the city, this time the RAF would outsmart them. Too late did they realise that the RAF

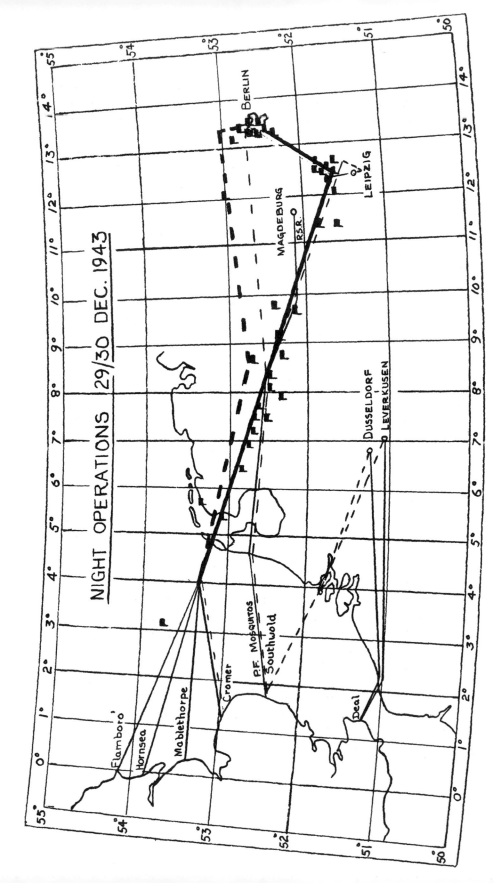

NIGHT OPERATIONS 29/30 DEC. 1943

had outsmarted them but not in the way they feared. Yet if they had immediately defended Berlin, then it was odds on that Berlin was not the target for that night. It really was a game of tactics, bluff and counter-bluff and of nerves. Also the Luftwaffe aircraft were as much affected by the severe winter weather as the RAF. It made nothing easier that they were flying over their own land. Weather can be a killer wherever one meets it. A German wireless message intercepted in England spoke of great difficulty caused by weather conditions.

Nevertheless, 45 interceptions were reported, resulting in twelve attacks, most of which occurred along the outward route. Thirteen interceptions were made in the Zyder Zee area alone but none at all for the next 100 miles and then a great many in the area of route markers north of Leipzig. Ten combats took place here resulting in six RAF losses. The fighters were first ordered to Magdeburg and few were seen over Berlin, not arriving in any force until zero hour plus 15 minutes.

One of the early interceptions involved Flying Officer Louis Greenburgh and his crew of 514 Squadron who were on their final Lancaster operation, were attacked by a Ju88 in the Meppen area at 6.15 pm. The rear gunner, Flight Sergeant Drake, exchanged fire with the German, but the Lancaster's petrol tanks were damaged which was to have an effect on the outcome of their flight home.

A Halifax gunner of 35 Squadron (in HX168 'Y') piloted by Squadron Leader Whetham, saw a Ju88 as it turned to attack and the rear gunner, Sergeant Rees, ordered a corkscrew to port, by visual signs as the intercom had failed. The fighter passed over them and attacked again, with Rees firing at it although both lower guns jammed. The 88 was hit and did not open fire.

A Lancaster of 50 Squadron flown by Pilot Officer Dobbyn, was over Berlin on a bombing run at 19,000 feet when his rear gunner, Sergeant Mason, saw a twin-engined aircraft on the port beam and opened fire with a burst of 180 rounds, the EA going away astern.

En route accurately predicted heavy flak was met at several points especially on the last leg from twenty miles north of Leipzig and on the northern leg out. One Ju88 was recorded as shot down by a Halifax. The flak was heavy but sparodic over Berlin, mostly in barrage form. Light flak was seen bursting near the PFF markers, hosepiping around them as they drifted down to the cloud top around a height of 15,000 feet. Some rocket flak and scarecrow flares were also observed in the target area, but only one aircraft was known to have been lost to Berlin's guns.

In Lancaster ED888 'V2' flown by Flying Officer Morgan, flew Sergeant Ben Frazier, an American staff correspondent. On his return, he wrote an article with the title 'Night Plane to Berlin'. His aircraft was a veteran of over 50 ops, and had the marking of the DFC ribbon painted on its fuselage to celebrate its 50th trip. The crew was of mixed nationality, the pilot being a Welshman, the navigator a Scot, and the bomb aimer an Australian.

It was all a great effort for the crew. The problems were flak, fighters and searchlights and last but not least, the weather. Ben Frazier wrote:

Suddenly the whole city opened up. The flak poured through the cloud, it poured up in streams of red as if shaken from a hose – it went off in bright white puffs. The Pathfinders had arrived. In another moment they had dropped the target indicators, great shimmering Christmas trees of red and green lights; you couldn't miss it. It would be impossible to miss such a brilliantly marked objective. Bright flares started going off under the clouds, that would be the Cookies of the plane ahead. V for Victor started the bombing run. 'Left, left, steady, now right a bit, steady, steady, Cookie gone.'

V for Victor shot upwards slightly. 'Standby!' came the voice of the rear gunner, Bob. 'Corkscrew, starboard!' he called. The pilot instantly went to starboard and dived headlong down.

A stream of red tracer whipped out of the dark, past the rear turret and on past the wing tip missing both, by what seemed inches. Then the fighter shot passed.

'A Me 109,' shouted Bob.

They went on corkscrewing over the sky and so the fighter was finally shaken off and a normal course resumed. The dark shapes of Lancasters could be seen all over the sky against the brilliant clouds below. The attack only took fifteen minutes.

Then came, 'Standby – Ju88, starboard corkscrew,' from the rear gunner again.

The aircraft went into a dive and the tracer from the Ju88 missed. From there on the journey was uneventful – the searchlights of the English coast sent out a greeting of welcome.

As the pilot of Victor circled over their base, the WOP called ground control, 'V-Victor', he said. A girl's voice came over the intercom. 'V-Victor, prepare to pancake.' From the WOP, 'V-Victor, in the funnels.' – the girl's reply, 'V-Victor, pancake.'

The aircraft landed and gently ran down the runway and turned off onto the perimeter track. 'V-Victor, clear of flarepath.' The ground crew met them with questions: 'How was it?' the reply: 'A piece of cake.'

The crew got out and the pilot had a look around the aircraft. One small hole through the aileron. Into the de-briefing by bus where a cup of hot tea laced with rum is waiting. Each pilot signed on the board as he came in.

*

Flight Lieutenant Greenacre of 460 Squadron had a problem with his Cookie – it would not release and so he decided to go round again. Sergeant G. Cairns, later to reach the rank of wing commander before retiring from the RAF in 1978, stood ready with a fire axe to make sure the Cookie went this time. On a signal from the bomb aimer, Cairns thumped the bomb slip with the axe and the bomb fell away onto the target.

Flying Officer Cyril 'Cy' Barton of 100 Squadron, later to be awarded the VC postumously on the famous Nuremburg raid in March 1944, bombed on the PFF markers and a large explosion was seen despite the cloud. On the return journey they found the compass was giving an incorrect reading and so their position had to be fixed by astronavigation. Their fuel situation was grave but they managed to make a field near Grimsby.

*

Halifax LL136 of 434 Squadron, piloted by Pilot Officer R.A. Pratt, was attacked by a night fighter. The engineer, Sergeant A. Bostock, was killed instantly while taking astro shots and Pratt was slightly wounded. The starboard inner engine caught fire, both outers were hit and the aircraft badly holed – at least 65 holes being counted later.

The second pilot, Sergeant Stinson, on his first operation, coolly pressed onto the target and bombed it, while Sergeant Samson, the bomb aimer, took over the engineer's duties. Both men were later commissioned and awarded DFCs.

Another Halifax (JD318) of 429 Squadron, was hit by flak over the target after bombing but managed to fly back to Holland where it was hit again, this time by a night fighter, forcing the crew to bale out. The pilot, Flying Officer A. Merkley of the RCAF, landed close to Borne and buried his parachute. He met up with the underground fighters at Hengalo and moved from safe house to safe house. On 15th April 1944 he was taken by train to Antwerp but was arrested as he left the station. After interrogation he was sent to Brussels where he spent 60 days in prison. On 26th June he went to Stalag Luft IIIA at Luckenwalde where he remained until liberated in April 1945.

A Lancaster of 115 Squadron (DS834 'F') flown by Flight Sergeant J. Lee, was attacked by a night fighter on the homeward journey, having just reached the Dutch coast when the attack came. Lee gave the order to bale out but before they could do so the aircraft blew up. Sergeant Herbert Pike found himself in mid-air with his parachute unopened. He pulled the rip cord and landed near to the Belgium border. He was captured at Liège on 6th January, remaining a prisoner until May 1945.

Another Lancaster (JB487 'S') of 103 Squadron, flown by Warrant Officer L.J. Grigg, was hit by flak after bombing. The two port engines were put out of action and the port fin and rudder shot away. They were down to 2,000 feet when Grigg finally gave the order to abandon the aircraft. Warrant Officer Alfred Warne baled out and landed in a field on the outskirts of Mettingen, about fifteen miles north west of Osnabrück. He hid his parachute harness and Mae West, and then began walking across country but was captured. He met up with three others of his crew, Sergeants Fletcher, Lamb and Cunning. Later that day a party of Luftwaffe guards arrived by lorry with two coffins, also Sergeant Hatherley, another of the crew. He was asked to identify the bodies, but only one coffin was opened which contained the rear gunner, Warrant Officer Henderson. The other was said to be the pilot but Grigg was himself a prisoner, and in fact met up with him later. They spent most of their captivity in Stalag IVB at Muhlberg.

Warne made three attempts to escape in February and June 1944 and then in February 1945. He was finally liberated by the Russians on 23rd April.

Meanwhile, at 10 pm over Germany, Flying Officer Louis Greenburgh, whom we met earlier this night when his aeroplane's fuel tanks were holed by a Ju88 attack, was now struggling on the homeward leg. They were then attacked by another Junkers, seen by both gunners, Sergeant Carey and Flight Sergeant Drake. Both men opened fire and appeared to hit the fighter as it apparently went out of control, and the mid-upper saw a red glow from the centre of the fuselage so it was claimed as a probable.

Fifteen minutes later another Ju88 was spotted. As it closed in and began firing, both gunners opened up and it broke away but came in for a second attack, but again broke off the engagement.

Shortage of petrol from the leaking fuel tank was now causing concern. There was a good chance they would have to ditch in the sea. Then it seemed they might make the English coast so no distress call was sent, but when the engines suddenly cut out and they began to go down, the wireless operator, Sergeant Stromberg, put out the call but was only able to give a quick position before clamping the key down. He just managed to make his ditching position before they hit the sea. He had lost his torch and told the navigator, Sergeant Butler, as they could not tell the height of the aircraft above the water. He was about to tell the pilot but as he put his hand to the microphone he lost consciousness. His next memory was getting out of the aircraft. He must have leant forward to talk to the pilot at the very moment the aircraft ditched.

The mid-upper was also in his ditching position and thinks he was hit on the head by shelves fitted to carry the special G-H equipment. The pilot, on feeling the spray on his cheek, pulled back on the stick and the aircraft hit the sea as he was flattening out. The tail broke off in the landing and because of this it took ten to fifteen minutes to get from the aircraft and into the dinghy which had not release itself through the action of the automatic or manual release mechanism. However, apart from cramp, the crew were okay.

A photograph taken from a search plane twelve hours after the ditching, showed the aircraft still afloat with the tail gone aft of the mid-turret. When the ASR launch arrived, sixteen hours after coming down, it passed the still floating aircraft, and a further report 36 hours later said it was, incredibly, still afloat! The aircraft was DS821 'S for Sugar'.

Pilot Officer Horsley of 166 Squadron was recommended for the award of an immediate DFC on 2nd January 1944, for his part in the raid. When 40 miles beyond the Dutch coast on the outward journey, the port inner engine caught fire and had to be closed down. Nevertheless he pressed on and bombed Berlin as detailed despite a gradual loss of height, for his load had pulled him down to 13,000 feet. Over Berlin he then discovered that his bomb doors would not open. He turned to make a second run across the target while the crew atempted to release the 4,000 pound load and open the doors. Then the starboard outer engine was hit by light flak and caught fire. By prompt cutting of the fuel supply the fire was put out but by now they were down to 6,000 feet. They finally succeeded in releasing the bomb which fell to the north of the city. Horsley, an experienced captain flying his 23rd op, managed to fly the aircraft home on two engines, without an artificial horizon or directional gyro, both of which had gone U/S. Passing over the Dutch coast he was coned by a couple of searchlights but fire from his gunners managed to douse them. He arrived back at base more than $2\frac{1}{2}$ hours overdue but made an excellent landing on a short runway.

Flight Sergeant George Burcher also had his problems flying a Halifax of 10 Squadron. He had his starboard outer engine hit by flak two minutes from Berlin but continued into the target area. Whilst over the city two incendiary bombs struck his aeroplane, one striking the starboard fuselage side which cut the leads to the instrument gauges while the other one crashed through the starboard flaps. On the return journey they discovered a 2,000 lb hung up in the bomb bay. It could not be released in the normal manner so the bomb aimer tried to release it manually and finally did so, though it took him $1\frac{1}{2}$ hours. Shortly after crossing the English coast their port inner engine failed completely. Permission was given for an emergency landing at Swanton Morley and Burcher made a perfect two-engine landing. For his action he was awarded an immediate DFM.

*

The alarm in Berlin sounded at 7.23 pm and the all clear came at 8.56. They estimated the number of aircraft as 200 and that 300 HE bombs, 50 mines, 3,000 phosphorus and 100,000 incendiaries were dropped. The casualties were 151 dead, 514 injured, with 10,000 made homeless. Eight industrial targets were destroyed, 30 more severely damaged and 27 slightly damaged. Seven military installations were destroyed with another 24 damaged. The raid was the 94th on Berlin since 1940 and the glow from the fires could be seen from 200 miles away.

The number of RAF aircraft missing was well down at 18 (2.8%) – nine Halifaxes and nine Lancasters. Another 104 were damaged – 84 to flak, three to fighters, and seventeen to other causes. Of the eighteen lost, at least ten went down to fighters, and five to flak (the other three are unknown). The aircraft fell to ground defences at Leipzig, Bernberg, Bitterfield, Terschelling and Texel. Six were lost to fighters on the outward route in the areas of Weppel and

Brunswick, and four over Bernberg and Leipzig. The other four went down on the homeward route to controlled fighters, mostly over Holland.

The rate of bombs per missing aircraft was 159.26 tons for Lancasters, and 63.43 for Halifaxes. The total tonnage overall was 2,314.5. During the year of 1943, Berlin had received 13,400 tons of bombs and was now the most heavily attacked city in the Reich.

In 115 Squadron a newsletter called *Bang On*, dated 31st December, gave a summary of the Berlin raids which read:

This summary reads like a tour on Berlin. Have patience, chaps, the Happy Valley is still there. Berlin it must be until the place is wiped out. It is the HQ of nearly everything that matters to Germany. Armaments, engineering, food stuffs, administration. Berlin is the 'London of Germany'. Until Berlin is Hamburged, Jerry's mainspring is wound up. 115 and the others will bust it. One point emerges from this summary, the 'returned early' figure is high. Cast your memories back, chaps, to May this year when the Happy Valley was the principal target. The May figures read 115 aircraft detailed, two returned early against the December figure of 66 detailed and 11 returned early. What about it, 115? Look at this Berlin – 29th December, detailed 19, attacked primary target 18, missing one. No early returns. Well done, chaps – one of your best shows! Preliminary evidence has shown extensive damage around the Tiergarten area and in Berlin's Whitehall. Goebbels, Göring and the whole bunch of those heathen sadistic Nazis have boasted that Berlin would never be bombed. The raid of the 29th was the 94th attack on Berlin.

At the end of 1943 the strength of the air defences of Germany was as follows: day fighters 450, night fighters 800, heavy flak guns 1,000, light flak guns 450, and searchlights 300. Considerable damage had been inflicted in the central district of Berlin where as in London the government and administration of the whole country have their officers in a well defined limited area. If the corresponding area of London had been bombed as Berlin had been, the government buildings in Whitehall would have suffered severely. The Treasury largely destroyed, the Foreign Office partially gutted, Scotland Yard would be soot black and ruined, the Ministry of Transport also. Downing Street would not have escaped, the Cabinet Offices at No 10 would be roofless and fire would have destroyed No 11. Many other well known landmarks in central London would have disappeared such as the British Museum Library, and the University would have been damaged, the Albert Hall and Drury Lane smouldering wrecks, office blocks like Shell Mex House and Bush House burnt out; the Ritz Hotel destroyed and the Savoy damaged by fire; the Café Royal would have been gutted from roof to basement. Hardly an embassy or legation would have escaped. Railway stations such as Euston, Victoria, King's Cross, would either be gutted or severely damaged by fire.

The Blitz in London early in the war could not be compared with the onslaught on Berlin. Fire services had to be called from as far as Frankfurt to deal with the fire. Over one third of the inhabitants and the largest part of the machinery of government have been driven from the capital.

Main devastated areas in central Berlin superimposed upon corresponding London areas

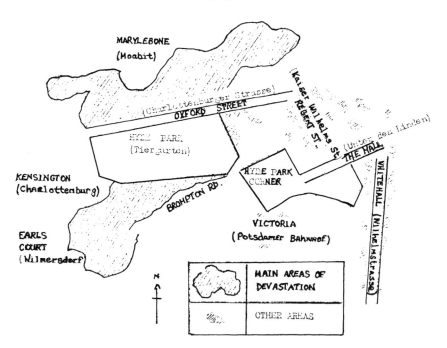

CHAPTER SIX

The New Year

The Ninth Raid
The New Year of 1944 began for Bomber Command with yet
another raid on Berlin on the night of 1/2nd January. The force of
421 Lancasters comprised:

    117 from No 1 Group
     31 from No 3 Group
    161 from No 5 Group
     31 from No 6 Group
     81 from No 8 Group
    ———

    421
    ———

The original take-off time was delayed for some four to five hours
because of deteriorating weather. While they waited, one ground
crew chalked 'Happy New Year' on a bomb and attached to it a
sprig of holly.

The weather forecast supplied to the Air Staff at 9.50 am that
morning, predicted variable cloud, with a base not below 1,500 feet
and in well broken layers to about 6,000 feet. Further broken layers
above to over 20,000 feet with good clearances. On route the cloud
would consolidate, becoming mainly 10/10th over the Continent,
with a base of 500 to 1,000 feet. By 4 am, over Berlin itself, the cloud
was expected to be thinly layered and probably well broken at 6 to
9,000 feet.

In fact the weather actually encountered was variable layer cloud
at about 2,000 feet over bases, broken layers on route, increasing to
10/10th over enemy-held territory. The winds at 20,000 feet over
Berlin were 70 mph.

The attack, according to the German commentators, fell on the
south-eastern section of the city. The Pathfinders dropped sky and

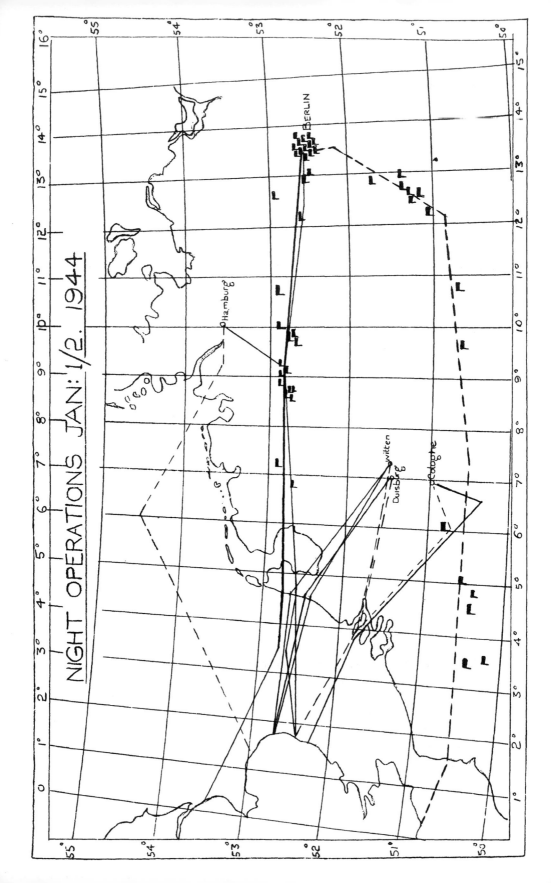

NIGHT OPERATIONS JAN: 1/2. 1944

BERLIN

Hamburg

Witten
Duisburg

Cologne

ground markers between 2.57 and 3.17 am but most crews reported sparse and somewhat widespread marking. While the ground marking was not visible under the cloud, the crews of 9 Squadron reported the PFF marking as well placed, which for them, resulted in a good attack.

*

As the Force droned its way to the Big City, the various problems that all too often occurred, began to happen. Squadron Leader Joseph Marshall of 101 Squadron had his intercom fail, and then had one of his crew suffer oxygen failure. Despite this he went on and bombed. He was put up for the DFC on 7th January, endorsed by Air Vice Marshal Don Bennett, AOC No 8 PFF Group.

There were large numbers of enemy fighters reported by returning bomber crews this night. A memory of one crew member, John McQuillan DFM, has lived with him ever since. Whilst sitting in his rear turret he saw the image of Christ, with a lamp of his shoulder. It followed the aircraft over the target and stayed with them most of the way back to the coast. He told his story to the others for the first time at a re-union in 1982 – it seemed to him to be an omen that they would get home. They in fact, landed at Wittering on the emergency runway at 8.30 am, following a trip of eight hours 50 minutes.

Flight Lieutenant G. Coldray of 405 RCAF Squadron, in Lancaster JB699 'S', was attacked by two enemy aircraft, a Ju88 and a FW190. After seeing tracer over the port wing, Coldray went into a diving turn to port. The Ju88 made an attack from dead astern and broke off above them to the left. The mid-upper, Flight Sergeant Renaud, fired about 50 rounds at it as it did so. The Focke Wulf made its attack from dead astern and at the same level. The rear gunner, Sergeant R. Daoust, fired a short burst but in the exchange the Lancaster received extensive damage. The 88 was claimed as probably damaged.

Flying Officer Bourke of 514 Squadron, in Lancaster LL672 'C', was attacked near Berlin at 3.13 am. His rear gunner, Sergeant Williston, reported a twin-engined aircraft which turned out to be a Me110, to starboard at 300 feet. Williston ordered a corkscrew to starboard at the same time as he opened fire as the 110 closed in. He suffered stoppages in two guns but despite this his tracer appeared to hit the fighter, which broke off into the darkness. A second attack came at 3.40, on the homeward journey, 25 miles east of Leipzig. Sergeant Williston was again alert, spotting a twin-engined aircraft

A message for the enemy

which he later identified as a Ju88, on the port quarter. He again gave the order to corkscrew and fired a four second burst, but again suffered stoppages. The 88 made one firing pass and was away.

Two enemy aircraft were reported being shot down on this raid, one by a Lancaster of 626 Squadron, west of Hannover at 2.23 am. One fighter attacked them four times before it fell away in flames. A few minutes later there was a violent explosion beneath the clouds, so it was claimed as destroyed.

The second was by a Lancaster of 7 Squadron whose gunners claimed an attacking Ju88 destroyed while making its third pass at them. It was seen to fall in flames.

Lieutenant Nick Knilans of 619 Squadron, flying Lancaster ED859 'V', had to make a sudden dive under about ten Me109s that suddenly came out of the darkness right over the target.

'Don't shoot,' he shouted to his gunners, 'they're not bothering us, don't attract their attention.'

His WOP tuned the rest of the crew into the intercom to listen to what he was receiving over his set. There seemed to be a terrible row going on between the German pilots and German Luftwaffe women on the ground. The WOP said that some of the girls' voices were English WAAFs giving wrong headings etc – in German – to the enemy pilots, causing them to run low on petrol while over the sea or over mountainous countryside.

*

The route to Berlin on this night was nearly direct. The return made via Le Tréport. The flak over the city was intense at first but moderated upon the arrival of the night fighters. Many combats took place over the target; one Lancaster seen shot down by two fighters. Some ten aircraft were seen shot down by fighters between the Dutch coast and Berlin and over the same area, aircraft were seen shot down by flak – one at Bremen, and three by individual salvos from single batteries at Meppel, Texel and north-east of Hannover.

On the return flight losses to flak were witnessed over Brussels and Lille. Returning to base, some aircraft met slight snow flurries, but for some Lincoln based squadrons, they met the dreaded fog. Lieutenant Knilans was diverted to Fiskerton where they had a FIDO system in operation. As he approached it was lit up and they broke into clear air at about 100 feet. The flames from the system shot two walls of fire up to 50 feet as Knilans brought his Lancaster down between them. It was very impressive and a little awe-inspiring.

A total of 28 Lancasters (6.7%) were missing from this operation. For each loss 50 tons of bombs had been dropped, the overall tonnage being 1,400.4. One of the missing aircraft was a Lancaster (DV307 'Z') of 101 Squadron, flown by Squadron Leader Robertson. He had in his crew Flight Lieutenant Duringer DFC, in the role of Special ABC Operator. He had taken the place of Pilot Officer Bill Parker. Parker had gone to London to collect his officer's uniform, having just been commissioned, and arrived back to find himself on that night's op. To let him settle into the Mess, Duringer took his place and asked him to look after his fiancée, Section Officer Knatchbull-Hugessen. Bill never forgot the tension of waiting for the aircraft to return, but it never did.

*

The Germans reported the raid lasting from 2.56 to 3.45 am, and that some 30 mines, 200 HE bombs, 10,000 incendiaries and 500 phosphorus bombs had been dropped. Damaged appeared somewhat lighter than previously; 21 houses destroyed, 28 severely damaged, 66 medium and 360 slightly damaged. Casualties were 79 dead, 117 injured. One industrial concern was destroyed and two damaged, while five military sites were also damaged. The target area and damage also embraced the Central Post Office, Exhibition Hall of the Fair Charlottenburg, Tempelhof goods station, a secondary flak battery at Wupperstraum and a gasometer in Neuhoellin.

Flight Sergeant E.G. Bacon of 542 PRU Squadron tried to take photographs in Spitfire EN685 but was unsuccessful.

Germany was becoming an even more dangerous place over which to fly. By January 1944 there were 6,716 heavy guns, 8,484 medium/light guns and 6,320 searchlights and 1,968 balloons in their defence arsenal. Also in January 1944 there came a reorganisation of night fighters, by the formation of Luftflotte Reich. This was responsible for entire direction of the air defence and controlled the directions of fighter units as well as directing the strength of flak artillery. Meanwhile the First Fighter Corps directed the operations of both night and day fighters as well as training fighter units.

CHAPTER SEVEN

The Weather Sets In

By the time many of the crews had run their engines down in their dispersal points on the morning of 2nd January 1944, the snow was falling thickly, and it was about 9 am before many of them got to their beds. Many went to sleep with the thought that the snow would curtail operations for at least that night. They were wrong. At around 3 pm, the men were being woken with the magic words: 'Ops again tonight, you lucky fellows!'

The Tenth Raid
On the affected airfields the snow had in fact been cleared by anyone who could hold a shovel, including even some Station Commanders. On some stations even aircrew who were flying that night had to give a hand in clearing the snow from the runways.

A force of 383 aircraft were prepared, 362 Lancasters, nine Halifaxes and twelve Mosquitos:

> 116 from No 1 Group
> 25 from No 3 Group
> 119 from No 5 Group
> 28 from No 6 Group
> 74 from No 8 Group plus
> 12 Mosquitos of 8 Group
> 9 Halifaxes
> ———
> 383
> ———

The weather forecast supplied to the Air Staff at 9.45 am was for a front expected at 11 o'clock near the Humber which would reach the Thames Estuary by 7 am. At take-off time, 5 and 6 Groups might be affected but it was regarded as unlikely that any airfield would be unable to get their aircraft away. Nos 3 and 8 Groups could expect no trouble at all. On route and over the target, 10/10ths stratus cloud with a base of 1,000 feet with tops at 5,000 feet was expected.

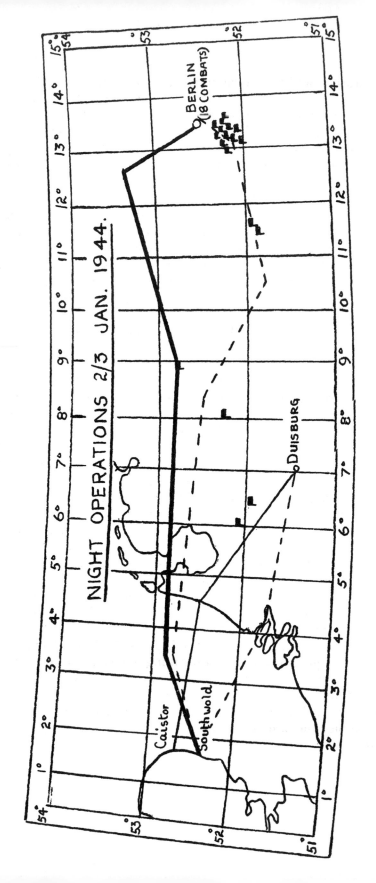

NIGHT OPERATIONS 2/3 JAN. 1944.

BERLIN (18 COMBATS)

DUISBURG

Caistor

Southwold

The return would be similar to the outward trip, but with frontal cloud to cross somewhere near Holland. The actual conditions experienced was 10/10ths cloud but the tops of this cloud varied from 6 to 16,000 feet. The winds at 20,000 feet were 85 mph with some icing at 20,000. On their return to England they found rain or drizzle in south Yorkshire and Lincolnshire. Visibility in this rain was two to four miles.

In the cockpit of Lanc Charlie II, of 626 Squadron, flown by Jack Currie, an unusual occurrence took place. The WOP picked up a broadcast on the Group operation frequency as they were climbing over base. It was a recall signal and they had to land at Exeter. As the weather looked all right they decided to press-on and wait for a repeat of the broadcast. Half an hour later when they were halfway across the North Sea, John Colles, the WOP reported to Currie again: 'Wireless operator to Skipper. You were right. I have just had a cancellation of the recall. We're to continue as briefed.'

It transpired that the original broadcast was intended for a small force of Wellingtons who were being kept out of the way of the Main Force effort, but the damage had already been partially done. 113 of the Main Force had indeed heeded the call and landed at Exeter. Of the 383 that took off, 295 Lancasters, five Halifaxes and 11 Mosquitos (total 311) attacked the target.

When Jack Currie and his crew reached Berlin they received a warm welcome from the flak gunners. It seemed more intense and was as accurate as ever. His rear gunner called that he seemed starved of oxygen and was feeling dizzy, so Currie sent Colles back to check the supply. He found the gunner semi-conscious, his oxygen tube probably frozen as ice could be felt in it. He also felt very cold so the heating to his electric suit must also have failed. The WOP was told to get him out of the turret and got in himself. This was easier said than done, as every time he touched the gunner he woke up and refused to leave his position. Currie told him he must be got out at once, he tried again, but it was impossible. Currie then ordered him back to his radio.

They then commenced their bombing run. Their bomb aimer was new on the squadron and was doing things by the book, much of the time, to the displeasure of the rest of the crew. He wanted to do a dummy run, but Currie told him as calm as he could in the circumstances: 'You don't do dummy runs on Berlin! Let them go!' Out tumbled the bombs and the aircraft lifted as it was lightened of its load.

On arrival back at Wickenby, their base, conditions were very poor and control suggested they divert to Acklington, north of Newcastle. The reply from Currie was that they had a casualty on board and requested permission to land. He was asked the nature of the casualty and told them his rear gunner was cold and anoxic, with possible frostbite. His landing was successful.

Flight Lieutenant Short of 50 Squadron was on the homeward journey when his bomb aimer, Pilot Officer Odgers, who was manning the front turret, sighted two lights approaching fast, below on the port bow at 600 yards. He identified it as a twin-engined aircraft and opened fire with long bursts of 250 rounds. The fighter did not attack but maintained its course and was lost to starboard.

Another Lancaster of 50 Squadron, flown by Pilot Officer Weatherstone, was also on the way home when two enemy fighters were seen – a FW190 and a Ju88. He immediately started to corkscrew; both gunners Sergeant Lineham and Flight Sergeant Collingwood, opened fire and continued to fire while the 190 flew out and above to 600 yards on the starboard side. Many hits were scored on the fighter and it broke off its attack. The Junkers then commenced its attack, the gunners hitting this also. Then both fighters joined up some distance to port where the gunners continued to fire at them until they were lost to sight, but both were claimed as damaged.

A Lancaster of 432 RCAF Squadron (DS792 'U-Uncle'), from Eastmoor in Yorkshire was on its third raid to Berlin in this series, flown by Pilot Officer Jim McIntosh from British Columbia. On the way to the target his airspeed indicator and altimeter went U/S. Just after turning for home at 3 am, an enemy fighter was seen by Sergeant Bandle, the rear gunner – a Me110. Both Bandle and the mid-upper, Sergeant Dedauw, opened fire as Bandle instructed the pilot to corkscrew. After a long burst from both gunners, the fighter was seen to stop firing but not before many shells had hit the Lancaster. The fighter's port engine caught fire and it was seen to go down in a dive, shrouded in smoke and flame. The engineer, Flight Sergeant Wally King, reported seeing the fighter spin out of control several times.

McIntosh was in trouble, for in making the corkscrew, hits were scored on the elevators which caused the control column to slam forward and sent the bomber into a dive. They lost twelve thousand feet but by putting both feet on the instrument panel and one arm around the control column and the other on the elevator trim, he

Winter 1944

Bomber Command fights the snow

managed by giving everything he had to force the aircraft up and out of the dive at about 10,000 feet. The compasses were out, the rudder controls jammed and there was now little response from the elevators. McIntosh, still keeping both arms around the control column to maintain height, made for Woodbridge aerodrome. Owing to shortage of fuel from a damaged tank, it was touch and go, and on landing he used all the runway, putting down on one wheel when they found the starboard tyre had been blown off, but he got them down safely. The damage to 'Uncle' was considerable. In addition to the damaged wheel, both starboard engine nacelles were gone, hydraulics smashed and twisted, two large tears in the starboard wing near the dinghy stowage (the dinghy itself was hanging out) and the tailplane riddled with cannon and machine guns hits. Through the fuselage there were five cannon shell holes, three of which had burst inside near the navigator. The rear and mid-upper turrets had cannon holes in them, one shell having travelled the entire length of the fuselage before exploding. Every propeller blade was holed and one split. Miraculously none of the crew was injured and Jim McIntosh was awarded an immediate DFC for his courage and determination to bring his machine and crew home.

Lancaster 'Q' of 12 Squadron encountered a Me110 over Potsdam. The engineer opened fire from the nose guns, his tracer seen to rake the Messerschmitt's fuselage from stem to stern. It broke away in a steep dive and was claimed as destroyed.

Lancaster 'K' of 49 Squadron was attacked by another 110 near Luckenwalde. The rear gunner fired and hits were observed, sending the fighter into a spin and was also claimed as destroyed. Lancaster 'A' of 550 Squadron shot down a Me109 which went down with smoke and flame pouring from the engine to be claimed as a probable. Lancaster 'X' of 83 PFF Squadron identified a 110 over Berlin, but a long burst from the rear gunner was right on target and the fighter exploded and burst into flames. Another PFF Lanc, 'M' of 97 Squadron, tangled with a FW190 north of Dessau. The rear gunner opened fire and the 190 caught fire, dived and seen later to explode on the ground.

Six Lancaster crews of 5 Group claimed damage to Ju88s, while one 6 Group and an 8 Group crew also claimed Ju88s as damaged. Most of the night fighter activity was confined to the Berlin area and for about 30 miles on the homeward track. As can be seen, there were many combats, and the encounters were mainly with Ju88s, some Me110s and about a dozen Me109s and FW190s. One of the more successful Luftwaffe pilots and CO of NJG/II, was Major Prince Sayn-Wittgenstein, who claimed six victories on this night.

Pilot Officer Derrick Bell in a Lancaster of 101 Squadron (DV308 'V') bombed successfully but on the return journey the main fuel tank was hit and set on fire. It could have been a flak hit or a night fighter; the crew had no idea! Bell gave the order to prepare to bale out and the crew started to put on their parachutes, but one man started to jump. The aircraft went into a dive and something hit the navigator, Sergeant Bailey, and he was knocked unconscious. When he recovered he was hanging in his parachute and landed in a wood near the village of Rance, twenty miles south of Charleroi. He saw the aircraft burning on the ground nearby and heard the ammunition exploding. Bell landed in a wood in the vicinity of Beaumont, twenty miles south-east of Mons. A little later he found the bomb aimer, an American, Lieutenant Albert. Picked up by the French they were moved around until 26th May, by the various escape movements in France, but on this day they were finally captured by the Luftwaffe, having apparently been betrayed. They were taken to Stalag Luft III at Sagan.

Over Berlin the crews experienced moderate heavy flak in a barrage at between 17,000 and 22,000 feet with intense light flak up to 16,000 around the marker flares. The Luftwaffe claimed to have destroyed 31 four-engined aircraft; in fact Bomber Command lost 27. There were no confirmed observations of any losses at all until Berlin was reached, but there seven aircraft were seen shot down between 2.44 and 3.04 am, of which five were seen to be hit by flak. After leaving the target a further four were seen shot down by flak in the Dessau area and three more by fighters.

Flight Sergeant Burke of 460 Squadron had his fair share of problems on the return journey. His mid-upper's oxygen tube came apart and he became unconscious. The WOP and the engineer went to assist him and both fell unconscious themselves, but the navigator managed to revive all three, though not before an hour or so had gone by. The mid-upper also suffered frostbite which put him in hospital.

*

The Germans sounded the air raid alarm at fifty minutes into the morning of 3rd January, and the all clear exactly five hours later. They reported strong penetrations over Holland to Central

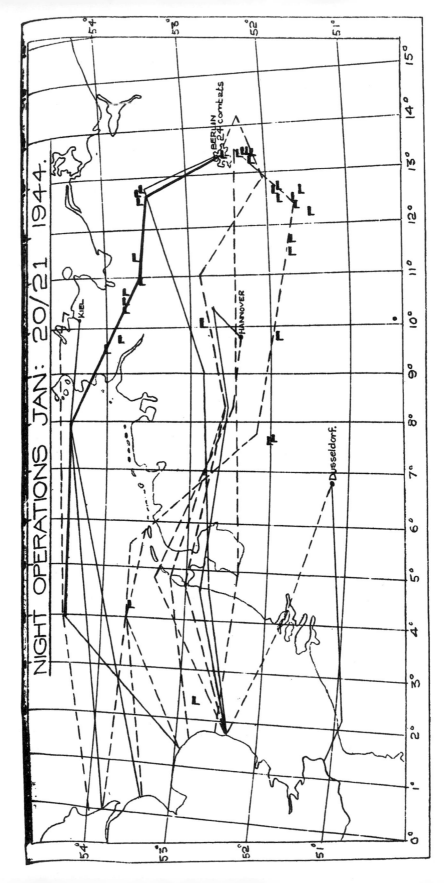

NIGHT OPERATIONS JAN: 20/21 1944.

Germany with the main attack centred on Berlin. About 300 aircraft, they estimated, attacked, 50 to 70 flying over the capital from a cloudy sky and in slight rain to drop their bombs. The main damage was caused to the east and south-east sectors of the city and they counted 60 mines, 35 HE bombs, 20,000 incendiary and 15,000 phosphorus bombs.

Some 141 houses were destroyed, 435 severely damaged, 106 with medium damage and 1,018 with slight damage. Casualties totalled 77 dead, 215 injured, 85 missing, while 5,000 were added to the growing figure of those made homeless. One industrial concern was destroyed and 12 damaged, eight severely.

The RAF dropped 1,116.4 tons on the city, which was 41 tons for each missing aircraft. The Mosquito force attacked Berlin four minutes before the attack began and then 40 minutes after the Main Force had passed over.

The following was extracted from a German High Command Communique dated 3rd January referring to an attack by 284 RAF Lancasters:

In the hours of yesterday evening the British directive made a terror attack against Nuremburg which caused heavy damage to houses and losses among the civilian population. Irreplaceable cultural monuments were among targets of the enemy's senseless fury to destroy. The British heavy bombers also attacked towns in south-west Germany and half attacked the Reich Capital. The air defences shot down yesterday, 22 enemy aircraft, amongst them 14 four-engined aircraft.

There was in fact no attack on Nuremburg on this date and on the whole the German reports were very inaccurate. Photographs of Berlin were attempted by Mosquitos of 542 PRU but again, weather was the biggest problem, with the city shrouded in cloud.

*

The Eleventh Raid

Over two weeks was to pass before the next raid was mounted. In between, Stettin and Brunswick were attacked by both the RAF and USAAF. Then on the night of 20/21st January, Bomber Command put into motion its biggest and heaviest raid in the series so far – 769 Lancasters and Halifaxes plus Mosquitos of 8 Group. There were

'Keep them flying at all costs'

Take off for Berlin Flight Sergeant Schuman and crew

RAF Driffield – Flight Sergeant Schuman and crew, and groundcrew

Y-Yorker 466 Squadron running up

also diversionary raids on Hannover, Düsseldorf and Kiel, all undertaken by 8 Group Mosquitos.

The weather, as supplied by the Met boys to the Air Staff at 3.55 that afternoon, promised mainly 10/10th cloud on route and over Berlin. Winds would be between 50 to 60 mph and the weather over enemy airfields cloudy to overcast with moderate to poor visibility and some local rain. The weather actually encountered was very near to that forecast, and for a change the weather over home bases remained fine all night.

The bombers approached Berlin from north-north-west, following land fall over Schleswig-Holstein, the route passing over the Kiel Canal, then between Hamburg and Lübeck. This route had not been followed previously in a large scale attack on Berlin and a small spoof attack was made on nearby Kiel.

A concentrated sky-marking attack was delivered on Berlin and flak was very slight at first but developed to moderate intensity later. Heavy flak was mainly in a loose barrage between 17,000 and 20,000 feet. Light flak was experienced above the marker flares.

A large number of enemy aircraft were reported along the route and over the target although the number of attacks and combats were comparatively few. Controlled night fighters could be heard between 5.30 and 10.20 pm of which twelve were active against British bombers. Identified areas of operation included the Schlising, Eindhoven, Enschede and Münster localities, but no claims were made.

The German running commentator control was heard operating at 5.35 pm passing directions to aircraft of NJG/I, II, III, IV, V and VI. Positions and heights of the bombers were passed and attempts were made to direct the fighters onto the bomber stream rather than to try and anticipate the likely destination. Berlin was mentioned as the probable target at 7.02 pm but specific instructions for the night fighters to proceed there were not issued until 7.34. Later, orders to remain over Berlin were heard while positions of the bomber stream continued to be passed after they left the target, to as far as the south-west of Magdeburg. In the Berlin area conditions appeared to be exceptionally favourable for night fighters. A layer of cloud at about 12,000 feet, illuminated by searchlights from below, formed a background against which aircraft could be silhouetted for the fighters and it is likely that many of the losses occurred as a direct result. An RAF Mosquito for instance, later reported that from 35,000 feet six Lancasters were quite visible below at one time, and many of the fighters were four to five thousand feet below the Mosquito's height.

Along the route, from the area between Hamburg and Lübeck to Berlin, and homewards as far as Bitterfield, fighters were active. In addition to directions from the running commentary they were guided into the bomber stream by a series of small red flares, apparently fired from the ground.

Although few crews reported intense flak, 46 aircraft suffered damage and there was some reports of aircraft known to have been shot down. From these, it appears that losses occurred at Neuruppin and four in the Berlin area. There is a possibility that further losses occurred over Hamburg, Ascherban and Leipzig but they cannot be definitely attributed to AA fire.

One Halifax (LW441), flown by Flight Sergeant Lewis of 640 Squadron, was attacked by a Ju88 which came out of the cloud. In the attack the starboard aileron was damaged but the rear gunner, Sergeant Everson, returned the fighter's fire. The attack came as they were on their bombing run and it seemed to Sergeant Tom Beckett, the mid-upper, that the Halifax went over onto its back, diving out of control. He struggled out of his turret, plugged in his intercom near to the rear door, just in time to hear the pilot shout, 'Don't jump, I think I have got her!' He went back to his turret and saw a gaping hole in the wing – about five feet across. They landed at Coltishall after a seven hour flight, but the aircraft was a write-off.

A Halifax of 102 Squadron encountered an enemy fighter at which the rear gunner fired about 500 rounds. It was seen to dive below in flames and was claimed as a probable. The mid-upper gunner of a 7 Squadron Lancaster, observed a Me110 as it opened fire. He let go a five-second burst which hit the fighter. It turned over, dived vertically and was claimed as destroyed. A Halifax of 578 Squadron also damaged a Ju88. In total, some 98 fighters were sent up to attack the bomber force, as the attack continued.

The crew of a Halifax (LK739 'P' of 428 Squadron, piloted by Flight Sergeant Reaine) were flying their first operation. They had been hit and began to lose height, twenty minutes from Berlin. The pilot then ordered the bomb load to be released as they were still losing height and already down to 12,500 feet. After releasing the bombs they managed to reach 19,000 and turned on a course for home. Fuel was pouring from No 3 petrol tank and the engineer, Flight Sergeant Fell, estimated they had enough fuel for another five minutes' flying. Reaine had little choice but to give the order to bale out.

The navigator, Flying Officer Fisher, engineer Sergeant Fell, and mid-upper Sergeant Lea Fryer together with the rear man, Sergeant Wynveen, all jumped from the front escape hatch. The bomb aimer, Flying Officer Lavoie, had been sick and when he jumped his feet were facing aft, so that his parachute pack got caught on the edge of the hatch. He put his elbows out and was unable to jump free. The WOP, Sergeant Banner, tried at first to pull him back in but was unable to do so; eventually Lavoie got himself free.

Sergeant Fryer landed in a pine tree in the Châlons area of France. After climbing down he spent the rest of the night under cover. In the morning he took down his 'chute and started to walk in a southerly direction. He eventually arrived in Switzerland on 3rd February. Sergeant Banner also fell into a tree and when he released his parachute, fell fifteen to twenty feet and was knocked out.

As the pilot left the aircraft, the port outer engine cut. Reaine opened his parachute but only one strap was attached, the other had pulled open, so he landed heavily hurting his spine. When the engineer's parachute opened, the straps hit him in the face cutting him about the jaw and mouth, but he made a safe landing.

Exceptionally, all the crew, apart from Sergeant Wynveen, evaded capture and got back home to England in the middle of 1944 – Wynveen was captured.

Squadron Leader Weetham's aircraft of 35 Squadron, flying over Berlin at 18,000 feet, was hit by incendiaries dropped from a Lancaster. Several smashed through the fuselage and port wing. The damage caused the dinghy to release and it, complete with ration packs, went floating down over Berlin. The brake pipes were also severed so on return Weetham was faced with a landing without brakes. He got down safely but swung off the runway and stopped dead when the starboard wheel went into a ditch. Still aboard was a 1,000 lb percussion fused bomb, which was swinging by its fins and held only by the spring doors. A member of the ground staff, an armaments warrant officer, was given a Mention in Despatches for making it safe before it was removed.

In Lancaster K-King (JB461) flown by Flight Lieutenant Roland King DFC, an Australian on his eleventh trip to Berlin, had just closed the bomb doors and was turning onto a new course when there was a crash and the aircraft went into a dive. The stick was dead in his hands, smoke and flames broke out in the port wing and he had somehow lost his flying helmet and intercom. He tried to check on the crew but could only see two of them. One, the flight engineer, Flight Sergeant Farmelow, was pressed to the roof of the aircraft, held there by the centrifugal force of the falling aeroplane. King released his harness and immediately shot upwards, hit the roof and bounced back in his seat. He tried to regain control but it was hopeless.

The next thing he remembered was falling through the air, his parachute unopen. He pulled the ripcord and the parachute spread out above his head. The raid was at its height. All round him was searchlights and exploding flak shells – the noise was terrific. He tugged on the parachute lines in an attempt to drift outside the city limits and eventually came down in a ploughed field south-west of Berlin, and soon afterwards, heard the 'all clear' sounded. He had hurt his head, and his face was covered in blood, while his left arm appeared to be broken while the right one he could not move at all. It was dark and raining. After walking for some while he was picked up by a German soldier and taken towards the burning city. At a barracks he was interrogated, then taken on a tour of Berlin, trying to find a hospital that would tend to his injuries but they were all full with air raid casualties. He was finally admitted to the Hermann Göring Luftwaffe hospital. Here he was taken to a room, his clothes cut off and then knew nothing until he woke up on an operating table. His left arm was operated on five times and he had two blood transfusions, both supplied by other RAF prisoners. After ten weeks he was taken to Stalag Luft III. A year later he went to Lamsdorf by hospital train to be exchanged with a German prisoner. When he eventually arrived back in England, he was reunited with his wife and saw his baby son for the very first time.

Pilot Officer Whitehead of 76 Squadron flying Halifax LL116 'X', successfully bombed the target but as the bomb aimer called 'Bombs gone', the aircraft was hit in the nose by flak. The machine shuddered violently and was thrown upwards. The instrument panel was hit and knocked out the direction indicator, climb and descent indicator and artificial horizon as well as all four boost gauges. The bomb aimer, Flying Officer Morris, had suffered terrible injuries to the head. The navigator went to his aid, tried his pulse but found none, and was told by Whitehead to leave his body where it was.

The navigator's table was completely wrecked and a large part of the window and fuselage opposite him was missing. All his logs, charts and instruments were missing or U/S. They were then hit by flak in the starboard inner engine area. Shell fragments sliced into the fuselage making another large hole in the starboard side while one fragment grazed the pilot's head, cutting his forehead and smashing his goggles. The WOP was also hit on the side of the head causing a long but not very deep gash, while the right side of his headphone earpiece was blown off. They also began to lose fuel and eventually forced to bale out when nearly out of petrol.

Whitehead landed at Lens in France, seeing his aircraft crash with a blinding explosion west of the town. He evaded capture and arrived back in England in the middle of the year.

Flight Sergeant Johnson of 434 Squadron had his aircraft hit twice by flak, first in the rear end of the bomb bay and then in the fuselage. The entrance door was badly damaged and the rudder controls sheared. The oxygen supply from the rest position back was U/S as well as all the electrical wiring. The ailerons were shot away and the directional range master unit destroyed. The crew baled out over the Driffield area of Yorkshire on their return. Johnson received a broken jaw, facial injuries and lost seven teeth; the bomb aimer, Sergeant Campbell, arm injuries and the rear gunner, Sergeant Tofflemeir, injured his head and leg.

Flying Officer Hall of 102 Squadron (HR716 'P') ran short of petrol and he and his crew made a successful parachute descent over Driffield. Flight Sergeant Proctor also from 102 (JD302 'D') crash-landed near Norwich and his bomb aimer, Flying Officer Turnbull, died of injuries received.

Flight Sergeant Cozens in a Halifax of 427 Squadron (LL191 'N') crashed on landing at Coltishall when running out of fuel. On his third attempt at landing he missed the flarepath, hit a tree, house and high tension cable. Four of the crew were critically injured, including Cozens, and died later. Another was slightly hurt but the other two escaped. Cozens had only been married a month, and when he was killed was becoming one of the most proficient pilots on the squadron.

*

In total 35 aircraft failed to return, 6% of those despatched. From crew reports it appears that eight fell to flak, eighteen to fighters and nine to unknown causes, although it was thought most probable to fighter attack as they were so active. Of the total, thirteen Lancasters and 22 Halifaxes. The tonnage of bombs dropped was 2,400.6

Unexploded bombs, Berlin

Berlin under attack

which was 69 tons for each aircraft that was lost.

A German report covering the period 5.05 to 8.30 pm, estimated some 400-500 bombers had penetrated the North Sea and Holland on an easterly and south-easterly course. In all about twenty were reported shot down. In Berlin the alert sounded at 8.25. The Germans estimated a medium attack, launched by about 200-250 aircraft of which ten were shot down over the city itself. Some 60 mines, 650 HE bombs, 4,500 phosphorus and 12,000 incendiary bombs fell during the raid. Damage to the city amounted to 463 houses destroyed, 657 severely damaged, 364 had medium damage and 1,800 were slightly damaged. Casualties were 243 dead, 465 injured, 40 missing and 10,000 made homeless. Five industrial concerns were destroyed, ten severely damaged while seventeen were listed as having medium damage and fourteen with slight damage. Some areas were without electric power, tramways, underground, while suburban railways were disrupted. In Brandenburg damage occurred in several places and a number of houses and business properties were destroyed and damaged.

*

The Twelfth Raid
Another week went by before the next raid on Berlin, scheduled for the night of 27/28th January. The aircraft detailed were as follows:

> 149 from 1 Group
> 62 from 3 Group
> 172 from 5 Group
> 48 from 6 Group
> 84 from 8 Group
> 21 Mosquitos of 8 Group
>
> ———
>
> 536
>
> ———

Of these 536 aircraft, 481 were to actually bomb Berlin.

The weather forecast supplied to the Air Staff at four o'clock that afternoon indicated weather over home bases fit for take-off. Over Berlin the weather should be 10/10ths cloud, which was indeed that experienced, with tops at 8-10,000 feet. They also met 90 mph winds at 20,000 feet, increasing to 95 at times.

Pathfinder aircraft dropped sky markers to indicate various turning points on route to keep the main bomber stream together. It also caused problems, for the night fighters would swarm round and round, knowing the bombers must pass the markers. The whole show was a remarkable vivid firework display, the colours being magnificent in their brilliance.

The attack opened with the Mosquitos going in to mark with flares of green and red and then the main Pathfinder force with their blind bombing technique. This they achieved with skymarkers – red and green balls of fire, dripping slowly on parachutes until they disappeared through the cloud layers. This cloud was too thick for accurate assessment, but crews reported a good glow of fire and several large explosions. The glow of fires was visible for 150 miles on the homeward route.

Mosquitos once again bombed the city an hour or so after the Main Force and surprisingly, flak was only moderate. Searchlights were unable to penetrate the thick cloud but night fighters appeared in force.

The only German broadcast intercepted after the raid referred to 'another terror raid on the residential districts of Berlin'. They later stated that the raid had fallen on the south-eastern and eastern districts, particularly on industrial targets on both sides of the River Spree.

The running commentary control was heard plotting the buildup of the bombers over the Norwich area as early as 5.36 pm and from 6.06 aircraft were being sent to intercept them over the North Sea. Meanwhile the bomber stream moved northwards to a point west of Vlieland, and on towards the Hamburg area. Fighters from NJG/I, II, III, IV, V, and VI were active. One claim was heard at 7.45 pm near Alkmaar, four more occurred between Minden and Magdeburg, seven over Berlin and two more by single-engined fighters on the way out near Frankfurt. Me110s, Me210s, and FW190s were reported, and over Berlin these were joined by Ju88s and Me109s.

In spite of this, a diversionary raid was successful in attracting the attention of a part of the enemy fighter force. This diversion was caused by 21 Halifax bombers of 8 Group who bombed Heligoland, and six Wellingtons from 1 Group with 74 Stirlings of 3 Group, who laid mines along the main sea route over which the Main Force aircraft flew.

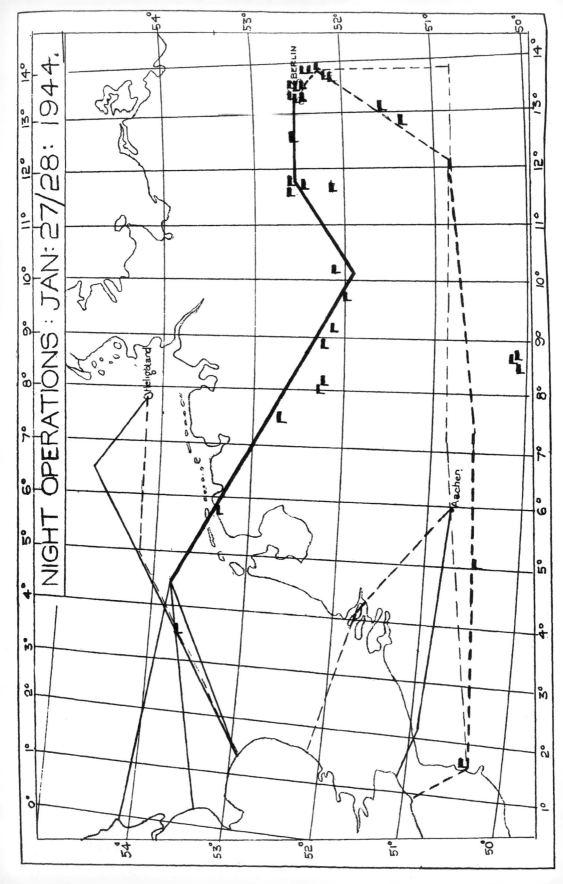

NIGHT OPERATIONS : JAN: 27/28: 1944.

BERLIN

Heligoland

Aachen

A Lancaster of 101 Squadron, flown by Squadron Leader Johnny Marshal AFC, was attacked by a Ju88. Hits were scored on the 88 by his gunners, Sergeant Fred Bence and Sergeant Jack Marsden, who claimed it as damaged. From the same squadron, a Lancaster was attacked twice by a FW190. Both gunners saw their fire bouncing off the fighter and it was last seen going down, trailing smoke behind it and was believed probably destroyed.

Flight Lieutenant Keith of 50 Squadron was attacked by a Ju88 over the target area. His mid-upper, Sergeant Brown, was the first to see it but as his intercom went U/S he had to give the pilot directions on its attack by the fighter attack indicator. The rear gunner, Sergeant Rowecliffe, got in one long burst but despite this their aircraft was hit amidships, damaging the upper turret and smashing the intercom to the rear gunner. The 88 attacked again opening fire from 500 yards, and again the Lanc was hit, this time in both wings and the tail unit as well as the fuselage. The starboard inner petrol tank caught fire, but this was soon put out by diving the aircraft several times. Meanwhile the 88 had been hit by the gunners and damaged.

One Lancaster of 207 Squadron was in combat with a Focke Wulf, the gunners claiming it as probably damaged. Other enemy fighters were damaged by other gunners and the rear gunner of a 408 Squadron Lanc claimed one destroyed.

The loss of a Lancaster of 626 Squadron (LM380 'S2') which crashed at Katzenel, was caused by an attack some twenty miles south-east of Koblenz. The fighter was a Me110 which attacked from below, once again a *Schräge Musik* attack. Its cannon shells hit the aircraft with a force which Arthur Lee, the navigator, described as like being hit with consecutive blows with an enormous hammer. He recalls three blows in as many seconds.

The Lancaster went into a steep dive and Lee emerged from his compartment to see flames streaming from both starboard engines. He slipped on his parachute knowing there could not be a lot of time left. The order soon came to abandon the aircraft. Prior to attaching his 'chute he had pulled off his helmet to ensure the leads from oxygen and intercom did not become entangled. He was to leave the aircraft by the forward hatch, but perhaps because of a brief lack of oxygen he became unconscious after moving forward. He came to lying on the floor and could smell burning – his hair was on fire! The Lancaster was spinning and he was pinned to the floor. He thought he was going to be killed as his harness and clothes were caught up in many projections. There seemed no quick way he could release himself before he would be burnt to death.

At this point he was miraculously flung through the escape hatch, from the intense heat of the burning aeroplane to the freezing January air outside. For some seconds he attempted to open his parachute but panic prevented him from doing so. Eventually he managed to pull the metal ripcord handle and the canopy cracked open above him. As he hung there, the blazing bomber howled passed him and disappeared into the cloud. Arthur Lee landed at the edge of a large wood on a hillside; the grass was wet and it was very cold. He felt alone and friendless, and not totally certain he was even alive! Perhaps he was dead, he thought, and this was the after life. The sound of heavy bombers overhead and the remains of his aircraft burning brightly in the wood nearby soon brought him back to reality. He had lost both his boots and was feeling pain from his burnt hands, face and head. In a short while a small party of men with torches came up the hillside towards him. He stood and raised his hands above his head – from then on he was a prisoner of war.

The rest of the crew were all killed and are buried in the Rheinburg War Cemetery. He understood they all died in the crash but the next day he was given the boots of John Lee, the bomb aimer, and they had no sign of burning or scorching. Another explanation was that his parachute had failed to open. The people of the village near where the Lancaster came down have erected a cross on the site. It is the custom of the village to read out the names of the men of that village who died in the war at the Sunday Service following the anniversary of their deaths. Now they do this for Flight Lieutenant William Belford (known as Noel Belford to his friends) and his crew. On an earlier raid 'Noel' Belford and crew had ditched in the sea returning from a raid on Stettin on 6th January but were rescued by ASR launch two hours later.

A Lancaster of 625 Squadron (ND461 'W') flown by Pilot Officer Cook DFM, detailed to support the PFF, took off at 8 pm and reached Berlin to bomb it from 22,000 feet. On the homeward route the navigator, Flight Sergeant Berger, had a problem with his plotting and the Lancaster's course was well south of track, before reaching the Rhine, where a route marker was expected north of Koblenz. The Lanc was then engaged by flak and hits sustained, causing fires in the Nos 1 and 2 tanks on the starboard side, also in the starboard engines, both of which stopped.

Suddenly there was a great sheet of flame from an explosion in

No 2 tank and the pilot put the aircraft into a dive hoping to extinguish the flames. The Lanc went down at a rate of about 1,000 feet per minute and it was down to 13,000 feet before the fires went out. The starboard inner was restarted using petrol from No 1 tank. Eventually with only twenty minutes juice left, the WOP asked for and got a fix for Southampton. At this time their estimated position was north-west of Paris so a second fix was requested which placed them north of Guernsey. After all engines cut, the pilot gave the order to bale out. The bomb aimer got the front hatch up and jumped out first followed by the navigator, WOP Sergeant Henderson, engineer Flight Sergeant Brown, then the pilot. The gunners appear to have gone out by the rear door and on one parachute, as the rear gunner, Sergeant Ringwood, in jettisoning all the surplus weight in the aircraft, had accidentally thrown out his 'chute. The records show that Ringwood was killed, but that the mid-upper, Sergeant Weller, survived. The crew, apart from Berger, were on their eighteenth trip, Berger being on his seventeeth. From the date of a report by Sergeant Brown – 23rd April 1944 – it would appear he escaped to fight another day.

Squadron Leader Lorraine Simpson DFC of 467 Squadron, flying a Lancaster (JB296), was shot down in the St Malo area on the return flight. He was captured on 2nd February and taken to Rennes civil prison, and then to a prison in Paris. After interrogation at the Dulag Luft Centre in Frankfurt, he was sent to Stalag Luft III. Flight Lieutenant Arthur Schrock, a fellow Australian in Simpson's crew, was also taken prisoner and sent to Stalag Luft IV.

Jack Currie, flying Lancaster JB559, which had previously been a 12 Squadron aircraft, and, as he described it, a very poor specimen of her type, was sluggish in control reponse and lacked the usual Lanc character of stability and flight. They bombed the target and turned south-west on the long route towards France, fighting a headwind of 100 mph. It seemed to take an age to reach the English coast. Despite this they were the first 626 Squadron crew to reach and land at their base at Wickenby.

In Lancaster W4315 of 61 Squadron, piloted by Pilot Officer E. Williams, the port engine was causing concern. It had been damaged by flak over Hannover on the outward journey and eventually they were forced to ditch. The engineer, Sergeant Beach, gunners Sergeants Acombe-Hill and Bowden, failed to reach the dinghy and were lost. Williams, his bomb aimer Sergeant Anderson and WOP Sergeant Parker were rescued at 6 pm on the 28th.

Flying Officer Colin Grannum, flying Lancaster JB650 'E' of 12 Squadron, was hit by flak three times on the bomb run. The port inner engine was knocked out, the roof of the cockpit blown off and extensive damage caused to the entire port wing, which eventually put the port outer engine out of action. In addition to these problems, all the petrol tanks had been holed. When down to twenty gallons, Grannum gave the bale-out order and they all went through the front hatch. The engineer, Pilot Officer Hoare landed successfully at Bannoux near Sprimont, Liège province. Grannum baled out at 9,000 feet and was told later that when he left the aircraft it rolled over onto its back. He landed on the side of a hill, and in doing so hurt his knee which did not help the situation. Despite this injury he and his wireless operator, Flight Sergeant Quinn, made it to Switzerland and safety by 9th May.

Some fifteen kilometres from Liège, Pilot Officer Hoare met up with Pilot Officer David Murphy, another member of the crew who came from Northern Ireland. They split up to make their way separately but Murphy was captured by a German patrol in the Tarbes area on 12th May after a month on the run. Flight Sergeant Harry Owen, the rear gunner, landed at Trees and was captured on 14th March at Liège. The navigator, Flying Officer Richard Taylor, from Nottingham and a former actor, managed to evade capture and after the invasion of France made contact with American forces in September.

Flying Officer Mike Beetham in LD744, was on his thirteenth trip and his eighth to Berlin. They were on their bomb run when a fighter was seen approaching. The bomb aimer, Les Bartlett, had rapidly to leave the bomb sight for the front guns. The fighter pilot threw caution to the wind and came tearing in amongst its own flak but all was well and he left without making a serious attack. They then made their bomb drop. On return to base they found at least ten aircraft in the circuit below 1,000 feet, all waiting to land. When their turn came it was rather hurried and Les had no time to leave his front 'office'. However, Beetham was an excellent pilot and made a fine landing.

Jimmy Flynn of 100 Squadron saw a Me109 hit over the target area. He remembers it being a lovely sight and was only sorry he had not shot it down. He also saw three Lancasters go down in flames and some parachutes open. It was the last trip of his first tour.

Pilot Officer William Parker was a special operator with 101 Squadron in a Lancaster (DV407 'V'), flown by Pilot Officer Norman Marsh, whom he described as a very cheerful Australian. On the return trip from Berlin his aircraft was attacked by a Ju88. The tail and port wing was damaged and on his ABC set he picked up an excited exchange between two German fighter pilots both claiming to have shot them down. They were obviously misled by the skilful evasive action of Norman Marsh. On this occasion his ABC set was modified to jam 'Benito'. Briefly, this was a method whereby individual fighters could be ranged and continually monitored while at the same time given the necessary control instructions from the ground station. It did not involve any radar principle, but depended upon the figher under control picking up a signal from his ground station which was alternately transmitted back to that ground station on a slightly different frequency. The essential feature of this Benito system was the re-transmitted ranging signal which was an audible tone of either 300 or 3,000 cycles, depending on the distance of the fighter from the ground station.

Regarding ABC, the theory was that if this audio tone could be simulated by an exactly similar signal from the jamming aircraft, it should so confuse the ground station working with one genuine, and one or more spurious return signals it would prevent the fighter from being ranged. Since the ABC type of radio transmitter jamming could not greatly affect reception of this tone, a suitable modulator was designed for jamming Benito. The method of

Me 109 German fighter

application was to tune the transmitter to the signal to be jammed, then adjust the modulator so that the audio note was exactly in pitch with the Benito tone. For his work with ABC during some 35 ops Parker received the DFC. In all he flew nine times to Berlin and later flew with 192 Squadron.

*

At 10 am on the morning of 27th January, Flight Lieutenant Stanley James, known as 'Jimmy', with his crew of 9 Squadron, checked over their aircraft as they were down for that night's attack on Berlin. They were the senior crew on the squadron at that time, having completed 23 ops, and after this trip, were on a posting to 617 Squadron.

As crews went they were very dedicated while in the air and knew what the job was all about. On the ground they liked to enjoy themselves. As Hal Croxson recalls, it seemed a little like flying and boozing – one night on ops, one night drinking, but of course the nights in the pub were more enjoyable. He had started as a trainee pilot in America but had to scrub it as he was sick for some while and could not catch up the course, so he re-mustered as an air gunner.

Having checked their Lancaster (LL745 'M-Mother'), they went for lunch, being careful not to drink too much liquid. Then came the briefing and preparation for the operation. At 4.30 they assembled at the aircraft, went through one or two final checks and at 5.15 they were airborne, circled, then set course towards Berlin. They were in the second wave of the five attacking waves, not a bad draw as the early waves often missed the majority of the fighter activity. Over Berlin 10/10ths cloud made the searchlights non-effective. They bombed the target satisfactorily and all seemed set for the return flight. They were slightly off course perhaps and because of this were picked up by radar and hit by either flak or *Schräge Musik* attack. They were hit in the bomb bay, the shock being felt throughout the bomber. A fire started in the bay, one engine was set ablaze and, unknown to them, one of the tyres had burst.

Jimmy James warned the crew of the situation, and the bomb aimer managed to open the panel into the bomb bay and extinguish the flames there. Then he discovered two incendiary bombs had hung up and tried to release them by using the hand release. This did not work, so he put his arm through and pulled out some pins which secured the shackled holding the canisters and out they or manually. The burning engine was feathered and the fire went out. Now on three engines and with the pilot's altimeter damaged, James was told that the navigator had been hit by flak in the leg and was being treated by the WOP on the rest bed. Once attended to, the navigator immediately returned to his table to assist the pilot with a course home.

They were now down to 16,000 feet and twenty minutes later a second engine failed. James felt they could reach England but later decided that he had been too optimistic and that a ditching in the sea was inevitable. All surplus weight was jettisoned. With the use of the axe, Hal Croxson chopped away the flare chute and the elsan toilet. He broke away the ammunition belts to the rear turret and threw out over 12,000 rounds of .303 ammo, while the mid-upper covered the rear of the aircraft. He even threw out the rest bed; it was not very heavy but everything would help. He then went back to his rear turret and clipped on his parachute.

Then a third engine went and controlling the aircraft became very difficult. With this James gave the order to bale out. Hal swung his turret full starboard, disconnected his intercom, collected all his bits and pieces, pushed his bottom out as far as he could, put his feet on the gun butts and launched himself out, remembering to take hold of the rip cord handle. His parachute opened immediately once he got out into the slipstream.

Hal Croxson found the silence after the noise of the aircraft, very lonely. Only the swish of his canopy could be heard. Descending into what he thought was a thick black cloud he hit the deck hard. It was not a cloud but one side of a valley. He pulled on the lines as he had been trained to do which stopped him being pulled along the ground. He had lost a boot in the jump and felt as thought the whole of Germany was looking for him. Taking out his .38 revolver he cocked it and put it ready by his side. He thought that it would be ready to use or to hand over! To calm his nerves he lit a cigarette without thinking that the light might be seen. He did not finish it, for he laid back and fell asleep for about a quarter of an hour or so. When he awoke he discovered that his fingers were cut, and bound them with strips of parachute silk, keeping them bent to stop the bleeding.

Shortly afterwards, having prepared himself, he set off into some woods where he buried everything he did not need, including his flying helmet. On the front was written 'Horizontal' – a nickname from the crew, for in his spare time he would lie down horizontally and either think or sleep! Despite only having one boot he set off, using his escape compass. He evaded for three days, dodging several German patrols but was then picked up by a hunting party with dogs and shotguns. He was taken to the local village who handed him over to the Luftwaffe. Following a period in Stalag Luft VI in Lithuania he was moved to Stalag Luft IV. a journey best forgotten, for at one time his party was chained inside a cattle truck – even at one time having the officer incite the guards not to hesitate in using their bayonets if they tried to escape for these were the men who had bombed their cities and killed their families. The final $3\frac{1}{2}$ kilometres had to be run, with prods from bayonets, clubbing if men fell, and with dogs barking and biting legs and arms as they staggered on.

In 1982 Hal returned to the crash sight. Four men had died in the crash and had been buried by local villagers and their names were entered in the village history book next to all the village men who had died in the war. When he returned home he sent the village a photograph of his crew showing the four men they had buried all those years before.

*

Thirty-two Lancasters failed to return from this night's mission which was a 6% loss ratio. Of these seventeen fell to fighters, and possibly even 21. Four were known to have been shot down by flak, two more had collided, and six others were missing from unknown causes. The tonnage dropped was 1,738.4, and, as Bomber Command liked to record, this was 53 tons for each aircraft lost.

For their part, the Germans estimated the raid had been carried out by a force of 200-250 aircraft. Their alert sounded at 7.58 and the all clear at 9.20. Two aircraft were shot down over Berlin. They reckoned over one thousand mines and high explosive bombs had been dropped, as well as 20,000 phosphorus bombs and 25,000 incendiaries – and 200 oil bombs! The casualties were 90 dead, 292 injured and 200,000 made homeless.

Local and long distance railway lines had been severely affected and of six gas works hit, three had been closed down and the area of Neukeolin was without gas. The Air Ministry, Ministry of Economics, Ministry of the Interior and a number of embassy buildings, as well as police, army and Luftwaffe barracks and installations were hit. Among the industrial targets hit was the AEG Company, Telefunken, Osram, Agfa, Siemens, the Deutsche Waffen munitions factory, Daimler Benz and the Bavarian Nitrogen Works.

*

The Thirteenth Raid

The very next night, Bomber Command set out for Berlin again – the 28/29th. A force of 682 aircraft were detailed:

            125 from No 1 Group
             39 from No 3 Group
            134 from No 4 Group
            155 from No 5 Group
            128 from No 6 Group
             96 from No 8 Group
              5 Mosquitos of 8 Group
            ───
            682
            ───

Split into types, this was 432 Lancasters, 245 Halifaxes and five Mosquitos.

The weather people supplied their daily report to the Air Staff which indicated weather fit for all night operations with considerable broken cloud, with a base of 1,500 feet or more. Over Berlin there was a good chance of 10/10ths cloud with tops below, 10,000 feet, which proved almost totally correct in the event. Winds were calculated to be between 70 and 95 mph.

Diversionary raids were flown by Mosquito aircraft of 8 Group against Hannover and the airfields at Gilze Reijen, Venlow, Deelan and Leeuwarden, plus four 8 Group Halifaxes and 63 Stirlings of 3 Group flying minelaying sorties.

As before the early attack was made by 8 Group Mossies. Three attacked from 27-18,000 feet through 7-10/10ths cloud using navigational aids. They met no opposition although they saw searchlights and some night fighters about. Behind them came the Main Force, led by Pathfinders who had laid good route markers. Over Berlin the PFF men did their job despite heavy flak fire, but searchlights were only occasionally able to penetrate the clouds but not in sufficient numbers to form cones.

On the way to the target, the force had met considerable opposition from flak but the diversionary raids took away some of the reported night fighters, although the route lay too far north to attract the whole of the fighter force. Some attempts were made to intercept minelaying aircraft while others were airborne in readiness against a possible land target. Fighters from NJG/I, II and V were heard

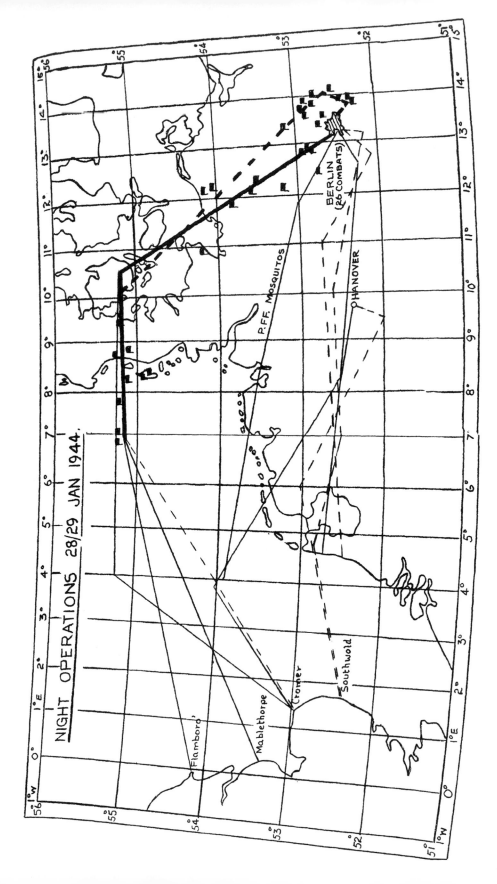

NIGHT OPERATIONS 28/29 JAN 1944.

Flamboro
Mablethorpe
Cromer
Southwold
P.F.F. MOSQUITOS
BERLIN (26 COMBATS)
HANOVER

operating in the Bremen area.

The fighter reaction to the Main Force stream was similar to that against the diversionary raids although aircraft from all night fighter units were used. It was thought that no great concentration of fighters was achieved in the bomber stream and that the main bulk of the fighters did not reach Berlin until the attack had started. There were, however, enough fighters in the stream across Denmark and from the north German coast to the target to claim a number of victims, possibly as many as twelve.

The Main Force was plotted at 1 am, 80 miles to the north-west of Texel and were followed from there along the route until 2.52 when it was announced that they were obviously making for Berlin. Aircraft from all night fighter groups were then heard being directed either into the stream or to rendezvous points on the way to the capital, depending on the areas in which they were based, and all that still had sufficient fuel had been ordered to Berlin by 3.10 am. Instructions to remain over Berlin were picked up until 3.33 after which positions of the bombers on their return route were passed on.

In the target area over 150 sightings were made including Ju88s, Me110s, Me109s and FW190s. Eleven attacks were recorded. Of the RAF losses of 43 bombers it was not possible to account for more than 28. Four were considered lost to flak, 24 to fighters. This could be representative of the losses as a whole. There was no RAF sightings of aircraft lost to flak over the city, but four losses were seen – two over coastal defence positions on the Danish coast and two at Flensburg.

Five fighter claims were made by air gunners. One Me109 by a Halifax of 77 Squadron at 3.05 near Parchim. Both gunners opened fire and the 109 was seen to turn onto its back with flames coming from its fuselage, then fall in a vertical dive. Over Sylt a Lancaster of 550 Squadron opened fire on a Ju88 and it was seen to go down with both engines on fire. A Lancaster of 463 Squadron saw a FW190 north of Berlin, and the rear gunner hit it with a long burst and the fighter exploded and fell in flames. When a Ju88 attacked a 15 Squadron Lancaster, the rear gunner's fire went into the 88's cockpit and engine, and it fell out of control. Two RAF Mosquitos of 141 Squadron in 100 Group found enemy night fighters and shot down a Me109 and a Me110. Eight other fighters were damaged, five being Ju88s.

Big fires were soon raging in Berlin and exceptionally large and prolonged explosions were reported at the start of the attack with two more later. The fires and explosions could be seen from beyond the Baltic coast on the return flight and many experienced crews considered this to be the most effective raid they had witnessed on the city. The Germans for their part claimed that:

> British Terror Raiders continued their attacks on the Reich capital. Damage was caused in various parts of the City, including many residential quarters, churches, hospitals and cultural institutions.

*

Although Mike Beetham did not get to bed until 4.30 am the previous day, the crew had been up by 9 am to pick up a 463 Squadron Lancaster from Waddington as theirs was U/S. They were on the battle order that night and take-off was due at 11.45 pm. Sergeant Les Bartlett intended to get about three hours sleep before the op, but instead started a card game which didn't finish until around 9.30. This was followed by the usual bacon and egg supper. At 10.30 they got dressed then into the transport for the ride to the aircraft. Dead on time they were racing down the runway to take off. The night was crisp and clear and aircraft could be seen in all directions, circling around, gaining height and setting course from their bases.

For Jack Currie and his crew it was a shock to find their names on the ops board again. The next op was to be their last of their tour. For it to be a Berlin trip made Jack a little hot under the collar, to the extent he went to see his flight commander about it. He had promised them an easy one to finish on and Berlin was anything but easy. It would also be his eighth Berlin trip. But orders were orders and they had to go. Take-off time was postponed twice but was finally fixed for midnight. To fill in the time they went to the camp cinema to watch *Casablanca*. It was eight minutes past midnight when they taxied from their dispersal point and it was 12.18 when they got the green light to roll.

The first leg for Mike Beetham was long and tedious, taking over an hour. They encountered heavy flak as they passed over north Heligoland. The first opposition was encountered when crossing the Danish coast not far from Flensburg, where two aircraft were seen to go down. Searchlights were more active than usual, but the Pathfinder boys were doing their job well and put down course markers very accurately. The 10/10th cloud gave maximum cover, but only until Rostock was reached where all cloud cleared leaving a clear sky about 40 miles from the target. The familiar red Very signals from fighter to fighter was everywhere in the sky.

Beetham was in the fifth wave of the attack and practically the whole of the Main Force was ahead of them. Combats would be seen everywhere but luckily the majority appeared to be 3-4,000 feet below. By the time they reached Berlin the fighters had laid a flare path right across their track from east to west. They actually saw a Ju88, flying flat out, dropping its global flares at intervals of about 1,000 yards, making the whole area as bright as day. The raid was in full swing and numerous huge fires could be seen. One particular explosion seemed to light up the whole sky in a vivid orange flash which lasted for about ten seconds. At the critical moment Les Bartlett yelled, 'Bomb doors open,' followed by 'Bombs gone – bomb doors closed!'

Just as he was about to make the usual checks to ensure that no bombs were left hung up, Beetham yelled, 'There's a bloody fighter dead ahead attacking a Lancaster.' It was a Ju88. On hearing this, Les jumped into the front turret and opened fire. The Junkers went into a slow turn to the left, and spiralled earthwards.

About 30 miles from the target on the homeward route, Les at last had time to check the bomb bay only to discover a bomb had failed to release. At the same time, through a break in the cloud he saw the lighting system of a German airfield, so he threw the jettison bars across and out went the bomb and much to his delight the lights went out also. On their return they found the cloud base down to 800 feet, so Beetham had to exercise great care when breaking cloud. He did this and to his great surprise were right over the English coast at Skegness. They landed at base at 8.40 am feeling tired and hungry. In the recommendation for Les Bartlett's DFM, this trip was mentioned with the shooting down of the Ju88.

Jack Currie, meantime, had set course for Denmark – distance of 360 miles, which took about two hours. At 2.19 am, they saw the first red marker flares go down. Their estimated time on target was 3.25. The first TIs went down at 3.10 and eight minutes later they saw a huge explosion. At 3.20 Currie's bomb aimer pressed the tit and the last trip of their tour was half over, and their last bomb load they would drop on Berlin was on its way down. The wind was estimated at 95 mph and being a tail wind it gave them a ground speed of 368 mph. The course that Currie should have held for three minutes did not look too healthy as it was lit on either side by fighter flares so he made for a darker piece of sky. At 3.26 the navigator estimated they had reached the turning point and altered course towards the north-west, straight into, instead of behind a wind of 95 mph and the ground speed fell to 144 mph.

Their journey home was quite uneventful. Currie was very aware of keeping away from known flak spots and soon Europe was behind them and only 360 miles of North Sea lay between them and England. One of the crew, a Welshman, sang on the intercom 'So Long Chop Land, and if I never see it again it will be too soon.' They saw their first friendly searchlight at 6.59 am and were over their home base at 7.17. They were given permission to land and congratulated by the controller on finishing their tour of ops. In the officers' mess a crate of beer had been put out by courtesy of the flight commander. Currie was told the CO was in the dining room having breakfast with the AOC, Air Vice Marshal Rice, and was invited to join them. Then it was off on two weeks' leave to London.

Unlike Jack Currie, for Flying Officer John Gray, a Canadian with 433 Squadron, flying a Halifax (HX265), the raid on Berlin was his first. It was to prove anything but uneventful. Just after crossing the enemy coast at 20,000 feet, his aircraft was hit by a chance shot of heavy flak which caused loss of petrol from No 3 tank, on the starboard side. He realised that if they carried on he would be short of petrol on return. Despite this he decided to carry on and did bomb the target. On their return his navigational aids and wireless went U/S and it was quickly evident he would not reach England and would have to ditch. They came down about 15 miles off the English coast off Hartlepool. The ditching was good, none of the crew was hurt and they all scrambled into the dinghy. They were soon picked up and brought to safety. Gray was awarded an immediate DFC.

Gray's was one of four ditchings on this night. The second was Flight Sergeant Corriveau of 431 Squadron flying Halifax LL150 'N'. The survivors were in the water for about 20-30 minutes but only four men were picked up when naval minesweepers reached the scene. Corriveau, Warrant Officer Barrie, and Sergeant Raymond all perished.

The third crew to come down in the sea was that of Flight Sergeant D.M.E. Pugh – Halifax JD165 'S'. It was only their second trip as a crew. They arrived over Berlin without mishap but after bombing the target their aircraft was hit and damaged by flak, the main damage being to the rudder controls and to Nos 5 and 6 starboard wing tanks. The flak had actually severed the block tube control at the tail end of the aircraft. The rear gunner, Sergeant Burgess, received a nasty head wound when a flak shell burst near to his turret. The explosion threw him against the side of the turret knocking him out and causing him slight concussion. When he came round he swopped places with the mid-upper, Sergeant Williams. The engineer, Sergeant Perkins, managed to repair the rudder controls when they reached the Danish coast, but as in the case of Gray's crew, they eventually became resigned to the fact that they were not going to make it. When down to 2,000 feet Pugh gave the order to prepare to ditch. It was now 8.45 am and they were something like 60-90 miles east of Dundee.

The WOP, Sergeant Cohen, had put the IFF to distress at 15,000 feet after leaving Denmark and at 8.25 he sent out an SOS. The engineer had just announced that they were down to 150 gallons of fuel while the rest of the crew took their ditching positions. The bomb aimer was lying on the starboard rest position with his feet braced on the front spa. The navigator was on the opposite rest spot, his intercom plugged in to listen to the pilot. The injured gunner was placed with his back to the main spa; then the mid-upper gunner collected the axe and No 7 pack with attached paddles and dinghy cover, and sat on the port side with his back to the spa. They were now down to 500 feet. The WOP clamped the transmitter key down and sat in the centre of the rest position, resting his neck on his parachute pack which he had placed against the spa, having collected the dinghy radio and handed the kite container to the bomb aimer. The engineer stood at his position until the last possible moment, so he did not have time to reach his ditching spot; he placed himself against the WOP and braced his feet against the centre rest strut of the front spa. He had already grabbed the Very pistol and cartridges. All the hatches were open, the pilot's jettisoned for him, and each member of the crew had collected rations and torches.

The sea was very rough with waves rising to 15 to 20 feet with a medium swell, the crest to crest was 100 feet, and crest to trough 20 feet. The waves were running across the swell with the wind strength at 30 mph in a direction west to east. The direction of the swell was the same. It was now daylight and visibility about ten miles. The weather was good although the sea was very rough. On coming down to ditch the starboard inner cut, possibly from lack of petrol. There was no time to feather it as they were now down to 200 feet. Pugh used a flap setting of 30-40% and with an airspeed of 130 mph reducing to 110, the tail struck the water, and the rest of the bomber dropped onto the sea. The front part of the nose broke off and water came pouring through the gap and through the open pilot's hatch. The bomb doors were probably smashed on impact; water came through the access hatch and the crew were immersed immediately.

The mid-upper operated the manual dinghy release and the 19-year-old engineer, Sergeant Royston from Bristol, was first out followed by the rest within two or three minutes. Mae Wests were inflated and they were soon in the dinghy, but some time afterwards a 20 foot wave overturned them, but after some difficulty, not the least through cold, most were back in, although the engineer, bomb aimer and rear gunner had to remain in the water, clinging to it by ropes. The injured gunner was losing interest rapidly and appeared too ill to care about rescue; they tried again but failed to pull him in. As the cold set in the three men in the water were unable to hang on and one by one drifted away without a word, except a faint 'Good luck' from the rear gunner.

The survivors were spotted by a rescue Warwick later that day but were unable to get to a Lindholme lifeboat that was dropped to them. The next day, the 31st, another boat was dropped but again they were unable to get to it. They were finally rescued on the 31st by an ASR launch from Tayport, captained by Flight Lieutenant Cook and coxswain Flight Sergeant Lewis, when about 95 miles east of Tayport. Flight Sergeant Graham, the navigator, died on his way to land, but the others survived. The sea and cold had claimed four of the seven men.

*

Severe icing was reported by some crews on this Berlin trip. Flight Sergeant Lew Lewis of the newly formed 640 Squadron, suffered icing and electrical storms on route; then his wireless transmitter broke down. In view of this he decided to abort. This was also the decision made by Pilot Officer Blundell of 35 Squadron when he encountered icing. They started to lose height and Sergeant Rhodes, in the upper turret, could see the build-up of ice and wondered if this, their fourth op, was going to be their last. They came under severe flak as they began to jettison all surplus weight, and managed to reach base, early, but safe.

Flying Officer Flewelling of the RCAF flying with 434 Squadron (ED256) had a port engine cut as the aircraft was about to run up to the target so he turned and headed for home. As he reached England he was low on fuel when the starboard inner engine cut, as petrol ran out. They were then forced to bale out and they came down near Scarborough. The rear gunner, Sergeant Demers, was killed and the engineer, Sergeant Dobney, was injured.

The night's losses totalled 43: 6.3% (twenty Lancaster and twenty three Halifaxes) and the tonnage dropped was 1,933.2.

CHAPTER EIGHT

The End is Near

The Fourteenth Raid

The next attack followed close on the heels of the thirteenth; the very next night. On the night of 30/31st January a force of 540 aircraft were made ready to hit again at the German capital, 446 Lancasters, 82 Halifaxes and twelve Mossies.

129 from 1 Group
 44 from 3 Group
 59 from 4 Group
156 from 5 Group
 47 from 6 Group
 93 from 8 Group
 12 Mosquitos of 8 Group
———
540
———

The all important weather forecast was for variable cloud over Bomber Command's bases with moderate to good visibility. The cloud extended from 1,500 to around 4,000 feet. Over Berlin the airmen could expect medium cloud, thin and well broken. The actual conditions met over the city were 7-10/10ths cloud, reaching to between 10-12,000 feet, with 60 mph winds. On their return to England visibility remained moderate except in the Midlands and South Yorkshire, where early mist and fog became more general nearer dawn.

As the bomber force left England and headed towards Germany, so the plots on the bombers began to be passed to the night fighters when the spearhead was only 40 miles out from the English coast, but no directions were given to the fighters to fly out to sea to intercept. Fighters from all the usual night fighter *Gruppen* were concentrated in the Hamburg area, from which point some of the earlier arrivals were then sent out to sea while others were sent northwards or to Berlin according to their time of arrival at the rendezvous points. Instructions to proceed to Berlin were issued at 8.11 pm and at 8.25 aircraft were ordered to remain over the target. Aircraft of NJG/V were also sent to Berlin. The planned time of attack was 8.15 to 8.27.

Flak was encountered along the route but was not particularly effective, except at Den Helder where it was very accurate. Heavy flak barrages of moderate intensity became more sporadic as the fighter flares appeared and the ceiling of the flak explosions lowered to 16-18,000 feet. There was considerable light flak below that height, concentrated in the main around the sky markers laid by PFF aircraft. Searchlights were unable to penetrate the cloud but were, in a small way, eliminating the cloud base.

Over and around Berlin a terrific air battle ensued, confirmed by the number of combats that were recorded. A Lancaster of 3 Group, at 8.07 pm, when still some 50 miles north of Berlin, spotted and recognised a Ju88. Both gunners opened fire and it was last seen diving enveloped in flames, to be claimed as destroyed.

A Lancaster of 5 Group, flown by Flying Officer Weatherstone, was fired upon by a Ju88 on the homeward journey. The rear gunner, Flight Sergeant Collingwood, saw the enemy aircraft dead astern and below at 400 yards, closing rapidly. As it opened fire Weatherstone was ordered to corkscrew to starboard which enabled Collingwood to get a short burst on the enemy's blind side. Hits were observed on its fins and rudder and it broke away at 250 yards climbing straight up. The rear gunner fired again as the 88 turned over and made a diving attack and the Junkers caught fire, and continued its headlong dive completely enveloped in flames.

Pilot Officer Dobbyn of 50 Squadron was in the target area on the bombing run when the flight engineer reported a Ju88 on the starboard beam, below at 1,000 yards, as it followed another Lancaster. It then moved to the port quarter at their level. At 150 yards both gunners, Flight Sergeant Dincomber and Sergeant Mason, opened fire and saw their tracer appear to enter the wings and fuselages of the fighter. By this time the Lancaster was in a corkscrew to port and the fighter broke off but it was claimed as damaged.

Lancaster T-Tommy of 467 Squadron opened fire on a Me110 over Berlin, tracer seen to enter the fighter's cockpit. It then rolled over on its back and dived below; it was claimed as destroyed. Near Berlin a Lancaster of 44 Squadron sighted a Me210, first spotted by

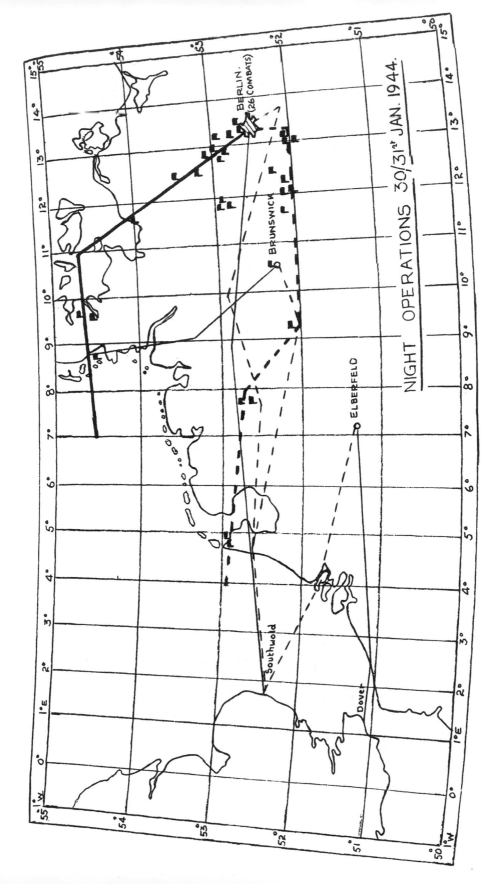

NIGHT OPERATIONS 30/31st JAN. 1944.

BERLIN.
(26 COMBATS)

BRUNSWICK

ELBERFELD

Southwold

Dover

Pilot Officer Noel Lloyd who was later to join 617 Squadron. He saw it attacking another Lancaster and he directed his pilot towards the fight and opened fire. His burst set the enemy's port engine on fire and it was later confirmed as destroyed. Noel Lloyd finished his tour of ops on 7th May, 1944. On this last op he was wounded in the legs but insisted on remaining at his guns. He received the DFC in July.

Halifax M-Mother (HX357) of 35 Squadron flown by Squadron Leader Wood, was south of Magdeburg when the mid-upper, Warrant Officer North, saw an enemy aircraft, later confirmed as a Ju88. It attacked from the port quarter and Warrant Officer Derek Tulloch, the rear gunner, opened fire. The bomber corkscrewed to port and the Junkers was lost without it having fired a shot. Tulloch completed some 80 operations and was awarded the DFC and DFM.

Flying Officer William Breckenridge of 626 Squadron in Lancaster Me584 'Y2', was on the approach to the bomb run when they were attacked by a fighter. Its initial burst of fire killed the WOP, Sergeant J. Hall, and wounded both gunners. The mid-upper, Pilot Officer William Baker, was wounded in the right side of his face by cannon shell fragments as it burst inside his turret, tearing away his oxygen mask and the right hand earpiece of his flying helmet. The rear gunner, Sergeant Joe Schwartz, was wounded in the foot. Both men fell unconscious. Now over the target, bomb aimer Sergeant Val Ponshinsky, dropped the bombs but a minute later the enemy fighter came in again firing a long burst. Bill Breckenridge took violent evasive action but the aircraft was once again hit and this time the navigator was seriously wounded. After a further two minutes the enemy attacked a third time and further damaged the bomber. Breckenridge himself was grazed by a passing bullet.

Just after leaving the target, Pilot Officer Baker regained consciousness. He discovered he had no intercom, no oxygen and his turret was U/S; he climbed out of the turret and found the WOP dead and the rear gunner slumped forward on the rest bed. The navigator, Warrant Officer Richard Meek, on his sixth op, had received a bullet through his left shoulder blade but despite loss of blood and in great pain he managed to give the pilot a new course for base. He remained at his post throughout the entire journey, navigating with great skill and accuracy despite many of his aids being out of action. For his gallant actions he was recommended for the CGM.

A Lancaster from 156 Squadron (JA702) was shot up by a fighter north of Hannover causing damage to the bomb bay. Ten minutes later it was attacked again. The bomber caught fire and then simply blew up. Warrant Officer Patrick Coyne, the wireless operator, found himself dropping through the clouds so he pulled his rip cord and the parachute opened. He landed about ten miles from Vollenhove in Holland, buried his 'chute and set off. After about fifteen minutes he met up with the navigator, Sergeant William Cottam. With the help of a Dutch policeman, who arranged for photographs to be taken and identity cards to be prepared, Pat Coyne, now in civilian clothes, was taken by car to an address in Hoogzand where he stayed until early August. Then he went to Antwerp, travelling by train, tram, horse drawn cart and bicycle. Two days later he was arrested by the Gestapo and remained a POW until April 1945.

Flight Lieutenant Thomas Blackham, from Dunoon, Scotland, was flying a 50 Squadron Lancaster (DV368 'S') and had already been to Berlin four times. He was attacked by a fighter whose approach had not been seen or detected. The hydraulics and oxygen supply were damaged by shell splinters. The rear gunner, Flight Sergeant J. Shuttleworth, an Australian from Brisbane, was wounded and slumped unconscious in his turret. The port fin and rudder and the tailplane were shot up in the attack – the hole later found was large enough for a man to crawl through. The mid-upper turret had also been hit and the gunner wounded in the head. They were later to discover the left tyre had burst and a cannon shell had gone through the port tailplane; it also holed the outer petrol tank, but the self-sealing there had held. There were cannon shell holes all along the fuselage, but despite this carnage, they carried on and bombed the target.

The engineer, Sergeant Walton, from Birmingham, went back with an oxygen bottle for the rear gunner who was trapped in his turret. He feebly waved to him, his face covered in blood. He tried to work the dead-man's handle to release him but because of the lack of oxygen, Walton kept passing out. The bomb aimer, Sergeant Godfrey, from Paisley in Scotland, went back to find out what was happening and when he too failed to come back, the WOP, Sergeant Wilkins went aft – and he too passed out. It was left to the Welsh navigator, Pilot Officer Jones, to help. He found Godfrey, brought him round, then went back to sort out the engineer, but then Jones too passed out.

The WOP, who then came too, gave a running commentary to the pilot, it went: 'The navigator is down, no it's the flight engineer, the navigator is up, no he's down, the engineer is kicking him, yes the nav's on his feet ...'

The engineer came around and the navigator got back to his seat. They were now about 30 minutes from the French coast and nearly out of oxygen, so Blackham got the aircraft down to 4,000 feet to cross the coast. They flew over the North Sea with their wheels down; it took the engineer twenty minutes to pump them down by hand. The rear gunner remained trapped until the aircraft was about to land, when the mid-upper, also from Wales, Sergeant Ridd, hacked the doors free with an axe and pulled him out. Despite a burst tyre they landed safely although petrol spilled out of ruptured fuel tanks. Shuttleworth had an operation on his damaged eye, as well as on a fractured forearm. Flight Lieutenant Blackham was shot down in May on a raid on Maily Camp and spent the rest of the war in a prison camp.

A Lancaster of 550 Squadron, flown by Flying Officer Godfrey Morrison on his ninth mission, was approaching the target and was within a few minutes of his zero hour when a fighter attacked. It fired rockets, cannon and machine guns at the bomber and both gunners were killed outright, and the starboard outer engine knocked out. The controls were severely damaged, intercom, compass and air speed indicator all rendered useless. The bomber lost a considerable amount of height, and the bombs had to be jettisoned but fell in the general area of the target. On their return flight the Lanc was again hit, this time by flak, but Morrison got them home and made a successful landing despite being overdue by some three hours. He received the DSO soon afterwards.

Warrant Officer Lew Lewis of 640 Squadron, flying a Halifax (LW463 'A'), was attacked by fighters in the Kiel area. The rear turret was knocked out and the mid-upper had stoppages after firing a short burst. They were unable to defend themselves, leaving Lewis little option but to abort. Pilot Officer Len Barnes, flying Lancaster ND530, was alerted by his rear gunner after passing Magdeburg, that a fighter was coming in astern. He took immediate evasive action. The fighter made three passes at them and then broke away. The gunner thought the fighter had been hit but they had got away without a scratch. However, on their return they found the aircraft had several holes and the fuel jettison tube was dangling down like an elephant's trunk, and later an unexploded cannon shell was taken from the starboard petrol tank. Len Barnes asked for it as a souvenir but was told, 'Sorry, sir, this has to go to the Air Ministry.' He was later shot down in March, but escaped to rejoin his squadron. He is now a member of the RAF Escaping Society, whose members either escaped or evaded capture after being shot down.

Pilot Officer Louis Greenburgh was piloting his 514 Squadron Lancaster (LL727 'C2'). After bombing he was 25 miles due south of Berlin on the homeward route when the rear gunner Sergeant Fox, reported a twin-engined Me110. It closed in to 600 yards and commenced its attack. The rear gunner ordered Greenburgh to corkscrew to starboard, opening fire at the same time with a burst of three to four seconds. The fighter did not return the fire, but broke away quickly and was not seen again.

One crew of 578 Squadron, who had just been posted from 'C' Flight of 518 Squadron from which 578 had been formed, set off on their trip to Berlin at 5.29 pm but were back by 11.34. An armourer, when loading the guns in 'Timber' Woods' turret had failed to close a small window on the right hand side when he had finished his work. During the flight it opened and fouled the fairing on the fuselage around the turret. As a result it was impossible to operate the turret in normal drive.

Despite all the night fighter activity, some crews reported the defence to be getting weaker. One crew commented that Berlin was like King's Cross in peacetime. Squadron Leader Chadwick of London, with some 53 ops completed in North Africa, and who was now on his fourth trip of his second tour, reported it being a very quiet operation. Added to the sky illumination, where dummy flares which the Germans set up from the ground to imitate the Pathfinder markers (though the colours were different, as well as the shape when they burst).

Pilot Officer Michael Foster, flying a Halifax (LW461 'D'), reported what he called a 'gen' trip: in other words everything went exceptionally well. He had no interference from anyone or anything on this raid. He had taken a second pilot, Sergeant Gibson from Canada, who was amazed at the lack of 'fireworks' over the city.

Mike Foster was serving with 51 Squadron at Snaith and he remembered 'Bomber' Harris visiting the squadron once, and earning great respect from everyone. Not by what he said, but by answering confidently questions on gunnery, aircraft, radio and navigation – in fact everything that was thrown at him. He certainly knew his stuff, 'even if he did choose his targets by getting Lady Harris to throw silver darts at the map of Europe.' (A popular aircrew myth.)

*

The Germans reported the alarm was sounded at 7.57 pm and the 'All Clear' at 9.15, and that it was a heavier raid than the previous night. They thought some 600 aircraft flew over their city, in rainy weather, and dropped an extraordinary large number of bombs of all kinds, estimated at 2,000 mines and 60,000 high explosive bombs, plus 40-50,000 phosphorus and 300 oil bombs. They recorded that the bombers made rendezvous to the north-west of the city and attacked in two waves in a south to east direction. The main weight fell on the districts of Charlottenburg Tiergarten, Wilmersdorf, Schoeneburg and Kreusberg. Seven aircraft were shot down over Berlin. German casualties were 102 dead, 531 injured with 20,000 made homeless.

All long distance railway lines, except that to Dresden, were closed. The surburban railway, underground and tramway system were similarly disrupted. The German radio admitted that extensive areas of Berlin were hit. The RAF lost 32 Lancasters.

*

The Fifteenth Raid
The next raid was well into February, on the 15/16th. 891 aircraft were assigned, the largest force ever despatched to the Big City. It comprised:

> 161 from 1 Group
>   66 from 3 Group
> 177 from 4 Group
> 226 from 5 Group
> 150 from 6 Group
>   95 from 8 Group
>   16 Mosquitos of 8 Group
> ———
> 891
> ———

There were 561 Lancasters, 140 Halifaxes and 174 of the new Halifax Mark IIIs. At the same time, 8 Group sent 24 Lancasters to

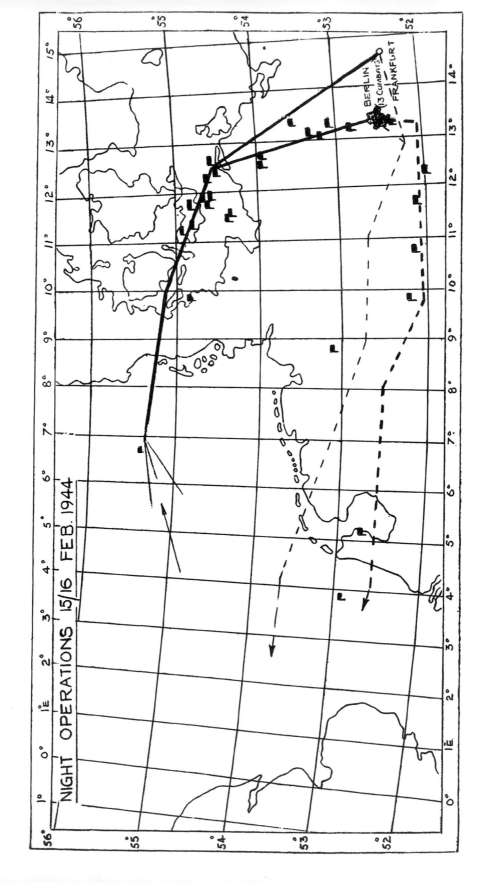

NIGHT OPERATIONS 15/16 FEB. 1944

BERLIN
(3 COMBATS)
FRANKFURT

Frankfurt-on-Oder and a force of Mosquitos operating against Aachen, Leeuwarden, Deelan, Gilze Reijen, Twente, Enschede and Venlo airfields.

At 3.45 pm that afternoon the Air Staff received the weather forecast. Variable cloud at 2-3,000 feet over England while the route out would be similar. Over Berlin the crews could expect 10/10th cloud below 8,000 feet and small amounts of stratus at around 30,000. In fact the weather experienced was moderate to poor visibility over England, aggravated in Yorkshire by smoke haze. The forecast of cloud increasing to 10/10ths over the sea and 10/10ths over Berlin proved correct; its base was down to 600-1,000 feet, topping at 6-8,000 feet. The wind speed was 35 mph.

The Luftwaffe directed its principal effort against the bomber stream along the route, leaving the target area to the flak gunners. The bombers were due over the enemy coast at 7.25 pm. However, at 6.16, the first bombers were plotted by German radar, 65 miles north-west of Harwich and fifteen minutes later a whole formation was reported as spread over a distance of 80 miles. From then on uninterrupted plots were given over the whole flight with particular concentrations at those points at which the German fighters hoped to intercept. That is to say, off the west coast of Denmark between Esbjerg and Flensburg, Odense and Kiel, and again on the return route and to the west of Magdeburg. At 10.29 the spearhead was estimated to be south-east of Emden and as late as 11.06 others were plotted three miles north of Amsterdam. Exceptionally few plots were made in the actual target area.

By 6.11 pm aircraft of NJG/I, II, III and V, were airborne. They were ordered to fire a green recognition signal as soon as they came into contact with the bomber stream but were also warned that there were many of their own fighters on similar courses as the bombers. Many green flares were seen by RAF crews between Magdeburg and Berlin, similar to ones seen in the Denmark area later on during the return flight.

At 6.37 NJG/I, II and II were ordered north to try to intercept the bombers between Westmerland and Esbjerg. As late as 7.43, German aircraft were still being directed north. The controllers of NJG/V instructed their fighters to a point east of Parchin and repeatedly said they must avoid Berlin on the account of the flak there. By 9.24 all German pilots were still being told of the whereabouts of returning bombers and those of NJG/V who still had sufficient fuel, were sent to south-west Berlin for a last attempt at intercepting.

The whole Main Force followed one route to the target, through southern Denmark, and approached Berlin from the north and north-west. The route home was split into two tracks, both fairly direct and on an average about 40 miles apart. There was little free-lance fighter activity along the homeward route but there was not enough evidence with which Bomber Command HQ could assess the success or otherwise of this tactic. The diversionary raid on Frankfurt had no effect at all. From observations the fighters appeared to have had success on the east coast of Denmark where fifteen bombers were seen to go down. It was on this leg that the greater number of enemy fighters were seen. Other losses were attributed to fighters south-west of Bork and another five on the return route, as the bombers re-crossed the Dutch coast. The very first exchange was when a four-engined aircraft tried to fire at a Halifax of 4 Group in the Denmark area – it was probably a nervous gunner from another RAF aircraft!

After leaving Denmark there were 22 attacks and about 40 to 50 sightings, chiefly Ju88s, FW190s, and two Dornier 217s, one of which made an attack. One Ju88 was destroyed by an 8 Group Lancaster and a 1 Group Lanc claimed another. In the target area, 30 enemy fighters were seen, Ju88s, some Me109s as well as 110s and 210s. Here there were thirteen attacks – eight attacks and fifteen aircraft were encountered on the return trip.

A Lancaster of 156 Squadron (JB444 'O'), flown by Flight Sergeant Doyle, had taken off at 5.46 pm as a blind backer-up. On the way to Berlin his rear gunner, Flight Sergeant Smith, sighted a Me110 dead astern and below at 700 yards, but it appeared to be a decoy for another aircraft. It closed in for an attack, however, and the gunners opened up as the fighter fired. The bomber was hit between the mid-upper turret and the radio transmitter, and the upper gunner, Sergeant Clarke, and Smith were wounded. Clarke received a compound fracture of the left leg from a cannon shell; Smith was hit in the right ankle. His leg was so severely injured that it was later amputated. Both turrets were put out of action, but Smith told Doyle that they had hit the Messerschmitt and that it had exploded. During the attack another fighter – a FW190 – attacked and opened fire but missed its target. Flight Sergeant Doyle came in on three engines at Woodbridge at 1.50 am. As he touched down the starboard tyre burst, but he landed safely.

Flight Sergeant Geoffrey Smith, aged 25 from Sydney, New South Wales, was recommended for the CGM two days later. His citation mentioned the loss of a leg and despite his turret being U/S he continued to manipulate the turret by hand until the Dutch coast was crossed. He was discharged from the service in November 1944.

Lancaster ND392 'Q', of 460 Squadron, was attacked by a Ju88 and an Me210. Its pilot, Pilot Officer R. Burke DFC, had previously been with 625 Squadron and he too came from New South Wales. He had just celebrated his 22nd birthday. In the action the Ju88 was shot down and the 210 damaged but the Lancaster suffered damage to the starboard wing and rudder, and had a hole in the starboard inner prop blade; the starboard outer engine also had a hole in it and there was a jagged hole in the fuselage. Cannon shell holes were found in the starboard inner engine. It was the crew's ninth op. Burke was killed in action in April 1944.

A Lancaster of 50 Squadron, flown by Squadron Leader Chadwick, was attacked in the target area at 9.27, by a Ju88. The mid-upper, Flight Sergeant McDiermid, also fired, his tracer seen to bounce off the nose of the fighter. It broke away and was claimed as damaged. Another Lanc from this squadron was attacked but the two gunners, Sergeant McCarthy and Sergeant Bacon, more than held their own and the fighter was claimed damaged.

Nineteen-year-old Pilot Officer Bradfield Lydon, known to the crew as Brian, his second Christian name, was flying Lancaster JB278 'L for London'. It was his fourteenth op to Berlin. He had been posted to 103 Squadron in September 1943. His aircraft was attacked by a FW190 and while taking evasive action he reported on the intercom that he had been hit. Then the flight engineer reported that the No 1 petrol tank had been hit and had drained. Having lost the 190, a discussion amongst the crew followed, as to whether they would reach England or play safe and head for Sweden. The rear gunner was for going home as he wanted to get back to the local pub in Scunthorpe – the 'Oswald' – for a drink. Having made some calculations, the engineer thought that they might make it if they flew a direct course. By using their H_2S set this they did and landed safely at their base at Elsham Wolds.

Brian Lydon was taken to hospital by ambulance and operated on by the Squadron MO, Flying Officer Henderson, who removed bits of metal and shrapnel from his head, face and right arm. To this day he still has some pieces in his head. While he was in hospital his crew were stood down for a week. During this period, his gunner, who had wanted his drink at the local, flew with another pilot and went missing.

Another crew of 103 Squadron, captained by Flight Lieutenant Berry (ND366) failed to return and were all killed. The navigator was Squadron Leader Harold Lindo DFC RCAF. His father, also named Harold, from Jamaica, donated a number of gold watches to be awarded to pilots who had contributed the most to the Battle of Berlin. Brian Lydon, who flew on fifteen of the sixteen raids, and rose from flight sergeant to pilot officer in that time, was one recipient, and he still wears the watch proudly to this day. He was recommended for the DFC on 19th January, by which time he had flown eighteen missions. Another 103 Squadron pilot, Len Young, also received a watch, which was presented to him by Lord Trenchard, known as the Father of the RAF. Len died in 1983.

Len Young's crew, in fact, took off sixteen times for Berlin but had to abort on three occasions. One of his crew, Paul Howthorn, the mid-upper, had lied about his age when he joined up, being only sixteen. He was just seventeen when he completed his tour. Four of the crew where in the mid-30's and the other two were eighteen and nineteen respectively.

*

The flak over Berlin was moderate to intense, in a barrage form over a wide area, between 16,000 and 25,000 feet, with a maximum intensity in the vicinity of the sky markers, but this decreased as the raid progressed. The searchlights were rendered ineffective by the cloud which on this occasion seemed to have been so thick as not even to allow a silhouette role. The usual defended areas were observed in action and flak was reported heavy in the Emden, Den Helder and Amsterdam areas. Between the Danish coast and the north coast of Germany, seven aircraft were seen to go down to flak. Another lost to flak was seen to go down to the north of Berlin and two more in the actual target area.

On the homeward run, flak claimed three over Den Helder and one over Amsterdam. From the crew reports it was assessed that of the 41 aircraft lost, fourteen had been shot down by flak, sixteen to fighters with the other twelve unaccounted for. Crews were reporting that the gunfire over Berlin was much heavier than usual and very accurate and heavier at the enemy coast. One crewman wrote, 'We were ten minutes late over Berlin, with the result Jerry was firing everything at us.'

Some of the crews were in the new Mark III Halifaxes, one being Pilot Officer Downes of 78 Squadron. The squadron had been stood down for three weeks while the conversion took place. He reported an excellent trip, especially with the greater performance, speed and increased altitude which gave a good deal more confidence to his crew. Another crew using the new Mark III was Flight Sergeant Schuman of 466 Squadron (LV837 'A'). Their old Halifax (HX336 also 'A') having been lost on operations while he and his crew were away on leave.

Flying Officer Moorcroft of 83 Squadron was on his last operation of his tour, flying as navigator to Pilot Officer McLean. With him on this trip was Squadron Leader Wilson, the blind bombing staff officer from 8 Group HQ, as the H$_2$S operator, but the set became unsatisfactory for marking so they bombed the target visually. Moorcroft remarked that the early days of H$_2$S Mk III were frustrating!

It was also the last trip for Pilot Officer Michael Foster flying with 51 Squadron. He was glad to report it had been a very quiet and peaceful operation despite having a second pilot – a Squadron Leader Kentish. Foster remembers the aircraft excelling itself and climbing to 23,400 feet over Berlin. He also recalls writing in a letter home:

> On the whole I shall say Berlin had rather a rough night with the heaviest attack ever. We were almost first in before they got organised. Everything indicated that Berlin is finished and I think we will probably be in at the death. That will be a fitting finish just as Hamburg was a fitting start.

In 1984 he observed: 'My prediction about Berlin's collapse was sadly wrong, but so were lots of other people's.'

Flying Officer Horner, flying with Pilot Officer Dobbyn of 50 Squadron, was another on his last mission. He had been fifteen times to Berlin out of the sixteen. Being a navigator and spending most of his time behind a curtain with his instruments and maps he remembers the long silence suddenly broken by the voice of the rear gunner, shouting that he had seen something. On one of these occasions he jumped six inches out of his seat. He had flown with four different pilots in his time with the squadron. One, an Australian, was so nervous on the ground, but once in the air he was ice cool. The second, a Canadian, kept everybody going by cursing all the way to a target and back. The third was an excellent pilot but would persist in calling him up every few minutes to ask for the route. The last, Dobbyn, was as solid as a rock and both men had the utmost faith in each other's ability. He would have liked to stay with the squadron at the end of his tour but this was not possible. He only hoped that his next squadron would be half as good as 50 had been.

Warrant Officer Lewis flying a Halifax (LW463), saw no sign of fighters and very little flak but he did have petrol problems. As it was very cold, his No 4 tank froze up. He just managed to get down at Binbrook flying on three engines and despite his hydraulics being U/S. He and his crew were later shot down in May. Only three men survived, but Lewis was not one of them.

*

Results were not observed in the early stages of the attack owing to the cloud, but later reports indicated that a good concentration had been achieved and several large explosions were seen. Mosquitos, over the target an hour after the main attack, dropped their bombs and the crews reported large areas of fires and columns of smoke rising to 20,000 feet. However, the Pathfinders reported a definite gap having developed in the sky marking. As a result the Main Force, for a short period of the raid, was forced to resort to bombing only the general area.

Photographic coverage of the Big City finally became available during the month of February. On the 19th, a PRU Mossie (LR424) of 540 Squadron flown by Flying Officer Holland, made four runs over Berlin to take photos. On the last run he came under intense ground fire. The next day a Spitfire, (EN666) flown by Flight Lieutenant Scargill of 541 PRU Squadron, found the city clear of cloud and he covered the whole area of Berlin with his cameras.

A study of the damage showed that a satisfactory amount of devastation had been achieved but there was still much to be done. It was once said of London that it was impossible completely to obliterate a large city by bombing and really the same applied to Berlin. It rather implies that after a certain stage the amount of new damage produced by successive raids must decrease and eventually a point is reached where the amount of new damage obtained fails to justify the loss – or risk of loss – necessary to obtain it. If on the first attack 50% of a city is destroyed, then a 50% wastage of effort is wasted on the next attack and so on. The wastage of effort is directly comparable to the percentage of the city already knocked out, and in time a point must be reached when only isolated areas exist to be

'Did we hit it, or not?'

A welcome drink

bombed and a great wastage of effort must be experienced to destroy it. There is no doubt that many areas of Berlin had been bombed and bombed again but there were districts were damage was comparatively light.

*

Of this latest raid, the Germans reported:

> British aircraft made another terror raid on the Reich capital. From a cloud-covered sky a large number of HE and IBs were dropped on various quarters of the town. These caused damage in residential areas, to cultural monuments, churches and a hospital. In spite of unfavourable conditions for the defences, air defence forces have destroyed 48 terror bombers.

In fact the losses of 42 were 4.7 of the force. They consisted of 26 Lancasters, nine Halifaxes and seven Halifax IIIs. In 39 minutes, 2,642 tons of bombs had been dropped. In addition to the losses, two aircraft crashed over England. An aircraft of 640 Squadron (LW439 'E') flown by Flight Sergeant Vicary, had been damaged by flak and was short of petrol. The crew was ordered to bale out and the Lancaster crashed near Thornaby, County Durham; all the men parachuted to safety. Flying Officer Barkley in another Lancaster of this squadron (LW500 'H'), while trying to contact base, flew into the high ground around Cloughton, near Scarborough. All the crew died in the 1.30 am crash.

*

Shortly after this raid, attacks on Berlin and other nothern targets in Germany, were temporarily halted. Raids on Leipzig and other southern cities were selected instead.

Up to the period 25/26th February 1944, the number of bombers that had attacked Berlin was 7,764. Of these 382 had been lost and the number of aircraft returning with heavy damage totalled another 355. The statistics were taken as from 24th July and so included the Berlin raids of August and September 1943. On the 24th February, there were 87 heavy flak batteries defending Berlin with 441 guns; 17 medium and light flak batteries with a further 445 guns and 35 searchlight batteries with a total of 420 searchlights. It was a formidable array and was, for instance, twice the strength of Hamburg's defences.

CHAPTER NINE

The End

The Sixteenth Raid

On the night of 21/22nd March 1944 came the final raid of the series, nearly five weeks after the fifteenth attack. Sir Arthur Harris sent the following message to be read out to the aircrews at their various briefing rooms:

> Although successful blind bombing attacks on Berlin have destroyed large areas of it, there is still a substantial section of this vital city more or less intact. To write this off, it is of great importance that tonight's attack should be closely concentrated on the aiming point. You must not think that the size of Berlin makes accurate bombing unimportant. There is no point in dropping bombs on the devastated areas in the west and south west. Weather over the target should be good. Go in and do the job.

Despite this build-up of morale, the operation was cancelled owing to the threat of cloud over the target, at target indicator level. On the 21st, an intelligence report on the damage to date to Berlin mentioned damage to the electrical precision instrument factories and other industrial centres of heavy electrical equipment, turbines, cables, transformers and high tension switch gear. The largest two were Siemens and AEG. The tank factory, Alkett, the largest single tank-building factory in Germany, was put out of action for several months.

More than any other large town, Berlin depended on gas for heating and lighting. One third of the total gas produced had been destroyed and production plant put out of action, by the destruction of mains and gas holders. The population were given one candle each by the government as an emergency measure! The loss of gas proved a serious handicap in restarting the industrial life of the city. This was also seriously retarded by the evacuation of labour into surrounding districts and the very heavy destruction of municipal transport which proved a great handicap in the daily movement of this large labour force.

The sixteenth raid was postponed to 24th March. It was to prove the last heavy bomber raid by the RAF in the war on Berlin. 811 aircraft set out while a diversionary raid by 147 aircraft from several Bomber OTUs, was carried out over France, 70 miles south of Le Havre. Twelve Mosquitos of 105 Squadron attacked the night fighter bases at Twente, St Trond and Venlo, and another seventeen Mossies went ahead and dropped Window over the Berlin area before the attack commenced.

The daily weather report and forecast was supplied to the Air Staff at 1.10 pm which showed that 6 Group bases would have good clearances through the cloud. Other Groups could expect stratus cloud cover to hold during take-offs. Visibility, they were told, would be about 2,000 yards but better in 6 Group's area. The route to Berlin would have considerable cloud, tops probably below 8,000 feet. Denmark would probably be clear of low and medium cloud, and then there would be a chance of practically clear skies all the way to Berlin.

The weather actually encountered was generally good for take-off, with visibility at 2,000 to 4,000 yards but it was 10/10ths over Lincoln and East Anglia with a base of 3,500 feet, topping at between 4,000 and 4,500 feet. Over Berlin variable stratus cloud from 8 to 9/10ths with tops at 5,000 to 5,600 feet with moderate visibility. The winds at 20,000 feet were 100 mph but at times up to 105 mph – very much higher than had been forecast!

The planned method of attack was code-named 'Newhaven', with emergency sky marking. The aiming point chosen for the visual markers was at the eastern end of the Tiergarten. It was hoped to centre the raid on the eastern side of the city, which had received much lighter damage than the rest of the city in the previous attacks. Blind marker illuminators were to drop green TIs with white flares, if there was less than 7/10ths cloud. If more they were to release greens and red flares with yellow stars. If H_2S failed to help, all the markers were to hold their TIs and flares and bomb with the supporters. Visual markers were to mark the exact aiming point with mixed salvos of reds and greens. Those blind backers-up detailed to attack before zero plus seven minutes, were to aim at the centre of all TIs, if a Newhaven was in progress, but if cloud prevented this they were to drop sky markers blindly. Late arrivals were to drop both reds and sky markers blindly. Visual backers-up

Gordon Ritchie – 429 Squadron before Berlin raid March 44

Norman Storey – 103 Squadron and crew

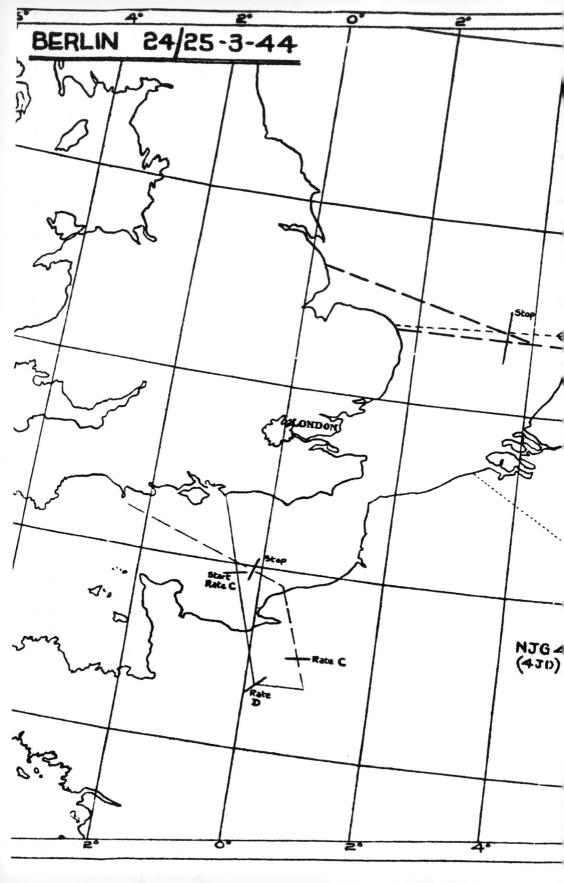

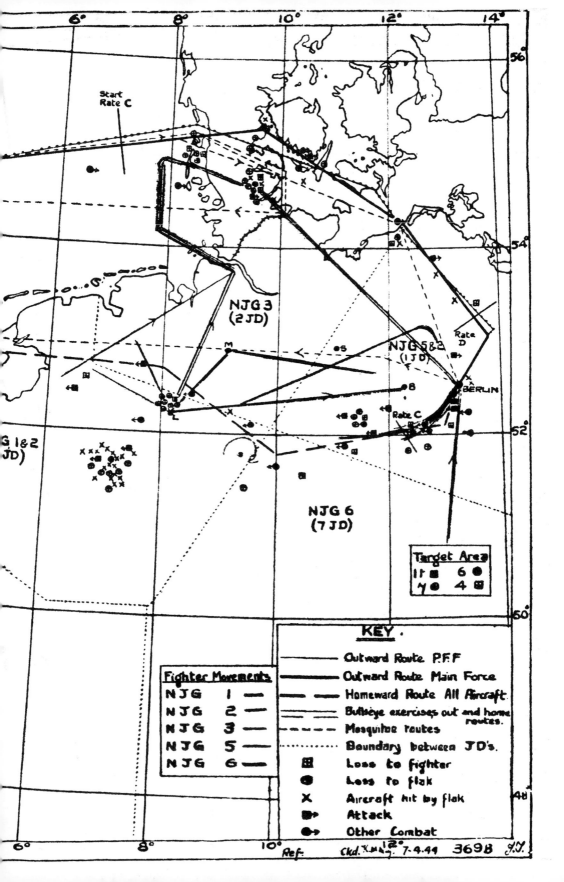

Ken Maun – 101 Squadron

Bombing up a Lancaster

were to aim reds at the centre of mixed salvos, or at the centre of all TIs with a two-second overshoot. Supprters were to bomb blindly. If possible, the Main Force crews were to aim at the centre of all mixed salvos in the early stages of the raid. The bombing was to be between 10.25 and 10.43 pm, in five waves, each of three minutes' duration. The planned concentration was thus about 40 aircraft per minute.

A Mosquito and a Lancaster crew acted as master bombers with a call sign for the Mosquito of 'Pommy' and 'Red Skin' for the Lancaster. The ordered route crossed the Danish coast just north of Sylt, proceeding direct to Wustrov on the Baltic Coast, then turning near Perenslau to approach the target from the north-east.

The diversionary raid over France did not appear to have any effect on the night fighter movement, and all German *Gruppen* were disposed to meet the main attack. The fighter plan apparently was to use aircraft from NJG/II and III for the route interceptions commencing at Sylt, with NJG/V for route interceptions between the Baltic Coast and Berlin; NJG/V and VI were to be in the target area and on the early part of the RAF's route home. It is possible that NJG/I and IV were held in reserve for use against the returning stream at a later stage. This sort of plan would normally have resulted in heavy fighter opposition for the bombers.

The winds found en route were far stronger than those forecast and became as high as 120-130 mph. All aircraft were being blown south of track, particularly on the return route. As the winds were nearly double those expected (and many H_2S aircraft operators thought their sets were unreliable) many bombers were blown way off course, while others overshot the target badly. Bombing was scattered but a considerable percentage of the bomber crews found Berlin and great credit was due to the many crews who made the best of a bad job. For example, one crew found themselves so blown off track as to be over Leipzig but returned to Berlin to bomb 45 minutes late! Because of the winds and crews over-shooting or arriving early, the bombing zero hour of 10.30 was brought forward to 10.25 pm. This change was only announced 23 minutes before the planned zero hour. In the opinion of some crews of 426 Squadron, it should have been ten minutes rather than five, which would have resulted in a better concentration of bombing. Radio commentaries by the master bombers helped to centre the raid by 'pulling in' many aircraft that would have otherwise overshot the target completely.

In the bomber stream all aircraft were to be spread evenly over a corridor of roughly 5,000 feet in depth while over enemy territory, and captains had to keep to this ordered corridor unless it impaired the success of their attack. Each group was given a varying height: 1 and 5 Groups, 20-24,000 feet; 3 and 6 Groups, 19-23,000 feet; and 4 Group, 19-24,000 feet. Despite the change in zero hour, 12% of the Main Force still managed to bomb before the briefed zero hour, 81% reported bombing within the planned period of twenty minutes, and 7% within 40 minutes (between 10 and 11 pm). The time between the first and last bombs was 62 minutes. The peak concentration was reached seven minutes after zero hour, when 38 aircraft were attacking each minute.

Numerous early arrivals were forced to orbit what they believed to be the target and had then to return to an area over which markers were seen to fall, while other crews reported overshooting the target completely and then turning back to it. Some 73% of the whole force bombed within the allotted period. Similarly, 80% of the aircraft carrying serviceable H_2S bombed in the same period. Losses among the H_2S aircraft were 9.4%.

*

Flight Lieutenant Alan Forsdike of 158 Squadron recalls the raid being basically a bad night for navigators. He flew as a spare navigator with Pilot Officer Lawrence, a Canadian pilot. Forsdike explained that good navigation depended on fixing the position of the aircraft at regular intervals, preferably every twenty minutes or so, plus calculation of the wind speed and direction, at the height flown. Once this was achieved the future movement of the aircraft could be predicted with some accuracy and confidence. The factors conspiring to defeat navigators on this night were, firstly, a strong north wind well in excess of that forecast, and a long sea crossing during which H_2S equipment, even for those lucky enough to possess it, was of no help. Forsdike did not have H_2S that night, as he was in an aircraft used by a relatively inexperienced crew. Seniority in a squadron tended not only to claim the best aircraft but also the H_2S-equipped aircraft, provided, of course, the navigators had been trained in its use. He normally used an H_2S when with his regular crew. All navigators carried forecast winds at heights up to 25,000 feet, however, on the long leg from the coast of Yorkshire to the East Coast of Denmark, a distance of 410 miles in a straight line, difficulties arose over fixing a position of the aircraft which seemed to escalate as the operation proceeded.

On crossing the North Sea his aircraft was drifting alarmingly to starboard of the required track, although corrections were made to port. The forecast winds of 45 mph at 15,000 feet, was later discovered to have increased to 92 mph at 21,000 feet. On approaching Denmark, Forsdike saw flak to port and guessed it was coming from the island of Sylt. He told the pilot to change course in that direction in order to regain track and the next concentration point, which was north of the island. The position of the aircraft was finally fixed by a pin-point at 9.39 pm over the island of Kegnaes on the east coast of Denmark. However, all this revealed was that their Halifax was still 35 miles south of track!

The problem was now resolved. It was clear that on the remaining legs of the route the ground speed of the aircraft would be high; in fact it reached 300 mph, so that they would arrived over Berlin ahead of the flight plan. Wireless messages from their Group controller in England were received at intervals giving increased wind velocity of 355% – to 90 mph. All the aircraft in the Main Force were required to keep their aircraft densely packed in an attempt to provide maximum cover from Würzburg (Radar) and night fighter attacks.

The revised forecast winds could not be transmitted from England until enough example winds found over the route had been relayed back to England by the WOPs. In certain aircraft with experienced crews, the navigators were known as wind finders. The wind samplings were then averaged out by the experts and a single velocity sent by wireless to the Main Force aircraft.

The time on target for wave number one was between 10.33 and 10.36, and their estimated time of arrival at Berlin, according to Flight Lieutenant Forsdike, was 10.34. On the final approach to the target nothing at all could be seen – it was completely dark and the crew began to doubt his navigations. However, at that very moment target markers fell immediately below. Being too early to bomb they went round again. Returning on the required bombing run, the bombs were released right on the markers. Turning from the target, the wind velocity was again calculated and was found to be 93 mph. This abnormally high wind, even at 21,000 feet, had not been encountered by him before or after this operation.

Flight Sergeant Les Bartlett of 50 Squadron, like the rest of Mike Beetham's crew, had just returned from a nine days' leave to find himself on the operation for that night. They took off at 7 pm and set course over the North Sea for a point off the German coast where they met their first spot of trouble. The winds were so variable that instead of passing the northern tip of Sylt they went bang over it and had to fly up the island's west coast, then round the top.

Many aircraft were off course. In fact, in his words: '... all over the place and some got a good pasting over Flensburg.' The next leg took them over Denmark, and down to the Baltic Coast. Many crews got into trouble with the defences of Kiel, Lübeck and Rostock, and Les Bartlett saw at least four aircraft go down in a very short space of time. They also had a scrape at Rostock when the wind blew them into the defences and they were coned by four searchlights, but after a few violent manouevres, Mike Beetham managed to shake them off before the flak got their range.

Once Rostock was behind them it was a straight run into Berlin. With a 100 mph tail wind they arrived in no time at all. Over Berlin they found a thin layer of stratus cloud which made it difficult for the searchlights to pick them up. They had no trouble on the bomb run but night fighters started to put down a ring of flares. They then saw a few fighters but their luck held and they were not attacked. On the return trip their work was cut out keeping away from the defences at Leipzig, Brunswick, Osnabrück and Hannover. Along this leg they cleared the Dutch coast, finding little cloud cover to help out, but before long it proved to be a nuisance. They received a message from their base at Skellingthorpe that they must divert to Docking in Norfolk. They found it and flew into the circuit with another aircraft from 50 Squadron but as they circled, a third aircraft in the landing order crashed on the flarepath which meant, as they were No 6 in line, that they were not able to land. They were given Coltishall as an alternative, and here they landed safely; then, however, they discovered how heavy the losses had been. 50 Squadron lost no aircraft at all, but it had been lucky. It was Beetham's twentieth trip of his tour.

Weather and visibility at bases for returning bombers was good till around 4 am in the Yorkshire area, but in the Lincolnshire area it deteriorated after 2 am. Meanwhile, aircraft strung out over Germany were having increasing difficulties with the wind speeds.

Navigator Fred Hall of 76 Squadron soon became aware that the wind was increasing from 90 to 140 mph. His pilot, Ray Bolt, steered to port to avoid Rostock, which was throwing up a lot of flak. Fred also found a tail wind to the target and prepared two plots which allowed for the wind forecast and the wind he was meeting. They bombed the target and made it successfully back to England, landing at a base in the south rather than their own in Yorkshire.

One navigator of 57 Squadron, Flying Officer Mackinnon, had already completed a tour of ops but these had been daylight missions on Boston aircraft, and night navigation was very different. His H_2S set was not working, but luckily it suddenly came on for a few minutes, allowing him to identify the north German coast. He was then able to plot a course around Rostock before they whistled down to the Big City at something over 300 mph, and, like many others, overshot the target. He was later told that the spread of the bomber stream at the coast was around 180 miles.

Pilot Officer Downes of 78 Squadron remembers nerves getting a little frayed as it was their seventh op that month. His mid-upper, Sergeant Joiner – an Australian – was stood down for this operation and was replaced by a Royal Artillery major, who had been trained as an air gunner; his main role was to assess the enemy's flak defences. They arrived quite easily over Berlin a minute or two after the first flares went down. The target area was virtually clear – the time, 10.44 pm. It was the first time on their ops to Berlin that the extent of the searchlights could be appreciated. It was a dark night but at 20,000 feet the visibility was almost as good as daylight. The bomb aimer called, 'Bombs Gone,' but the flight engineer, Sergeant Jupp, checked through the inspection panel to the bomb bay and reported a 2,000 lb HE bomb had hung up. It was out of the question to go round again so they made for home with the bomb still aboard. Downes asked for a course to Magdeburg and gave instructions to release the bomb on H_2S. The run-up to Magdeburg, which showed up clearly on the H_2S screen, was without incident and Jupp released the bomb manually. They then altered course to regain track, when the flak opened up and began to creep nearer and nearer. The Artillery major wanted Downes to maintain as steady a course as he could to enable him to observe the shell fire, but Downes knew better. An isolated aircraft in range of radar predicted flak was no place to hang about so he took evasive action, but the flak still stayed too close for comfort. This continued for five to ten minutes, which at the time seemed like hours. Eventually they cleared the range of the guns and were hopefully back on track.

As they looked ahead they could seen an unexpected mass of searchlights and heavy flak explosions. They were heading directly for the middle of a massive defence area, which extended from Dortmund to the south of Cologne; they were 70 to 80 miles south of track! Downes thought the navigator, Sergeant Hendry, had made a mistake, but once again it was the wind blowing them off

(*Above*) Groundcrews, a welcome break

(*Left*) Return from Berlin – 78 Squadron

course. It seemed pointless now to try to regain the right course, so Downes decided to alter course to the south of Cologne, and then make a beeline for the nearest part of the coast. This seemed to work as they completed the run home successfully.

In the target area at 10.31, Lancaster ND648 'B', flown by Squadron Leader Creswell of 35 Squadron, was about to turn away from his bomb run when the mid-upper – Sergeant Rhodes – saw a FW190 at 300 yards astern in a steep dive, and closing rapidly. He yelled for Creswell to corkscrew and as the Lancaster began to do so, the fighter opened fire. Red and green tracer lanced into the bomber, hitting the starboard tailplane. As the 190 broke away, both gunners opened fire and claimed hits on its underside before it appeared to roll over and dive.

The German fighter controllers could see from their radar screens that the bombers were being scattered over a wide area. They guided some fighters over the coast as the bombers began to come in and others sent after bombers in the Kiel area, north-east of Lübeck. Plots on the bombers were passed to the fighter pilots over the radio, reporting three main concentrations. One had approached the Danish coast, another converging from the North Sea, and later the largest one was to the west of Berlin. As Berlin as the target was confirmed, so too was the realisation that part of the bomber force was considerably off track to the south. NJG/I, II and III operated in the bomber stream along the whole route, while NJG/V and VI were finally ordered to the city at 10.16 pm. The RAF tried to jam over the whole VHF band and ABC was heard on 30 frequencies. It was then that the air battle began in earnest.

Flight Lieutenant Blackham, as on previous occasions, was involved with a fighter. He was attacked over the target at 10.49 by a Ju88. Both of his gunners concentrated their fire on it as it fired at them. Strikes were seen on the 88 and it was claimed as damaged.

Pilot Officer Giddens in a Lancaster of 207 Squadron (DN521) was attacked by a FW190 over the target at 10.51. Standard corkscrew action was taken and the rear gunner, Sergeant Hall, fired. The mid-upper could just bring his guns to bear on the fighter, but the rear gunner kept up the return fire. As the attack continued, the mid-upper, Sergeant James, was found slumped in his turret. His oxygen supply had been shot away. Sergeant Walker, the WOP, managed to get him out and gave him the emergency oxygen supply, and plugged the gunner into the intercom. When Giddens later checked his crew over the radio, James replied, 'I am searching.' Giddens replied, 'Your turret has gone U/S!' However, James wasn't delirious and said, 'I am searching through a hole in the side.'

On reaching England, Giddens made an emergency landing at Shipdown, Norfolk, an American base. Owing to a burst tyre the aircraft slewed off the runway and finished up the opposite way round on another runway. By the time it stopped an ambulance and fire engine had drawn up by its side. An American shone a light into the rear turret and remarked, 'Gee, Buddie, were you in there when that happened?'

On examining the aircraft the following morning, the turret door showed several hits by cannon shells and the bulk-head door blown off. The rudder controls and trimmer tabs were also severely damaged and the aircraft had to be written off.

Flying Officer Greenburgh of 514 Squadron, in Lancaster LL727 'C2', was attacked by a fighter south of Berlin. It was a Ju88 and the mid-upper saw it first, giving the order to corkscrew as he opened fire, followed by a burst from the rear gunner, Flight Sergeant Drake. The fighter opened fire almost at the same moment and then broke away. Two minutes later the rear gunner reported a Ju88 coming in at 400 yards. Sergeant Carey in the top turret and Drake opened up and strikes were seen on the 88. Eight minutes later the engineer reported an aircraft making an attack from starboard. It fired, putting a burst into the Lanc's starboard outer engine that knocked it out. This caused the aircraft to begin a series of vicious spirals which soon became uncontrollable. All the instruments were knocked out and the aircraft was rapidly losing height, all but completely out of control. Greenburgh had no choice but to give the order to abandon the aircraft.

The engineer and bomb aimer jumped immediately and Greenburgh was half out of his seat but then decided to have another attempt at regaining control. He was also told that the navigator's parachute had been thrown out of the escape hatch during the spin. At about 7,000 feet he managed to get the aircraft on a more or less even keel. They returned to base at 9,000 feet and made a safe landing. The mid-upper and WOP had been literally standing by the hatch on the point of jumping when they realised the aircraft was under control and returned to their posts.

An aircraft of 83 Squadron, Lancaster ND529 'D' flown by Flight Lieutenant Eeggins, was homeward bound from Berlin when attacked by a Me109. The rear gunner opened fire and hits were observed on its fuselage and it broke off to be claimed as damaged. Immediately afterwards the mid-upper reported a FW190 approaching, and both gunners began firing as did the 190. Hits were seen on the 190's wing and engine by the WOP and gunners. A few seconds later it came in again and the rear gunner continued to fire. This time the 190 broke away with smoke coming from its engine. It then burst into flames and was seen to hit the ground.

Soon after leaving Berlin, Flight Lieutenant Picton of 550 Squadron, in Lancaster ME581 'D', was in combat with another 190 and both gunners, Sergeant Keen and Sergeant Porteous in the rear turret, received serious injuries from cannon fire. Sergeant Williams, the WOP, went into the astrodome, warning the pilot and giving him evasive instructions. With the attack apparently over, he then went back to the rear gunner whose oxygen tube had been severed, gave him his own oxygen mask and assisted him out of the turret. Williams later sent a radio message back to base, giving details of the casualties so that medical aid was waiting when the aircraft landed.

Pilot Officer Bowen-Bravery had his rear turret rendered U/S and bombed a flak emplacement on the west coast of Denmark. Soon afterwards he was attacked by a single-engined aircraft and the mid-upper gave it a short burst from very short range. A short while later a burning aircraft was seen going down by three of the crew and then burning on the ground.

Flight Lieutenant Everest, flying a Halifax (HX355 'D') of 78 Squadron, was attacked by a fighter over Berlin but was able to hold a course till over Rockanje, south of the Hague. Pilot Officer Alan Sinden baled out and was helped by Dutch farmers. They tried to get him back to England but this was found to be impossible and he was moved from house to house until December when he was captured and sent to Stalag 1, where he met the rest of his crew.

*

The flak was far worse than the fighters on this night. It was estimated to have accounted for at least 45 of the RAF's missing bombers. Because of the dispersion of the aircraft, many must have been without sufficient Window cover. This would have given ample scope to predicted flak on a night particularly suitable for co-operation with searchlights. Some aircraft reported being hit by flak at 22,000 feet and above. Another 30 aircraft were hit by flak between 16,000 and 22,000 feet. Altogether seventeen bombers were reported as being shot down on the outward route and 21 on the homeward. These were mostly in the area of Sylt, Flensburg, Kiel, Wilhelmshaven, Leipzig, Museburg, Magdeburg, Osnabrück, Münster, Deusau, Aachen and the Ruhr.

Over Berlin the flak was reported as mainly in barrage form at 18,000 to 24,000 feet and there was intense searchlight activity. One pilot said, 'It seemed as though no aircraft could possibly get through the thick forest of their beams but there proved to be many ways round them.' Seven aircraft were reported to have been brought down over Berlin. Flight Lieutenant Clark of 625 Squadron was flying Lancaster ME684 'Z' when he was hit by flak and came down over the German frontier on the outward journey. Three members of the crew managed to evade capture. Sergeant Donald Beckwith baled out and landed three miles east of Haaksbergen. He was found by a farmer and taken from house to house in Holland and France, the aim being to get him into Switzerland. During August he fought with the Maquis in France and at the beginning of September he contacted the American Army and was soon on his way home. Flight Lieutenant Peter Armytage, from Victoria, Australia, landed on the German side of the Dutch/German border and eventually got into Holland. He was, however, later picked up in Antwerp and sent to Stalag Luft III where he stayed until liberated in April 1945. Two other members of the crew successfully evaded, Sergeant Rimmington and Sergeant Munro, the rest were taken in captivity.

Flying Officer Hentsch, flying Lancaster ND650 'Y', of 12 Squadron, was hit and shot down over Duisberg on the outward journey. Two men were taken into captivity, four died and the seventh, Sergeant Albert Keveren, baled out and swam across the river Maas. On the other side he was contacted by a Dutch boy who took him to the local organisation HQ where he remained for six weeks. He then crossed into Belgium and remained there for four weeks with nine other British and American airmen. They were given Belgium identity cards and remained in a farmhouse until mid-July when they walked to Eelen. From there they travelled to Seraing via Liège where they waited for advancing American soldiers.

Flight Sergeant Hall of 106 Squadron made two runs over Berlin despite his aircraft being damaged by flak, and brought his machine back on three engines. It was a wonderful effort considering it was his first operation.

Pilot Officer McIntosh of 432 Squadron in a Halifax (LW593 'O') was shot down over the city and he and three of his crew taken prisoner; the other three died. Some time later McIntosh sent a message back to England: 'Please forward two Caterpillar Badges, one for myself and one for Flying Officer Small.' (These badges were given to all airmen whose lives had been saved by a parachute descent.)

One crew of 61 Squadron, led by Flight Lieutenant Burgess, a Canadian, were on their thirteenth trip, of which eleven had been successful and two aborted – both because of engine problems. Although John McQuillan, the rear gunner, had gone through the usual ritual of relieving himself against one of the aircraft's wheels, he found that soon after they had crossed the enemy coast he needed to go again. It was impossible, however, just to leave his turret at such a time to use the Elsan. He asked the pilot how long before he could do so with reasonable safety and was told, four to five hours, the rest of the crew finding his predicament somewhat amusing! An hour later he was feeling very uncomfortable but trying his hardest not to think about it. By the time they had bombed he was in agony. He saw aircraft going down in flames and wondered who was suffering most, them or him!! After leaving the target he again asked, 'How long now, Frank?' and was told about two hours by Frank Burgess. 'I cannot wait that long,' stated McQuillan. With all the fighters and flak about he managed to, or perhaps his mind was taken off his problem, although the rest of the crew were smiling and thinking it a bit of a joke. Eventually nature could not be ignored. It was impossible for him to stand up in the turret so he had to relieve himself where he sat.

On their return they were diverted to Metheringham where they landed at 2.30 am. He was, to say the least, uncomfortable after his experience and his presence in the sergeants' mess at Metheringham was not a popular one! McQuillan was later shot down in February 1945, but still the agony he suffered that night was never surpassed by anything before or since.

Flight Sergeant Pydden, from Dover, was on his thirteenth trip of his second tour. He got through to the target successfully, and as it was his seventh op to Berlin, he found it the easiest. There was no heavy flak and very little light stuff coming up. They saw little until they were about 60-70 miles into the homeward trip, when a big flash lit up the night sky behind them, which they thought must be an oil or fuel dump going up. Their route took them just south of Magdeburg, then between Hannover and Osnabrück, crossing the Dutch coast south of Den Helder. No route markers were seen, but they made it home safely.

Halifax 76 Squadron in flight

(*Left*) Bob Thomas, killed hours later, March 1944 (*right*) Fred Brownings and crew.
L to R Arthur Richardson, Ron Walker, Bob Thomas and in cockpit Fred Brownings

Flying Officer Wimberley, flying Halifax LW510, had taken off at 6.59. A fix on him was made at 10.45 and later a message was received, 'Aircraft returning to base – one engine U/S,' followed by another fix at 10.55 when the Halifax was given permission to land at Cranfield. It crashed one mile ahead of the runway and all the crew were killed.

Pilot Officer K.S. Simpson, flying Halifax LW718 'T', had his WOP send a message when they were over the Dutch coast at 10.40. It stated that one engine on the port and one on the starboard side had failed. He then apparently carried on across the North Sea on two engines, crashing at the water's edge at Ingham, near Cromer, Norfolk at 11.11 pm, ploughing into a minefield where it blew up. All the crew were killed.

Flight Sergeant Brownings in a 103 Squadron Lancaster (ND572 'M') took off at 9.30. When over the Danish coast the rear gunner, Bob Thomas, spotted a Ju88 but Brownings managed to shake it off and went on to bomb the target successfully. As they cleared the target they saw a fighter coned by its own searchlights and with flak all around it. It promptly fired off a red and white star Very flare and the searchlights went off and the flak stopped. Some while later a voice from the rear turret yelled for Brownings to corkscrew as a FW190 was coming in for the attack. This time Fred Brownings could not shake it off and they were raked from stem to stern, and believed they were only saved because the fighter ran out of ammunition. Their intercom was put out of action so Brownings had no idea of any damage or injuries to his crew.

It was left to Jack Spark to go back with a clip-on oxygen bottle and find out. He found it very cold and draughty down the fuselage, but the mid-upper, Sergeant Ken Smart was all right though his foot rest had been shot away, and the hydraulics that powered his turret had been shot out. Right down the tail, he found a very different story. Bob Thomas had taken a direct hit in the attack and was dead in his turret.

To add to their problems there was a five-foot gap in the top of the port wing and one of the tanks was open to the elements and the flaps damaged beyond repair. Brownings was having to use his legs to control the column to prevent the aircraft from stalling. The crew were told to strap on their parachutes but Jack Spark found his in shreds, having been hit by a cannon shell. They were then coned by searchlights so Jack, remembering the fighter's flare shot, fired off the only ones they had, three reds and three white stars. It worked, and the searchlights went straight out and the firing ceased.

With only about twenty minutes of fuel left they came down on Dunsfold airfield but all the lights were out as German intruders had been over the south of England that night. Without any air to ground radio, which had also been hit, they fired a red Very cartridge at intervals and eventually the lights came on and they came into land. His first attempt was too high so he went round again. On his second attempt he managed to get down but then they slewed off the runway and hit something, which brought them to an abrupt halt. They had hit an American B17 Flying Fortress named 'Passionate Witch' that had crashed two days earlier.

The body of the rear gunner was extricated from his turret; all the rest of the crew were uninjured apart from shock, to the extent that they could not sleep. In July, four of the crew were decorated. Fred Brownings was commissioned and together with Norman Barker and Arthur Richardson received the DFC, Jack Spark the DFM. Strangely, their trip to Berlin was not mentioned in their citations.

Pilot Officer Davies, flying Lancaster LW587 'V', was airborne when the WOP, Flight Sergeant Woodward, discovered he had left his parachute harness behind, so they jettisoned the bombs into the sea and returned to base. One wonders what sort of reception he got back at base.

Many aircraft landed at Coltishall, a fighter station, having been diverted from their own bases due to weather. The quantities of surplus petrol in tanks on landing makes interesting reading. No 1 Bomber Group recorded that only nine of its aircraft returned with less than 100 gallons, but it is unlikely that petrol shortage through the strong wind, contributed to any losses.

*

The German European Service in English, broadcast at 10.30 pm on 25th March announced:

> The general impression in Berlin after last night's raid was that the raid had been one of the lightest sort. Berliners on their way to work this morning, looked in vain for the bomb craters. It was not until military HQ issued the first reports that it was realised that a big raid had been planned, and had been frustrated by the German night fighters.

A continuation of the report was made on the 26th when an air raid warden at one of the big Berlin bunkers described his experiences of the raid:

> I realised at once that something out of the ordinary was happening, for in previous raids I've always been able to notice the arrival over the City of the different waves of enemy bombers, but this time they came over all at six's and seven's, like an armada that had been scattered by the storm.

The German Telegraphic Service at 1.32 am on the 26th, reported:

> English bombers again made a large scale attack on Berlin in the evening hours of Friday. The raid has definitely the character of a terror raid. The raiders dropped a large number of HEs and IBs on all parts of the city. German ack-ack batteries and night fighters attacked the raiders. How many enemy planes were shot down is not yet known as only incomplete reports are yet to hand.

A further report at 2.16 am recorded:

> British formations approached the Reich and were intercepted between 9.00 and 10.00 on the evening of the 24th of March by strong German night fighter formations. The first of a series of aircraft shot down was between Freiberg and Kiel. Four streams of enemy bombers reached the Reich capital from the north west for more than an hour without pause. According to reports so far available, very heavy RAF losses may be expected. The attack was again aimed at Berlin, bombs were dropped at random in moderate visibility all over the built up area of the city – the terror nature of this attack is obvious. Many four-engined bombers were shot down over Berlin itself and the south-west suburbs. The enemy aircraft continued to be attacked as they flew off. In the west, small formations bombed the Leipzig and Weimar areas. 2,240 tons of bombs were dropped.

*

When the crews had been debriefed and gone finally to their beds to try and sleep for what was left of the night, many could still feel and hear the throb of their engines. Often the RAF police would come into a billet and collect the kit of the crew who had not returned.

(*Above*) 550 Squadron Lancaster damaged over Berlin

(*Left*) 'One of our aircraft is missing'

The next day only the memory of them remained.

On this night, when the last heavy bomber raid on Berlin by the RAF was made, another historic situation was developing not far away. Today it is known as 'The Great Escape', when 76 RAF and Allied airmen escaped from Stalag Luft III at Sagan. Of these 76, three reached safety. Of the others who were recaptured, 50 were murdered by the Gestapo.

*

The RAF losses on this night were 72 aircraft, which was a loss ratio of 8.9%. Broken down it showed that out of the force of 809 bombers, the Group's totals were:

    1 Group 189 Lancasters despatched, 19 missing – 10.3%
    3 Group 61 Lancasters despatched, 7 missing – 11.1%
    5 Group 192 Lancasters despatched, 11 missing – 5.6%
    8 Group 91 Lancasters despatched, 7 missing – 6.2%
    4 Group 132 Halifaxes despatched, 16 missing – 11.9%
    6 Group 108 Halifaxes despatched, 12 missing – 14.4%
    8 Group 18 Mosquitos despatched,   0 missing – –

    ───   ──
    809   72
    ───   ──

Of the force, 43 returned early. Of the 72 lost, 45 were estimated to have fallen to flak, 18 to night fighters, the other 9 unknown. Statistics shown another way record:

    8 Group   112 PFF aircraft   – losses 7
    1 Group   27 Supporters   – losses 5
    First Wave   125 aircraft   – losses 10
    Second Wave   125 aircraft   – losses 13
    Third Wave   128 aircraft   – losses 15
    Fourth Wave   125 aircraft   – losses 13
    Fifth Wave   123 aircraft   – losses 9
                                            ──
                                            73
                                            ──

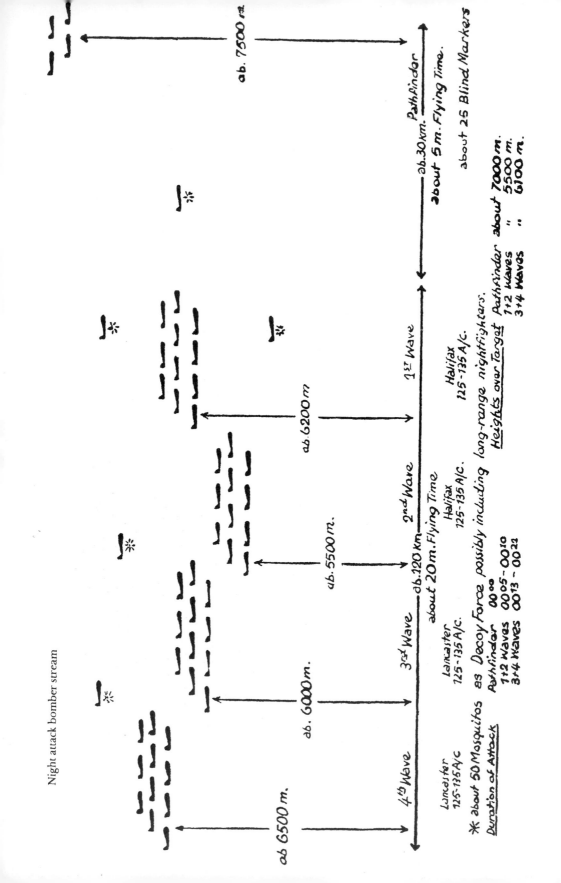

Night attack bomber stream

ab. 7500 m.

Pathfinder

about 5 m. Flying Time.

about 25 Blind Markers

ab. 30 km.

1ˢᵗ Wave

Halifax
125-135 A/c.

Heights over Target

Pathfinder   about 7000 m.
1+2 Waves   "   5500 m.
3+4 Waves   "   6100 m.

ab. 6200 m.

2ⁿᵈ Wave

Halifax
125-135 A/c.

ab. 120 km.

about 20 m. Flying Time.

ab. 5500 m.

3ʳᵈ Wave

Lancaster
125-135 A/c.

✳ Decoy Force possibly including long-range nightfighters.

ab. 6000 m.

Duration of Attack

Pathfinder   00⁰⁰
1+2 Waves   00⁰⁵ – 00¹⁰
3+4 Waves   00¹³ – 00²²

4ᵗʰ Wave

Lancaster
125-135 A/c

✳ about 50 Mosquitos

ab. 6500 m.

The Pathfinders marked between	10.25 and 10.27 pm
The first wave bombed between	10.30 and 10.33 pm
The second wave bombed between	10.32 and 10.36 pm
The third wave bombed between	10.36 and 10.30 pm
The fourth wave bombed between	10.39 and 10.42 pm
The fifth wave bombed between	10.42 and 10.45 pm

There were 26 ABC aircraft from 1 Group but all returned safely. The losses to flak were, seventeen on the outward journey, seven in the target area and 21 on the way home. To fighters, six on the outward, four over the target, eight on the homeward run. The German Fighter Corps IJ claimed 80 aircraft shot down and reported losing one fighter themselves. Goebbels Overseas News Agency claimed 110 aircraft destroyed.

The German AA Batteries at this time were using 128 mm guns with much higher and greater radius of bursts, concentrated in *Grossen Batterien*, huge groups of up to 40 guns that worked in rectangular patterns known as box barrages. This night resulted in the best score for German flak guns in the war thus far.

Undoubtedly the major factor in the night's saga had been the wind. On the 25th March, the Meteorological Section of Bomber

'A missing Lancaster'

Command HQ was visited by the Director of the Met Office of the
Air Ministry, Doctor Petterssen, to discuss the difficulties in
forecasting winds from available data over enemy territory. It was
agreed, particularly in the light of winds forecast, and the actual
winds found on the night of the 24th/25th, that more upper air data
from Sweden would be of assistance on these occasions. An analysis
of navigation for this Berlin raid was undertaken to discover reasons
for the wide scatter of the force and its displacements to the south of
the ordered track. The southerly displacement obviously resulted
from a systematic error in the broadcast winds, both past and
forecast, the strength being in all cases too low. This under-estimate
of the strength was due in about equal proportions to:

    a. Lack of belief in the unusual wind strength on the part of the
        many wind finders.
    b. The time delay between the transmissions, by wind finders,
        and their reception at Bomber Command HQ.

The wind finders transmitted less than half the winds that they
found, 40% used the recommended period from 15 to 30 minutes
for wind determination. The main reason for the scatter was that
only about 55% of the winds used by navigators was the correct
broadcast winds. Very simply this meant that the wind finders just
could not believe the winds speeds they were reading and reduced
them by anything from 5 to 15 mph. In turn, the Met boys in
England could not believe even these reduced figures. So winds of
115 mph were reduced to around 110 by the wind finders and down
to around 95 mph by the Met people at Bomber Command. The
estimated true winds coming from the north and the use of the
slower wind estimations when calculated to courses to fly, caused the
aircraft to drift more and more to the south off track and into the
flak defences of towns they should have not flown near – hence the
heavy losses. It really was a case of a war with the elements – and the
elements won.

CHAPTER TEN

The Outcome

The most important factor in the Battle of Berlin was its contribution to the Second Front created by Bomber Command's air attacks on Germany. The defences in Berlin along with the other defences throughout Germany and the occupied countries, took vital guns and fighters away from the Eastern (Russian) Front, which was the main campaign as far as Germany was concerned at that time. With the huge numbers of Russian tanks on that front, the use of the hundreds of German 88 mm guns used as anti-aircraft guns against the RAF and American Air Forces, could have caused untold casualties amongst our Russian allies and decimated its armour.

Also, under the German dispersal plan, hundreds of private homes in Berlin were factories in miniature. Since the battle began on 18th November 1943, Bomber Command had dropped nearly 45,000 tons of high explosives and incendiary bombs on the City. In thirteen of the sixteen raids, 30,000 tons went down.

When the four-month battle came to an end, some 326 factories were left destroyed or damaged, including five priority ones, such as Krupps. The effect of the constant blitz was felt throughout the entire German war production. For instance, the destruction of the electrical engineering plants in Berlin, vital for synthetic oil production. Albert Speer, when interrogated in 1945, stated of this fact: 'There is no doubt!'

The effect of the German people having to live in this atmosphere of smoke and foul air caused by the severity of the fires was very upsetting and disturbing for their morale. Even in the daytime this was noticeable with the traffic jams in and around the city. The flak defences were under severe criticism and a jibe was made by the people: 'Flak is not a weapon, but an article of faith.'

The reactions to the bombing offensive on German morale was mentioned by Sir Arthur Harris on 25th February 1944. He stated that from secret sources he had found that the highest Nazi circles were regarding the bombing as something which would assure a German defeat comparatively quickly by producing a collapse of

4,000 cookie being loaded into a Mosquito

Siemens Berlin

morale as well as of production on the Home Front. The Nazi Propaganda machine under Goebbels, spread the news of the bombing as one of 'apathy' to the German people.

Harris had wanted the Americans to join in the battle but this was not to be. Would it have made a diference? We shall never really know but of course, round the clock bombing would obviously have had a considerable effect on the German people and production would have suffered so much more because of this. The American 8th Air Force did, however, contribute to the latter part of the battle with six raids in March 1944, beginning on the 3rd. This raid was foiled by bad weather and only the fighter escort reached the outskirts of Berlin. But when the raids on Berlin ceased by heavy bombers of the RAF, the Americans continued to attack the city right up until March 1945.

The British contribution to these attacks were taken up by the Mosquitos. They had also made attacks in between the heavy raids during the actual battle and they continued raiding it right through 1944, but it was in 1945 that the full weight of their attacks built up to a maximum. One must remember that the Mosquito could carry more bombs than the American Flying Fortress with its very small bomb bay.

On one raid on 1/2nd February 1945, 116 Mosquitos from 8 Group dropped 133.9 tons of bombs on the city. Between 20/21st February and 27/28th March 1945, 36 consecutive operations were mounted on Berlin. A message of congratulation was sent for the raid of 1/2nd February and at the end of all 36 raids, by Sir Charles Portal, Chief of Air Staff. The first message, dated 3rd February, to 8 Group says:

> Last night's attack was a fine contribution to the great and growing battle under which the enemy will finally succumb. Please convey my congratulations to all concerned and particularly the ground crews, without whose skilful effort the job could not have been done.

A tribute of sorts was made to the Mosquito boys by the Germans at the end of the war. They said there was no answer to their kind of raid and their attacks were very effective.

*

The losses in the battle were high, but no higher than Sir Arthur had predicted the previous November. He said it would cost his Command 500 aircraft and 495 had in fact been lost, and this was without the support of the Americans, certainly in the first three months of the battle. The loss percentage to Bomber Command's Main Force was 6% and to the Path Finder Force, 13%. One must also realise that if Berlin had not been attacked during this period there would have been other major targets to go for and losses would probably have been around the same figure. Up to the last raid the casualties were very moderate, especially considering the time of year and the weather conditions.

In a letter to the Under Secretary of State, dated 10th April 1944, Sir Arthur was commenting on the statements released to the press by the Directorate of Public Relations concerning the activities of Bomber Command. He stated that a lot of publicity had been given to the heavy losses on the Berlin raid of the 24th, and on Nuremburg on 31st March. Also a very successful raid on Frankfurt and notable achievements against Essen and Berlin itself. They had rather given the impression that the month of March as a whole was a failure. He pointed out that March had the second best minelaying figures of the war so far and included much outstanding and accurate work on factories and marshalling yards in occupied territory – mainly France. He ended by saying that at the end of March, all previous records in sorties and bomb tonnage had been greatly exceeded despite unfavourable weather and fierce enemy opposition and at the lowest rate of casualties experienced during the previous thirteen months.

*

A seventeenth raid was arranged for 21st June 1944 with a force of up to 2,000 heavy bombers which would have included 700 from Bomber Command. It was hoped that 6,500 tons of bombs might be dropped of which the RAF would drop 4,000 tons. A fighter escort from the Americans would have been provided as it was to be a daylight attack. It came at a time when London was being subjected to V1 attacks from the Continent, just days following the invasion of Europe.

In a letter to the Prime Minister on 20th June, Portal ended his outline of the proposed raid saying it was to be an experiment of the US Air Force and Bomber Command working together in daylight, and that it would in any event be a pretty good answer to the German V1 attacks. The PM replied, 'I entirely agree.'

Lancaster DV 372-F crew and groundcrew

DV 372-F today – IWM

Up to this time a 1,000 flying bombs had been launched on London and only three days before a flying bomb had made a direct hit on the Guard's Chapel in Birdcage Walk – a stone's throw from Buckingham Palace – and killed or injured over 200 people.

However, this raid was cancelled on the 21st, on the basis that only 600 US bombers would be able to attack instead of 1,800. The Americans had decided to split their force and use only 600 on Berlin, and the remainder on other targets. Also, the original plan was for not less than 300 escort fighters at any one time but the plan showed this liable to a reduction of around 150 or even less. The Americans did however make the attack with the 600 bombers and only Mosquito aircraft of the RAF attacked Berlin that night.

It was a difficult period with so many targets needing attention from the heavy bombers and the continued threat of rockets and flying bombs. With Allied troops having now landed in Normandy and in constant need of direct or indirect support if their offensive was to succeed, the air forces had many things to contend with.

*

One aircraft that took part in the raids on Berlin, completing six of the sixteen operations, was Lancaster S for Sugar (R5868). She had started her operational period on 8/9th July 1942 as Q for Queenie (W5868), with 83 Squadron at Scampton and completed some 70 ops before going to 467 Squadron at Bottesford, when she became 'Sugar'. Here she flew some ten ops before 467 moved to Waddington, from where this grand old lady took part in the first raid of the battle, on 18/19th November. She went on to complete a further 60 ops, ending on 23rd April 1945, against Flensburg. During her time with 83 its pilot on many occasions was Squadron Leader (later Wing Commander) R.L. Hilton DFC and bar, who was later to be killed in the Battle of Berlin. After the war Sugar became a 'Gate Guardian' at RAF Scampton for many years, but in 1972 was moved to the RAF Museum at Hendon where she can be seen today in all her splendour in the Bomber Command Museum, still wearing the wartime slogan, 'No Enemy Plane Will Fly Over Reich Territory, signed, Hermann Göring.' On each of its engines is the name of one of the many pilots who flew it during its operational work. Former members of 467 paid a visit to Sugar in May 1975.

Another living memory of the battle is the fuselage of another Lancaster, also of 467 Squadron – DV372 'F'. It took part in some 49 operations between November 1943 and June 1944, with 467, including fourteen on Berlin. Its first op was 18/19th November to Berlin and its last against Orléans on 10/11 June 1944. It was struck off the RAF's charge in October 1945. Since 1946, the fuselage of this Lancaster, has been housed in the Imperial War Museum in London, still in its wartime markings of the goofy-figure from *Brer Rabbit*, with the words 'Old Fred' beneath it and its 49 trips marked on its side.

*

It is not always possible to determine to the letter the ultimate success of a battle. One certainly can't in this case, judge its contribution to the war as a whole, but without doubt it kept many men, guns and fighters pinned down in the defence of Berlin, which otherwise would have been used on the Russian front and later in Normandy. These men, guns and aircraft could have made a vital difference and changed the course of history.

At the end of the war damage assessment for Berlin revealed that 6,427 acres of the city had been devastated. Of this 750 to 1,000 acres is credited to the American 8th Air Force. As no further major attacks were made on the city after March 1944, it is certain that the

Winston Churchill and daughter, Berlin 1945

major portion of 5,427 acres of devastation must have been achieved by Bomber Command during the Battle. This was achieved in 9,112 sorties plus 162 Pathfinder Mosquitos — 90% of whom actually bombed the City. It was a definite battle that Harris wanted to fight, but Bomber Command during the period flew a total of over 26,000 sorties against Germany, so Berlin only took up around a third of his effort. Harris had hoped that devastating Berlin and its war industry would herald the final collapse of Germany. If there had been a combined RAF/USAAF assault it might have done, though probably it would have not caused a surrender, but merely written off the German capital. To be fair to Harris, he only promised that the destruction of Berlin would cost Germany the war, rather than the immediate collapse of the Nazi regime and with it the end of the war. What can no longer be in doubt is that his Battle against Berlin went a long way to costing Germany the war.

Remains of Berlin

The damage all but stopped production of war materials from the capital. The Armaments Minister, Albert Speer, was gradually able to bring production up to the level achieved before the bombing but as Speer himself stated, to catch up on lost production was not enough. Production of the essential needs of her Army, Navy and Air Force was far below what was desired. Any halt in this production had to cut deep into the German war machine. From that point of view alone, the Battle of Berlin was certainly no failure.

Generalfeldmarschall Erhard Milch, the Armaments Chief of the Luftwaffe, told his staff officers on 23rd February 1944:

Everyone should pay a visit to Berlin. It would then be realised that experience such as we have undergone in the last few months cannot be endured indefinitely. That is impossible. When the big cities have been demolished it will be the turn of the smaller ones.

Berlin War Cemetery

(*Left*) Air Vice Marshal Don Bennett,
(*right*) G/Capt Hamish Mahaddie 1983

Les Bartlett in Berlin

Bomber Command Association – 1983

A Tribute

4th May 1984

I am writing this in a free country, without fear thanks to Allied airman and all the others, fighting for a free world.

I am only thirty one years old so I am an 'After the war-kid', but I and most people of my generation do realise the great things you did for us. Thanks!

Eric Leÿenaur, Dronten, Holland.

'View from the Cockpit' by Alf Huberman

Appendices

The Battle of Berlin

Losses

Aircraft missing:

Lancasters	381
Halifaxes	110
Stirlings	4
Mosquitos	2
Total	497

Aircraft lost or crashed in the United Kingdom:

Lancasters	60
Halifaxes	12
Total	72

Aircrew:

Killed	2938
POW's	716
Evaded or escaped	36
Injured or wounded	92
Total	3782

The Battle of Berlin

The following information is drawn from operational records
on file at the Public Record Office, Kew,
Commonwealth War Graves, Air Historical Branch

Missing Aircraft
18th/19th November 1943

Squadron and Aircraft	Crew
9 Sqdn:- Lanc ED 871-Z on loan from 467: Crashed Bornicke, Germany. Sgt Harris Buried in Berlin. Collided with another Lancaster	P-O F.J. Lees POW Stalag L1 (Barth) Sgt N. Hunn POW Stalag III Sgt H. Fisher POW Stalag IVB Sgt Drake POW Stalag IVB Sgt D.T. Cordon POW Stalag IVB Sgt S. Hand Killed SGT L. N. Harris Killed
9 Sqdn: Lanc DV 284-G Crashed west of Burgwurben, Germany. All the crew buried in Berlin. Hit by flak at 21.55	PO G.A. Graham RCAF Killed F/S J.G.Mc Comb Killed Sgt W.G. Stratham Killed F/O D. McDonald Killed Sgt R .M.C. McInness Killed Sgt A.F. Williamson RAAF Killed F/S H.F. Altus RAAF Killed Sgt K. Mellor Killed
57 Sqdn: Lanc JB 418-1 Crashed Barnsdorf, Germany. Those killed have no known grave but are recorded on the Runneymede Memorial.	F/Lt A.F. Gobbie POW Stalag L1 (Barth) Sgt J.A. Hemming POW Stalag LIII (Sagan) F/O A.E.W. Gardner DFC Killed F/S R.W. Newcoms Killed F/O T. Scott POW Stalag IVB Sgt T. Pool POW StalagIVB F/S F.J. Lamble POW Stalag IVB
97 Sqdn: Lanc JB 367-S Crashed Château at Voort, Belgium. F/Sgt Johnson is now buried in Heverlee War Cemetery, Leuven, Belgium. Hit by flak over Acchen.	F/Sgt A.A. Johnson DFM RNZAF Killed Age 27 F/Lt A.P..W Pepper DFC Evaded P/O F.T. Williams DFC Evaded F/S J.J. Sansam POW Stalag IVB F/S T Hesselden Evaded F/S C.J. Billows Evaded F/S W. Jackson POW Stalag 4B
100 Sqdn: Lanc JB 991-H Crashed Salzwedel, Germany.	F/S R.B. Doughty RCAF POW Stalag IVB Sgt H.N. Loton POW Stalag IVB Sgt R.E.. McPherson RCAF POW Stalag VB Heydekruge) later F/Sgt Sgt W.G. Gray RCAF POW Stalag IVB J.H. Kerr POW Stalag LIII Sgt D.S.G. Wynbergen POW Sgt F.R. Marsh POW
101 Sqdn: Lanc DS 370-K2 Crashed Schoonebeek, Holland. All the crew buried in Schoonebeek, Drenthe, Holland. F/O McManus hailed from Dublin, Ireland.	F/O C.P. McManus Killed age 25 Sgt K. Jones Killed F/O G.D. Spyers Killed Sgt A.E. Rosen Killed F/O B.K. Petyt Killed F/S G.H. Gittins DFM Killed Sgt C.H. Downs Killed WO II G.P. Herman RCAF Killed

Squadron and Aircraft	*Crew*
115 Sqdn: Lanc DS 680-L All the crew buried in Heverlee War Cemetery, Leuven, Belgium. Shot down by a nightfighter flown by Oblt Eckart Wilhelm von Bonin of II/NJG1 crashed at Hermee (Liege)	Sgt N. MacKay Killed F/Sgt F.B. Collenet Killed P/O M.L. Richardson RCAF Killed WO II S.A. Anderson RCAF Killed Sgt G.V. Sharrat Killed Sgt H.G. Bannister Killed P/O N.R.Shaw Killed
156 Sqdn: Lanc JB 363-K Crashed Doberitz Crew buried in Berlin.	W/C J.H. White DFC Killed age 28 F/Lt R. Robers DFC Killed P/O M.J.E. Stonely DFM Killed P/O W. Wilkinson DFC Killed P/O J.C. Otter DFC Killed F/Lt E.M. Thompson DFC Killed P/O D.M.C Silverman DFM Killed
207 Sqdn: Lanc DV 361-V Sgt E.H. Shimeild, flying with P/O W.H. Baker, was in collision with another Lanc over Berlin. He fell to his death and is now buried in the Hamburg War Cemetery.	Sgt E.H. Shimeild Killed
460 Sqdn: Lanc DV 341-C2 Crashed Zornigall, Germany. All the crew buried in Berlin.	F/Sgt J.G. Gibson RAAF Killed F/Sgt W.F.J. Manning RAAF Killed Sgt D.O. Jones Killed F/S J.D. Malcolm RAAF Killed Sgt R.K. Megit RAAF Killed F/O C.G. Slennett RAAF Killed P/O H.S. Spain Killed

22nd/23rd November 1943

Squadron and Aircraft	*Crew*
7 Sqdn: Lanc EE 119-N The crew are buried in the Rheinburg Cemetery.	W/O S.G. Dorrell Killed later P/O Sgt G. Hawgood Killed Sgt F.E. Deavin Killed W/O D. Gadson Killed later P/O F/S C.L. Hartman RCAF Killed Sgt J.W. Harvey Killed Sgt I.A. Hastings RAAF Killed later F/Sgt
7 Sqdn: Lanc JB 115-G Crashed near Hanover, Germany. Crew buried in Hanover.	S/L H.M. Nesbitt Killed F/Lt J. Perfect DFC Killed F/S FL. Chapman Killed F/S W.M. Wilson Killed F/Lt A. Seymour MID Killed F/Lt G.J.B. Neil Killed F/O A. Barker Killed
10 Sqdn: Halifax JD 146-V The crew have no known grave, but are on the Runneymede Memorial.	F/Lt D.S. Pont Killed Sgt A. Buchan Killed Sgt J. McMillan Killed Sgt K. Lance Killed Sgt D. McKensie Killed Sgt T.H.R. McKeag Killed F/O M.F. Baxter Killed
10 Sqdn: Halifax JD 367-Z The crew are buried in the Reichswald War Cemetery.	F/O T. Hall Killed Sgt G.L. Skelton Killed Sgt S.P. Rogers Killed Sgt C.J. Ashton Killed Sgt H.L. Anderson Killed Sgt W.R. Zastrow Killed Sgt J.R. Colebrook Killed

Squadron and Aircraft	*Crew*
49 Sqdn: Lanc JB 368-G The crew have no known grave, but are on the Runneymede Memorial.	F/O CM, Cottingham RCAF Killed Sgt A.J. Mathieson Killed F/O R.B. Richard RCAF Killed Sgt G. Tabenor Killed F/S C.E. Byers RCAF Killed F/O MW. Wright Killed Sgt G.F.A.J.. Falck Killed F/O G.C. Bailey RCAF Killed
50 Sqdn: Lanc DV 366-R The crew are all buried in the Berlin War Cemetery.	W/O J.H. Saxton Killed Sgt P.H. Fryer Killed F/S J.H.Jowett Killed Sgt J.C.E. Rees Killed F/S W.E. Coates Killed F/S J.J. Zunti Killed Sgt C. Watson Killed
51 Sqdn: Halifax TR 726-B Crashed Grunewald, Germany. Crew names on the Runneymede Memorial.	W/C C.L.Y. Wright Killed age 29 Sgt A.A. Brandon Killed Sgt S. Grognet POW P/O W. Martin POW Stalag Ll Sgt A. Spurr Killed Sgt R. Thorn Killed Sgs W.E. Pyne Killed
51 Sqdn: Halifax LW 286-H Crashed at sea. Crew names on the Runneymede Memorial.	P/O H.F. Farley Killed F/O F.H. Moynihan Killed F/O H. Hetterley Killed Sgt A. Springett Killed Sgt S.H. Godfrey Killed Sgt F. Dyer Killed Sgt J.E. Whitehead Killed
75 Sqdn: Stirling U 453-K The crew are buried in the Rheinburg War Cemetery.	F/Sgt K.R. Dingle Killed F/O J. Brothwell Killed F/S J. Margetts Killed Sgt E.R. Whittington Killed Sgt I.G. Holbrook Killed Sgt V.S. Hughes Killed Sgt A.G. Bernard Killed
75 Sqdn: Stirling EF 148-R The crew are buried in the Reichswald War Cemetery.	F/S J.C. Turner Killed P/O S. MeKensie Killed P/O W.G. Pagett Killed F/S J.L. Cowie Killed Sgt G.J. Blackman Killed Sgt R. Mc. More Killed Sgt T. McGloin Killed
77 Sqdn: Halifax LW 290-IA Crashed at Kloster Zimma. Crew buried in Berlin.	F/S J.A. Smart RCAF Killed later WOII Sgt W. Eaton Killed Sgt J. Robertson Killed F/S W.E. Ackland Killed F/S E.A. Davies Killed Sgs L.L. Green Killed Sgt W. Allen Killed
83 Sqdn: Lanc JB 424-B The crew are buried in Berlin. Crashed in the Schiller Park, Berlin.	P/O R. Henderson DFM Killed Sgt J.P. MeAdam Killed F/S H.E.M. Dulieu Killed Sgt F.J. Fay Killed F/S J. Prendergast Killed Sgt D.M. Rutter Killed Sgt T. Cubitt Killed

Squadron and Aircraft	*Crew*
97 Sqdn: Lanc JB 238-A Crashed near Osnabruck. Those killed buried in Reichswald War Cemetery, Germany.	F/O E.F. McEgan RAAF Killed age 21 P/O PA. Spencer POW Stalag LI F/O J.V. Tyler Killed Sgt J.J.Johnson POW Sgt W.S. Gibb POW Stalag LIII W/O J.R.A. Burke DFM RAAF POW F/S F.A. Williams RCAF Killed
97 Sqdn: Lanc JB 227-J The crew have no known grave, but are on the Runneymede Memorial.	F/Lt J.F. Munro RCAF DFC Killed F/S W.G. Waller Killed F/Lt A.J.W Silk DFM Killed F/Lt F.P. Burbridge DFC Killed F/S J.N. Underwood Killed F/S R.S. Bennett DFM Killed W/O W. Hill DFM RCAF Killed
115 Sqdn: Lanc DS 782-K The crew have no known grave, but are on the Runneymede Memorial.	Sgt J. Harris Killed Sgt M. Bools Killed Sgt A. Wilson Killed P/O S.M. Smith RCAF Killed F/S D.C. Morley RAAF Killed Sgt H.A.R Hurn Killed Sgt D.H. Hughes Killed
115 Sqdn: Lanc DS 764-S Sgt Smith found in the aircraft.	Sgt H. Smith Killed Sgt F.C. Downs POW Stalag IVB Sgt C. Deakin POW Stalag LVI Sgt R. Strong POW Stalag IVB Sgt J.H. Ferguson RCAF POW Stalag IVB Sgt T.H. Schotchmer RCAF POW Stalag IVB Sgt E. Miller POW Stalag IVB
115 Sqn: Lanc JB 238-A Those killed buried in the Reichswald War Cemetery Crashed Achmer	P/O E.F McEgan RAAF Killed F/Sgt F.A Williams RAAF Killed P/O P.A.Spencer POW Stalag L1 F/O J.V.Tyler Killed Sgt J.J.Johnson Stalag Wistritz Tephlitz Sgt W.S.Gibb Stalag LIII WO1 J.R.A.Burke RCAF Stalag IVB
156 Sqdn: Lanc JB 694 Crashed in the Doeberiw Area; the crew have no known grave but are on the Runneymede Memorial. Crew buried 7/12/1943 but now no trace of graves.	F/Sgt T.G. Stephens DFM Killed Sgt M.N. William Killed Sgt T. Stocks DFM Killed Sgt S.J. Ryan Killed Sgt H. Truscott Killed Sgt F. Phelan Killed Sgt L. Bettaney Killed
156 Sqdn: Lanc JB 304-Z The crew have no known grave, but on the Runneymede Memorial.	S/L D.C. Anset DFC Killed F/Lt J.T. Smith DFC Killed F/Lt W.A.G. Clark Killed Sgt J. Walker Killed P/O G.J.H. Stokes Killed F/S R.O. Buckle Killed W/O J.A.C. Lovis DFC Killed
158 Sqdn: Halifax HR 977-A Crashed at Lingen. Crew buried in the Reichswald War Cemtery, Germany.	P/O J. Wood-Brown Killed P/O L.A. Smith Killed Sgt J.M. Phillips Killed Sgt J.T. Sykes Killed Sgt K. Williams POW Sgt W.J. Middleton Killed Sgt S.T. Hazel Killed

Squadron and Aircraft	*Crew*
?14 Sqdn: Stirling EF 445-J Crashed at Lingen. Both are on the Runneymede Memorial; the remainder of the crew were saved.	Sgt W. Sweeney Killed F/Sgt G.A. Atkinson Killed
218 Sqdn: Stirling EF 180 Crew names on the Runneymede Memorial.	S/L G.W. Prior DFC Killed Sgt E.J. Lovell Killed Sgt G.A. Wright Killed Sgt F.C. Stoney Killed W/O H.J. Hansell Killed Sgt W.A.J. Baldwin Killed Sgt J.A. Gartland Killed
419 Sqdn: Halifax LW 231-F An all-Canadian crew; Hunter was on his fourth trip and Lisage his 25th - he had filled in on Hunter's crew because of illness. Buried at Diever, Holland.	Sgt W.L. Hunter Killed F/O R.J. Newman Killed Sgt M.A. McKellar Killed Sgt B.A. Howitson Killed Sgt W.B. Jones Killed Sgt C.H. May Killed F/S J.A. Lisage Killed
428 Sqdn: Halifax LK 906-D Crashed Scherenbostel, Germany. Crew buried in Hannover.	Sgt J.M. Jacobs Killed Sgs W.R. Boucher Killed Sgt A.B. Radhourne Killed Sgt A. Ackland Killed Sgt W.D. Bracken Killed Sgt M.F. Donaldson Killed Sgt G. Kemp Killed
434 Sqdn: Halifax LK 702-F The crew have no known grave, but are on the Runneymede Memorial.	F/S B. Tedford Killed P/O I. Armitage Killed Sgt J.G. Tomlinson Killed Sgt K. Plummer Killed Sgt J.R. Wilson Killed P/O J.R. Mayo Killed Sgt N. Speight Killed
434 Sqdn: Halifax LK 953-C Those killed buried Sage, Oldengerg, Germany.	F/O R. Savage POW Stalag LI F/O J.A. Higgins POW Stalag LI P/O J.E. WheellerPOWStalagLI Sgt G. Woodruffe POW P/O R.F. McGregor RCAF Killed Sgt G.L. MacKay RCAF Killed Sgt J.R. Molesworth Killed
622 Sqdn: Stirling FE 150-F The crew's seventh trip.	F/Lt K.H. Denham POW Stalag LI F/O D.E. Woodward POW Stalag LI Sgt E.Johnson POW Stalag LI Sgt W. Hoggan POW Stalag LIII F/S G.E. Bartholmew POW Stalag LVI F/O J. Carter POW Stalag LI Sgt A. Littlewood POW Stalag LIII

Aircraft crashed in United Kingdom

Squadron and Aircraft	*Crew*
77 Sqdn: Halifax 264-K Collided with an aircraft of 102 on return at Barmby Moor, Pocklington; time 2355; crew killed.	Pilot: F/S C.C. Linehan. *Remainder of the crew* Sgt A.D. West, F/S E.B. Gosden, Sgt S. Tweddle, Sgt S. Elder, Sgt J.L. Bennett, Sgt W.G. Thomson.
101Sqn: Lancaster DV 291-V Crashed on Take Off Ludford Magnor	Pilot: P/O E. Wallace Remainder of crew Sgt L Crooks. Sgt P.L. Cairns, Sgt R Grundy, Sgt L Condon, Sgt Dunbon, Sgt Powney, P/O C Clothier

Squadron and Aircraft	*Crew*
102 Sqdn: Halifax LW 333-K Collided with an aircraft of 77 on return both crews were killed.	Pilot: P/O W. Hughes. *Ramainder of the crew* Sgt W.W. Cottle, Sgt R.B. Bainbridge, F/S D. Willington, Sgt J. Boxall, Sgt F.T. Dunn, Sgt R.A. Dabnor.
166 Sqn: Lan W4966-C2 Hit by flak over target area and over Hannover on return also again at the Dutch Coast crashlanded at Bradwell Bay airfield 0035. On injuries to the crew.	Pilot : Sgt W.V.Butler. Remainder of the crew Sgt R.E.W Cheeseman, Sgt J.W.Thomas, Sgt J. Holden, Sgt F.C.Collins, Sgt McIntyre, Sgt J.M.Preston
467 Sqn: Lancaster L7574 Crashed on Take Off Waddington	Pilot: Sgt C C Schombery RAAF Remainder of crew Sgt H Steels, F/Sgt L. R. Seton RAAF, Sgt C. Gifford RAAF, F/Sgt B.W.Fitzgerald, Sgt H.A.Brown RAAF, P/O L.J. Calderwood RAAF

23rd/24th November 1943

Squadron and Aircraft	*Crew*
7 Sqdn: Lanc JA 932-M Crashed at Oudeschild on the island of Texel. Crew buried in Denburg Cemetery, Holland. Hit by flak.	F/Sgt G.W. Tindle RNAF Killed age 23 Sgt C.H. Hollingsworth Killed Sgt J.H. Pepper Killed Sgt A.D. West Killed Sgt J. Forrest Killed Sgt G.W. Smith Killed Sgt F.W. Harris Killed
7 Sqdn: Lanc JB 480-N The crew have no known grave, but are on the Runneymede Memorial.	F/Sgt F.R. Page Killed F/Lt J. Bannon Killed F/Sgt L.J. Allum DFM Killed Sgt A.J. Stanton Killed Sgt E.H. Blanks Killed Sgt W.J. Davies Killed Sgt W.N. Kinsey Killed
12 Sqdn: Lanc JB 537-N The crew are buried in the Reichswald War Cemetery. Crashed at Vrees.	F/O C.E Jones Killed F/Lt G. Soulsby Killed Sgt S. Knight Killed F/Sgt T.W. Boynton Killed Sgt B.H. Farndale Killed Sgt W. Hazeldine Killed Sgt H.E. Petersen RCAF Killed later F/Sgt
44 Sqdn: Lanc DV 329-W Crashed Rastdorf. Crew buried Reichswald War Cemetery, Germany.	F/Lt C.E. Hill Killed P/O E.G. Wright Killed P/O J. Marsden Killed F/O C.W. Nunn Killed F/Sgt T.W. Myerscough Killed Sgt P.B. Kiewan POW Stalag 4B Sgt R. Ledsham Killed
44 Sqdn: Lanc LM 373-V Crew buried in Berlin.	P/O W. Buckel Killed age 19 Sgt E. Ambrose Killed F/Sgt J. Beebe Killed Sgt P. Middleton Lees Killed Sgt G.J. O'Brian Killed Sgt J. Taylor Killed F/Sgt M.H. Hardy RAAF Killed Sgt P.M. Lees Killed

Squadron and Aircraft

Crew

44 Sqdn: Lanc LM 374-S
The crew have no known grave, but are on the
Runneymede Memorial.

P/O C.K. Hanscomb Killed
Sgt C.C. Langley Killed
P/O H.J. Whitticks Killed
Sgt A. Reeves Killed
F/O C.S. Laxton Killed
Sgt A.C..M. Seaman Killed
Sgt R.C. Strickland RCAF Killed

83 Sqdn: Lanc JB 284-C
The crew are buried in Berlin.
Hit by flak crashed in the target area.

W/C R. Hilton DSO DFC Killed
Sgt F.E. Burton-Burgess Killed
F/Sgt S.J. Davis Killed
F/O G. Ainsworth Killed
S/L A.F. Chisholm DEC Killed
Sgt B.G. Tucker DFM Killed
F/Lt J.P. Crebbin DFC Killed

97 Sqdn: Lanc JB 218-Y
Those killed are on the Runneymede Memorial.

F/Sgt J.A. Penny POW Stalag LVI
Sgt R.T. Fathers Killed
Sgt J. Graham Killed
Sgt R.A. Campbell Killed
Sgt J.R. Cowan Killed
F/Sgt R.S. Mortham Killed
F/Sgt P.W. Dries RCAF Killed

100 Sqdn: Lanc JB 564
Those killed are on the Runneymede Memorial.
Abandon aircraft over target area and it came down
into a river or lake near Berlin.

WO S.C. Leman POW
Sgt L.F. Daniels POW Stalag IVB
P/O J.R. Lake POW Stalag LI
F/Sgt W.E Jefferies RCAF POW Stalag IVB
Sgt F.A. Fuller Killed
Sgt W.E. Lloyd Killed
Sgt A.G. Chandler Killed

103 Sqdn: Lanc JB 528-Q
Crashed at Werder-Havel, Germany. Those killed
buried in Berlin.

F/O J.D. Johnston Killed
Sgt R. Crossley POW Stalag LIII
F/O R.H. Kerr RCAF Killed
Sgt A.H. Stanton POW Stalag 357
F/O R.T. Jones POW Stalag L1
Sgt D. Clark Killed
Sgt J.B. Reilly Killed

139 Sqdn: Mosquito DZ 614
Crashed at Borkheide through flak over Berlin.
P/O Booker buried in Berlin.

F/Lt A.R. Head DFC POW Stalag LIII
P/O G.R. Brooker RAAF Killed

156 Sqdn: Lanc JB 223-M

F/Sgt King, F/O McDonald, F/Lt Stewart buried in
Berlin. Remainder names on the Runneymede
Memorial.

P/O W.H. Rose RAAF DFC Killed age 22
F/Lt C.V. Harvey DFC MID Killed
F/O E.R. Mitchell DFM Killed
P/O W. Anderson DFC Killed
P/O M.M. Patrick RAAF DFC Killed
F/O R.H. McDonald RAAF Killed
F/Lt H.W.J. Stewart RCAF DFC Killed
F/Sgt F P King Killed

166 Sqdn: Lanc JA 865-A
Those killed are on the Runneymede Memorial.

Sgt Iverson buried in Berlin remainder name on the
Runneymede Memorial.
Crashed in the Leluin/Emstal area.
Sgt Davies did survive descent.

W/O E.R. Grove POW Stalag III
Sgt A. Rossi POW Stalag IVB
E/Sgt E.W.D. Hunt RNZAF POW Stalag IVB
Sgt A.C. Smith POW Stalag IVB
Sgt S.G. Paterson POW Stalag IVB
Sgt J.F.M. Davies Killed
Sgt J.E.W. Iverson Killed

207 Sqdn: Lanc W 4959-S
The crew has no known grave, but are on the
Runneymede Memorial.

F/Lt D.E. Reay Killed
Sgt C. Burton Killed
F/Sgt A.J.C. Williams Killed
Sgt C. O'Connor Killed

Squadron and Aircraft	*Crew*
	P/O R.E. Mair Killed
	Sgt J. Richardson Killed
	Sgt L.J. Lewis Killed

405 Sqdn: Lanc JA 939-C
Crashed Ter Apel Holland in Friesland Province.
Those killed buried Vlagtwedde, Grongien,
Holland.

F/Lt H. Le Froy RCAF DFC Killed
F/Lt C.W. Cole DFC POW Stalag Ll
F/O W.J. Lawrence RCAF Killed
F/Lt R.A. Gardiner RCAF DFC Killed
F/Sgt J.G. O Dell RCAF Killed
F/Sgt J.G.S. Kavanugh RCAF Killed
P/O P J Mc Scott Killed

405 Sqdn: Lanc JB 182-O
P/O Scott is buried at Vlagtwedde Gen Cemetery,
Groningen, Holland. The remainder of the crew are
recorded on the Runneymede Memorial.

F/O H.T. Clark RCAF Killed
P/O E.J.B. Moss Killed
Sgt R.N.P Critchlow Killed
Sgt A.P. Hateley Killed
Sgt W.C. Higgs Killed
Sgt J.E. Goss Killed

405 Sqdn: Lanc LL 623-J
The crew has no known grave, but are on the
Runneymede Memorial.

F/O D.M. Bell Killed
F/O R.A. Quinney Killed
F/Sgt R.G. Williams Killed
F/Sgt H. Smith Killed
Sgt L.G. Hanton RCAF Killed
F/Sgt R.O. Hiscock Killed
Sgt R.G.B. Shea Killed

460 Sqdn: Lanc ED 664-CJ2
Those killed are buried in the Reichswald War
Cemetery.
Crashed near Modlen Bahonof

F/Sgt M.J. Freeman RAAF Killed age 28
F/Sgt A.F. Ashley POW Stalag IVB
Sgt P.A.F. Liddle POW Stalag IVB
E/Sgt C.R. Kingsmill RAAF POW Stalag IVB
Sgt D.A. Jackson POW Stalag IVB
Sgt D.B. Aberle Killed
Sgt T. Elliott Killed

460 Sqdn: Lanc W 4162-A2
Those killed are buried in Berlin.
Exploded near Luben after a nightfighter attack.

F/Sgt R. Brown RAAF Killed age 23
F/Sgt R.M. Henderson RAAF Killed
F/Sgt D. Louthean RAAF Killed
Sgt G.S. Camm Killed
Sgt G. White Killed
P/O D.A. Crookston RAAF POW Stalag LIII
F/Sgt J.W. Muntz RAAF Killed

630 Sqdn: Lanc JB 135-L
Crew names on the Runneymede Memorial.

P/O J. Howe Killed
F/Sgt N.J.Y. Goulding Killed
F/O D.E. Caudrey Killed
P/O A.J. Matthews Killed
Sgt T.N. Blanc Killed
Sgt R. Inglis Killed
Sgt J.G. Smith Killed

630 Sqdn: Lanc JB 236-0
Crashed on the bombing range at Fassberg. Those
killed buried in the Hannover War Cemetery.

F/Lt F.L. Perrers RNZAF Killed age 30
Sgt C.H. Pell Killed
F/Sgt J. Clapperton Killed
F/Sgt J.F. White Killed
F/Sgt R.B. Mutum POW Stalag LVI
Sgt L.H. Cooper Killed
F/Sgt E.C. Crowe POW

Aircraft which crashed on returning from Berlin

Squadron and Aircraft	*Crew*
7 Sqn: Lan JA 971-J2	F/O P.K.B Williams

Squadron and Aircraft   *Crew*

Hit by flak over target, elevator blown away   Sgt N R Sefton
five of the crew bales out and pilot and naviator   W/O J.M. Alexander
baled out later about 20 miles north of UK airfield.   Sgt G. Stainforth
                                                          F/Sgt A.Frewin
                                                          Sgt L.G. Glaus
                                                          Sgt F.W.Harris

9 Sqdn: Lanc DV 327-N   P/O G. Ward
On making a turn to port for second approach at   Sgt J. Sutton
height of 500 feet, the aircraft made a shallow dive   Sgt F. Keene
to starboard, did not respond to the controls and   Sgt G.L. James
crashed landed near Bardney. The crew were   Sgt G.E.K. Bedwell
unhurt.   Sgt N.F. Dixon
                                                          Sgt W.L. Doran RCAF

9 Sqdn: Lanc ED 656-V   P/O N.J. Robinson Killed B Derrinton, Ireland
Crashed at 2345 ten miles NE of Bardney at   F/O C.G. Hinton Killed B Cheltenham, Glos
Ludford Magna, Sgt Casey and F/Sgt Mitchell   Sgt R.G. Taylor Killed Cambridge City Cem
taken to RAF Hospital Rauceby.   F/Sgt T.R. Davis Killed Withernsea, Yorks
                                                          F/Sgt T.B.J. Pitman Killed B Stanford Orcas,Dorset
                                                          Sgt W.E.Jones Killed B Birkenhead, Cheshire
                                                          F/Sgt L.E. Mitchell Injured
                                                          Sgt J. Casey Injured

12 Sqn: Lanc JB 465-V   Sgt D.C.H. Maxwell
Crashed on take off at Wickenby.   Sgt P.H. Lambert
                                                          Sgt Harrison
                                                          P/O C.W. Kruger RCAF
                                                          Sgt Wilcock
                                                          Sgt F.W. Peppeiatt
                                                          Sgt W.F.H Smedmore

49 Sqdn: Lanc JB 229-S   F/O D.G. Turner Unhurt
Crashed on the beach at Chapel St Leonard's,   Sgt J.K. Finlayson Injured
Skegness.   Sgt J.N. Hughes Injured
                                                          Sgt L.H Nightingale Injured
                                                          Sgt J.N. Bennett Injured
                                                          F/O W. Pearce Injured
                                                          Sgt T.D. Horne Unhurt

156 Sqdn: Lanc JB 293   F/Sgt G.W. Fordyce RCAF Killed
Crashed at Bercham Newton at 2322 (Manor Farm,   B Cambridge City Cem
Harpley).   Sgt L.J. Collins Injured
                                                          F/Sgt A.E. Egan Injured
                                                          Sgt G. Johnson Killed B Leeds(Arnley) Cem
                                                          Sgt R. Harries Injured
                                                          Sgt R.M. Hodges Killed B Cambridge City Cem
                                                          F/Sgt J.S. Minogue Injured

426 Sqdn: Lanc LL 629-G   P/O D.R. De Bloeme Injured
Crashed into rising ground at High Mowthorpe   F/Lt J.B. Cleveland Unhurt
Farm nr Malton, Yorks after being hit by flak over   Sgt W.H. McGarrigan Unhurt
Berlin, causing damage to one engine; it returned   F/O G.D. Huffman RCAF Killed
on three engines.   B Harrogate Cemetery
Hit high ground Marthorpe, Yorks.   Sgt F.C. Borst Injured
                                                          F/Sgt W.G. Martin Injured
                                                          F/Sgt C.D. Manders RCAF Killed
                                                          B Harrogate City Cem

26th/27th November 1943

Squadron and Aircraft   *Crew*

7 Sqdn: Lanc JB 538-G   W/C. F.W. Hilton POW Stalag LI
P/O Leonard buried in the Durnbach War   Sgt J.C. Naylor POW Stalag IVB
Cemetery, Germany.   Sgt J. Lamb POW Stalag III

Squadron and Aircraft	*Crew*

Sgt D. Spence POW
Sgt C. Dunmall POW Stalag 4B
F/Sgt C.H. Moody POW
P/O A.M. Leonard Killed

7 Sqdn: Lanc JB 303-F
Crashed north of Frankfurt. Those killed buried in
Hannover.
Attacked by a nightfighter.
Crashed at Winkels & Mergerskirchen

F/O G.A. Beaumont Killed
F/Sgt D. Wilson Killed
Sgt D. Ashworth Killed
Sgt W.A. Meek Killed
P/O A.E. Ansfield POW Stalag 1
Sgt P.J. Palmer Killed
F/Sgt A.C.Turner RNZAF POW Stalag 4B

49 Sqdn: Lanc JB 362-D
Crashed near Gransee. Those killed buried in
Berlin.

W/O R. Brunt Killed age 21
Sgt H. Bronsky Killed
Sgt F. E. Ashman Killed
Sgt R.W. Norley DFM Killed
Sgt A. Wilson Killed
Sgt J.G. Burrows POW
Sgt R.P. O'Dea RAAF Killed

50 Sqdn: Lanc DV 178-N
Sgt Billett buried in Becklingen War Cemetery,
Saltau, Germany.
Sgt Ward buried Sage War Cemetry.

P/O J.C. Adams RAAF POW Stalag I
Sgt T. Midgley POW 2/Pilot
Sgt T. Raweliffe POW Stalag III
F/Sgt D.R.Crawford RAAF POW Stalag IVB
Sgt G.M. Hastie POW Stalag IVB
Sgt W.J. Ward Killed
Sgt C.W. Billett Killed
F/Sgt C Thomas POW Stalag 4B

51 Sqdn: Lanc W 4198-H
Crashed at Bad Zwischenahn.
Crew buried Sage War Cemetery, Oldenberg,
Germany.

P/O A.J. Eaves Killed age 24
Sgt J. Robertson Killed
Sgt R.C. Cantin Killed
F/O D.C. White Killed
F/Sgt F.K. Fuller RAAF Killed
F/Sgt H.L. Sweet Killed
Sgt J.A. Weston Killed

57 Sqdn: Lanc JB 485-L
Crashed at Neuenlandrmoor. Those killed buried
Sage, Oldengerg, Germany.
Shot down by a nighfighter and crashed near
Bookholzberg-Neuenlands.

Sgt H. Beaine Killed
Sgt L.A Williamson Killed
Sgt B.N. Deas POW Stalag LIII
F/Sgt J.A. Armstrong RCAF POW Stalag IVB
Sgt W. Dwyer Killed
Sgt J. MacKay Killed
Sgt F/O R.G. Pickard RCAF Killed

61 Sqdn: Lanc DV 297-O
Sgt Johnson is on the US Cemetery Margaten
Memorial, Holland, remainder on the Runneymede
Memorial

P/O A.P.E. Strange Killed
P/O C.J.B. Cogdell Killed
F/Sgt J.B. Toombs RCAF Killed
F/O D.H. Calman Killed
Sgt E. Smith Killed
Sgt E.F. Johnson USAAF Killed
F/O J.A. Stephens RCAF Killed

61 Sqdn: Lanc DV 339-W
Crew names on the Runneymede Memorial.

P/O J.C. McAlpine RAAF Killed
Sgt E. Vine Killed
F/Sgt H.W. Harris RAAF Killed
F/Sgt V.A. Martin RAAF Killed
P/O S. Heald Killed
Sgt B.H. Varey RCAF Killed
Sgt H.S. Oldfield Killed

61Sqn: Lanc W 4198-H
Crashed Borgermoor, South of Sorwold.

P/O A.J.D. Eaves Killed
Sgt J.Robertson Killed
F/O D.C. White Killed

Squadron and Aircraft	Crew
Crew buried Sage War Cemetery.	Sgt R.C.H. Cantin Killed Sgt J.A. Weston Killed F/Sgt K.R. Filler RAAF Killed F/Sgt H.L. Sweet Killed
83 Sqdn: Lanc JB 459-T Crashed at Seelenberg. Crew buried Durnbach War Cemetery, Germany.	F/O A.B. Smeaton Killed Sgt A.W. Savoury Killed F/O V.W.J. Nunn Killed Sgt R.A. Gillam Killed F/Lt R.M. Smalley DFC Killed F/Sgt R.S. Nelson RAAF Killed Sgt W.S. Walton Killed
83 Sqdn: Lanc JA 913-G Crew names on the Runneymede Memorial Crashed at Schonnalde nr Berlin. Crew buried Doberitz but could not be found after the war.	P/O K.R.G. Millar RCAF Killed age 22 Sgt F.R. Birks Killed F/Sgt R.H. Pennells DFM Killed F/Sgt J.H.S. Harsley Killed F/Sgt M.H.. King Killed W/O S.T. Stacey DFM Killed F/Sgt K.G. Davis RCAF DFM Killed Later WOII
101 Sqdn: Lanc DV 268-0 Crashed at Astrup (Visbek). Those killed buried in Sage War Cemetery, Oldenburg, Germany. Sgt Josa repartriated 6/2/1945.	SGT P. R. Zanchi Killed later F/Sgt Sgt L.A. Crooks Killed Sgt J.C.Jossa POW Sgt H.S. Waller Killed Sgt W. Rowland Killed Sgt D.W. Timms Killed Sgt A.G. Lovesay Killed
101 Sqdn: Lanc DV 289-T Crashed at Heuchelbein, Germany. All of those killed buried Berlin, F/O Spofford died 21 July 1944, and is also buried in Berlin.	F/Sgt J.G. Bennett RCAF Killed Sgt R.W. Hodgson Killed F/Lt F.G.T. Collins Killed Sgt H. Feeney Killed F/Sgt M.J. Kennedy RCAF Killed Sgt E. North Killed Sgt A. McKeenan POW Stalag 357 F/O G.L. Spofford RCAF Died as a POW at Stalag L1
101Sqn: Lanc DV 285-Q Shot down by a nighfighter flown by Hptm Eckart Wilhelm von Bonin II/NJG1 Crashed Aywaille (Liege) Those killed buried at Heverlee War Cem	P/O A.J.S Walker POW P/O S. Mayer CGM Killed P/O J.G. Blandford Evaded F/O A.W. Gadd DFC Killed Sgt J.K. Robertson Killed Sgt R.A. Hebditch POW Stalag 357 F/O K.N. Hicklin DFM Killed P/O R. Scott DFM Killed
103 Sqdn: Lanc JB 458-V Crashed at Oberan, nr Altenstad, Germany. Those killed buried Berlin War Cemetery, Germany.	Sgt E.S. Siddall Killed age 20 Sgt W.C. Buzan Killed Sgt D. Blue Killed Sgt AM. Grimson RCAF Killed Sgt D.J.J Evans Killed Sgt H. Wood POW Stalag IVB Sgt N.D. Taylor Killed
103 Sqdn: Lanc JB 350-L Those killed buried in Berlin.	F/O A.J. Sumner Killed Sgt J. Gibson POW F/Sgt R. Butler Killed Sgt A.H. Masters Killed P/O P.J. Duffy RCAF POW Stalag L1 Sgt P. Gallagher Killed Sgt R.H. Bussell Killed

Squadron and Aircraft	*Crew*
103 Sqdn: Lanc JB 527-B All the crew are buried in the Berlin War Cemetery. Crashed Ahiensfolde, near Berlin.	F/O R.E.V. Pugh DFM Killed Sgt P.A. Barnes Killed F/O D.S. Thom RAAF Killed F/O M.H. King Killed Sgt G.W. Prescott Killed Sgt A. Mavromatis Killed F/O G. Booth Killed
106 Sqdn: Lanc JB 592-W Crashed at Gross Karben, the Sqdn's first loss for a month. Crew buried in Durnbach War Cemetery F/O Hoboken from Belgium.	F/O J.R.C. Van Hoboken DFC Killed age 32 Sgt G E.G Lucas DFM Killed F/O J.P.J.Jenkins Killed P/O J.C. Graham Killed F/O AW. Read Killed Sgt E.W. Davies Killed F/O H.G. Stuffin Killed
115 Sqdn: Lanc DS 793-L Crashed at Stockheim, Germany. Crew buried in Durnbach War Cemetery.	F/O E.B. Woolbouse Killed Sgt W. Bell Killed P/O W.A. Mitchell RCAF Killed Sgt A.V. Baker Killed Sgt H.H. Falls Killed Sgt T.A. Monk Killed Sgt J. Pallanca Killed
166 Sqdn: Lanc DV 247-F Those killed buried in the Reichswald War Cemetery, Germany. Sgt Collins went to help Sgt O'Malley who was trapped but both perished.	W/O J.E. Thomas DFC POW Stalag 357 Sgt J.J. Robshaw POW Stalag LVI Sgt D.J. Edwards POW Stalag LVI Sgt W.G. Bell POW Stalag L III Sgt E.M.L. Davies POW Stalag IVB Sgt A.V. Collins DFM Killed Sgt W. O'Malley Killed
166 Sqdn: Lanc DV 387-W Crew buried in the Rheinberg War Cemetery, Germany. F/O O'Brian from Tipperrary, Ireland. Crashed in the Mondengladbach area	F/O D.H.P O'Brian Killed age 26 Sgt G.E.J. Ballard Killed Sgt H.J. Beattie RCAF Killed F/O J. Howe Killed Sgt D.J. Howell Killed F/Sgt F.E. Nowland RAAF Killed Sgt W.A. Green Killed
408 Sqdn: Lanc DS 723-L They have no known grave, but are on the Runneymede Memorial. F/O North was the Sqdn Navigation Leader and F/Lt Glasspool, the Signals Leader.	S/L/A/W/C A.C. Mair RCAF DFC Killed F/O W.R.E. North DFC Killed F/O A.W. Douglas Killed F/Lt S.A.H. Glasspool Killed F/Sgt G. Fielding Killed Sgt L.H. Matthews Killed Sgt C.F. Kirsch Killed
426 Sqdn: Lanc DS 679-R They have no known grave, but are on the Runneymede Memorial.	S/L A.J. Hughes RCAF Killed P/O W.H. Boles RCAF Killed PLO F.D. Rawlings Killed F/O G.H. Buchanan RCAF Killed Sgt W.J. McLean Killed Sgt F. Wikinson Killed F/Sgt K.W. Sawyer RCAF Killed
460 Sqdn: Lanc ED 370-B2 Crashed near Grossenkneten Railway Station, Oldenburg. Crew buried Berlin.	Sgt E.J. Stones RAAF Killed Sgt R.G. Jones Killed Sgt N.W. McNair RCAF Killed Sgt K.G. Smith Killed Sgt W. Belton Killed Sgt J.H. McIvor Killed Sgt G.D. Arnott RCAF Killed

Squadron and Aircraft   *Crew*

463 Sqdn: Lanc DV 338-N   F/Sgt J.W. Fowler Killed
All this crew are buried in Berlin. 463 had only   Sgt J.L. Williams Killed
been formed on 25th November and this was their   Sgt J.W. Barker Killed
first casualty. The first man that took off for Berlin   Sgt J.E. Thomas Killed
from 463 was P/O G.F. Baker DFC at 1710 in V   Sgt J.P. Eerier Killed
for Victor.   Sgt W.T. Sherwin RCAF Killed
                                                 Sgt A.E.G. Thomas Killed

467 Sqn: Lanc DV331-N   P/O J.W.Fowler RAAF Killed
Crashed at Trechwitz   Sgt J.L.Williams Killed
All are buried in Berlin.   Sgt J.W. Barker Killed
                                                 Sgt J.E.Thomas Killed
                                                 Sgt J.P Ferrier Killed
                                                 F/Sgt W.T. Sherwin RAAF Killed
                                                 Sgt A.E.G Thomas Killed

514 Sqdn: Lanc DS 814-M   F/O M.R. Cantin RCAF Killed age 21
Crew buried in Berlin.   Sgt S.E. Smith RCAF Killed
                                                 Sgt W.G.F. Saddler Killed
                                                 Sgt W.E.T. Mitchell Killed
                                                 Sgt L.F. Eyre Killed
                                                 Sgt R.N. Walne Killed
                                                 Sgt K.G. King Killed

550 Sqdn Lanc LN 379-S (late 100 Sqdn)   F/Lt P.J.M. Prangley Killed age 22
Crashed at Havel Bie, Potsdam, on the outskirts of   Sgt A.K. Ward Killed
Berlin. 550 had been formed on 25th November   F/O G.H.R.F. Harris Killed
from 'C' Flight of 100 Sqdn. Those killed buried in   P/O J.W. Lowe RCAF POW Stalag LI
Berlin.   F/Sgt P.W. Smith POW
                                                 Sgt R. Redfern Killed
                                                 Sgt F.C. Diggle Killed

619 Sqn: Lanc DV 381-B   F/Lt R.D.Rayment Killed
                                                 Sgt M.J.Lynch Killed
                                                 F/O J.Kellett Killed
                                                 Sgt G.

625 Sqdn: Lanc ED 809-T   F/O M.C McSorley RCAF Killed age 22
Crashed at Apeldoorn. Gelderland, Holland.   P/O J.D. Lynch RCAF Killed
Sgt Lynch buried Groesbeak, Sgt Green Buried   Sgt B.L. Gooding Killed
Ughelen, Sgt Foulkes Buried Ughelen, Sgt Bolt   F/O G.F.R. Green Killed
buried On Runneymede Memorial, Sgt Paice   Sgt E.L. Foulkes Killed
buried at Ugchelen, F/O McSorley buried at   Sgt N. Bolt Killed
Ughelen.   P/O P.R. Paice Killed

Shot down by a nighfighter flown by Uffz Amsberg
of III/NJG1.
Crashed at theVarenna south of Apeldoom.

626 Sqdn: Lanc DV 388-S2   F/Sgt C.J.E. Kindt RCAF Killed Later WO2
Crashed at Finow nr Berlin. Buried in Berlin.   F/Sgt J.R.R. Small RCAF Killed
                                                 Sgt T.G. Brady Killed
                                                 Sgt A.S. McDonald RCAF Killed
                                                 Sgr J.A. Calloway Killed
                                                 Sgt C.Johnson Killed
                                                 Sgt F. Matthews Killed

Aircraft crashed in the United Kingdom

Squadron and Aircraft	*Crew*
12 Sqn:Lanc JB 354-O Swung off the runway on returning from Berlin.	P/O R.S. Yell RAAF Sgt W.J.C. MacDonald RCAF P/O K.R. Middlemiss RCAF Sgt T.A. Finch F/Sgt J.H. Nutt Sgt K.B. Reeves Sgt S.Bates
12 Sqn:Lanc JB 464-D Hit by flak and landed wheels up on return to Binbrook	Sgt A.G. Twitchett Sgt D. Leatherbarron Sgt D. Robertson Sgt S. Burnell Sgt C.W. Farrant P/O M. Hewitt Sgt P.F.J.Sykes RCAF
49 Sqdn: Lanc JB 235-C Crashed on the outer circuit on return from Berlin to Fiskerton and caught fire.	Sgt R.J. Richardson Killed Sgt H.G Boswell Killed Sgt Carr Killed Sgt Cartwright Killed P/O Lane Injured Sgt Winterborn Injured Sgt M.O Mahoney Injured P/O H. Lowe Killed P/O Richardson buried-Cambridge City P/O Lowe buried Biddulph,- Staffs Sgt Boswell buried- Manchester Sgt Carr buried –Stockton-on-Tees Sgt Cartwright buried -Bournemouth P/O Lowe buried Biddulph, Staffs
50 Sqn:Lanc DV 377 Struck a van whilst landing at Skellingthoorpe and then collided with Lanc JA 961 which was bogged down in wet ground, both caught fire	P/O E.F. Weatherstone Sgt D. Gregory F/Sgt P.E. Thompson Sgt P.H. Lane Sgt A.D.F. Spruce Sgt H.J. Lineham Sgt R.A. Collingwood
50 Sqdn: Lanc ED 393-K K-King had been trying to land for some while when it finally hit a farmhouse at Hayton nr Pocklington, killing the farmer and his wife; the cause was lack of fuel.	F/Sgt J.W. Thompson Killed Sgt R.W. Laws Killed F/Sgt S. Chapman Killed Sgt A.F.Conlon Killed Sgt C.R. Corbett Injured Sgt T.A. Wyllie Injured Sgt A.D. Spiers Killed F/Sgt Thompson buried – Greenford Park F/Sgt Champman buried-Wimbledon Sgt Conlon buried-Heworth. Durham Sgt Spiers buried- Harrogate
50 Sqn: Lanc JA 961-A On return became booged down and then hit by DV 377 after it had collided with a van.	P/O D.R Toovey Sgt R.G.C. Pagett Sgt J Olsson Sgt W.J. Kelbrick F/O F.T. Bedingham Sgt J.P. Flynn Sgt J.B. Knight

Squadron and Aircraft	*Crew*

100 Sqn: Lanc JB 554-K2
Crashed and burnt out at RAF Grimsby.

P/O L J Stow
Sgt J.E. Lamb
Sgt A.D.Walker
Sgt D.R. Tapper
Sgt R.K.A. Grainger
Sgt. M.R. Shear
Sgt. D.J. Derlin

103 Sqdn: Lanc ED 417
Collided with a Halifax JN966 while approaching
the base for landing. Crashed at Middleton-St-
George.

F/O R.W. Brevitt Killed
Sgt M.W. Cartmell Killed
Sgt J.K. Cubey Killed
Sgt S.T.K. Bowyer Seriously Injured
Sgt I.B. Morgan Killed
Sgt S.T.K. Ingle Killed
Sgt G. Bruce Killed

F/O Brevitt buried – Harrogate
Sgt Cartmell buried – Keswick
Sgt Cubey buried-Harrogate
Sgt Morgan buried – Llaneli, Wales
Sgt Ingle buried - Harrogate
Sgt Bruce buried -Caddonfoot, Selkirk

103 Sqn: Lanc JB 423
Landed at Croft a mile from Elsham Wolds on
return.

W/O W.H. Frost
Sgt J. Woodward
Sgt L.H. Wise
Sgt R. Huddart
P/O J.W. Lowrie
Sgt A. Burdett
Sgt C.H. Seldan

106 Sqn: Lanc ED 873
Lost power on take off and turned back crashing in
a field near Metheringham at 20.15.

P/O R.F. Neil
Sgt M.J. Sherwyn
Sgt J.F. Harmes
F/O G.L. Ashman
F/Sgt T.J. Robertson
Sgt R.P. Prothero
Sgt A.L. Parker

408 Sqn: Lanc DS 712-G
Hit by flak over Magdeburg on the return leg
wounding Sgt Robert in the foot.
attacked by a nightfighter over Ijssemeer damaging
the starboard inner engine and then the starboard
outer failed over Fiskerton crash landed 2 miles SE
of Lincoln.

F/Sgt R.T. Llloyd RCAF
Sgt H. Nightingale
F/O J.F. Fowler RCAF
F/Sgt G.E. Cameron RCAF
Sgt. L.Lowe
Sg E. Williams
Sgt M.A. Robert RCAF Injured

619 Sqdn: Lanc DV 381-B
Ditched in the Sea.

Names on the Runneymede Memorial

F/Lt R.D. Rayment Killed
Sgt M.J. Lynch Killed
F/O J. Kellett Killed
Sgt D.W. Archibald Killed
F/Sgt J.T. Richards Killed
F/Sgt C.S. Cook Killed
F/Sgt J.A. Fowler Killed

619 Sqdn: Lanc DV 336-U
Crashed on return just south of Elvington airfield.

P/O K.J. Mears Killed
Sgt L. Pearse Killed
P/O G.G. Salt Killed
Sgt D.W. Blundell Killed
Sgt A.R. Wilcher Killed
SgtW.W.N. Knights RAAF Killed
Sgt H.V. Birch Killed

P/O Mears buried Twickenham, Middx
F/Sgt Pearse buried-Harrogate

Squadron and Aircraft	*Crew*
	P/O Salt buried-Harrogate
	F/Sgt Knights buried- Harrogate
	F/Sgt Birch buried Brompton,London
	Sgt's Blundell and Wilcher names on the
	Runneymede Memorial
619 Sqn: Lanc EE111 Crashed on to Fourholme Sands on return, crew baled out over Humber Estuary.	F/Lt W.E.D. Bell Sgt M.V. Pink F/Sgt J.A. Featherstone F/Sgt J.A. Walsh Sgt J. Webster F/O T.K. Graves F/O J. Kemp
619 Sqn: Lanc EE168 Crashed on return near Hutton Cranswick Airfield, York caught fire.	F/Lt Tomlinson F/Sgt E.G. Cass P/O T.A. Peatfield F/Sgt J. Simkin Sgt H.W. Thompson Sgt W. Dunham F/Sgt P.D. Mitchell
626 Sqn: Lanc LM 362-A2 Crashed at Lissington.	F/Lt V. Wood F/O J. Wilkinson Sgt C.G. Davis P/O L.N. Kirby F/Sgt G.H. Wood Sgt W. Cruickshank Sgt S.F. Hare F/Sgt R. Hornby
630 Sqn: Lanc JB 597 Crashed Holme-on-Spallding-Moor on return.	F/Sgt S.A. Edwards Sgt D.H. Ryder F/Lt R. Heap Sgt H. Grant Sgt H.M. Kent Sgt G. J. Hill Sgt. L. Diggle

2nd/3rd December 1943

Squadron and Aircraft	*Crew*
9 Sqdn: Lanc DV 332-D The crew are buried in the Berlin War Cemetery. Crashed N.E of Brunsenddorf at 23.00	F/Lt R.F. Wells Killed Sgt D.J. Nutunan Killed P/O A.U. Duncan Killed F/Sgt K. Garnett Killed F/Sgt F. Smith Killed Sgt W.E.. Gough Killed F/Sgt S.V. Moss Killed
12 Sqdn: Lanc JB 478-C The crew are buried in the Berlin War Cemetery. Crashed near Bernan crew originally buried here.	W/O L. Lawrence Killed Sgt S.O.J. Boxhall Killed Sgt H. Johnson Killed Sgt J.L. Selkirk Killed Sgt R.E. Ward Killed Sgt G.H. Reveley Killed Sgt E.W. Pritch Killed
12 Sqdn: Lanc JB 463-R Crashed Blankenfelde. Sgt Forward buried Berlin remainder names on the Runneymede Memorial	F/O E.A. Taylor Killed F/Lt C.T. Bassage Killed Sgt A. Wiles Killed Sgt J.F. Cole Killed Sgt F.D. Beattie Killed

Squadron and Aircraft

Crew

Sgt Forward;s body found elswhere possibly
having baled out.

Sgt J. Broadhurst Killed
Sgt E.L. French Killed
Sgt A.H. Forward Killed

12 Sqdn: Lanc JB 285-G
Flt Lt Goldsmith buried in Reichswald War
Cemetery.
Harris repatriated in 1945.

F/O G. Goldsmith Killed age 25
Sgt G.B. Robertson POW Stalag III
Sgt J.W. Kirkbride POW Stalag LIII
Sgt R.W. Robinson POW Stalag 4B
Sgt J.D. Veals POW Stalag LIII
Sgt A.J. Harris POW Stalag LVI
Sgt R.T. Prestage POW stalag IVB

35 Sqdn: Halifax HX 167-C

Lt G. Hoverstad Killed
Sgt S.V. Brazier POW Stalag 4B
F/Sgt J.C. McDougall later F/O POW Stalag 4B
Sgt A.G. Briggs POW Stalag IVB
F/Sgt W.J. Cooke POW Stalag IVB
Sgt A.J. Williams POW Stalag IVB
Sgt A. Storme POW Stalag IVB

35 Sqdn: Halifax HR 876-S
The crew are buried in the Reichswald War
Cemetery.

F/Sgt H.V. Stinson Killed
Sgt M.J. Day Killed
Sgt D. Richardson killed later P/O
F/Sgt G. Allso Killed
F/Sgt F.C. McCubbin shown as WO Killed
Sgt R.H. Wells Killed
Sgt G. Merrill Killed

44 Sqdn: Lanc JA 700-P
The crew are buried in the Berlin War Cemetery.
F/O West's DFM Gazetted 12/3/1943

F/O G.A. West DFM Killed
Sgt A. Woodley Killed
P/O F.G. Cox Killed
F/O A.W. Hazell Killed
Sgt G.C. Cone Killed
F/Sgt W.J. Smith Killed
F/Sgt H.L. Clayton Killed

44 Sqdn: Lanc EE 179-B
The crew are buried in the Berlin War Cemetery.
Crashed at Gross Kientz

F/O W.F. Newell Killed
Sgt W.B. Curie Killed
P/O F.A. Dell Killed
P/O T. Rosser Killed
Sgt R.W. Jones Killed
P/O G.H. Kay Killed
Sgt W.P. Johnson Killed

49 Sqdn: Lanc JB 371-J
Sgt Walker buried in Berlin, Sgt Smith has no
known grave, but is on the Runneymede Memorial.
Attacked by a nightfighter and then hit by flak in
trying to get away from a seconds fighter.
Abosnon in the air and crashed near Berlin.

W/O R.W. Petty POW Stalag LIII
Sgt G. Lumsden POW Stalag IVB
Sgt T. Tulloch POW later F/Sgt Stalag IVB
Sgt S.J. Richards POW later F/Sgt Stalag IVB
Sgt O. Roberts POW later F/Sgt Stalag IVB
Sgt W.A. Walker killed later F/Sgt
Sgt E. Smith Killed
Sgt A.M. Tucker 2/Pilot POW Stalag 4B

50 Sqdn: Lanc DV 325-B
Sgt Moody is buried in Berlin.
Shot down by a nighfighter and crashed in the
target area.

F/Lt I.D. Bolton DEC POW Stalag I
Sgt G.E. Brown later F/Sgt POW Stalag 4B
P/O A.Mc. Watson DFC later F/Lt POW Stalag
  LIII
Sgt D. McCall POW Stalag 357
Sgt R.E. Moody Killed age 19
F/Sgt R.C. Forrester DFM POW Stalag 4B
F/Sgt A.A. McDougal RCAF POW Stalag 4B
Mr. L.L. Bennett POW War Correspondent

57 Sqdn: Lanc JB 372-R

F/O J.A. Williams Killed

Squadron and Aircraft	*Crew*
The crew have no known grave, but are on the Runneymede Memorial.	Sgt E. Hibbert Killed
	F/O B.P. Duval Killed
	Sgt B. Thomasberg RCAF Killed
	Sgt J.H. Chambers Killed
	Sgt E.W. Graves Killed
	P/O A.T. Hook RCAF Killed
57 Sqdn: Lanc JB 529-P	P/O E.H. Tansley Killed
The crew are buried in the Berlin War Cemetery.	Sgt J.P. Dalton Killed
	Sgt L.C. Brown Killed
	Sgt D. Park Killed
	Sgt E.H. Patrick Killed
	Sgt I. Groves Killed
	Sgt R.A. Lewis Killed
	F/Sgt H.A. Moad RCAF Killed
97 Sqdn: Lanc JB 190-V	S/L J.M. Garlick DFM& Bar Killed age 25
S/L Garlick 'B' Flight Commander. This crew was	P/O A.G. Boyd POW Stalag LI later F/O
left out of the order of battle. S/L Garlick is buried	F/Sgt E.O. Charlton DFM POW Stalag III
in Kiel War Cemetery, Germany.	F/Sgt F. Edwards Killed
F/Sgt Edwards on the Runneymede Memorial.	W/O F.O.A. Dawkins POW Stalag 4B
Abandon near Kiel.	F/Sgt J.M. Anderson POW Stalag 4B
	F/Sgt M.T. Ward RAAF POW Stalag 7B
101 Sqdn: Lanc JB 128-U2	S/L H.M. Robertson POW Stalag 7B
	Sgt S.T. Kones POW
	Sgt A.K. Hill RAAF POW Stalag 4B
	Sgt J. Ferguson POW Stalag 4B
	Sgt J. English POW Stalag 4B
	Sgt D. Lester POW Stalag 7B
	Sgt E.G.C. Fennell POW
	F/Sgt P.L.H. Fox POW Stalag 4B later W/O
101 Sqdn: Lanc LM 364-N2	Sgt L.V. Murrell Killed later F/Sgt
Crashed at Rehfelde. Crew buried in Berlin War	Sgt E. North Killed
Cemetery.	Sgt R.W. Webb Killed
	Sgt R.W. Hayes Killed
	Sgt R.H. Kirby Killed
	Sgt J. Cockroft Killed
	Sgt J.W. Garland Killed
	Sgt T.C. Bramley Killed
101 Sqdn: Lanc LM 363-P	F/Lt G.A.J. Frazer-Hollins DFC Killed
Crew names on the Runneymede Memorial.	Sgt C.H. Mortimer Killed later P/O
	F/O J.W.F. Deane Killed
T/Sgt buried US Cemetery Neuville-en.Condroz.	Sgt H.W. Witham Killed
Sgt's Heap, F/Lt Frazer-Hollins,F/O Deane,P/O	P/O H. Tiller Killed
Tiller, Sgt'sWelson and Witham buried in the	Sgt E. Heap DFM Killed
Rheinberg War Cemetery.	Tech/Sgt J.J. Kelly USAAF Killed
Crashed near Diepholz	F/O A. Weldon DFM Killed
103 Sqdn: Lanc JB 400-K	F/O C.P. Ready Killed age 33 later F/Lt
At 42 P/O Wakefield was much older than the	Sgt W.G. Neale Killed
remainder of the crew. Sgt Fox and F/O Ready	P/O A.J. Wakefield Killed
buried in Berlin. Remander names on the	Sgt W. Ainscow Killed
Runneymede Memorial.	Sgt S. Williams Killed
	Sgt H. Fox Killed
	Sgt W.E. Cheal Killed
103 Sqdn: Lanc JB 401-P	F/LtE F.T. Hoppo DFC Killed
The crew are buried in the Berlin War Cemetery.	Sgt R.S. Imeson Killed
	P/O F.J. Roberts RCAF DFM Killed
	Sgt J.B. Daniel Killed
	Sgt W.L. Sargent Killed
	Sgt R. Thomas Killed
	F/Sgt R.E. Black RCAF Killed later WOII

Squadron and Aircraft	*Crew*
103 Sqdn: Lanc JB 403-T The crew are buried in the Berlin War Cemetery.	W/O J.E. Bellamy Killed Sgt H. Brown Killed Sgt G.A. England Killed Sgt T.M. Robbins Killed Sgt E.G. Wyatt Killed Sgt H.C. Haslam Killed Sgt R.H. Tomlin Killed
106 Sqdn: Lanc ED 874 The crew are buried in the Berlin War Cemetery. Crashed at Lindenberg	P/O R.F. Neil Killed Sgt M.J. Sheryn MID Killed Sgt J.F. Harnes Killed F/O G.L. Ashman Killed F/ Sgt T.J. Robertson Killed Sgt R.P. Prothero Killed Sgt G.H. Stubbs Killed
156 Sqdn: Lanc JB 472-Z Crew buried in Becklingden War Cemetery, Soltau, Germany. Crashed near Fallingbostel where they were first buried.	W/O R.R. Wicks RAAF Killed F/ Sgt N. MacDonald RAAF POW F/Sgt N.J. Edmonds RAAF Killed Sgt P.E. Wells Killed W/O R.K. Thomas RAAF Killed P/O R.E. Inglis RAAF Killed W/O K.A. Wood RAAF Killed
156 Sqdn: Lanc JA 697-V Crew names on the Runneymede Memorial.	F/Lt B.J. Staniland Killed age 22 Sgt L.W. Fisher Killed Sgt P.J. Smart Killed Sgt C. Butler Killed Sgt D.G. Craig Killed Sgt W.A. Cox Killed F/Sgt W.E. Robinson Killed
156 Sqdn: Lanc JB 179-F F/Sgt Tinman, and Sgt Wood are buried in Berlin the remainder are recorded on the Runneymede Memorial.	F/Sgt J.G. Redfern Killed Sgt B. Carroll Killed F/Sgt J. Richmond Killed P/O L.J. Johnson RAAF Killed F/Sgt W.R. Clarke RCAF Killed showing later WOII Sgt K. Wood Killed F/Sgt W.R. Tinman RAAF Killed
166 Sqdn: Lanc JB 145-D Crashed at Hannover. Those killed buried in Hannover.	F/Sgt C.A. Cox Killed age 21 later WO Sgt T. Lafferty Killed P/O F.A. Denney Killed F/Sgt F.A.C Efemey Killed Sgt D.E.E Pitcher POW Sgt S.J. Pope Killed Sgt E. R. Claxton Killed
207 Sqdn: Lanc ED 601 All are buried in the Berlin War Cemetery. Crashed near Saalon	P/O A. Mann Killed Sgt S. Martin Killed F/O H.F.C. Bonner Killed Sgt A.S. Rusby Killed F/O E.V. Harley Killed Sgt F.L. Brisco RCAF Killed Sgt N.E. Petty Killed
426 Sqdn: Lanc DS 770 All are buried in Berlin War Cemetery.	P/O M.C. Shaw RCAF Killed F/O R.F. Waddington RCAF Killed Sgt D.E.P. Pearson Killed F/Sgt F.T.A. McKernon RCAF Killed Sgt A.B. McDonald Killed P/O J.T.E. Cummings-Bart RCAF Killed Sgt H.A. Keast RCAF Killed

Squadron and Aircraft	*Crew*
432 Sqdn: Lanc LL 618-F The crew are buried in the Berlin War Cemetery. Crashed at Mahlow originally buried at Kreis- Teltow	F/Sgt A.E. Slegg RCAFKilled F/Sgt G.P. Lowle RCAF Killed P/O S.W.F Baker RCAF Killed F/Sgt A.R. Morgan RCAF Killed later WOII Sgt W.E. Stinson RCAF Killed Sgt W H. Green RCAF Killed Sgt J. Wadsworth Killed 2/Pilot F/Sgt J.R. Goodwin RCAF Killed
460 Sqdn: Lanc DV 296-E2 All are buried in the Berlin War Cemetery. Crashed at Teltow.	F/Sgt C.H. Edwards RAAF Killed age 23 Sgt R. Tarlig Killed Sgt A. McDougall Killed Sgt D.J. Hobbs Killed F/Sgt J.I. McKee RAAF Killed Sgt P.R. Webber Killed Sgt F. Sullivan Killed
460 Sqdn: Lanc LM 316-H2 P/O's Boyd, Ellis and Sgt Keir are on the Runneymede Memorial the remainder are buried in Berlin. Crashed near Doberitz	F/O A.R. Mitchell RAAF Killed age 23 Sgt G.H. Cooper Killed F/Sgt I.R. Phelan RAAF Killed F/Sgt R.O. Cole RAAF Killed P/O J.0. Boyd RAAF Killed P/O L.J. Ellis Killed Sgt K.G.V. Keir Killed Captain Nordahl Greig Killed
460 Sqdn: Lanc W 4881-K Those killed buried in the Berlin War Cemetery. Exploded after an attack by a nightfighter.	P/O J.H.J. English RAAF DFC Killed age 22 Sgt A.G. Cole Killed P/O N.J. Anderson later F/G POW Stalag LI F/Sgt A.E. Kan RAAF Killed F/Sgt A.W. Catty POW Stalag IVB Sgt W.L. Miller POW Stalag IVB F/Sgt I. Rodin RCAF Killed Mr Norman Stockton War Correspondent Killed
460 Sqdn: Lanc JB 608-J Both F/O Alford an Australian and P/O Howe-Brown are buried in Berlin War Cemetery. Crashed at Bucholz	F/O T.D.H. Alford RAAF Killed F/Sgt A.E. Daley RAAF POW Stalag IVB F/Sgt L. Leask RAAF POW Stalag IVB F/Sgt N.L. Ginn RAAF POW Stalag IVB Sgt H.J. Follard POW Stalag IVB later F/Sgt P/O *F.D.K.* Howe-Brown Killed Sgt S.T. Mason POW Stalag IVB
460 Sqdn: Lanc JB 61 l-R The crew are buried in the Berlin War Cemetery.	*S/L E.*G.M. Corser DFC MID Killed F/Sgt A.J.J. Brown RAAF Killed Sgt WA. Young later F/Sgt Killed Sgt L.R. Price Killed F/Sgt W.W. Harrington Killed W/O L.A. Kent RAAF DFC Killed Sgt H.G. Keymer Killed
514 Sqdn: Lanc DS 738-J Sgt Curle's name is on the Runneymede Memorial.	F/Lt G.H.D. Hinde POW Stalag LI F/Sgt J.D. Alford POW F/O M.S.C. Emery POW Stalag LI Sgt W. Muskett POW Stalag IVB Sgt R. Galloway POW Sgt R. Curle Killed age 20 Sgt W.J. Stephen POW
514 Sqdn: Lanc DS 783-B Buried Cambridge City Cemetery.	Sgt L Wilton RCAF Killed age 26 in action over the target
550 Sqdn: Lanc LM 301-V Crashed at Washbuttel. Those killed buried in	W/O A.T.S. Collier RAAF Killed Sgt F. Turner Killed

Squadron and Aircraft	*Crew*
Hannover. Crashed at Wasbuttel crew were at first buried here.	F/Sgt P.A. Lee Killed later P/O F/Sgt H.S. Bennett Killed F/Sgt J.A. Cromie RAAF POW Stalag 4B Sgt W.E. Dowser Killed Sgt E.A. Topham Killed
576 Sqdn: Lanc W 4337-R2 Crashed at Berlin (Stratum). Crew buried in the Rheinberg War Cemetery. Crashed near Monchengladbach crew were at first buried here.	F/Sgt J.M. Booth RAAF Killed age 21 Sgt G.H. Kaye Killed Sgt L.W.L. Godfrey Killed F/Sgt R.E.D. Richards RAAF Killed F/Sgt M.N.Jennings RAAF Killed Sgt M.W. Jones RAAF Killed F/Sgt D.R.G. Taskis RAAF Killed
619 Sqdn: Lanc EF 170-N Those killed are buried in Berlin War Cemetery. Hit by flak and burst into flamses and exploded to the north of Magdeburg	P/O J.F. Ward Killed Sgt C.W. Cross POW (wounded)Stalag 4B P/O E.T. Hargraves Killed Sgt J.H. Duncan Killed Sgt W.J. Scott Killed Sgt R. Smithers Killed SGT G.W. Arlett Killed
619 Sqdn: Lanc JB 847-C F/O Bower buried in Berlin the remainder killed are on the Runneymede Memorial Crashed into the Tegel, a wooded area near Berlin.	F/O J.F. Bower RCAF Killed F/O F.E. Staker POW Stalag 1 Sgt E.C. Parrott POW F/Sgt T.G. Conway POW Stalag LIII Sgt E.R. Thornhill POW Stalag L III F/O R.W. MeManaman RCAF MID Killed Sgt A.C. Leitch Killed
626 Sqdn: Lanc JA 864-D2 Crashed at Glienwick. Sgt Brittle and Whitmore are on the Runneymede Memorial the remainder killed are buried in Berlin.	S/L G.A. Roden DFC Killed Sgt L.C.J. Street Killed Sgt G.H. Brittle Killed Sgt T.R. Jackson Killed Sgt HA. Van Hal Killed Sgt H.W. Whitmore Killed Sgt A.G. Luke Killed 2/Pilot Sgt J.W. Stewart POW
627 Sqdn: Mosquito DZ 479-F	F/Sgt L.R. Simpson Evaded Sgt P.W. Walker Evaded
630 Sqdn: Lanc ED 777-Q Crashed NE of Gross Schubzendorf. Crew buried in the Berlin War Cemetery.	P/O W.A. Clark Killed Sgs G. Crowe Killed F/Sgt R.H. Banks Killed F/O L.R. Rinn RCAF Killed Sgt J. Ford Killed Sgt R. Hughes Killed F/Sgt C.R. McLaren RAAF Killed

Aircraft crashed in United Kingdom

Squadron and Aircraft	*Crew*
9 Sqdn: Lanc DV 334-C Crashed at RAF Gamston a satellite of RAF Ossington.	P/O K.E. Warwick Killed Buried Winkfield Sgt R.W. Davison Killed Buried Longbenton, Northumberland F/Sgt T. Butterfield Killed Buried Middleton, Yorks F/Sgt J. Graham Killed Buried Carlise Sgt D.I.T. Munn Killed Buried Much Cowarne, Hereford Sgt R.E. Jones Killed Buried Wallasey

Squadron and Aircraft	*Crew*
	F/Sgt N.B. Owen RCAF Injured
	Sgt C.W.A Rickard Injured
432 Sqn: Lanc DS 851-D Shot up by a nightfighter and crashed on return to base.	F/O C Wales Sgt J Dickinson F/S J Evans Sgt J Garvey Sgt J Aplin Sgt D Thomas F/Lt G Ranville
467 Sqn: Lanc JB 140 Both port engines cut on take off and collided with JB 138 of 61 Sqn.	F/O R.I. Reynolds RAAF Sgt W. King F/S E.A. Joyce RAAF F/S K.N.B Davies RAAF F/S H.M. Kellenweth Injured Sgt R.H Keating F/S C.R. Frizzell Dided of Wounds 5/12/43 Buried Cambridge City Cemetery
625 Sqn: Lanc W 4999-G Returned to base after both port engines cut colldied with an obstruction and was wrecked.	W/O P.R. Aslett Sgt D.M. Blackmore Sgt J.W. Bott Sgt H.B. Cooper Sgt H.B Jennings F/S R.A. Kerry P/O R.O. Budd Sgt E.B. Thomas

16th/17th December 1943
Missing Aircraft

Squadron and Aircraft	*Crew*
7 Sqdn: Lanc JB 552-K Crashed at Werte. Crew buried Sage War Cemetery, Oldenberg.	F/Lt J.R. Petrie RNAF DFC Killed age 26 S/L A. Gibson DFC Killed F/O A. Jackson-Baker Killed P/O A.W. Osborne Killed F/O I.R. MacDonald Killed F/Sgt A.H. Hartshorn Killed F/Sgt C.J. Seery Killed
7 Sqdn: Lanc JB 543-J Those killed buried the Reichswald War Cemetery.	P/O G. Tyler RAAF Killed age 21 F/Sgt A. Smillie POW Sgt A.A. Tucker Killed Sgt C.R. Underhill Killed Sgt D. Woolford POW F/Sgt R.R. MacMillan RAAF Killed Sgt W.R. Wilson Killed
7 Sqdn: Lanc JA 803-K Watson and Butterworth are on the Runneymede Memorial. The remainder of the crew are buried at Lemmerland Gen Cemetery. Shot down by Major Heinz Wolfgang Schnaufer of IV/NJG1 using the Schrage Music(Upwar Firing Gun) method of attack. There is an interesting contrast of ages in this crew, F/Sgt Hedges was 35 and Sgt Hurst only 19. Crashed on farm land at Follega.	W/O W.A. Watson RAAF Killed age 21 W/O W.M. Wateman RAAF Killed F/Sgt J. Butterworth RAAF Killed F/Sgt R.E. Hedges Killed F/Sgt L. Robinson RAAF Killed Sgt J. Hurst Killed Sgt R.D. McWha RAAF Killed
7 Sqdn: Lanc JB 656-D Crashed Oberlegk (Alkmaar). Those killed buried	F/O F.W. Rush RAAF Killed age 23 Sgt K. Wightman Killed

Squadron and Aircraft	*Crew*

Oterleek, Noord Holland, Holland.

Sgt H.B. Bushell Killed
Sgt J.S. Ogg Evaded
F/O W.V. Scott RAAF Killed
P/O C.P. Luther RAAF Killed
Sgt W.R. Buntain Killed

9 Sqdn: Lanc EE 188-B
The crew are buried in the Reichswald War
Cemetery.

P/O I.C.B. Black Killed
Sgt N.E. Adams Killed
Sgt D.T. Gordon Killed
F/O G.E. McTaggart RCAF Killed
Sgt G. Brothers Killed
Sgt A.E. Baumann Killed
SGT E.L. Button

9 Sqdn: Lanc DV 293-Y
The crew are buried in the Berlin War Cemetery.
Crashed at Eberswalde Finow

P/O R.A. Blaydon Killed
Sgt F.E. Cope Killed
F/O B. Otter Killed
Sgt J.K. Widdop Killed
Sgt E. Egan Killed
Sgt R.J. Baroni RCAF Killed
Sgt A. Richardson Killed

44 Sqdn: Lanc DV 238-M
Crashed Wetcher-Wissen. Those killed are buried
at Hannover.

P/O DA. Rollin DFC Killed age 22
Sgt J.C. Blackmore Killed
F/Sgt T.B. Melia Killed
F/Sgt E.J. Tocher Killed
Sgt L. Barker POW Stalag 4B
Sgt B. Chew Killed
Sgt R. Standing Killed
2/Pilot P/O A.T. Moodie Killed

49 Sqdn: Lanc JB 545-O
Crashed Wolvega. Crew buried Weststellingwer,
Friesland, Holland.
Shot down on utward leg by a nighfighter flown by
Oblt Heinz-Walfgang Schnafer IV/NJG1
crashed Sonnega.

P/O G.L. Ratcliffe Killed
Sgt A.E.A Marsland Killed
Sgt E. Holloway Killed
Sgt W.T. Rees Killed
Sgt R. Losa RCAF Killed
Sgt W.R. Day Killed
F/Sgt B.J.V. King RAAF Killed

57 Sqdn: Lanc JB 373-N
Ditched in the sea. Crew names on the
Runneymede Memorial.
On return at the time. Hurley picked up and
continued to serve with 57.

Sgt J.W. Hinde Killed age 21 later P/O
Sgt D.F. Faulkner Killed
Sgt W.J. Bellinger Killed
F/O H. Clark Killed
F/Sgt C.H.T. Hunley Safe
Sgt A.W. Watson Killed
Sgt D.F. Butler Killed

97 Sqdn: Lanc JB 963-Q

P/O's Butler, Little, F/Sgt Battle and F/O McIntrye
are buried in Berlin and the remainder are on the
Runneymede Memorial

F/Lt D.J. Brill Killed age 22
F/Lt R.E. Handley DFM Killed
Sgt J. Stone Killed
F/O N.G. McIntyre RAAF Killed
P/O R. Butler Killed
Sgt H. Chappell Killed
P/O G.J. Little RCAF Killed
F/Sgt E.J. Battle RAAF Killed

97 Sqn: Lanc JB 531-Y
Crew baled out near Ely
crashed 4 miles NW of Oxford Ness, Suffolk

P/O E.Smith
Sgt F.E. Surn
P/O J.W. Arthuson
F/Sgt J.A.Wilson
Sgt G.H. Townsend
Sgt N. Stewart
Sgt N.Stewart
Sgt C.A. Bradshaw

Squadron and Aircraft	*Crew*

101 Sqdn: Lanc DV 299-K2
Crew names on the Runneymede Memorial.

F/Sgt P.E. Head Killed age 29 later P/O
Sgt W. Welby Killed
Sgt R.A.C. Wilson Killed
Sgt H. Street Killed
SGT D.J. Gibson RCAF Killed
Sgt R. Betts Killed
Sgt H.R. Lintern Killed
F/Sgt W.M. Green Killed

101 Sqdn: Lanc DV 300-W
Crashed at Lemsterland. Buried Lemsterland,
Friesland, Holland.

F/O R.E. MacFarlane RCAF DFM Killed age 21
Sgt J.E. Clark Killed
Sgt L.D. Wilson Killed
Sgt D.B. Harvey Killed
Sgt F.R. Westall Killed
Sgt J. Ireland Killed
Sgt E.R.E. Jordan Killed
P/O L.E. Thompson RCAF Killed

103 Sqdn: Lanc JB 658
Crashed at Doberitz. Crew buried Berlin.

F/Sgt H. Campbell RAAF Killed age 27 later WO
Sgt P.W. Alderton Killed
F/Sgt M. Hartley Killed
Sgt C. O'Neil Killed
Sgt D.J. McGrath Killed
Sgt T.W. Moore Killed
Sgt W.H. Chambers Killed

106 Sqdn: Lanc 638-G
Crashed at Achmer. Crew buried Reichswald War
Cemetery, Germany.

P/O C.H. Storer Killed
F/Sgt J. Coulton Killed
F/Sgt E.G. Grundy Killed
F/Sgt R.E. Hackett Killed
Sgt F.W. Kite Killed
Sgt C. Frankish Killed
Sgt M.J. Martin Killed

115 Sqdn: Lanc DS 835-K
Crashed Heemskirk 9 miles from Alkmaar,
Holland. Crew buried Heemskwek, Noord-Holland,
Holland.

P/O N.T. Newton RNZAF DFC Killed age 23
P/O E.J.H Downs Killed
F/Sgt I. Lewis Killed
Sgt G.A.W Ray Killed
F/Sgt A.G.R Cowdrey Killed
Sgt R. Hawkins Killed
Sgt M. Saetter Killed

156 Sqdn: Lanc JR 216-W
Crew names on the Runneymede Memorial.

F/Lt C.O. Aubert RAAF DFM Killed
F/Lt J.F. Samuel RAAF DFC Killed
S/L R. Hadley RAAF DFC Killed
P/O R.S. Smith DFC Killed
F/Sgt W.S. Fisher Killed
F/Lt N.T.R. Poulton RAAF DFM Killed
F/Lt T. Trilsbeck RCAF DFC Killed
F/Lt L.J. Powell RAAF DFC Killed

166 Sqdn: Lanc ED 411
Crashed at Hannover. Crew buried Hannover.
Crashed at Diepholz where they were originally
buried.

F/O P.W.R. Pollett Killed age 22
Sgt F.R.M. Squair Killed
Sgt F.F. Clarke Killed
F/O G. Drake Killed
Sgt E. Speirs Killed
Sgt C. Cushing Killed
Sgt R.C. Clifford Killed

207 Sqdn: Lanc EE 141-P
Crashed at Hemsdorf. Crew that were killed are on
the Runneymede Memorial.
Shot down by a nightfighter and crashed at
Hemsdorf.

F/Lt R.J. Allen POW Stalag LIII
Sgt D.J. Peppall POW Stalag 4B
P/O E.H. Stephenson POW Stalag LIII
Sgt W.J. Vowles POW Stalag IVB
F/Sgt J.A. Brindle POW Stalag LIII

Squadron and Aircraft

Crew

Sgt R.J. Stone RCAF Killed Chute did not open.
Sgt E.J. Takle Killed

408 Sqdn: Lanc LL 676-E
The pilot was on the first trip of his second tour.
Crew names on the Runneymede Memorial.
Maitland DFM London Gazette 29/5/1942 with 420
Sqn.

F/O W.J. Maitland RCAF DFM Killed
F/Sgt J.E. Saunders RCAF Killed 25th trip later
WOII
Sgt J.J.Robertson Killed 2nd trip
F/O T.C. Gierulski BA RAAF Killed 2nd trip
F/Sgt C.A. Besse RAAF Killed 1st trip
F/Sgt R. Pettitt RCAF Killed 4th trip
Sgt M. Maher Killed 1st trip

426 Sqdn: Lanc DS 846-Y
Crashed at Hoya, Hannover, shot down by a night
fighter. Crew that were killed are buried in
Hannover.

P/O L.P. Archibald RCAF Killed age 21
P/O J.L.R.R Lachance Killed
P/O N.B. Morrison Killed
P/O J.L. Wilson POW Stlaga LIII
Sgt R. Atkin Killed
P/O H.J. Hurley RCAF Killed
WOII J.D. Newcombe RCAF Killed

426 Sqdn: Lanc DS 762-V
Crashed at Lake Asan, near Urshult Southern
Sweden.
Sgt George awarded an immediate DFM LG
9/5/1944

P/O A.C. Davies RCAF Interned
P/O H.F. Gariock RCAF Interned
Sgt R. Engel RCAF Interned
F/Sgt F.T. Mudry RCAF Interned
P/O R.F. Richards RCAF Interned
Sgt E.O. George RCAF Interned injured
F/Sgt R.H. Ginson RCAF Interned

432 Sqdn: Lanc DS 831-N
Crashed at Huizum. Crew apart from F/O Fisher
that were killed are buried in Leeuwarden,
Friesland, Holland. He is buried in the US
Cemetery at Neuville-on-Condroz
Shot down by a nighfighter by Oblt Henry-
Wolfgan Schnauden IV/NJG1

F/O W.C. Fisher USAAF Killed
2/Pilot F/Sgt O.D. Lewis RCAF POW
W/O J.S. Briegel Killed
F/Sgt T.W. Pragnell RAAF Killed
F/Sgt M.A.T. Brudell POW Stalag LIII
W/O R.K. Saunders RAAF Killed
F/Sgt H.A. Turner RCAF KilledI
Sgt R. Hughes Killed

576 Sqdn: Lanc DV 342-G2
Crashed at Lichtenberg, Berlin.
F/Sgt's Chapman and Russom are buried in Berlin
the remainder are on the Runneymede Memorial

F/O R.S. McAra Killed
Sgt J.L. Barrett Killed
F/Sgt C. Chapman Killed
F/O G.L. Blackmore RAAF Killed
F/Sgt E. Russom Killed
F/Sgt M.G. Western RAAF Killed
F/Sgt A.A. Harris RAAF Killed

619 Sqdn: Lanc JA 867-X
All the crew are buried in Berlin.
Crashed Eberswalde-Finow

P/O G.B. Loney RCAF Killed
F/Sgt J. Gray Killed
F/O H.A. De Vries Killed
P/O M. Gennis RCAF Killed
Sgt L. Banks Killed
Sgt D. Corbitt Killed
Sgt R.F. Dearden Killed

625 Sqdn: Lanc LM 424-B
Crashed at Wetcher Wiesen. Those killed are
buried in Hannover.

W/O D. Baker Killed age 20 later P/O
Sgt W.H. Pallett POW
Sgt B.G Robinson Killed
F/Sgt G.W.F. Batchelor Killed
W/O G.E. Adams DFC Killed
Sgt K. Watmough Killed
F/Lt W.D. Crimmins DFC Killed (625 Gunnery
   Leader)

Aircraft crashed in the United Kingdom

Squadron and Aircraft	*Crew*
12 Sqdn: Lanc JB 715-U The rear gunner Sgt R.A. Whitley died on the afternoon of 17th December at Louth Hospital. The aircraft crashed at Hainton on return.	F/Sgt H.R. Ross RAAF Killed buried Cambridge F/Lt A. Walker Killed buried Whitehaven Sgt H.R. McDowell RAAF Killed Sgt H.P. Aldiss Killed buried East Dereham Sgt F.G. Clark Killed buried Sunningdale Sgt A.T. Broome Killed buried Bishops Castle Sgt R.A. Whiteley injured died later buried Throop, Bournemouth
83 Sqdn: Lanc JB 344-K Aircraft crashed at Wyton.	P/O F.F. McLean RAAF Injured Sgt H. Day Inj F/Sgt R.A. Lindsey RNZAF Unhurt Sgt J. Henderson Injured F/Sgt V.G. Tankard RAAF Died F/Sgt L.E. Faithorn Injured Sgt C.C. Reid Injured F/Sgt Tankard is buried in Cambridge
97 Sqdn: Lanc JB 119-F Crashed at Bourn while trying to land.	S/L D.F. MacKenzie DFC Killed F/Sgt R.F. Marshall Injured F/Sgt A. Hunter Injured F/Sgt W.A. Lang RAAF Injured F/Sgt K.L. Kirby Injured P/O J.T. Pratt DFM Killed F/O W.A. Colson DFM Killed S/L MacKenzie buried in Cambridge P/O Pratt is buried in Clitheroe, Lancs F/O Colson is buried in Willesden, Middx
97 Sqdn: Lanc JB 176-K Crashed at Bourn on landing due to fog and low cloud.	F/O E. Thackway Killed Sgt G. Grundy Killed Sgt J. Powell Killed P/O L.K. Grant RCAF Killed Sgt R. Lawrence Killed Sgt PH. Mack Injured Sgt L.A. Laver Uninjured F/O Thackway is buried in Killinghall Sgt Grundy is buried Bradford Sgt Powell Buried in Wakefield F/O Grant in Cambridge
97 Sqdn: Lanc JB 117-C Crashed near Gravely.	F/Sgt I.W.Mc Scott RAAF Killed Sgt E.W. Collishaw Killed Sgt S. J. Peek Killed Sgt D.R. Irvine RCAF Killed Sgt K.E. Foxcroft RAAF Killed Sgt C.L. Hope RCAF Killed Sgt S.G.Parrott Killed F/Sgt Scott, Irvine, Foxcroft and Sgt Hope Is buried in Cambridge. Sgt Collishaw is buried in Nottingham Sgt Peek is buried in the City of London Sgt Parrott is buried in Liss, Hamps
97 Sqdn: Lanc JB 243-P Crashed at Graveley on return.	S/L E.A. Deverill DFC AFC DFM Killed F/Sgt A. Russell Killed P/O J.T. Brown Killed F/Sgt J. Farr Killed F/Sgt R. Crossgrove RNZAF DFM Killed

Squadron and Aircraft   *Crew*

W/O D J Penfold DFM
Mid Upper W/O J. Benbow DFM Injured taken to
  Ely Hospital and died later

S/L Deverill buried Cocking, Norfolk
F/S Russell buried Epsom, Sy
F/O Brown Buried Belfast
F/S Farr buried in Windsor
P/O Crossgrove buried in Cambridge
W/O's Benbow and Penfold are buried in
  Worthing, Sx

97 Sqdn: Lanc JB 219-B   P/O J. Kirkwood DFC Killed
Crashed near Gransden.   F/Sgt E.G. Hubbard Killed
                                Sgt R.C. Stewart Killed
                                F/O G.A. Wigley Killed
                                Sgt R.G. Cleeve Killed
                                Sgt L. Madeley Killed
                                Sgt J. Killon Killed

                                P/O Kirkwood buried in Kilwinning, Ayrshire
                                F/S Hubbard is buried in Croxton, Staffs
                                Sgt Stewart is buried Braemar, Aberdeenshire
                                F/O Wigley is buried in Carshalton, Sy
                                Sgt Cleeve is buried in Worth Matravers, Dorset
                                Sgt Madeley is buried in Manchester
                                F/S Killen is buried in Hollinfare, Lancs

97 Sqdn: Lanc JB 482-S   F/O R.L. Mooney
Crew baled out owing to conditions at base, and all   Sgt F.B. Gray
landed safely.   Sgt G.A.Johnson
Aircraft crashed in the North Sea.   F/S J Worsdale
                                             Sgt N.D. Cameron
                                             F/Sgt G Woolf
                                             F/Sgt L Smith

100 Sqdn: Lanc JB 560-N   W/C D.W. Holford DSO DFC Killed
Crashed on return near Kelstern near the runway.   Sgt J. Winderley Killed
W/C Holford was the Commanding Officer of 100   W/O H.B. Wareham RCAF Killed
Sqdn.   Sgt R.E. Mason Killed
                                             Sgt R. Mackay Dangerously Injured
                                             F/Sgt H. Whybrew Killed
                                             F/Sgt D. Bolinbroke Dangerously Injured

                                             W/C Holford buried in Cambridge
                                             W/O Wareham buried Cambridge
                                             Sgt Wunderley buried Salford, Lancs
                                             Sgt Mason buried Winchcomb, Glos
                                             F/Sgt Wybrow buried Over, Cambs

100 Sqdn: Lanc JB 678-F   Sgt G.C. Denman Killed
Crashed at Binbrook, after collision with another   Sgs A.H. Johnson Killed
aircraft of 100 Sqdn JB 674 letter Q.   Sgt I.A. Redman Killed
                                             Sgt H.L. Blackwell Killed
                                             Sgt J.W. Christmas Killed
                                             Sgt R.G. Read Killed
                                             Sgt C B Wallace RCAF inj died later on 8/1/1944

                                             Sgt Denman buried in Croydon
                                             Sgt Johnson is buried in Stalham, Norfolk
                                             Sgt Redman is buried Shaw, Wilts
                                             Sgt Blackwell is buried in Cheltenham
                                             Sgt Christmas is buried in Wandsworth, London
                                             Sgt Read is buried in Little Stanmore, Middx
                                             Sgt Wallace is buried in Cambridge

Squadron and Aircraft	*Crew*

100 Sqdn: Lanc JB 674-Q
Crashed at Binbrook, after collision with another aircraft of 100 Sqdn JB 678 letter F.

F/Sgt A.J. Kevis Killed
Sgt D.S. Watson Killed
W/O W.H. Harras MID Killed
F/Sgt J.R. Bateman RCAF Killed
Sgt R.M.J. Saffney Killed
P/O R.A. Van-Walwyk DFM Killed
Sgt T.E. Cain Killed

F/S Kevis is buried in Sevonoaks, Kent
Sgt Watson is buried in Cambridge
W/O Harris is buried in Cambridge
Sgt Bateman is buried in Cambridge
Sgt Gaffney is buried in Mount Jerome, Dublin, Ireland
F/O Van-Walwyk is buried in Brentford, Middx
Sgt Cain is buried in Warrington

100 Sqdn: Lanc JB 596-H
Crashed at Rarnoldby-Le-Roeck.

F/O R.L. Proudfoot Killed
Sgt S.D. Viggers Killed
Sgt L. Noyes Dangerously Injured
Sgt J. Bamford Killed
Sgt B. Phillips Dangerously Injured
Sgt F.H. Taylor Dangerously Injured
Sgt B Heaton Killed

F/O Proudfoot buried Orsett, Essex
Sgt Viggers buried in Cardiff
Sgt Bamford buried Beeston, Notts
Sgt Heaton buried Crigglestone, Yorks

101 Sqdn: Lanc LM 389-Y
Crashed at Holme, Yorks

Sgt V.M. Cooper Killed
Sgt W.O. Ross Injured
W/O H.P. Davis Injured
Sgt J.K. Watson Killed
Sgt R.K. Rye Killed
Sgt R.W.M. Spelman Killed
Sgt J. Gayden Killed
Sgt R.C. Custan Killed
Sgt Cooper buried in Cambridge
Sgt Rye, Hayden buried in Harrogate
Sgt Custance buried Highgate, London
Sgt Spelman buried Manchester

101 Sqdn: Lanc DV 283-P
F/O Lazenby was awarded an immediate DFC.

F/O A.C. Lazenby and crew haled out at Ingham, all landing safely

101 Sqn: Lanc LM 389-Y
Crashed into a hillside Eastrington, Yorks

Sgt N.M. Cooper Killed
Sgt R.K. Rye Killed
Sgt R,C. Custance Killed
Sgt R.W. M. Spelman Killed
Sgt J.G. Hayden Killed
Sgt J.K. Watson Killed
WO H.P. Davis injured
Sgt W.O. Ross injured

Sgt Cooper Buried Cambridge
Sgt Rye Buried Harrogate
Sgt Custance Burried Highgate
Sgt Spelman Buried Cambridge
Sgt Hayden Buried Harrogate

103 Sqdn: Lanc JB 670
Crashed at Ulceby after take-off; believed to have

F/Sgt V. Richter Killed
Sgt F.S. Copping Killed

Squadron and Aircraft

Crew

collided with an aircraft of 576 Squadron LM 322-
Letter B2

F/O C.R. Jacques Killed
Sgt C.W. Plampton Killed
F/Sgt T.L.H. Kay Killed
Sgt P. Coopman Killed
Sgt F.A. Furie Killed

All but Sgt Furrie are buried in Cambridge
He is buried in New Stevenson, Scotland

103 Sqdn: Lanc JB 551
Crashed in a ploughed field at Barton.

F/O G.M Russell-Fry and crew uninjured.

156 Sqdn: Lanc JB 282
Crashed two miles south-west of Sutton, 1½ miles
from Garth.

F/Sgt W.H. Watkins Killed
Sgt C.H. Reeve Killed
Sgt J.A. Watson Killed
Sgt H.A. Hadlow Killed
Sgt J. Beever Killed
Sgt E.W. Crouch Killed
Sgt L.F. Darlison Injured taken to Ely Hospital

F/Sgt Watkins buried in Lllaran, Glam
Sgt Hadlow buried in Poole, Dorset
Sgt Reeve is buried in Cambridge
Sgt Beever is buried in Holmfirth, Yorks
Sgt Watson is buried in Long Eaton, Derbys
Sgt Crouch is buried in Cambridge

166 Sqdn: Lanc JB 639
Crashed near Barton on Humber.

F/Sgt A.E. Brown Killed
Sgt C.G. Thompson Killed
Sgt D.W. Inglis Killed
Sgt N.P. Perry Killed
Sgt E.V. Smith Killed
Sgt H.A. Williams Killed
Sgt W.N. Griffin Killed

F/Sgt Brown is buried in Ipswich
Sgt Thompson, Sgt Perry, are buried in Cambridge
Sgt Williams is buried in Crystal Palace
Sgt Griffin is buried in Hove, Sx
Sgt Smith is buried in Romford, Essex
Sgt Inglis is buried in Brigg, Lincs

166 Sqdn: Lanc LM 385
Crashed at Caister time 2359.

Sgt S.F. Miller Killed
Sgt T. Rudden Killed
Sgt B.W. Haney Killed
Sgt H.G.A. Hine Killed
F/Sgt J.H. Murphy Killed
Sgt H.E Miles Killed
Sgt W.W.A. Allen RCAF Killed

F/Sgt Miller is buried in Scarborough, Yorks
Sgt Rudden is buried in Brigg, Lincs
Sgt Hine is buried in Cambridge
F/Sgt Haney is buried in Cambridge
F/Sgt Murphy is buried in Cambridge
Sgt Miles is buried in Wasperton, Warks
Sgt Allen is buried in Cambridge

405 Sqdn: Lanc JB369 D
Crashed near Gravely.
Sgt Nutting DFM LG 10/9/1943

F/O B.A.Mc. McLennan RCAF Killed (17th trip)
Sgt G.R. Schneider RCAF Killed
F/O W.F. Sheppard RCAF Killed
Sgt E. Halliwell Killed
W/O S.H. Nutting RCAF DFM Injured (45th trip)
Sgt .H.L. Cornwell Killed
Sgt M.F.V. Roobroeck RCAF Killed

Squadron and Aircraft	*Crew*

F/O McLennan is buried in Cambridge
Sgt Cornwell is buried in Bottisham, Cambs
F/O Sheppard is buried in Cambridge
WO2 Schneider is buried in Cambridge
Sgt Halliwell is buried in Blackpool
Sgt Roobroeck is buried in Cambridge

405 Sqdn: Lanc JB 481- R
Crashed near Marham at 0130.

F/O E.B. Drew RCAF Seriously Injured
F/Sgt V. Mienert RAAF Killed
F/Sgt H.M. Saunders RCAF Killed
WO2 W.L. Dohson RCAF Killed
Sgt H.R. Bessent RCAF Killed
Sgt L.A. McCrea RCAF Uninjured
Sgt W. Corrigan Uninjured

F/Sgt Mienert is buried in Cambridge
WO2 Dobson is buried in Cambridge
F/Sgt Saunders is buried in Cambridge
Sgt Bessent is buried in Cambridge

405 Sqdn: Lanc JB 477-O
Crashed 2 miles from Graveley.

F/Lt W.C. Allan RCAF Seriously Injured died later
28/1/1943
F/O D.H. Stamers RCAF Killed
P/O M. Collier RCAF Killed
Sgt E.S. Joslyn Injured
Sgt G.L. Strang RCAF Killed
Sgt J.C. Egan RCAF Injured
Sgt A.E.S. Kiff Injured

F/Lt Allan buried in Botley, Oxford
F/O Stamers is buried in Cambridge
P/O Collier is buried in Cambridge
Sgt Strang is buried Cambridge

406 Sqdn: Lanc JB 613
Crashed at Ludford Magna.

F/Lt Greenacre and his crew. None of the crew was
injured.

408 Sqdn: Lanc DS 737-C
Crashed near Hawnby, Yorks, into a mountain.
Clark died later of his injuries; he was on his eighth
trip of his second tour. Peek, Wood, Marynowski
and Yeo were also on their second tours.

F/O B.S. Clark RCAF Seriously Injured
Sgt T.A. Dee Killed
Sgt N. Wood Killed
F/Sgt J.G.E. Boilly RCAF Seriously Injured
Sgt L.A. Moran Slightly Injured
F/Sgt L.J. Yeo Injured
F/O M.R. Marynowski RCAF Killed

F/O Marynowski is buried in Harrogate
Sgt Dee is buried in Croxton, Lincs
Sgt Wood is buried in Brighton

426 Sqdn: Lanc DS 779-Q
Crashed at Hunsingcre on the north side of the river
Nidd

F/Sgt R.D. Stewart RCAF Killed
F/O H.P. Norris RCAF Killed
Sgt J. Greeenwell Killed
F/O W. Hamilton Killed
Sgt L. Sale Killed
Sgt A.S. Jamieson Injured
Sgt D.E. Stewart Injured

F/Sgt Stewart is buried in Harrogate
Sgt Sale is buried in Mexborough
Sgt Greenwell is buried in Willesden
F/O Hamilton is buried in Hove

426 Sqdn: Lanc DS 837

S/L T.M. Kneale RCAF Killed

Squadron and Aircraft

Crew

Crashed at Yearsley.

P/O G.M.A.C Jones RCAF Killed
P/O M.M. Prill RCAF Killed
F/O J. MacKay RCAF Killed
P/O R.P. Marks Injured
Sgt A.A. Johnston RCAF Killed
Sgt G C Foster Injured

All those killed buried in Harrogate

460 Sqdn: Lanc DS 832-K
They had been diverted to Leeming for landing but
were unable to see the ground because of the poor
visibility. Abandon the aircraft in the air.

F/O H.B. Hatfield RCAF and his crew baled out
near Thornaby; all uninjured apart from the W/Opt
Sgt W.H. Poole who broke an arm.

460 Sqdn: Lanc JB 657
Aircraft crashed into an ammunition dump in a
wood at Market Stainton.

F/O F.A. Randall RAAF DFC Killed
F/Sgt W.K. Halstead RAAF Killed
F/O H.G.D. Dedman RAAF Killed
Sgt H.H. Petersen RAAF Killed
Sgt J. McKenzie Killed
F/Sgt C.G. Howie RAAF Killed
Sgt R.A. Moynagh RAAF Killed

All buried in Cambridge

460 Sqdn: Lanc DV 173
Crashed into a field in Normandy near Caister.

W/O M. Stafford Uninjured
Sgt W.F.H. McIntyre Uninjured
P/O C.E. Hanson Uninjured
F/Sgt R. Mansfield Uninjured
Sgt E.D. Dixon Severely Injured
Sgt J. Davies Uninjured
P/O H.H. Garment Killed

P/O Garment buried Ruislip, Middx

460 Sqdn: Lanc JB 704
Crashed in a field short of the runway at Rinhrook.

F/Sgt K.J. Godwin and his crew. All uninjured.

576 Sqdn: Lanc JA 957-X2
Overshot the flare path at Wickenhy, having been
diverted there, and made a crash landing with the
under-carriage up in bad weather.

W/O T.J. Bassett and his crew. Three crew injured.

576 Sqdn: Lanc JB 746-B2
Collided with an aircraft of 103 JB 670 and crashed
at Ulceby.

F/Sgt F.R. Scott RAAF Killed
Sgt S.V. Cull Killed
Sgt G.G. Critchley Killed
Sgt J.H. Caldwell Killed
Sgt B.P. Wicks RAAF Killed
Sgt J.W. Ross Killed
Sgt P.M.C. Ellis Killed

All buried in Cambridge

619 Sqdn: Lanc EE 15O-F
Crashed on return near the outer beacon at
Woodhall Spa; the crew were all unharmed.
F/Lt Tomlin was awarded an immediate DFC.
Had been attacked by a nighfighter on outward trip.

F/Lt A.H. Tomlin and crew.

625 Sqdn: Lanc ED 951-A
Crashed at Gayton Le Wold at 2325 pm. The
injured were taken to Louth County Infirmary.
F/O Woolley was attached from the USAAF.

F/O G.E. Woolley USAAF Injured
Sgt G.A. Draycott Killed
Sgt S.A. Taylor Killed
F/Lt G.E. Shannon Injured
Sgt D. Pascoe Injured
Sgt F.R. Johnson Injured
Sgt G.A. Richards Injured

Squadron and Aircraft	*Crew*
	Sgt Taylor is buried in Leicester
	Sgt Draycott is buried in Wigston

625 Sqdn: Lanc W 4993-K
Overshot the base at Kelstern and hit the ground
slowly with the inner wing and belly landed
without any injury to the crew.

W/O E.S. Ellis and crew.

625 Sqdn: Lanc LM 317-U
Landed on three engines at Blyton.

P/O R.G. Bowden DFM and crew uninjured except
    navigator P/O S.N. Cunnington, wounded.

463 Sqdn: Lanc ED 949
Hit by flak.

P/O D.C. Dunn and crew uninjured except bomber
    P/O Coals wounded.

23rd/24th December 1943

Squadron and Aircraft	*Crew*

44 Sqdn: Lanc R 5669-Z
Crashed at Waldhof Elegeshausen (Greifenstein).
Crew buried Hanover.

P/O T.H. Knight Killed
Sgt K.T. Cooper Killed
Sgt D.J. Symmonds Killed
Sgt A.R.C. Yeatman Killed
Sgt E. Birchall Killed
Sgt R.G. Tutt Killed
Sgt S.W. Whitney Killed
2/Pilot Sgt E.J. Blackley Killed

44 Sqdn: Lanc ED 999-X
Crashed at Graftlage-Wetchen. Crew buried in
Hanover.
Shot down by a nightfighter said to be Oblt Paul
Zorner of 1/NJG3
crashed at Diepholz

Sgt R.L. Hands Killed age 22
Sgs H. Bowles Killed
Sgt J.A. Wilde Killed
Sgt A.P. Coombe Killed
Sgt G.E. Phillips Killed
Sgt K.A. Beech Killed
Sgt C. Burgess Killed

50 Sqdn: Lanc ED 445-L
Crashed at Gotzen. Crew buried in Hannover.

F/O D.W. Herbert Killed age 21
Sgt J. Russell Killed
Sgt P.A.E.Philip Rex Killed
Sgt D.J. Poole Killed
P/O C. Hughes Killed
Sgt C.H. Kewley Killed
Sgt T.L. North Killed

57 Sqdn: Lanc JB 233-F
Crashed at Meppen near Lingen. Those killed
buried in the Reichswald War Cemetery.

F/Sgt H.J. Knights RCAF POW Stalag 4B
Sgt D.A. Fisher,Killed
F/Sgt I.D. Forsyth RAAF POW Stalag 7B
Sgt J. Low RCAF POWStalag 4B
Sgt A.E. Eley Killed
Sgt J.Mc. Adamson RCAF Killed
Sgt R.R. Mutton Killed

100 Sqdn: Lanc JB 594-O
All are on the Runneymede Memorial.

F/Sgt D.B. Jameson Killed age 29
Sgt W. Phillips Killed
F/O F.M. Connolly Killed
Sgt J.R. Jones Killed
Sgt R. Smith Killed
Sgt V.De. P. Brown Killed
Sgt A.B. Burke Killed

103 Sqdn Lanc JB 730-P
Crashed at Oborsair. Crew are buried in the
Rheinberg War Cemetery.

F/Sgt M. McMahon RCAF Killed
Sgt R.B. Stocks Killed
Sgt J.W. Brewster Killed

Squadron and Aircraft   *Crew*

	Sgt G.E. Crawford Killed
	F/O A.G. MacDonald RNZAF Killed
	Sgt A.R. Fleming Killed
	Sgt T. Thompson Killed

115 Sqdn: Lanc DS 773-T
All but Sgt Davidson killed buried in Berlin.
He is on the Runneymede Memorial.

P/O D.L. Pirie Killed
P/O K.D. Pearce Killed
F/Sgt W. Hardaker Killed
Sgt K. Davidson Killed
Sgt J. Southwell Killed
Sgt J. Calvert Killed
Sgt R.J. Heal Killed

156 Sqdn: Lanc JB 711-W
Crew names on the Runneymede Memorial.

F/O N.J. Warfield DFM Killed
Sgt J. Hill Killed
P/O R.R. Stain RAAF DFM Killed
Sgt T.E. Rees Killed
Sgt F.J. Manley Killed
F/Sgt F.H. Morgan Killed
F/Sgt R.N.V. Daniel (Welsh Football Cap) Killed

207 Sqdn: Lanc DV 188-J
Crashed at Luckenwalde. Sgt Davies aged 20 is on
the Runneymede Memorial.

P/O G.E. Moulton-Barrett POW Stalag III
Sgt T.H. Gladders POW Stalag 4B
F/O L.R. Roberts POW Stalag III
F/Sgt E.W. Burl POW Stalag 4B
F/Sgt J. Sherlock POW
F/Sgt I.W. Robinson RAAF POW Stalag 357
Sgt D.O. Davies Killed

463 Sqdn: Lanc ED 420-L
Crashed at Kaulsdorf.
Sgt Ryan and Sgt Tunnicliff are on the
Runneymede Memorial remainder are buried in
Berlin.

P/O A.W. Heap RAAF Killed age 21
Sgt W.H. Carter Killed
F/O R.S. Gall Killed
Sgt D. McCreadie Killed
Sgt L.M. Ryan RAAF Killed
Sgt F.J. Tunnicliffe Killed
F/Sgt K.R.R. Glover RAAF Killed

514 Sqdn: Lanc LL 671-A2B
Crashed at Ostheim-Friedberg. Those killed buried
in the Durnbach War Cemetery.

P/O K.G. Whitting RAAF Killed age 25
F/Sgt D. Edwards Killed
F/Sgt R.W. Basey Killed
Sgt W.A. Casey Killed
F/Sgt J.E. Moloney RAAF POW Stalag IVB
Sgt P.A.T. Nelson RCAF Killed
Sgt L.F. Bostock Killed

550 Sqdn: Lanc DV 343-X2
Crew names on the Runneymede Memorial.

P/O D.C. Dripps RAAF Killed age 27
Sgt J.C. Scott Killed
F/O J.E. Stewart RCAF Killed
Sgt W.T. Sibley Killed
Sgt D. Campbell Killed
Sgt R. Gillies Killed
P/O G.C. Orme Killed

576 Sqdn: Lanc ED 913-U2
Those killed are buried in Berlin.

F/O J.H. Richards Killed age 29
F/O B.J. Marks Killed 2nd Pilot
Sgt G. Evans POW Stalag LIII
Sgt A.E. Hooper Killed
Sgt S.W. Irons Killed
Sgt C. Milburn Killed
Sgt H. Johnson Killed
Sgt H.S Mitchell Killed

576 Sqdn: Lanc ED 713-W2
Crashed at Lanzonhain in deep snow. Those killed

P/O R.L. Hughes Killed later F/O
Sgt J.E.F. Paton Killed

Squadron and Aircraft	*Crew*
buried in Hannover.	Sgt F.H. Lanxon POW Stalag LIII
	Sgt D.A.H. Morris POW Stalag IVB
	Sgt J. Woodruff POW Stalag IVB
	Sgt J.P. Gray Killed
	Sgt F.E.A. Rivett Killed
625 Sqdn: Lanc LM 421-Q	Sgt G.F. Clark Killed age 22
Crashed at Mittenualde east-north-east of	Sgt D.W. Walker Killed
Rangsdoff.	Sgt R. Parkinson Killed.
Sgt's Walker and Whitmarsh are on the	Sgt W.E. Whitmarsh Killed
Runneymede Memorial remainder are buried in	F/Sgt C.R. Harrison Killed
Berlin	Sgt F.A. Sugden Killed
	Sgt A.E. Naylor Killed

Aircraft crashed in the United Kingdom

7 Sqn: Lanc JB730-P	*Crew*
	P/O H C Williams RNZAF Inj
Crashed after take off from Oakington	P/O G H Falloon Inj
	F/O Hewitt Inj
	F/Sgt A L B Carson Inj
	P/O W Swain Inj
	F/O S A Strong Inj
	P/O I G Kaye Inj
207 Sqn: Lanc DV361-V	*Crew*
	Sgt G A Baker
Abandon in the air	Sgt P W Groom
	Sgt R Wellfare
	Sgt L A Hinch
	F/Sgt C E Ryall RCAF Killed
	Sgt G C O'Neil Killed
	Sgt T G Higgins Killed
	Sgt Ryall buried in Oxford
	Sgt O'Neil buried Port Glasgow, Renfrewshire
	Sgt Higgins buried Caerlaverock. Dumfiesshire

Squadron and Aircraft	*Crew*
550 Sqdn: Lanc LM 319-G2	Sgt H.F.J. Woods Killed
Crashed at Fulstow, having collided with JB 604-K	Sgt D.G. Davies Killed
also of 550 Sqdn.	Sgt M. Giles Killed
	F/Sgt J.R. Legere RCAF Killed
	Sgt W.F. Wright Killed
	Sgt J.C. Atherton RCAF Killed
	Sgt J. McConnell Killed
	Sgt Woods buried Bristol
	Sgt Davies buried Neath, Wales
	Sgt Giles buried Gloucester
	F/Sgt Legere buried Cambridge
	Sgt Wright buried Hereford
	F/Sgt Atherton buried Cambridge
	Sgt McConnell buried Dalziel, Lanarkshire
100 Sqdn: Lanc ND 327-	F/Sgt W.R. Cooper Killed
Crashed at Fulstow, having collided with LM	Sgt G.W. Clayden Killed
319-G2 also of 550	Sgt A.R. Laurence Killed
	F/Sgt G.W. Guest Killed
	Sgt R.W. Theobald Killed
	Sgt J.A. Jordan Killed
	Sgt J. Rawson Killed

Squadron and Aircraft   *Crew*

F/Sgt Cooper buried Harrow
Sgt Claydon buried Walgrave, Northants
Sgt Laurence buried Bishops Hatfield, Herts
Sgt Guest buried Cambridge
Sgt Theobald unknown
Sgt Jordan buried Cambridge
Sgt Rawson buried Wickersley, Yorks

550 Sqn:Lanc ED 730-G2   Sgt H.F.J Woods
Collied in mide air with Lanc ND 327-100 Sqn   Sgt D.G. Davies
Crashed near Fulston   Sgt M.E. Giles
                                                F/Sgt J.R.E. Legere RCAF
                                                Sgt L.F. Wright
                                                F/Sgt J.C. Atherton
                                                Sgt J. McConnell

                                                Sgt Woods Buried Bristol
                                                Sgt Davies Buried Neath, S outh Wales
                                                Sgt Giles Buried Gloucester
                                                F/Sgt Legere Buried Cambridge
                                                Sgt Wright Buried Hereford
                                                F/Sgt Atherton Buried Cambridge
                                                Sgt McConnell Buried Dalziel, Lanarkshire

29th/30th December 1943

Squadron and Aircraft   *Crew*

10 Sqdn: Halifax JC 314-X   F/Sgt P.B. Green Killed age 22
Nuinerwold Gen Cemetery, Drenthe, Holland.   Sgt A. Colbourne Killed
                                                 Sgt R.E. Roos Killed
                                                 F/Sgt S. Webb Killed
                                                 Sgt D.R.C. Appleyard Killed
                                                 Sgt W.D. Hall Killed
                                                 Sgt P.J. Greruman Killed

12 Sqdn: Lanc JB 407-A   Sgt J.H. Hawkesley-Hill POW Stalag IVB
Hit by light flak. Aircraft abandon near Dutch   P/O F.A. Hodgkinson POW Stalag LIII
Coast.   Sgt A.A. Mortimer POW Stalag IVB
Crashed at Gangett where those killed were   Sgt W.E. Doak USAAF POW
originally buried.   F/Sgt C. Toulson POW Stalag LIII
                                                 Sgt E. Podborchinski RCAFKilled
Those killed buried in the Rheinberg War Cemetery   Sgt R. Cooke Killed

35 Sqdn: Halifax HR 986-G   F/O R.C. Williams DFC Killed
Those killed buried in Berlin.   P/O J. Hooson DEM Killed
                                                 F/O E.J. Stone DFC Killed
                                                 F/O G.R. Davidson DFM Killed
                                                 Sgt F.C. Redman POW Stalag LIII
                                                 F/Sgt W.E.C. Dillow Killed
                                                 Sgt W. Laverick DFM Killed

50 Sqdn: Lanc DV 375-E   F/Lt D.G. McAlpine Killed age 29
Crashed in the sea. Groves was picked up by a   Sgt W. Hope Killed
destroyer, with minor injuries. F/O Hales washed Sgt J. Greenwell Killed
up on a German beach buried Sage. The remain der F/O C.N. Hale Killed
are on the Runneymede Memorial   Sgt J. Biggs Killed
                                                 F/O H. Mordue Killed
                                                 F/Sgt H.E. Groves RAAF inj picked up

51 Sqdn: Halifax JD 264-H   F/Sgt A.R. Baird POW Stalag IVB
                                                 Sgt R.M.Jones POW

Squadron and Aircraft	*Crew*

P/O P.O. Coryton POW
Sgt J.A. Horrell POW
Sgt G.B. Mowbrey POW
Sgt A.D. Gunn POW Stalag LIII
F/Sgt C.D. Wilkes POW Stalag LIII

---

61 Sqdn: Lanc DV399-R
Hit by flak caused a fire in the fuselage P/O
Thomas tried to extinguished this seeing the rear
gunner Sgt Stuart preapring to bale out and not in
intercom contact he baled out at that moment the
aircraft blew up.

All those killed are buried in Berlin.

F/Lt G.H. Harvey RAAF Killed age 22
Sgt J.S. Kennedy Killed
F/Sgt R.W. Carver Killed
F/Sgt K. Prouten Killed
Sgt N.S.J. Meehan Killed
P/O D.F. Thomas RCAF POW Stalag LIII
Sgt R.S. Stuart Killed

---

101 Sqdn: Lanc LM 371-T
Crashed at Schillerslage, near Hanover. Sgt Morton
aged 22 buried in Hanover.

F/Sgt J.W. Shearer POW Stalag IVB
Sgt R.M. Lloyd POW Stalag LIII
F/Sgt W.M. Smith RNZAF POW
Sgt D. Naylor POW Stalag IVB
Sgt N.F. Worsnup POW Stalag LIII
Sgt W.R. Coleman POW Stalag IVB
Sgt J. Morton Killed
Sgt M. Cohen RCAF POW Stalag IVB

---

102 Sqdn: Halifax HR 867-A
Hit by flak.

P/O A.C. Fraser POW
F/O H.H. Hesketh POW
Sgt R. Day POW
F/Sgt N.L. Pearce Killed
Sgt R. Mundy POW
Sgt R.R. McWhinnie POW
F/O Carlson 2/Pilot POW

---

102 Sqdn: Halifax JD 412-X
Sgt Stokes is on the Runneymede Memorial.

Sgt F.F. Stokes RAAF Killed age 29 later P/O
Sgt H.W. Parr POW
Sgt C.E. Habberley POW
Sgt E.H. Ricketts POW
SgtJ. Thomson POW
Sgt T.G. Hatton POW
F/Sgt E. Bretherton POW

---

103 Sqdn: Lanc JB 748-G
Sgt Henderson age 19 is buried in the Reicswald
War Cemetery.
Hit by flak and suffred dameg to the tailplane and
and loss of both port engines crashed Mettingen.

W/O L.J. Grigg POW Stalag IVB
Sgt A.R.G. Warne POW Stalag IVB
Sgt A. Fletcher POW Stalag IVB
Sgt R.W. Hatherley POW Stalag IVB
Sgt W.A. Lamb RCAF POW Stalag IVB
Sgs C.H. Cunning POW Stalag IVB
Sgt T.C. Henderson Killed

---

115 Sqdn: Lanc DS 834-F
Those Killed buried Weert (Tungelroi) Holland.
Hit by a nightfighter and crashed at Tungelroi

F/Sgt J. Lee POW Stalag IVB
Sgt H. Pike POW Stalag LIII
Sgt L.H.Jones Killed
Sgt K.S. Bell RAAF Killed
Sgt A.M. Wilkinson RCAF Killed
Sgt G. Johnson Killed
Sgt A.F. Gunnell Evaded

---

408 Sqdn: Lanc DS 718-R
Shot down Wietmanschen near Lingen,
crew originally buried here.

F/Lt Wilton buried in the Reichswald War
Cemetery
Sgt Feran, P/O McCabe, WO2 Raban, Sgt Landing,
F/O Pildrem and P/O Hoyle all buried in Hooton
War Cemetery

F/Lt W.T. Wilton RCAF Killed age 24
F/Sgt D.A. McCabe RCAF Killed
F/Sgt H. Landing Killed
F/Sgt W.E. Raban RCAF Killed
F/O R.A. Pildrem Killed
F/O F.H. Hoyle Killed
Sgt B.H. Kearn Killed

Squadron and Aircraft	Crew

Squadron and Aircraft

419 Sqdn. Halifax LW 282-Y
Shot down over Berlin.

F/Sgt R.L. Thompson POW Stalag IVB
Sgt F.H. Webb POW Stalag IVB
Sgt S.J. Maloney POW Sealag IVB
Sgt R.G. Bilyard POW Stalag IVB
Sgt G. Cooper POW
Sgt A.J. Carrol POW Stalag IVB
Sgt W.J. Barry POW Stalag LIII

429 Sqdn: Halifax JD 318-F
Shot down by a night fighter. Those killed buried
Tubergen, Overijssel, Holland.

P/O A.L. Merkley POW Stalag LIII
F/O R.O. Marion POW Stalag LIII
F/O C.W. Peasland RCAF Killed
Sgt B.S. Ranson Killed
F/Sgt E.N. Parker Killed
Sgt R.H.J. Walsh Killed
F/Sgt A.G. Innes Killed

431 Sqdn: Halifax LK 701-L
Those killed buried Hanover.

F/O G.E. Bishops Killed
F/O R.A. Holtby RCAF Killed
F/Sgt G. Cummive Killed
Sgt N. Roffie POW
Sgt J.J. Whelan Killed
Sgt G.D. Kehoe Killed
Sgt A.E.F. Banning Killed

431 Sqdn: Halifax LK 659-A
Crew are buried in Berlin.

F/O J.N. Nelson RCAF Killed later F/Lt
Sgt P. Walker Killed
F/O F. Spencer Killed
Sgt L.C. Nosworthy Killed
Sgt A.H.R. Fielding Killed
Sgt J.R. Ruthvein Killed
Sgt F.G. Goodall Killed

460 Sqdn: Lanc JB 298-Q

F/O Poole. F/O Beattie, F/Sgt Irvin, buried in
Berlin the remainder are on the Runneymede
Memorial

F/O R.K. McIntyre RAAF Killed age 20
F/O J. Poole RAAF Killed
Sgt R. Gartside Killed
F/O J.P. Grant RAAF Killed
F/O G.P. Beattie RAAF Killed
F/Sgt G.H. Irvin RAAF Killed
P/O W.R. Read Killed

460 Sqdn: Lanc JB 607-N
Those killed buried in the Reichswald War
Cemetery.

P/O S.J. Ireland RAAF Killed age 30
Sgt W.A.H. Squire Killed
F/Sgt F.J. Seery RAAF POW Stalag LIII
W/O A.E. Blight RAAF Killed
Sgt C. Seddon Killed
Sgt R.J. Poulter Killed
F/Sgt M H Squires RAAF Killed

467 Sqdn: Lanc ED 547-M
A new crew to 467, the pilot only had three trips,
two as second pilot. The aircraft M for Mother was
on its 65th trip. Crew buried in Berlin.

P/O R.A. Tait RAAF Killed age 22
Sgt R.A. Yale Killed
Sgt F.A. Spencer Killed
P/O F.M.C. Allen Killed
F/Sgt L.E. Lambert Killed
Sgt S. Allom Killed
Sgt D. Wetherell Killed

514 Sqdn: Lanc DS 821-S
After combat with a fighter, the aircraft ran out of
petrol and had to ditch picked up by ASR.

F/O L. Greenburgh and crew rescued uninjured.

Crashed in the UK

100 Sqn: Lanc JB 605-O
Abandon in the Air

Crew
F/O R M Parker Inj
Sgt C W Ellis Inj
F/o H Ferguson Inj
Sgt G Wilverwood Inj
Sgt T Campbell Inj
Sgt E Stalkie Inj
Sgt G A Orchard Inj

405Sqn:Lanc JB 668-T
Hit by flak while bombing, damage to port inner
and starboard outer engines then hit again by flak
near Bremen on return.
Landed safely at Woodbridge airfield, Suffolk.

F/Sgt A.R. McQuade RCAF
Sgt J. McCreadie
WO2 D.M. Lunney RCAF
F/Sgt R.H. Law RCAF
F/Sgt J Fraser
Sgt W.C.Palater RCAF
F/Sgt G.E. Foster RCAF

1st/2nd January 1944

Squadron and Aircraft
7 Sqdn: Lanc EE 129-V

Crew
F/Lt K.C. Kingsbury RNZAF DFC POW Stalag
LIII
F/O D.W. Souchen RCAF POW Stalag LIII
F/Sgt G.F. Mortimer POW
Sgt A.W.D. King POW Stalag LVI
Sgt D.T.M. Ingram POW Stalag LIII
F/Sgt E. Parr POW Stalag IVB
F/O E.G. Bedwell RCAF POW StalagLIII

7 Sqdn: Lanc JB 682-A
Crew buried in the Reichswald War Cemetery.
Crashed at Ramsel

S/L H.R. Jaggard Killed age 27
F/Lt AF. Taylor DFM Killed
F/O J.C. Osborne Killed
F/Sgt G.V. Roberts Killed
F/O C.J. Donahue RCAF DFM Killed
W/O J.T. Williams Killed
F/Sgt R.G. Warwick Killed

9 Sqdn: Lanc JA 711-A
Crew buried in Hanover.

P/O C. Ward Killed Later F/O
Sgt J. Sutton Killed
Sgt E.D. Keene Killed
F/Sgt G.L. James Killed
Sgt G.F.K. Bedwell Killed
F/Sgt N.F. Dixon Killed
F/Sgt W.L. Doran RCAF Killed

12 Sqdn: Lanc ND 325-G
Crashed at Wingshach. Sgt Smith aged 21 is buried
in Durnbach. Sgt Smith chute failed to open.

P/O K.C. West POW Stalag LIII
Sgt R.H. Pearce POW Stalag LIII
Sgt D.L. Smith Died of injuries as a POW
W/O E.A. Walters RCAF POW Stalag IVB
Sgt E. Waterhouse POW Stalag IVB
Sgt K. Apps POW Stalag IVB
Sgt V.A. Panniers POW Stalag IVB

44 Sqdn: Lanc W4 831-C
Crew buried in Berlin.

P/O W.A. Holmes A'Court Killed
P/O J.W. Woods Killed
F/O O.D. Blaha Killed
Sgt A.R. Morris Killed
Sgt R.A. Kidley Killed
F/Sgt T.W. Black Killed
Sgt H.A. Norton Killed

57 Sqdn: Lanc JB 548-Q

P/O G.L. Grimbly POW Stalag III

Squadron and Aircraft   *Crew*

Sgt E.S.J. Michael POW
F/O J.R. Upton POW Stalag LIII
Sgt W.A. Turner POW Stalag IVB
Sgt C. Walker POW Stalag LIII
F/Sgt D.F. Hall POW Stalag IVB
F/Sgt R.C. Lowe POW Stalag IVB

61 Sqdn: Lanc LM 377-F   F/O G.E. Sharpe RCAF Killed age 23
Crew buried in Hanover.   Sgt B.G. Imber Killed
                                                 F/O E.A.C. Willard Killed
                                                 F/O A.V. Shirley Killed
                                                 Sgt A. Ross Killed
                                                 Sgt W.J. Churcher Killed
                                                 Sgt H. Pattrick Killed

61 Sqdn: Lanc DV 344-V   F/O R.P. Cunningham Killed
Crew are buried in Berlin.   Sgt A.F. Gleadle Killed
                                                 F/O J. Storey Killed
                                                 SGT M.S. Williams Killed
                                                 Sgt R.R. Barbour Killed
                                                 Sgt E. Lunnis Killed
                                                 F/Sgt W.C. Butler Killed

83 Sqdn: Lanc ND 354-A   W/C W. Abercromhy Killed age 33
Those killed buried in Sage War Cemetery,   F/Sgt A.F. Nairn Killed
Oldenberg.   Sgt L.H. Lewis POW
Crashed at Lutten.   F/Sgt W.R. Halloran Killed
                                                 Sgt W.A. Wall Killed
                                                 P/O W.J.James Killed
                                                 Sgt R.W. Allen Killed
                                                 F/Sgt A.B. Earson Killed

97 Sqdn: Lanc JA 960-E   F/O R.L. Mooney DFM Killed age 23
Crew buried in the Rheinberg War Cemetery.   Sgt F.B. Grey Killed
Hit by flak near Acchen and crashed.   Sgt G.A. Johnson Killed
                                                 F/Sgt J. Worsdale Killed
                                                 Sgt N.D. Cameron Killed
                                                 F/Sgt G. Woolf Killed
                                                 F/Sgt G.E. Smith Killed

100 Sqdn: Lanc JB 740-R   F/Sgt R.W. Chinery Killed age 23
Crew buried in Hanover.   Sgt D.S. Fawcett Killed
Crashed at Rottorj on outward leg.   F/Sgt J.A. Dwelly Killed
                                                 Sgt D.R. Jessop Killed
                                                 Sgt G. John Killed
                                                 Sgt J.B. Gooravitch Killed
                                                 Sgt G. Monk Killed

101 Sqdn: Lanc DV 308-V   P/O D.J. Bell POW Stalag LIII
Those killed are buried at Gosslies, Charleri,   Sgt L.F. Somers POW
Hainaut, Belgium. P/O Zubic was only 18.   Sgt H. W. Bailey Evaded
                                                 Sgt E.H. Harris POW Stalag I
                                                 1st Lt M.H. Albert (USAF) POW
                                                 P/O F.J. Zubic RCAF Killed
                                                 F/O W.E. Suddick Killed
                                                 Sgt G.C. Connon Killed

Squadron and Aircraft	*Crew*

101 Sqdn: Lanc DV 3O7-Z
Crew names on the Runneymede Memorial.

S/L I. Robertson DFC Killed age 22
Sgt R. Calvert Killed
F/O S.I. Kennedy Killed
F/Sgt S.T. Player Killed
P/O B.W. Zeal Killed
P/O T. Wright Killed
Tech Sgt E. Jones USAF Killed
F/Lt A.H. Duringer DFC DFM Killed

106 Sqdn: Lanc JB 645-F
Crew are buried in Berlin.

P/O E.C. Holbourne Killed
Sgt H.V. Walmsley Killed
Sgt E.N. Burton Killed
Sgt T.T. Powell Killed
Sgt J.H. Dyer Killed
Sgt T.H. Mallett Killed
F/Sgt S.R. Mattick Killed

106 Sqdn: Lanc JB 642-J
Those killed buried in Hanover.
Crashed at Hoya on outward leg.

P/O F.H. Garnett Killed age 21
Sgt D. McLean Killed
F/Sgt T.J. Thomas Killed
Sgt E.M.J. Pease Killed
Sgt E. Edge Killed
Sgt J.A. Withington Killed
Sgt A.A.E. Elsworthy POW

156 Sqdn: Lanc JB 476-R
Crew buried in Berlin.

F/O T. Doherty Killed
P/O C.L. Gynther Killed
W/O L.F. Gill Killed
F/O W. Raper Killed
F/O W.A. Robertson Killed
F/Sgt W. Lumsden Killed
F/Sgt J. Murray Killed

156 Sqdn: Lanc ND 384-D
Buried Chievres, Hainaut, Belgium.
Crashed at Glandreu on return leg.

P/O G.P.R. Bond DFC Killed age 22
P/O A. Morassi Killed
Sgt G. Barry Killed
P/O C.E. Blanchette Killed
F/O A.R. Relsover Killed
F/O V. Waterhouse Killed
F/Sgt R. Underwood Killed

156 Sqdn: Lanc JB 703-X
Crew buried in Berlin.

S/L R.G.F. Stewart DFC Killed age 23
F/Sgt R.J. Hudson Killed
P/O C.M. Handley Killed
F/Sgt F. Thorington Killed
F/Lt M.S. Fletcher Killed
F/Lt C.F. Horner Killed

156 Sqdn: Lanc JA 925-L
Crew names on the Runneymede Memorial.

S/L R.E. Fawcett DFC Killed
P/O P.R. Lyford Killed
F/Sgt J. Bell Killed
F/Sgt R.J. Bowen Killed
P/O G. Vickers Killed
F/Sgt G.M. Headley Killed
F/Sgt B.C. Hinks Killed

207 Sqdn: Lanc DV 370-L
Crew names on the Runneymede Memorial.

P/O W.J. Bottrell Killed age 29 later F/O
Sgt F. Holland Killed
Sgt S. Ecelestone Killed

Squadron and Aircraft

Crew

Sgt F.W. Porteous Killed
Sgt K.H.H. Wardle Killed
Sgt J. O'Mahony Killed
Sgt R Clark Killed

207 Sqdn: Lanc W 4892-T
Solmon had completed 24 trips and was due to
complete his tour with the USAAF. He and
Debardcleben Buried in the US Military Cemetery
Neuville-en-Conoz
Remainder of Crew buried in Berlin

Lt F. B. Solmon USAF Killed
Sgt W.J. Cant Killed
Lt W.A. Debardcleben USAF Killed
Sgt A.W. Lawrie Killed
Sgt F. Morgan Killed
F/Sgt H.M. Scot Killed
P/O P.S. Watt Killed
F/S L.D. Gosney RCAF 2/Pilot Killed

405 Sqdn: Halifax JR 280-K
Crashed at Berle, Holland. Crew buried
Schoonebeek, Drenthe, Holland.

F/O T.H. Donnelly RCAF DFM Killed
F/O A.J. Salaba Killed
F/Sgt W.L.J. Clark Killed
Sgt B.S.J. West Killed
Sgt R.E. Watts Killed
Sgt R. Zimmer Killed
Sgt L.G.R. Miller Killed

405 Sqdn: Halifax JR 737-R
Those killed buried St Pol, Pas de Calais, France.
Crashed on the home leg near St-Pol-Sun Ternoise.

F/O A.P. Campbell RCAF Killed age 22
P/O T.D. Gavin Killed
F/Sgt J.B. Dunne Killed
Sgt J. Redhead Killed
P/O D.N. Thompson POW
F/Sgt B.C. Cameron Killed
Sgt D.J. Leslie POW

460 Sqn: JB 606-H
All are buried in Berlin.
Crashed at Muckenderf

F/Sgt R.W. Rowley RAAF
Sgt W. Fleming
F/O E.C. Truscott RAAF
F/O A Robinson RAAF
F/Sgt L.A.Chester
Sgt R.H. Lawn RAAF
P/O H.E. Bennett

463 Sqdn: Lanc W 4897-Q
Crew name son the Runneymede Memorial

F/Sgt S.W. Lawson RAAF Killed later P/O
Sgt P. Chittenden Killed
Sgt A.G. Smith Killed
F/Sgt C.D. Redgrave Killed
F/Sgt M.E. Sadler RAAF Killed
F/Sgt W.A. Sampey RAAF Killed
Sgt F.C. Eggleson Killed

467 Sqdn: Lanc LM 372-K
Crew are buried in Celle,Germany.

F/O L.B. Patkin Killed
Sgt R. Chambers Killed
F/O R.J.A. Maidstone Killed
Sgt G.A. Litchfleld Killed
F/Sgt W.D. Blackwell RAAF Killed
F/Sgt H.D. Scott RAAF Killed
F/Sgt A.N. Boetteher RAAF Killed
F/Sgt J. Mudie RAAF Killed

550 Sqdn: Lanc DV 189-T2

F/O J.G. Bryson Killed

Crew buried Hannover.
Attacke dby a nightfighter on outward leg crashed
to the south of Hoya.

Sgt T.F.M. Roxby Killed
Sgt D.F. Fadden POW
F/Sgt P.H. Evans POW Stalag IVB
Sgt J.E. Donnan POW Stalag IVB
Sgt J.J. Saukins POW
Sgt W.C. Gundry POW Stalag IVB

Squadron and Aircraft	*Crew*

626 Sqdn: Lanc DV 190-B2
Crew buried in Berlin.
Crashed at Garselegen

Sgt E. Berry Killed
Sgt J.B. Edwards Killed
Sgt S. Henderson Killed
Sgt R.H. Doull Killed
Sgt E. Atkinson Killed
Sgt V.H. Trayler Killed
Sgt J. Waters Killed

630 Sqdn: Lanc JB 532-X
Crew buried in Berlin.
Crashed at Grossbeuthen

F/Lt D.A. MacDonald RCAF Killed age 20
S/L K.F. Vare 2/Pilot Killed
Sgt R.F. Smale Killed
F/O N.E. Westergard Killed
F/Sgt J.M. Turubull Killed
Sgt W.R. Tyrie Killed
F/Sgt W. Jenkins Killed
F/Sgt W.J. Roche Killed

Crashed in the UK

)S 796-E
orce landed at Stertham nr Ely

F/Sgt R.E. Chantler
Sgt G Ralwings
P/O D.M.Drew
F/Sgt R/L. Francis RCAF
Sgt D.P. Nash
Sgt K. Farmer
Sgt W.N.W. Brown

)V 345-Z
'rashed on return at Whaphole Grove

F/O R.H Mawle
Sgt P.P. O'Meara
F/O. de Menten de Home
Sgt J.R. Ransing
Sgt M.G. Capel
Sgt C.W. Taylor RCAF
Sgt E. Skelton

F/O Mawle buried Eastbourne
Sgt O'Meara buried Tiiperary
F/O de Menten buried Melveren, Belgium
Sgt Ransing buried Harpham
Sgt Capel buried Cambridge
Sgt Taylor Buried Cambridge
Sgt Kelton buried Wold Newton

2nd/3rd January 1944

Squadron and Aircraft	*Crew*

7 Sqdn Lanc JB 677-U
Crew names on Runneymede Memorial.
Crashed at Fursteriwolde

F/Lt I.M. Pearson DFC Killed
F/Sgt W. Curie Killed
F/Sgt L.T. Wilmshurst Killed
P/O R.J. Wheway Killed
F/Sgt M. Davies POW
F/Sgt S.W. Raynor Killed
F/Sgt J.J. Davenport Killed

49 Sqdn: Lanc JB 727-S
Crew have no known grave, but are on the
Runneymede Memorial.

F/Lt C.J.E. Palmer Killed
Sgt P.O. Camm Killed
F/O G.T. Young Killed
Sgt H. Conrad Killed

Squadron and Aircraft

Crew

Sgt D.F. Prusher Killed
P/O R. Stobo Killed
Sgt D.D.R. Dallaway Killed

49 Sqdn: Lanc JB 231-N
Beleived shot down by flak in target area.

F/O J.E.M. Young RCAF POW Stalag LIII
Sgt A.W. Vidow POW Stalag LIII
P/O J.M. Scott POW Stalag LIII
Sgt E.B. Cachart POW Stalag 357
Sgt M.R.A. Mahony POW Stalag IVB
P/O L.M. Orchard POW Stalag LIII
Sgt L.C. Crossman POW Stalag LIII

57 Sqdn: Lanc JB 681-J
Crew buried in Berlin.

F/Sgt G. Ely RAAF Killed age 28 later P/O
Sgt S.. Lewis RCAF Killed
Sgt R.W. Homewood Killed
F/O A.W.C. Nixon RCAF Killed
Sgt A.W.C. Ball RCAF Killed
Sgt A.S. Pilbeam Killed
Sgt K.H. Harper Killed

57 Sqdn: Lanc JB 364-M
Shot down over Berlin. Crew buried in Berlin.
Crashed at Luhme

F/O D.A. Shewan Killed
Sgt E.R. Hughes Killed
F/Sgt R. Stevenson Killed
F/O W.G. Cockwill Killed
Sgt A. Cohen Killed
Sgt D.A. Dixon Killed
Sgt P.J.. Parraball POW Wounded

61 Sqdn: Lanc DV 401-Z
Crew buried in Gaasterland, Friesland, Holland.
Crashed at Mims

F/O G.A. Tul Killed age 22
Sgt G.E. Heasman Killed
Sgt J.G. Holden Killed
F/Sgt J.S. Baldwin Killed
Sgt J. Stock Killed
Sgt C.G. Crosby Killed
Sgt C. Ablett Killed

83 Sqdn: Lanc JB 355-J
Crew are buried in Berlin.
Crashed nr Neuenhagen to Honow Road

F/O F.C. Allcroft DFC Killed
Sgt A.W. Bell Killed
P/O A.W. Blakeman DFC Killed
F/Sgt R. Ellwood Killed
P/O R.P. Watts Killed
F/Sgt J.A. Thomas Killed
F/Sgt J.B. Wood Killed

83 Sqdn: Lanc JB 114-Q
Crew are buried in Berlin.

F/Lt L.W. Munro Killed
F/Sgt D. Cromer DFM Killed
F/O P.H. Ewin Killed
P/O J.T. Hitchen Killed
P/O C.D. Wall Killed
F/Sgt R.J. Hunter Killed
F/O G.R. Harris Killed

83 Sqn: Lanc JB 453-F
Crew buried in Berlin
Crashed at Blankenburg

P/O E.B.Stiles RCAF Killed
F/Sgt P.Traynor Killed
P/O D.C.J. McKendry Killed
F/O W.H. Dyke Killed
Sgt J. Banks Killed
Sgt J. McDunlop Killed
F/O I.G. Allan Killed

83 Sqn:Lanc ND 330-O
Crew buried in Hannover
Crashed at Wahoenholz

W/O A.W.Robinson Killed
Sgt. W.J.Blakely RCAF Killed
F/O D.J.Elliott RCAF Killed
F/Sgt G.R.Evans Killed

Squadron and Aircraft	*Crew*

F/Sgt J.D.Clarke Killed
F/Sgt J. Anderson Killed
WOII T.H. Nolan RCAF Killed

100 Sqdn: Lanc JB 549-C
Crew names on Runneymede Memorial.

P/O G.W. Henderson RCAF Killed age 22
Sgt L.J. Loewenson Killed
F/O J.McVie. Ogilvie Killed
Sgt G.H. Hendry Killed
Sgt N. Bowman Killed
Sgt R.E.L. Stoneman Killed
Sgt E.C. McLaughlin Killed

101 Sqdn: Lanc DV 269-M
Crew buried in Berlin.
Crashed at Michendorf on retuen leg,

F/Lt A.L. Lazenby DFC Killed
Sgt C. Lindsay Killed
F/O W. Craig Killed
Sgt A.A. Walton POW
F/O J. McClure POW
Sgt G.A. Beckett Killed
Sgt D.H. Stephens Killed
Sgt C.D. Browne Killed

103 Sqdn: Lanc JB 747-M
Crew are buried in Berlin.
Crashed at Zehrensdorf

W/O E..T. Townsend Killed
Sgt H.A. Joint Killed
F/O G.S. Palin Killed
Sgt C.R. Greenwell Killed
Sgt A.J. Larby Killed
Sgt J.W. Bateman Killed
Sgt R.G. Creber Killed

115 Sqdn: Lanc DS 667-G
F/Sgt Hayes died 26 Jan 1944 aged 22 and is buried
in Berlin.

F/Sgt R.J. Hayes Died while a POW age 22
W/O B.N.M.A. Booth POW Stalag 4B
Sgt F.W. Wardale POW Stalag L3
F/O E.F. Bridgman POW Stalag L3
Sgt F. Pearson POW Stalag LVI Repatriated
2/2/1945
Sgt J.R. Dodds POW Stalag LIII Repatriated
6/2/1945
Sgt J. Weatherstone POW

156 Sqdn: Lanc ND 380-T
Crew names on Runneymede Memorial.
Crashed at Riesdorf.

F/O C.G. Cairns DFM Killed age 23
F/Lt R.C. Blockley Killed
Sgt C.T.R. Morris Killed
Sgt H. Martin Killed
Sgt J.F. Haywood Killed
Sgt E.J. Sutton Killed
F/Sgt J.P.R. Mount Killed

156 Sqdn: Lanc JB 640-V
Crew names on Runneymede Memorial.

P/O J.D.R. Cromarty Killed age 23
Sgt P.E. Woolven Killed
Sgt N.H. Colebatch Killed
F/Sgt L.M. Lapthome Killed
F/Sgt D.F. Burtenshaw Killed
F/Sgt R.J. Collens Killed
F/Sgt K.S.J. Chapman Killed

156 Sqdn: Lanc JB 553-J
Crew names on Runneymede Memorial.
Shot down over Berlin and crashed on Reinkendafe
Street 3/1/1944.

P/O J. Borland Killed age 20
F/Lt A.N. McGlashan Killed
W/O V.R. Purnal Killed
Sgt D.B. MacKensie Killed
Sgt J.S. Scott Killed
F/Sgt D.C.G. Snelling Killed
Sgt A. Wailer Killed
W/O L.J. Adair Killed

Squadron and Aircraft

Crew

156 Sqdn: Lanc JB 317-C
Those killed are on the Runneymede Memorial.
Attacked by a nightfighter near Bremen on outward
leg.

Sgt A.D. Barnes Killed age 20 later F/Sgt
P/O R.S. Smith POW Stalag LIII
Sgt R.V. Huliman Killed
Sgt W. Hall POW Stalag IVB
F/Sgt F.C.G. Colk POW
Sgt R. Davis POW
Sgt A.J. Hackett Killed

156 Sqdn: Lanc JB 810-O
Crew buried in Berlin.

F/Lt J.C. Ralph RNAF DFM Killed age 24
Sgt C.R. King Killed
Sgt K. Aspinall Killed
Sgt K. Hunt Killed
F/Sgt A.H. Hayward Killed
Sgt G. Griffiths Killed
Sgt P.E. Pout Killed

166 Sqdn: Lanc W 4780-H2
Crew names on Runneymede Memorial.

Sgt G. Firth Killed age 23
Sgt E.A. Oldham Killed
Sgt J. Birthwhistle Killed
Sgt P. Murray Killed
F/Sgt W.P. Harrison Killed
Sgt J. Hamilton Killed
Sgt H.F. Hales Killed

405 Sqdn: Lanc ND 380-O
Crew buried in Hanover.

W/O A.W. Robinson Killed age 30
F/O D.J. Elliott Killed
F/Sgt G.R. Evans Killed
F/Sgt J.D. Clarke Killed
F/Sgt J. Anderson Killed
W/O T.F. Nolan Killed
Sgt W.J. Blakely Killed

408 Sqdn: Lanc LL 681-G
F/Sgt Hilker from Canada was on his fourth trip.
Those killed on the Runneymede Memorial.

F/Sgt D.E. Hilker RCAF Killed age 20
F/O E. Deakin POW Stalag LIII
P/O G.C. Morlock POW Stalag LIII
WO2 L.P. Toepe POW Stalag IVB
Sgs H.J. Mouland Killed
Sgt S.R. Sweetzir POW Stalag 357
Sgt H.C. Hawkins POW Stalag IVB

426 Sqdn: Lanc DS 760-M
Crew names on Runneymede Memorial.

P/O CA. Griffiths RCAF Killed age 21
F/Sgt L. Offer Killed
F/Sgt P. Allwell Killed
P/O R.H. Filby Killed
P/O G. Spooks POW Stalag LIII
Sgt G. Jowett Killed
Sgt R.A. Cridland POW Stalag IVB
WO2 F.R. Symons Killed

432 Sqdn: Lanc DS 739-Y
All the Crew apart from Sgt Corbett are buried in
Berlin. He is buried in Choloy in France having
been re-interned by a US Graves investigation unit.

F/Lt J.A. Allen RCAF Killed age 23
F/O H. Doull RCAF Killed
F/O K. Crawford RCAF Killed
W/O J.E. Scott RCAF Killed
Sgt A.S. Dupois RCAF Killed
Sgt J.A. Corbett Killed
Sgt W.R. Collier Killed

460 Sqdn: Lanc JB 606-H
Crew are buried in Berlin.

F/Sgt R.W. Rowley Killed
Sgt W. Fleming Killed
P/O A.J. Robinson Killed
F/O E.C. Truscott Killed
F/Sgt L.A. Chester Killed
Sgt R.H. Lawn Killed
P/O H.E. Bennett Killed

Squadron and Aircraft	*Crew*
463 Sqdn: Lanc JA 902-D Crew buried in Vollenhove, Overrijssel, Holland. Crashed on what is now the Noord-Oost-Polder, the Netherlands.	F/Sgt J. Weatherill RAAF Killed age 20 later P/O Sgt A.E. Cowell Killed P/O J.W. Cage Killed Sgt F.N. Looney Killed Sgt W.D. Toohey Killed P/O P.L. Symonds Killed Sgt C. Hemingway Killed
619 Sqdn: Lanc JB 123-D Crew buried in Hamburg. Crashed at Wense.	F/O J.A.F. Heffernan RCAF Killed age 25 Sgt K.W. Cheshire Killed F/O L.C. Keeling Killed F/O A.B. Bearcroft Killed F/O W.C.J. Lord Killed F/Sgt K.M. MacDonald Killed W/O E.S.I. Evans Killed
619 Sqdn: Lanc LM 423-H Shot down by a fighter over Zyder Zee. Those killed buried in the Reichswald War Cemetery. Abanson after a nighfighter attack.	F/Lt J.K. Cox Killed Sgt G.J. Hawkins POW Stalag 4B F/O R.W. Braid POW Stalag LIII Sgt C.G. Payne Killed Sgt D. Burden Killed Sgt J. Cooksey Killed Sgt G.M.Braid Stalag LIII

Aircraft crashed in the United Kingdom

Squadron and Aircraft	*Crew*
460 Sqdn: Lanc JB 738-T	F/Lt B.A. Knyvett Killed
Took off at 2380 completed a half circuit, then dived into the ground at 2336, a quarter of a mile east of Binbrook Village.	Sgt R.D. Trett Killed Sgt J. Dobinson Killed F/Sgt J.W.A. Farthing Killed F/Sgt H.J. Gill Killed P/O E.J. Ross Killed P/O C.R. Pickworth Killed
560 Sqdn: Lanc DV 845 Crashed at Whaphole near Spalding on take off.	F/O R.H. Mawle Killed Sgt P.P. O'Meara Killed F/O G. Home Killed Sgt J.R. Rounding Killed Sgt M.G. Capel Killed Sgt C.W. Taylor Killed Sgt E. Skelton Killed

20th/21st January 1944

Squadron and Aircraft	*Crew*
7 Sqdn: Lanc ND 368-U Shot down by a nightfighter. Those killed buried in Berlin. Bartholmew was only 18 was brought in to hospital with a broken neck, having been hit with a rifle butt after bailing out. He was taken to the operating theatre and not seen again. But is known to have died six days later. Crashed at Doberitz.	S/L M.J. Baird-Smith POW Stalag LIII F/O F.O Waddington POW Stalag LIII F/Lt R.J. Andrews Killed P/O D.C. Johostone Killed Sgt E.F. Bartholmew died while a prisoner F/Lt R.N. Ridley Killed W/O W.D. Brown Killed
10 Sqdn: Halifax JD 470-S Those killed are recorded on the Runneymede Memorial	F/Sgt D.A. Arthur Killed age 21 Sgt D.Jackson POW Sgt D.H. Laraman POW Stalag LIII Sgt L. Dryer Killed

Squadron and Aircraft

Crew

Sgt D.C. Bolton Killed
Sgt R.W. Branchflower Killed
Sgt A.J. Gilders Killed

10 Sqdn: Halifax JN 899-T
Crew buried in Berlin.

P/O F. Crothers Killed age 22
F/Lt H.C. Eaton Killed
Sgt D. Logue Killed
Sgt W. Good[ellow Killed
Sgt C. Mason Killed
Sgt R. Scotland Killed
Sgt T. Stones Killed

57 Sqdn: Lanc JB 419-E
Those killed buried in Berlin.
Crashed at Kienberg

P/O J.C. MacGilvray Killed
Sgt F. Wilson Killed
Sgt N. Cottrell Killed
Sgt J.S. Whittle POW Stalag 357
Sgt R.S.W. Cowdrey Killed
Sgt D.R. Mills Killed
F/Sgt J.P. Irwin Killed

76 Sqdn: Halifax LK 958-Q
Crashed at Luckstedt. Those killed buried in Berlin.

P/O G.C. Ive RAAF Killed age 24
Sgt K.C. Buchan POW Stalag LVI
Sgt K.F. Hutson Killed
F/Sgt M.F. Curry POW Stalag LVI
Sgt J.C. Stones Killed
Sgt R.V. Turner Killed
Sgt A.J.E. Raven Killed

76 Sqdn: Halifax LK 921-R
Crashed 15 km NW of Burgkemnitz; crew all
buried in Berlin.

F/Sgt V. Parrott Killed
F/Sgt A.L.P. Gibson Killed
F/Sgt J.L. Miriams Killed
F/Sgt F.W. Hickman Killed
Sgt J.T. Hadland Killed
Sgt J. Vicary Killed
F/Sgt L.J. McCrathy Killed

76 Sqdn: Halifax LL 116-X
Crash-landed at Lievin, 5 km west of Lens, France.
F/O Morris age 25 buried at Longuenesse(St
Omer), Pas De Calais, France

P/O G.G.A. Whitehead Evaded
Sgt R.G. Prior 2/Pilot POW Stalag LVI
F/O H.D.G. Morris Killed
W/O J. McTrach Evaded
Sgt L. Stokes POW Stalag LVI Wounded
Sgt J.M. Fisher Evaded
Sgt B. Compton Evaded

77 Sqdn: Halifax HR 946-X
Those killed are recorded on the Runneymede
Memorial.

F/Lt V.H. Surplice DFC Killed
Sgt A.A. Timson Killed
Sgt H.P. Hopkins Killed
Sgt J.L. Duffy DFM POW Stalag LI
Sgt T. King DFM Killed
Sgt K. Emeny Killed
F/Sgt B.H. Stevens Killed
Sgt L. Ashton Killed

78 Sqdn: Halifax LW 291-M
Those killed buried in Berlin.

F/Sgt F.R. Moffat RCAF Killed later WO age 20
F/O R.L. McGregor POW Stalag LIII
F/O R.G. Selman Killed
Sgt H. Bennet POW
Sgt N. Legg Killed
Sgt H.W. Rudlehoff Killed
Sgt J.A. Sewart Killed

83 Sqdn: Lanc ED 974-Y
Those killed are buried in Berlin.

P/O G.I. Ransome RCAF Killed later F/O
Sgt G.S. Mc MacKinnon POW
F/Sgt C.F. Plumb Killed.

Squadron and Aircraft	*Crew*
	Sgt A.W. Coote Killed
	Sgt F.T. West Killed
	Sgt P.V. De Villies Killed
	F/Sgt A.E. Millard DFM Killed

83 Sqdn: Lanc JB 461-L
Hit by flak and exploded. Those killed buried in Berlin. F/Lt King was taken to the Herman Goring Luftwaffe hospital in a motor bike and side car. He had a bad arm wound but apart from that was okay. He wasrepatriated on the Letitia 2/2/1945

F/Lt R. King RAAF DFC POW Stalag LIII
F/Sgt K.E.L. Farmelow Killed
F/Sgt H.E. Borrow DFM Killed later P/O
F/Sgt D.J. Phelan Killed
F/Lt W.G. Ross DFC DFM Killed
F/Sgt E.D.McPherson DFM Killed
F/Sgt R.A. Adams DFM Killed

83 Sqdn: Lanc ND 414-K
Those killed buried in Berlin. S/L Jones had already served one tour with 75 NZ Squadron and F/Lt Butler a tour with 99 Sqn.

S/L A.P. Jones DFC Wounded and POW Stalag LIII
F/Lt N. Butler DFC Wounded and POW Stalag LIII
Sgt A.J.H. Gainsborough-Allen Killed
Sgt W.S. Travers Killed
P/O E. Anderson Killed
F/Sgt E.R. Jacobs Killed
F/O H.L.G. Dobson DFM Killed

97 Sqdn: Lanc ND 367-K
Crew buried in Berlin.
Crashed at Zahrensdorf.

P/O C.A. Wakley Killed
Sgt G. Taylor POW Stalag IVB
Sgt A.J. Alexander POW
Sgt E. Lowe POW Stalag IVB
Sgt R.G. China Killed
Sgt J. Tye Killed
Sgt B.H. Stedman Killed

101 Sqdn: Lanc LM 387-O
Crew have no known grave, but are on the Runneymede Memorial.

F/O S.W.W. Perry Killed
Sgt T.W. Dune Killed
F/Sgt N.G. Dowler Killed
Sgt P.F.. Searle Killed
Sgt R.A. Hart Killed
W/O F. Stokes Killed
Sgt W. Whifield Killed
F/O R.J. Wilson Killed

102 Sqdn: Halifax EW 337-F
Those killed buried in Berlin.

F/O G.A. Griffiths POW Stalag LIII
Sgt K.F. Stanbridge RAAF Killed
F/Sgt R.C. Wilson POW
F/Sgt E.A. Church Killed
F/Sgt C.G. Dupieis Killed
Sgt H.J. Bushell POW Stalag LVI
Sgt J. Bremner POW Stalag LIII
F/O L.A. Underwood POW Stalag LIII

102 Sqdn: Halifax HX 187-H
Those killed buried in Berlin.

P/O A.W. Dean POW
Sgt A. Whittle POW Stalag LVI
Sgt S.R. Stone POW Stalag LVI
Sgt D.S. Veale POW Stalag LVI
Sgt J.H.L. Towler POW Stalag IVB
Sgt A. Watson Killed
Sgt A. Landen Killed
F/O J. Nelson Killed

102 Sqdn: Halifax JN 951-N
Those killed buried in Berlin.

F/Sgt E. Render POW Stalag LVI
F/Sgt F.A. Dobson Killed
Sgt F.M. Obray Killed
Sgt J.E. Lyons Killed
Sgt R. Frankish Killed
Sgt G.H. Gayer Killed
F/O E.A. Richardson Killed

Squadron and Aircraft	Crew
102 Sqdn: Halifax 227-X Shot down by a fighter.	W/O R.G. Wilding POW Stalag LVI Sgt R.W. Chandler POW Stalag LVI Sgt T.K. Buxton POW Stalag LVI W/O F.F. Yeager POW Stalag IVB Sgt H. Sheppard POW Stalag LVI Sgt J.L. Corrigan POW Stalag LVI Sgt J.C. Heap POW Stalag LVI
102 Sqdn: Halifax JD 461-V F/Sgt Moss buried in Berlin.	F/Sgt R. Compston POW Stalag LIII Sgt E.W.B. Evans POW Stalag LIII Sgt W.J.M. Eastwood POW Stalag LIII Sgt E.R.P. Smith POW Stalag LIII Sgt DV. Metcalfe POW Stalag IVB Sgt D. Courtney POW Stalag IVB F/Sgt F. Moss Killed
115 Sqdn: Lanc LL 650-J Shot down by a nightfighter. Those killed buried in Berlin. Crashed at Tetlow	P/O D. Canning Killed age 21 Sgt J.D. Groves Killed Sgt J. Hill Killed F/Sgt B.J. Lobb Killed Sgt A. Mickus Killed F/Sgt W.F.J. Hocking POW F/Sgt R. Brotherton Killed
158 Sqdn: Halifax LV 773-R Crew buried in Hamburg.	F/Sgt R.H. Thompson RCAF Killed Sgt A.J. Poulton Killed Sgt A. Radley Killed Sgt R.J. Standley Killed Sgt H.W. Spackman Killed Sgt L.G. Neary Killed Sgt D. Fowler Killed
166 Sqdn: Lanc R 5862-N2 Shot down by a night fighter over Berlin. Those killed buried in Berlin.	F/Sgt R.W. Sutton Killed age 21 Sgt D.J. Edwards Killed F/Sgt L.W. Mattin Killed Sgt M.F. Early POW Stalag LVI F/Sgt C.B. Jeffery Killed Sgt A.A. Mansfield Killed Sgt C.H. Rusk POW Stalag IVB
419 Sqdn: Halifax DT 731-M Shot down by a night fighter, SW of Leipzig.	F/Sgt I.V. Hopkins POW F/Sgt W E. McKenzie POW F/Sgt F.A. Paules POW P/O A. Cormack POW Sgt J. Chambers POW Sgt E.R. Jenkins POW Stalag IVB Sgt W.D. MeCaghey POW Stalag LIII
419 Sqdn: Halifax HX 162-X Shot down by a night fighter. Most of the crew who survived were wounded in the action. Those killed buried Kiel, Germany.	P/O H.L. Bullis POW Stalag LIII W/O A.H. Towers POW Stalag LVI F/Sgt B.H. Boisvert RCAF POW Sgt R. Bonathan RCAF Killed Sgt D.J. Ferguson Killed Sgt E.S. Sanderson Killed Sgt M.A. Potter POW Stalag IVB
426 Sqdn: Halifax LL 628-Y P/O Polson's father had been killed in action on 14th November 1917 with the 1st Ontario Regiment. Crew buried in Berlin. P/O Ketcher's DFM Gazetted 15/2/ 1944 This crew had already sruvived a crash landing 23/24/9/1943 in Lancaster DS 714.	F/Lt L.N. McCaig RCAF DFC Killed age 28 P/O R.J. Orr Killed F/Sgt T.J. Preece Killed P/O R.D. Poison Killed P/O R.W. Elliott Killed P/O G.R. Ketcher DFM Killed WO2 E.S. Hawkes DFC Killed

Squadron and Aircraft	*Crew*
427 Sqdn: Halifax EB 246-S Crew are buried in Berlin.	P/O N.E. Cook Killed F/Sgt J.G. Goflin Killed P/O R.S. Thompson Killed F/Sgt C. Cook Killed Sgt B.C. Prill Killed F/Sgt B.E. Findlay Killed Sgt J.S. Child Killed
428 Sqdn: Halifax LK 739-P Crew baled out over France; Banner arrived back in the UK on 24th March 1944, Fryer evaded via Switzerland.	F/Sgt F.E. Reaine POW F/O A.R. Fisher POW F/O J.G.Y. Lavoie POW F/Sgt W.E. Fell POW F/Sgt W.T. Banner Evaded Sgt L.R. Fryer Evaded Sgt W.R. Wynveen POW
429 Sqdn: Halifax LL 197-L Crew buried Berlin.	F/O H.D. Paddison RCAF Killed P/O B.N. Forster Killed F/O J. McRamsay Killed Sgt W.H. Bryant Killed F/O A.A. Ares Killed Sgt N.E. Carter Killed Sgt R.A. Saffran POW
434 Sqdn: Halifax LL 141-H Crew are buried in Berlin.	P/O J.T. Clinkskill Killed F/O W R. Sloan Killed Sgt C.J. Jones Killed Sgt C.C. Casey Killed Sgt E.W. McCaffrey Killed Sgt D.J. Gillam Killed Sgt V.G. Baker Killed
434 Sqdn: Halifax LL 179-K Shot down by a night fighter. Those killed are on the Runneymede Memorial.	Sgt G.C. Mould RCAF Killed later F/Sgt F/Sgt A.M. Wilson POW P/O W.C. Drumm POW Stalag LIII Sgt R.T. Cox POW Sgt P. Dack POW Sgt J.A. McKenna Killed Sgt E. Porter Killed
434 Sqdn: Halifax LL 135-R Those killed buried in Berlin.	F/O C.S. Brest RCAF Killed P/O W.M. Kipp POW P/O J. Snowesell POW Sgt L.H. Doe Killed P/O M.C. Gnius Killed Sgt H.B. Hill Killed Sgt J. Morgan Killed
460 Sqdn: Lanc JB 739-E Those killed buried in Berlin. Attacked by a nightfighter and abandon in the air crashed at Mecklenburg	F/Sgt A.J. Lynch Killed age 27 Sgt E. Mortimer Killed P/O J.D. Vaughan POW Stalag LIII F/Sgt .S. Trinder POW Stalag 357 F/Sgt J.A. Cassidy POW Stalag 357 P/O D. Alexandtros POW Stalag LIII P/O L.J. Lawler POW Stalag LIII
466 Sqdn: Halifax HX 278-Z Crew buried Becklingen, Soltau, Germany.	F/Lt W.G. Baldwin RAAF Killed age 33 P/O M.R. Sparrow Killed W/O J.P. Morrow Killed F/Sgt J.T. Gilchrist Killed F/Sgt F. Rushworth Killed W/O K.E. Rimmington Killed Sgt J.McM. Fleming Killed F/O W.L. Clemo Killed

Squadron and Aircraft	Crew
622 Sqdn: Lanc W 5483 D Crew buried in Berlin.	F/Lt D.A. Claydon RCAF Killed age 22 P/O W.H. Davies Killed Sgt D.F. Bache Killed Sgt P.J. Maher Killed Sgt S.E. James Killed F/Sgt F. Mosley Killed Sgt H. Graham Killed
622 Sqdn: Lanc R 5915-P Shot down by a night fighter. Those killed buried at Becklingen, Soltau, Germany. Crashed near Bad Bevensen	F/Sgt R.G. Deacon Killed F/Sgt P.J. Irwin POW Wounded F/Lt K.R. Miller POW Stalag LIII Sgt J.H. Kidman Killed Sgt N. Butler Killed Sgt A.W. Woodcock Killed Sgt J. Cunningham Killed Sgt J.B. Strange Killed
630 Sqn: Lanc JB 294- All but Walker buried in Berlin. A diversionary Berlin operation,	F/Sgt J.W. Homewood Killed Sgt W.G. Yorke Killed F/Sgt A.W. Reedman Killed Sgt G.S. Walker Stalag 357 Sgt A.C. Stopp Killed Sgt J.D.Morris Killed F/Sgt M.S. Marks RCAF Killed

Aircraft crashed in the United Kingdom

Squadron and Aircraft	Crew
102 Sqdn: Halifax JD 302-D Crash-landed near Norwich.	F/Sgt Proctor and crew uninjured except bomb aimer F/O Turnbull who died of his injuries.
102 Sqdn: Halifax HR 716-P	F/O Hall and his crew had to bale out owing to fuel shortage; all landed safely. Aircraft crashed in the United Kingdom.

427 Sqdn: Halifax LL 191-N
After three attempts overskidded the runway on landing, crashing into tree tops and ending up in a nearby field. The pilot F/O Cozens, Navigator F/O L.G. Biddicombe, F/E Sgt J. McGowan, and Bomb Aimer Sgt W.L. Stockford were killed or died later. Sgt H.P. Whittaker was seriously injured and F/Sgt C.L. Bernier and Sgt R.B. Naim were uninjured. F/O Cozens had only been married for a month.

| 484 Sqdn: Halifax LK 656
Aircraft crashed in Driffield area crew baled out. | F/Sgt F. Johnson Injured
P/O R. Davis Uninjured
Sgt J. Campbell Injured
Sgt A. Hessian Uninjured
Sgt W. Whitton Uninjured
Sgt D. Tofflemeir Injured
Sgt S. Phillips Uninjured |
| 622 Sqdn: Lanc L 7576 | F/Sgt T. Hargreaves |

The pilot, navigator Sgt R.L. Unwin and F/E Sgt F. Williams were all hurt by flak, but despite this Sgt Urwin navigated the aircraft back to base then collapsed. He was recommended for an immediate DFM.

27th/28th January 1944

Squadron and Aircraft	Crew
9 Sqdn: Lanc LL 745-M F/Lt James was only 19; he had joined the RAF at	F/Lt S. James Killed age 19 Sgt G.R. Tomlinson Killed

Squadron and Aircraft	*Crew*

the age of 16. Those killed buried in the Durnbach
War Cemetery.
Last heard on the WT at 19.32

F/Sgt A.W. Archer Killed
F/Sgt A.H. Howie POW Stalag LVI
Sgt R.E. Burke Killed
Sgt R.E. Chivers POW Stalag LVI
F/Sgt H. Croxson POW Stalag LVI

12 Sqdn: Lanc JB 650-E
Crashed between Gornze and Andoumont

F/Lt C. Grannum Evaded
P/O R.H. Taylor Evaded
F/Sgt J. Quinn Evaded
P/O D.R. Murphy POW Stalag LI
P/O R.G. Hoare Evaded
Sgt K. Singleton POW Stalag 357
F/Sgt H. Owen POW Stalag 357

12 Sqdn: Lanc JB 283-W
Shot down by a night fighter. Those killed buried in
the Rheinberg War Cemetery.

S/L H.W. Goule DFC Killed age 26
Sgt S. Moller POW Stalag 357
P/O F.M. Kelleher Killed
Sgt D.W. Price Killed
Sgt H.S. Howie Killed
F/Sgt P.S. Carran Killed
F/Sgt B.K. Maunsell Killed

12 Sqdn: Lanc JB 358-J
Abandon after a nightfighter attack over Franfurt
and running out of fuel

F/Sgt E.A. Webb POW
F/Sgt G.J. Munro POW
F/Sgt R.W. McLean POW Stalag VII
Sgt D.C. Bruce POW
Sgt E.J.T. Boardman POW
Sgt R..Jenks POW
Sgt F.C. Vaughan POW

15 Sqdn: Lanc ED 323-D
Those killed are on the Runneymede Memorial.

P/O G. Clarke Killed
Sgt N.A. Mitchell POW Stalag 357
F/Sgt EL. Gold POW Stalag 357
W/O E.L.P. White Killed
F/Sgt L.I. Probert POW Stalag LI
Sgt I.A. McPhee POW
Sgt R.F. King POW Stalag IVB

49 Sqdn: Lanc JB 360-N
Those killed are buried in Berlin.

P/O K.O. Barnes RAAF DFC Killed age 20
Sgt G.E. Greenwood Killed
F/Sgt J.C. Atkinson POW Stalag LIII
Sgt A. Marshall POW Stalag LIII
F/Sgt D.W. MePhee RCAF POW
F/Sgt D. Grimley POW Stalag VI
W/O J.T. Hill RCAF Killed

57 Sqdn: Lanc JB 366-N
Shot down over Berlin. Those killed are on the
Runneymede Memorial.

P/O A.O. Wright Killed age 20
Sgt J.K. English POW Stalag LVI
F/Sgt D.N. Marsh POW Stalag 357
F/Sgt J. Rennie POW Stalag 4B
Sgt G.J. Huxtable POW Stalag LVI
Sgt R. Anderson Killed
F/Sgt R.A. Cook RAAF Killed

61 Sqdn: Lane DV 400-Y
Crew buried in Hannover.

P/O R.A. West Killed age 23
Sgt W. Warburton Killed
F/O A.V. Beetch Killed
F/Sgt L.O. Cuming RCAF Killed
Sgt C.B. Clark Killed
Sgt A.P. Brander RAAF Killed
P/O F. Langley Killed

61 Sqdn: Lanc W 4315-Q
Ditched in the sea north of Guernsey

P/O E.A. Williams Uninjured
Sgt W. Beach Killed

Squadron and Aircraft   *Crew*

after flak damage in the Hannover area.   F/Sgt A. D. Beesley Uninjured
Sgt Beach age 21 is buried in Fort George Military   Sgt A.D. Anderson Uninjured
Cemetery, St Peter Port Channel Islands.   Sgt J.L. Parker Uninjured
                                                     Sgt T. Bowden Killed
                                                     Sgt C.A. Acombe-Hill Killed

83 Sqdn: Lanc JB 724-V   F/Lt S.H. Alcock DFC Killed age 24
Crew buried in Hotton War Cemetery, Hotton,   Sgt S. Bullomore Killed
Luxemberg, Belgium.   F/Lt E.W. Sargant DFC Killed
Shot down a by a nighfighter flown by Maj   F/Lt L.G. Davis Killed
Wilhem Herget I/NJG4   P/O R.H. Adainson Killed
Crashed at Sautour   W/O V.G. Osterloh Killed
                                                     P/O W.H. Hewson Killed

101 Sqdn: Lanc DV 231-A   F/Sgt A.J. Sandford Killed age 22
Those killed buried in Hanover.   Sgt A.H. Smallman POW Repatriated 6/2/1945 on
Hit by flak and a nighfighter crashed beleived   Arundel Castle
Hollenstredt Northeim.   Sgt E.E. Baron Killed
                                                     Sgt T.D. Simpson Killed
                                                     Sgt R.T. Ottowell Killed
                                                     Sgt K. Bartholmew Killed
                                                     Sgt E.H. Alcock Killed
                                                     F/O J. Clark Killed

103 Sqdn: Lanc JB 277-M   P/O F.A. Whitehead Killed age 30 later F/Lt
Crew buried in Berlin.   Sgt A.G. Palmer Killed
                                                     P/O L.J. Slatter Killed
                                                     F/Sgt J.M. Cassady Killed
                                                     Sgt D.W.A. Udall Killed
                                                     Sgt W. Speakman Killed
                                                     Sgt D. Minor Killed

115 Sqdn: Lanc LL 682-P   Sgt A.C.N. Morris Killed age 23 later F/Sgt
Crew on the Runneymede Memorial.   Sgt W. Ornnet Killed
                                                     Sgt R. Browne Killed
                                                     P/O J.R. Booth Killed
                                                     Sgt L. Stone Killed
                                                     Sgt A. Kell Killed
                                                     Sgt F.W. Booth Killed

115 Sqdn: Lanc LL 668-H   F/O W.W. Ryder Killed age 20 Later F/Lt
Crew buried in the Durnbach War Cemetery.   F/Sgt R.J. Rouse Killed
Crashed at Steinberg   Sgt R.C.J. Iles Killed
                                                     P/O H.B.D. Pringle Killed
                                                     Sgt AM. Miller Killed
                                                     Sgt G.W. Rawlings Killed
                                                     Sgt P.Niel Killed

166 Sqdn: Lanc W 4996-R   P/O R.E. Hicks Killed age 22 later F/O
Crew are all buried in Berlin.   Sgt J.W. Swann Killed
                                                     Sgt D.K. Ashton Killed
                                                     P/O A.E. Cook Killed
                                                     Sgt J.T. Ravenscroft Killed
                                                     Sgt A.J. Holdom Killed
                                                     Sgt H.B. Bell Killed

408 Sqdn: Lanc DS 710-A   S/L C.W. Smith RCAF DFC Killed age 26
S/L Smith was on his 22nd Operation. For P/O   F/O D. Mc Sim Killed
Wilson it was his first. Crew buried in the   P/O J.D. Teskey RCAF Killed
Rheinberg War Cemetery.   P/O C.W. Frauts Killed
                                                     P/O T.K. Canning Killed
                                                     P/O J.G. Bennett RCAF Killed
                                                     Sgt M.F.R. Sorton Killed
                                                     2/Pilot P/O H.R. Wilson RCAF Killed

Squadron and Aircraft	*Crew*
408 Sqdn: Lanc DS 709-P F/L Kearl on his 17th trip, Sgt Brown on his first. Crew buried in Berlin. Crashed at Reichenwalde	F/Lt E.E. Kearl RCAF DFC Killed P/O J.P.D. Parise Killed F/Sgt A. Smith Killed P/O J. Adamson Killed F/Sgt J.A. McLean Killed F/Sgt J.F. McManus Killed 2/Pilot P/O E.R. Proud Killed
408 Sqdn: Lanc DS 849-X Crew are buried in Hannover. F/Lt Laine on his 20 trip and P/O Baker's his first. Crew buried in Hannover. Shot doiwn by a nighjfighter flown by Obt Wilhem Engel of III/NJG6 crashed at Wurges.	F/Lt S.R.W. Laine RCAF DFC Killed age 23 P/O J.G. Broadfood RCAF Killed F/Sgt R.J. Bradley RCAF Killed P/O D.L. Wright RCAF Killed F/Sgt G.H. Scott RCAF Killed F/Sgt R.A. MacKay RCAF Killed P/O A.E.Jones Killed 2/Pilot P/O J.J. Baker RCAF Killed
426 Sqdn: Lanc LL 688-R Crew have no known grave, but are on the Runneymede Memorial. WOII Patterson attached for operational experince.	P/O R.E. Countess Killed WOII L.H. Patterson Killed 2/Pilot from 420 Sqdn P/O KA. Solmundson Killed F/Sgt W.G. Filer Killed F/Sgt M. Kwas Killed Sgt A.P. Readdy Killed F/Sgt T.A. Thomson Killed F/Sgt V.M. Lawson Killed
426 Sqdn: Halifax DS 686-D Those killed are recorded on the Runneymede Memorial.	F/Lt T.R. Shaw RCAF Killed age 27 P/O B.E. Lynn Killed Sgt L.V. Langston POW Stalag LVI P/O J.H. Dodge Killed Sgt D.L. Huband Killed F/Sgt H. Ellis Killed Sgt T.R. King Killed
426 Sqdn: Lanc LL 721-U Those killed buried in Berlin. Attacked 3 times by a nighfighter over target area out of control and burning crashed at Rausslitz.	F/Lt M.C. Wilson POW P/O J.P.A.R Jacques POW F/Sgt M. MacDonald RCAF Killed P/O L.H. Power POW Stalag LIII Sgt W. Lawson Killed Sgt A. Carlson Killed WOII W.A. Park RCAF Killed
426 Sqdn: Halifax DS 775-W Those killed buried in Berlin. Attacked by a nightfighter crashed 2 KM east of Kade.	F/Lt A.T. Mattens Killed F/Sgt F.J. Trevithick POW Stalag LVI Sgt A.J. Belton Killed WOII E.J. Houston RCAF POW Stalag LVI Sgt W.L. Pritchard Killed Sgt R.S. Chesters Killed Sgt A.Brooks Killed
432 Sqdn: Lanc LL 638-M Crew names on the Runneymede Memorial. Crashed at Schmocklinz Where crew were at first buried.	F/O D.J. Patterson Killed F/O A.D.G. Bell RCAF Killed F/Sgt C.A. Sherwood RCAF Killed Sgt F.W. Heinen Killed RCAF F/Sgt R.P. Wilson Killed RCAF P/O A.S. Gates Killed RCAF Sgt W.R. Greenway Killed
460 Sqdn: Lanc JB 296-K Lost due to fuel suply problems	S/L L.J. Simpson RAAF DFC POW Stalag LIII F/Sgt J. Nairn POW Stalag 357 P/O C.W. McLeod POW Stalag LIII P/O A.G. Osborn POW Stalag 357 F/O J.A. Rydings POW Stalag 357

Squadron and Aircraft

Crew

F/O A.R.B. Sherock POW
P/O A. Kennedy POW Stalag LIII

463 Sqdn: Lanc ME 563
Crew buried in Berlin.
Crashed Teltar area

F/O A.J.D. Leslie RAAF Killed age 26
P/O T.V. Finn Killed
F/Sgt D.G. Barnett Killed
Sgt R.R. Jones Killed
F/O F.S.G. Chidgery Killed
Sgt A. Wiggins Killed
Sgt J. Falconer Killed

467 Sqdn: Lanc JA 860-C2
Those killed buried in Poznan, Poland.

F/Sgt W.R. McLachlan RAAF Killed age 23
Sgt W.V. Murray Killed
Sgt J.M. Jones Killed
Sgt R.C. Yates Killed
F/Sgt R.J. Rofe RAAF POW Stalag 357
F/Sgt S.W.A. Jonas RAAF POW
Sgt R.D. White POW Stalag 357

467 Sqdn: Lanc ED 589-P
Crew names on the Runneymede Memorial.

P/O C. O'Brien RAAF Killed age 27
Sgt D.J. Coombe Killed
P/O G.H. Sudds Killed
Sgt H. Boardley Killed
F/Sgt W.J. Simpson Killed
Sgt J.J. Melling Killed
Sgt F.H. Doncaster Killed

467 Sqdn: Lanc ME 575-G
Crew buried in Hannover.
Crashed at Schiedel

P/O S.C. Grugeon Killed
Sgt D. McKechnie Killed
F/Sgt A. Bryce Killed
Sgt W.A. Taylor Killed
Sgt K. Molyneux Killed
Sgt D.A. Taylor Killed
F/Sgt K E. Sehiedel Killed

576 Sqdn: Lanc ME 593-T2
Crew buried in Berlin.

F/Sgt E.W. Ebsworth Killed
Sgt J.E. Novell Killed
P/O T.C. Laing Killed
Sgt G.A. Porter Killed
Sgt G. West Killed
Sgt L.R.H. Miehell Killed
Sgt W.C. Boot Killed

622 Sqdn: Lanc ED 624-G
Shot down by night fighters. Crew buried in Berlin.
Attacked by a nighfighter when leaving target order
given to abort the aircraft which wa sout of control
and burning.

F/Sgt H.H. Craig Killed age 25
F/Sgt E.B. Sutherland POW
Sgt B.P. Dineen Killed
P/O G.G. Sproule POW
Sgt F.W. Flower Killed
Sgt F.G. Aldred Killed
Sgt D. Dart Killed

625 Sqdn: Lane ND 461-W
Hit by flak over Leipzig, damage to boith
satraborad inner engines and shortage of fuel but
pilot managed to keep it flying to get to Gournay
area of France before crashing. Those killed buried
Marissel, Oise, France.

P/O R.J. Cook RCAF DFM Killed age 22
F/Sgt D. Brown POW Stalag LVI
Sgt V.H.N. Thompson POW Stalag VII
F/Sgt J. Berger POW Stalag 357
Sgt R. Henderson POW Stalag 357
Sgt R.V. Weller POW Stalag L III
Sgt J. Ringwood Killed

626 Sqdn: Lane LM 380-S2
Crashed at Katzenel. Those killed buried in the
Rheinberg War Cemetery.

F/Lt W.N. Belford RAAF Killed age 23
F/Sgt A.J.P. Lee POW
Sgt T.S. Trinder Killed

Squadron and Aircraft	*Crew*
	Sgt A.J.P.. Lee Killed
	Sgt H. Hill Killed
	Sgt H.H. Mewburn Killed
	F/Sgt R. Gould Killed

28th/29th January 1944

Squadron and Aircraft	*Crew*
7 Sqdn: Lanc JB 717-V All the killed are buried in Berlin.	W/C R.E. Young POW Stalag LIII F/Lt T. Burger Killed F/Sgt A.G. Ryder POW Stalag 357 F/Sgt I.T. Taylor POW Stalag 357 F/Lt F.S. Whittlestone DFC Killed F/Lt H.J. Miller Killed Sgt S.G. Cohen Killed
7 Sqdn: Lanc JA 718-T Those killed apart from Sgt Liddle buried in Berlin. He has no known grave and is on the Runneymede Memorial. Crashed at Zuhlen.	W/O N.J. Clifford POW Stalag 357 Sgt W. Fraser Killed Sgt R.G. Brown Killed F/Sgt S. Jarvis POW Stalag LVI Sgt R.W. Willmott Killed Sgt S.M. Liddle Killed Sgt R.G. Sharp Killed
10 Sqdn: Halifax JP 133-D Shot down by a fighter over Berlin. Crew killed are on the Runneymede Memorial.	F/Lt N.W. Kilsby Killed age 20 F/Sgt D. Collumbell POW P/O G.P. Woods POW P/O S. Daggett Killed Sgt P.B. Capper POW Wounded Sgt W.R.C. Davies POW P/O D.P. Shipley POW
10 Sqdn: Halifax JN 891-P Those killed buried in Berlin or on the Runneymede Memorial.	Sgt D. Ling Killed age 21 Sgt J. Christie POW Stalag LVI Sgt G.W. Rushton POW Stalag LVI Sgt R. Biekell POW Sgt J.B. Foster Killed Sgt V. McQueen POW Stalag LVI Sgt J.C. Smith Killed
10 Sqdn: Halifax HR 952-T Those killed on the Runneymede Memorial.	P/O C. Large Killed Sgt J.G. Hodgkinson Killed later F/Sgt Sgt J.B. Spark POW Sgt R. Martin Killed Sgt G. Armstrong Killed Sgt K.R. Corbett Killed Sgt C.E. Trebilcock Killed
10 Sqdn: Halifax JD 273-Y Crew buried Aabenraa, Denmark.	Sgt A. O'Connor Killed age 24 P/O V.L. Miles Killed F/Sgt G.A. Twigge Killed F/Sgt A. Mayes Killed Sgt A. Saxty Killed Sgt J. Watters Killed Sgt T.K. Dudley Killed
15 Sqdn: Lanc ED 610-C Crew names on the Runneymede Memorial.	F/Lt D.C. Woodruff DFC Killed age 28 P/O A.J. Burcham Killed P/O R.V. Newlyn Killed P/O J.E. Hussey Killed

Squadron and Aircraft   *Crew*

Sgt R.J. Batham Killed
F/Sgt P.K.R. Gericke DFM Killed
Sgt E.E. Appleby Killed

50 Sqdn: Lanc LM 428-O   F/Lt R.P. Burtt Killed
Crashed at Steinberg.   Sgt R. Taylor Killed
                                               P/O G.R. Presland Killed
                                               P/O R.D. Betty Killed
                                               Sgt E. Brookes Killed
                                               P/O H.E. Daynes Killed
                                               Sgt J.A. Parkman Killed

51 Sqdn: Halifax LW 466-H   F/Sgt T.G. Griffin Killed
Crew are buried in Berlin.   Sgt H.J.C. Gwynn Killed
                                               Sgt L.S. Hammett Killed
                                               W/O R.F. Woods Killed
                                               Sgt A.W. Canty Killed
                                               Sgt M.A. Martin Killed
                                               Sgt S. Cameron Killed

57 Sqdn: Lanc JB 311-B   P/O K.C. McPhie Killed
Crew buried in Berlin.   Sgt F.S.G. Reeves Killed
                                               W/O K. Moreton Killed
                                               W/O J.F. MacMillan Killed
                                               Sgt S.H. Davis Killed
                                               F/Sgt W.H. Andrews Killed
                                               Sgt W.R. Weston Killed

77 Sqdn: Halifax LK 711-V   F/Sgt J.K. Pertigrew POW Stalag LVI
Shot down by a fighter over Berlin.   Sgt L.G. Sandlands Killed
                                               F/O A. Pawliuk POW Stalag LVI
                                               Lt L.D. Runshe POW
                                               Sgt J.E. Connor POW Stalag LVI
                                               Sgt A. Hague POW Stalag LVI
                                               Sgt E. Yates POW Stalag LVI

77 Sqdn: Halifax LK 729-F   P/O J. O. R. Webster Killed age 33
Crew names on the Runneymede Memorial.   P/O B.J. Kearley Killed
                                               Sgt G.C. Garner POW
                                               F/Sgt L.R. Lewis Killed
                                               F/Sgt J.W. Robinson Killed
                                               Sgt E.R. Prince Killed
                                               F/Sgt R.D. Morrison Killed

77 Sqdn: Halifax LK 709-R   F/Sgt A.B. Walker Killed
Crew buried in Berlin.   Sgt T.E. Edwards Killed
                                               F/Sgt N.T. Steele Killed
                                               Sgt D.W. Jenkins Killed
                                               Sgt K.J. Bray Killed
                                               Sgt L.R. Bright Killed
                                               F/Sgt W.P. White Killed

77 Sqdn: Halifax HR 841-T   F/Sgt R. Mc. Duncan Killed
Sgt Jarvis buried in Berlin. F/Sgt Chalk's name is   Sgt W. Cannon Killed
on the Runneymede Memorial.   F/Sgt H.H. Strecting Killed
                                               F/Sgt W.C. Thom Killed
                                               Sgt F. Jarvis Killed
                                               Sgt G.M. Jandron Killed
                                               F/Sgt K.W. Chalk Killed

83 Sqdn: Lanc JB 412-B   P/O W. Simpson POW Stalag LIII
Those killed buried Aabenraa, Denmark.   Sgt T.K. McCash Killed

Squadron and Aircraft	*Crew*
	F/Sgt J.J. Martin Killed
	Sgt W. Livesey POW Stalag LI
	P/O R. Pilgrim POW Stalag LIII
	F/Sgt J.R. Tree Killed
	F/Sgt J.A. Fell POW Stalag 357
83 Sqdn: Lanc JA 967-S Crew buried Aabenraa,Denmark. Collied in the air with HK 537-S of 463 Sqn and crashed at Broballe on the Danish Coast of Als.	F/Lt H.R. Hyde Killed age 32 Sgt R. McKerlay Killed F/Lt C.C. Lockyer Killed F/O W.B. Robson Killed F/O B.A. James Killed F/Sgt A. Waite Killed F/O P.G. Davies Killed
97 Sqdn: Lanc JB 353-L Crashed at Haagelsburg. Crew names on Runneymede Memorial.	F/Lt C.T. Smith DFC Killed Sgt T.W. Smith Killed F/Lt G.W.S. Borthwick Killed F/Lt G.A. Watling Killed F/Sgt L.G. Jones Killed F/Sgt G.K. Harper Killed F/Sgt H.J. Pleydell Killed 2/Pilot F/Lt C.T. Wilson DFC Killed
97 Sqdn: Lanc JB 712-U Crew names on the Runneymede Memorial.	F/O F. Allison DFM Killed Sgt E.S. Monaghen Killed Sgt J.C. Reynolds Killed F/Sgt T.W. Elder Killed Sgt N.D.J. Vincent Killed Sgt W. Woodward Killed Sgt A.R.E. West Killed
102 Sqdn: Halifax LW 277-Y Hit by flak over Berlin. Those killed buried in Berlin.	P/O E.W. Linsell POW Stalag LIII P/O M.J. Connolly POW Sgt G. Cullis POW Sgt L.D. Hammond Killed age 19 F/Sgt W.H. Coderre POW Stalag LI Sgt J.R. Coward POW W/O W.T. Scott POW Sgt D.E. Ward POW
115 Sqdn: Lanc DS 833-S Crew names on the Runneymede Memorial.	F/Lt K. Harris Killed age 20 F/O J. Horn Killed F/Sgt A. J.A. Chappel Killed F/O J. Harrigan Killed Sgt J. King Killed F/Sgt T.F. McLeans Killed Sgt D.R. Edmands Killed
115 Sqn: LL 649-G	P/O F.G.G. Tinn Killed P/O G.R. Adamson POW Stalag LIII Sgt. H. Roberts Killed P/O A.L.Prince Killed Sgt. C.R.L Todd Killed Sgt. P.G.Topping killed P/O A. Chaulk Killed
158 Sqdn: Halifax HX 333-J Hit by flak; aircraft abandoned over Holland.	F/Sgt D.A. Robinson POW Stalag LIII Sgt D.A Wilkinson POW Stalag LVI P/O D. Rosenthal POW Stalag LIII F/O S.E. Chapman POW Stalag LIII Sgt G.E. Hale POW Stalag LIII

Squadron and Aircraft

Crew

Sgt C.N. Durdin POW Stalag LIII
W/O L.E.J Cote POW Stalag LVI
SGT L.A. Cradell POW Stalag LVI

166 Sqdn: Lanc ND 382-Z
Crew buried in Berlin.

P/O J. Horsley DFC Killed age 22
Sgt A.W. Pilgrim Killed
F/Sgt W.G. Morgan Killed
P/O K.F. Cornwell DFC Killed
Sgt M. Smith-Crawshaw Killed
Sgt J.R. McCourt Killed
Sgt J. Davies Killed

166 Sqdn: Lanc DV 180
Those killed buried in Berlin.
Collided in the air when changing course on the
return leg and explosion followed blowing off the
nose and three of the crew were blown clear.

P/O C.C. Phelps POW Stalag LIII
Sgt E.P. Hillyard Killed
Master Sgt W.W. Mitchell (USAAF) Killed
P/O E.D. Nesbitt POW Stalag LIII
Sgt R. Winder Killed
Sgt W.H. Clarke Killed
Sgt H.R. Gibbon Killed

207 Sqdn: Lanc LM 366-H
Those killed buried in Berlin.

F/Lt J.G. Taylor Killed age 21
Sgt T.F. Westmorland Killed
P/O I. Mitchell Killed
Sgt L.A. Croxton POW
Sgt R. Hughes Killed
Sgt J.P. Rothera Killed
F/Sgt I.P. Chalmers Killed
2/Navigator Sgt D.A. Turner Killed

419 Sqdn: Halifax JP 119-O
Crew buried in Berlin.

F/Sgt P.H. Palmer Killed
P/O P. Forrest Killed
P/O G.E. Lemerick Killed. Brother also died on
    service.
F/Sgt P.T. Reilly Killed
Sgt J.H. Parrott Killed
Sgt R. Tarbet Killed
Sgt E. Milner Killed
P/O S.J. Gibson Killed

429 Sqdn: Halaifax LK 697-D
Crew are buried in Berlin. The pilot had done three
trips, the remainder of the crew two. Crew buried in
Berlin.

P/O T. Siltala Killed age 28
P/O W.A. Cook Killed
P/O A.C. McKersaic Killed
Sgt E.C. Richards Killed
WOII E.H. Cornfield Killed
Sgt H. Howson Killed
P/O K.B. Malcolm Killed

429 Sqdn: Halifax LK 746-K
Crew buried in Berlin.

P/Sgt J.L. Wilkinson POW Stalag LVI
P/O W.G. Hicks RCAF Killed
F/Sgt J. Begg Killed
Sgt R.S. Green POW Stalag LVI
Sgt J.W. Ward Killed
Sgt R.S. Drewett Killed
Sgt H.C. Clay Killed

431 Sqdn: Halifax LK 963-H
Hit by flak. Those killed on the Runneymede
Memorial.

F/Sgt M.J.J. Maher POW Stalag LVI
P/O M. Davis POW Stalag LIII
F/Sgt D. Bonokoske Killed
Sgt D.H. Lockyer POW
Sgt B.S. Rowe RCAF Killed
Sgt J.R. Bothwell Killed
Sgt T. Boyd POW

Squadron and Aircraft	*Crew*

431 Sqdn: Halifax LL 181-Q
Crew are buried in Berlin.

P/O W.R. Hewetson Killed
P/O R. MacLean Killed
Sgt AC. Thompson Killed
F/Sgt G.T. Moody Killed
Sgt NA. Bell Killed
Sgt J. Melvor Killed
Sgt G.F. Carter Killed

431 Sqdn: Halifax LL 150-N
Ditched in the sea; three crew lost with the aircraft; the others were picked up by HM Minesweepers Varonga, Prospect and Property. Sgt Raymond on the Runneymede Memorial.

F/Sgt J. Corriveau Killed
WOII J.D. Bane Killed
F/Sgt M.J. Charlebois Uninjured
Sgt S.C.B. Parker Uninjured
Sgt G.S. Webber Uninjured
Sgt J.P. Raymond RAAF Killed
Sgt R.S. Cole Uninjured

434 Sqdn: Halifax LK 649-X
Crew buried in Berlin.

F/Sgt R.H. Stanley RCAF Killed later WO age 21
P/O R.C. Crompton Killed
Sgt D.I. Rose Killed
Sgt J.C.W. Olliffe Killed
Sgt D.L. Silverman Killed
Sgt J. Ledus Killed
Sgt S.J. Groucott Killed

434 Sqdn: Halifax LL 134-U
Shot down by a fighter over Berlin.

S/L J.E. Hockey POW Stalag LIII
F/Sgt L.C. Bannister POW Stalag LVI
P/O J. Perguson POW Stalag LIII
F/Lt G.B. Poad POW Stalag LIII
P/O J.P. Acquier Stalag LIII
WOII S. Saprunoff Stalag LIII
P/O P.G. Hearsley Stalag LIII
P/O G. Borrett Stalag LIII

434 Sqdn: Halifax LK 916-D
Crew have no known grave, but are on the Runneymede Memorial.

P/O E.P. Devaney Killed
WOII C.T.E. Lee Killed
P/O W.K. Maxwell Killed
Sgt K.J. Scales Killed
Sgt V.H. McKeown Killed
F/Sgt W.H. Martin Killed
Sgt R.E. Parker Killed

434 Sqdn: Halifax LK 740-V
Crew buried in Berlin.

S/L L.M. Linnell Killed age 26
P/O A.V. Heaton Killed
P/O A.W. Hornby Killed
P/O S.W. Taylor Killed
Sgt P.P. Wicks Killed
Sgt O.D. Culverwell DFM Killed
Sgt P.J. Elms Killed

463 Sqdn: Lanc HK 537-S
Crew buried Aabenraa, Denmark.
Crashed on the Danish Coast after colliding with Lanc JA 967- of 83 Sqn while changing course for the homeword leg.

F/Lt N.P. Cooper Killed age 31
Sgt P.C.W. Bull Killed
F/Sgt L.H. Christmass Killed
W/O G.J. Kerr Killed
Sgt F.E. Robson Killed
P/Sgt H. Suthers Killed
Sgt R.J. Grist Killed

466 Sqdn: Halifax HX 294-A

S/L A.O. McCormack POW Stalag L3
F/Sgt G. Walker POW Stalag LVI
P/O J.W. Tyler Killed

Squadron and Aircraft   *Crew*

F/Sgt J.R. Clark POW Stalag LVI
F/Sgt R.A. Whitfield POW Stalag LVI
F/Sgt S.L. Smith POW Stalag LVI
Sgt R. Collings POW

466 Sqdn: Halifax HX 233-C
Shot down by a night fighter near Berlin. Those
killed buried in Berlin.

F/Lt P.W. Mack Killed
F/Sgt D.J. Cowin Killed
P/O H.G. Hunt POW
P/O N.E. Ward POW
Sgt C.J. Barton POW
F/Sgt D.S. Alexander RAAF Killed

466 Sqdn: Halifax HX 345-Y
Shot down by a night fighter. Those killed buried in
Berlin.

P/O G.B. Coombes POW Wounded
F/Sgt R.D. Hughes POW Stalag LVI
P/O R.R. Last POW
P/O L.D. Anderson RAAF Killed
F/Sgt P.P. Balderston POW LVI
P/O C.J. Trotman Killed
Sgt R. Nelson Killed
Sgt J.T. Causier POW

467 Sqdn: Lanc ED 867-L
Crew names on the Runneymede Memorial.

F/Lt I.G. Durston DFC Killed age 32
Sgt F.A. Aver Killed
F/Sgt S.J. Grifiliths Killed
F/Lt H.L. Fry Killed
F/Sgt R.L. Ludlow Killed
F/Sgt P.R. Gill Killed
F/Sgt J.W.A. Sutherland Killed

576 Sqdn: Lanc ED 888-V2
Crew buried in Berlin.

P/O E.H. Childs Killed
Sgt V.E.T. White POW Stalag LVI
Sgt R. Johostone Killed
Sgt E. Bardsley POW Stalag LVI
Sgt H.R. Bowles Killed
Sgt C.M. Brewster Killed
Sgt C.A. Giffard Killed

576: Lanc ND 386
Crew buried in Berlin.

F/Sgt E.G.Hart Killed
Sgt W.F. Ledingham Killed
F/Sgt W.D. Grant RCAF POW Stalag 357
F/Sgt J.A.L. Martel RCAF Killed
Sgt A. Thompson Killed
Sgt W.A. Owen Killed
Sgt R.V. Fairley Killed

625 Sqdn: Lanc DV 364-D
Crew names on the Runneymede Memorial.

F/Lt G.A. Spark DFC Killed
Sgt W.H. Lyssington DFM Killed
Sgt R. Latham Killed
Sgt J.E. Alves Killed
Sgt G. Bone Killed
F/Sgt L.G. Carson Killed
P/O H.J. Watkins Killed

630 Sqdn: Lanc JB 654-C
Crew have no known grave, but are on the
Runneymede Memorial.

P/O D.W. Story RAAF Killed age 24
Sgt D.E.James Killed
P/O F.J. Peacock Killed
P/O H.L.W. Cairns Killed
Sgt G.H. Barrington Killed
F/Sgt G. Dove Killed
Sgt H.J Barrons RCAF Killed

Squadron and Aircraft	Crew
630 Sqdn: Lanc JB 666 Crew buried in Berlin.	W/C J.D. Rollinson DFC Killed age 32 Sgt P.G. Kempen Killed F/Lt L. Ehrman Killed F/Sgt W.J. Rosser Killed F/Sgt A.E. Broomfield Killed Sgt S.R. Loades Killed W/O L. Christie Killed

Aircraft that crashed in the United Kingdom

Squadron and Aircraft	Crew
76 Sqdn: Lanc DK 245-G	F/Sgt W.B. Ward crashed on take off Sgt Munson and Sgt Channon killed.
102 Sqdn Halifax JD 165-S Ditched in sea.	F/S D.M.E. Pugh Pilot Safe Sgt E. Campbell Died Sgt A.A. Burgess Died Sgt R.F. Purkiss Died Remainder of the crew saved.
433 Sqdn: Halifax NK 285 Crashed at Catfoss.	F/Sgt W.A. Stiles Killed Sgt Ludlow Sgt Boissevain Injured
433 Sqdn: Halifax 231 Crew baled out eight miles NE of Thirsk, Yorks having ran out of petrol after being attacked by a Ju88. The rear gunner F/O Cox was killed after his chute fouled the aircraft on baling out.	F/Sgt J.E. Mitchell Uninjured.
433 Sqdn Halifax HX 265 Ditched in the sea.	F/O J.M. Gray All of the crew picked up safe.
434 Sqdn: Halifax EB 256 Crew baled out owing to a shortage of petrol and landed near Scarborough. Sgt W. Demers, the RIG, was killed and Sgt Dobney was injured. Sgt Demers was buried at Harrogate on 2nd February, and all his crew attended.	P/O M. Flewelling
466 Sqdn: Halifax HX 239 Crash-landed with hardly any fuel at Madask. The navigator P/O A.F. Studdes and 2nd Pilot F/Sgt F.C. Pope were slightly injured.	
466 Sqdn: Halifax HX 239 Crash-landed with hardly any fuel at Matlask. The navigator P/ A.F. Studdes and 2nd Pilot F/Sgt F.C. Pope were slightly injured.	

30th/31st January 1944

Squadron and Aircraft	Crew
44 Sqdn: Lanc ND 514-C Shot down by a fighter over Berlin. Crew buried in Berlin. Ordee given to bale out by Lyford.	P/O N.J. Lyford RAAF Killed age 22 F/Sgt A. Semple POW Stalag LVI F/Sgt J.R. Tijou POW StalagL1 F/Sgt G. Owen POW Stalag LVI F/Sgt R.G. Keen POW Stalag LVI

Squadron and Aircraft

Crew

Sgt H. Marrs POW Stalag I.1
Sgt J.A. Wainwright POW Stalag LVI

44 Sqdn: Lanc JA 843-O
Hit by flak over Berlin. Those killed buried in
Berlin.
Aircraft began to fall and then exploded in the air
throwing P/O Johnston clear.

P/O A. Johnston POW Stalag LIII
Sgt G.R. Parker Killed
Sgt C.H. Gow Killed
F/Sgt S.J. Wareham Killed
Sgt J.W. McDonald Killed
Sgt F. McPrae Killed
Sgt T.M.Jones Killed

83 Sqdn: Lanc JB 352-C
Shot down by a nightfighter on the outskirts of
Berlin. And then fell out of control.
Crew buried in Berlin.

F/Lt A.H.J. Sambridge DFC Killed
P/O H.O Scathard Killed
P/O T.E. Wilkins Killed
F/Sgt J.J. Taylor Killed
F/Sgt J.R. Maycock Killed
F/Sgt J.B. Gilbertson Killed
P/O R. Cass Killed

97 Sqdn: Lanc JB 535-Q
Crew buried Barsingerhorn, Noord-Holland,
Holland. F/Lt Clarke came from Belfast, Northern
Ireland.
Crashed at Kolhorn.

F/Lt E.S. Clarke Killed age 22
Sgt R.V.T. Bowerman Killed
P/O E.J.L. Carpenter Killed
F/O N.C. Law Killed
Sgt G. Ridley Killed
P/O T.E. Charles Killed
F/Lt R.P. Wishart Killed

97 Sqdn: Lanc JB 659-J
Crew on their 13th Operation. The aircraft was shot
down by a night fighter And crashed on a
farmhouse at Halfweg home of the Van de Bilj
family both the husband and wife plus four children
died. P/O Hart and WO Williams were buried
shortly after the crash at Haarlemmermeer but the
remainder of the crew were not recovered until
2001 and are now buried as a crew at
Haarlemmermeer. Relatives of all seven were
present at the burial.
This was a BBC TV documentry.

P/O A.R. Hart RAAF Killed age 22
Sgt K.F. Hicks Killed
Sgt L. Clifton Killed
F/Sgt H.K. Boal RAAF Killed
Sgt C.l. Williams Killed later WO
Sgt W.J.Jones Killed
Sgt C.M. Price RCAF Killed later F/Sgt

100 Sqdn: Lanc ND 360-N
Shot down by a nightfighter over Berlin. Crew
buried in Berlin.

W/O J.K. Ives Killed
Sgt D.C. Cornes Killed
W/O2 I.F. Ruppel Killed
F/Sgt R.G. Fenton POW Stalag LIII
Sgt D.P.J. Savage Killed
Sgt Johnson RCAF Killed
Sgt D Sissons Killed

100 Sqdn: Lanc ND 398-B
Crew buried in Berlin.
Crashed at Karwe

W/O J.A. Crabtree Killed age 22 later P/O
Sgt R.J. Davies Killed
F/O M.O. Rees Killed
Sgt J.W. Knight POW
Sgt F. Helm Killed
Sgt J.J. Whelan Killed
F/Sgt G.W. Box Killed

100 Sqdn: Lanc JB 673-P
Crew buried in Berlin.

F/O R.M. Parker Killed age 21
Sgt C.S. Ellis Killed
F/Sgt K.R.J.. Bradhury Killed
Sgt G. Silverwood Killed
Sgt T. Campbell Killed
Sgt E. Starkie Killed

Squadron and Aircraft	*Crew*
	F/Sgt G.A. Orchard Killed
101 Sqdn: Lanc DV 3O3-U Shot down by a fighter over Berlin. Crew buried in Berlin.	Sgt D.W. Froggatt Killed later F/Sgt Sgt L.V. Houlton Killed Sgt A.F. Graves POW Stalag VI Sgt P.E.J. Carmichael POW Stalag VI Sgt F. Charnnock POW Stalag 357 Sgt R.C. Wilson Killed Sgt G.T.J. Heath Killed P/O M. Marder Killed
106 Sqdn: Lanc ND 336-Q Crew buried Vlieland, Friesland, Holland. Crashed in the North Sea.	P/O K.H.W. Kirkland RAAF Killed age 26 Sgt W.G. Mann Killed Sgt K.W. Barry Killed F/O J. Inston Killed Sgt D. Naylor Killed Sgt R.M. Winfindale Killed Sgt R.J. Charters Killed
115 Sqdn: Lanc LL 648-J Crew buried in Berlin.	F/Lt H.G. Hicks RNAF Killed age 28 F/O B.A.W. Beer DFC Killed P/O C.F. Farquharson Killed F/Sgt A.W. Todd Killed P/O J.A. McLoughlin RAAF Killed F/O M.G. Gladwell Killed Sgt A.E. Elms Killed
156 Sqdn: Lanc JB 302-W Shot down by a nightfighter over Berlin. Those killed buried in Berlin.	W/O P. Batman POW Sgt F.E. Darycott POW Sgt F. Habbershaw Killed Sgt R.C. Crockett Killed F/Sgt W.E. Reay POW Sgt J.E. Beattie Killed Sgt D. McDonnell Killed
156 Sqdn: Lanc JA 702-Z Those killed buried Vollenhove, Overijssel, Holland.	W/O J.E. Rule RNAF Killed age 28 later P/O Sgt W.W. Cottam POW Sgt P. Coyne POW Sgt E.A. Shorter Killed F/Sgt K.R. Ball Killed Sgt G.A. Race Killed Sgt J.J. Sloan Killed
166 Sqdn: Lanc DV 406-Y Those killed buried Berlin. Nightfighter and probaly crashed into one of the Berlin lakes.	P/O J.F. Tosh Killed Sgt D. Alletson POW Sgt R.A. Morris Killed Sgt F.H. Mosen Killed Sgt E.J. Martin POW Stalag LIII Sgt R.L. Brown RCAF POW Stalag LVII Sgt R. Walton Killed
207 Sqdn: Lanc EE 173-K Shot down by a nightfighter over Berlin. Abandon with port wing on fire.	P/O R. Burnet POW Stalag LIII Sgt G. Reed POW Stalag VI Sgt K.W.C. Brown POW Stalag LVI Sgt L.J. Barnes POW Stalag 357 Sgt R.R. Hawkins POW Stalag LVI Sgt G.M. Gibb POW Stalag 357 Sgt A. Pullman Killed
207 Sqdn: Lanc ED 758-V Crew buried in Berlin.	P/O A. Moore Killed age 29 later F/O Sgt K. Burrell Killed F/O W.T. Tranmer Killed

Squadron and Aircraft   *Crew*

                                                 Sgt J. Wilson Killed
                                                 Sgt A.J.O. Archer Killed
                                                 F/O E.L. Keeler Killed

207 Sqdn: Lanc DV371-M   P/O H.D. Broad Killed
Those killed buried in Berlin.   Sgt S.K. Chalkin Killed
                                                 F/O C.E. Pointon Killed
                                                 Sgt E.W.D. Downey POW Stalag VI
                                                 Sgt J.B. Stewart Killed
                                                 Sgt C.R. Bailey Killed
                                                 Sgt G.A.N. Thompson Killed

405 Sqdn: Halifax JA 924-R   F/Lt H.L. Shackleton POW Stalag LIII
Shot down by a nightfighter at 20,000 feet when Sgt R.C. Gibson Killed
leaving Berlin. Port wing on fire and spiraled out of F/O A.H. Ashford Killed
control at 15,000 feet exploded two of the crew Sgt H. Williams POW Stalag LVI
blown clear.   Sgt J.W. Walker Killed
Those killed on the Runneymede Memorial.   Sgt T. Newton Killed
                                                 Sgt W.R. Palmer Killed

405 Sqdn: Halifax ND 493-S   F/Sgt A. Bonikowsky POW Stalag LIII
Shot down by a nightfighter on outward leg caught F/O A.R. Laberge DFC POW Stalag LIII
fire and crashed at Teschendorf. Crew names on   F/Sgt G.M. O'Neil RCAF Killed later P/O
the Runneymede Memorial.   W/O G.R. Buchanan POW Stalag L IIII
                                                 Sgt S. Einarsson Killed
                                                 F/Sgt J.M.A.L. Charest Killed
                                                 Sgt F.S. Cole POW Stalag LVI

405 Sqdn: Halifax ND 462-J   F/Lt W.A. Roberts RCAFKilled age 23
Crew buried in Berlin.   F/O E.S. Guiton Killed
Crashed at Loburg.   F/O D. Hackett DFC Killed
                                                 W/O A.B. Hazlehurst Killed
                                                 W/O 2 J.P.R. Boileau RCAF Killed
                                                 P/O A.B. Schultz RCAF Killed later F/O
                                                 Sgt I.E. Smedley Killed

463 Sqdn: Lanc ED 545-J   F/Sgt L.S. Fairclough RAAF Killed age 20 later
Crew buried in Berlin.   P/O
Crashed at Luthendorf   Sgt N.A. Vemer Killed
                                                 F/Sgt L.R. Carius RAAF Killed
                                                 F/Sgt P.K. Giles RAAF POW Stalag LIII
                                                 F/Sgt A.J. White RAAF Killed
                                                 F/Sgt J.G. McLean RAAF Killed
                                                 Sgt D. Robinson Killed

463 Sqdn: Lanc JA 973-O   P/O P.E. Hanson RAAF Killed age 23
Crew buried in Berlin.   Sgt E.A. Hughes POW Repatriated 6/2/1945
Crashed at Repente.   Sgt M.A. Stevens Killed
                                                 F/Sgt G.E. Edgecombe Killed
                                                 Sgt L. Bowes Killed
                                                 Sgt N.N. Bligh Killed
                                                 Sgt J.M.M. Wilson RAAF Killed

463 Sqdn: Lanc ED 772-G   P/O G.L. Messenger RAAF Killed
Crew buried in Berlin.Crashed at Jabel   Sgt H.W.H. Marshall Killed
                                                 Sgt M.F. Holmes POW Stalag LIII
                                                 Sgt E. Brown POW Stalag LIII and 357
                                                 Sgt F. Wooldridge Killed
                                                 Sgt R.W. Young Killed
                                                 Sgt G.C. Borradaile Killed

463 Sqdn: Lanc ED 949-A   P/O D.C. Dunn RAAF Killed age 22 later F/O

Squadron and Aircraft	*Crew*

Those killed buried in Berlin.
Shot down and crashed at Newruppin.

Sgt F.T.H. Adams Killed
F/O F.G. Fidler Killed
F/Sgt M.Y. Smith POW Stalag LVI
Sgt A.C. McConnell Killed
Sgt H. Deakin Killed
F/Sgt E.F. Gloster RAAF Killed

467 Sqdn: Lanc DV 378-C
Hit by flak and aircraft exploded. Crew buried in Berlin.

P/O A.D. Riley RAAF Killed age 28 later F/O
Sgt S.T. Tupper Killed
W/O 2 J. Valastin RCAF POW Stalag LIII
F/Sgt N.W. Allen Killed
Sgt J. Nixon Killed
W/O C.S. Baker Killed
Sgt F. Barrett Killed

514 Sqdn: Lanc DS 706-G
Crew names on the Runneymede Memorial.

F/Lt G.K. Boyd DFC killed age 25
F/Sgt P.D. Martindale Killed
Sgt L.S.J. Adkin Killed
Sgt J. Dowding Killed
Sgt R.A.D. Mirams Killed
Sgt A. Nicholson Killed
Sgt P.W. Webb Killed

514 Sqdn: Lanc DS 735-A
Those killed buried in Berlin.
Sgt Mortimer killed as a pow on a route march when attacked by RAF Typhoons 19/4/1945.

F/Lt G.J. Chequer RCAF Killed age 22
F/Sgt E.J. Wallington POW
F/Sgt K. Mortimer Killed
Sgt R. Montgomery Killed
Sgt J.L. O'Brien RAAF Killed
F/Sgt A.J. Robertson RAAF POW Stalag LVI
Sgt J.S. Carey Stalag 357
F/Sgt R.L. Gulliford POW Stalag 357

550 Sqdn: Lanc ND 396-D
Hit by flak over Berlin.
Hit by flak and crash landed 1st Operation.

Sgt G. Hunter POW Stalag LVI
Sgt J.C. Cartwright POW Stalag 357
F/O G. Pickavance POW Stalag LIII
Sgt L.I. Smith POW Stalag LVI
Sgt W.C. Frost POW Stalag 357
Sgt T.W. Vittle POW Stalag LI
Sgt C.V. Gale POW Stalag 357

576 Sqdn: Lanc W 4245-S2
Crew buried in Berlin.
Sgt Bardsley killed on a pow route march when attacked by RAF Typhoons 19/4/1945.

P/O E.H. Childs Killed
Sgt V.E.T. White POW Stalag 357
Sgt RE. Johnstone Killed
Sgt E. Bardsley Died while a POW 9/4/1945 357
Sgt H.R. Bowles Killed
Sgt C.M. Brewster Killed
Sgt C.A. Giffard Killed

622 Sqdn: Lanc ED 364-Q
Crew names on the Runneymede Memorial.

F/Lt R.J. Brown Killed age 23
Sgt A.T.W. Woolhouse Killed
Sgt F.E. Tidmas Killed
Sgt F.M. Forde Killed
F/Sgt R.W. Robertshaw Killed
Sgt W.F.S. Wootten Killed
F/Sgt .J.L. Piche Killed
Sgt W.J.T. Brodie Killed

625 Sqdn: Lanc JB 122-H
Crew buried in Berlin.

F/Sgt R. Gallop Killed later P/O
Sgt S.J. Harrison Killed
Sgt P. Rawlings Killed
Sgt G.A.J. Prigg Killed
F/Sgt P. Moylan Killed

Squadron and Aircraft	Crew
	F/O A.J. Normandin Killed
	W/O D.W.T. Johnson Killed
626 Sqdn: Lanc ME 587-X2	F/O J. Wilkinson Killed
Crew name son the Runneymede Memorial.	F/Sgt C.A.S. Noad Killed
	F/Sgt A.J. Neeson Killed
	F/Sgt A.E. Lafferty Killed
	Sgt W.A.M. Anderson Killed
	Sgt J.S. Pomeroy Killed
	Sgt R.E. Allan Killed

Aircraft that crashed in the United Kingdom

Squadron and Aircraft	Crew
50 Sqdn: Lanc DV 368-S	F/Lt Blackham
	F/Sgt H.G. Ridd Wounded
	F/Sgt J. Shuttleworth Wounded
405 Sqdn: Halifax Letter D	F/O D.E. Biden
Crashed at Coltishall with its wheels retracted, the	F/Sgt Wilkinson injured by flak in the right arm.
undercarriage being U/S after combat with a	F/O Farb and W/O Weaver wounded in the fighter
fighter.	attack.
550 Sqdn: Lanc DK 305	F/O R. Warren misunderstood an order in the air
Landed at Woodbridge with both gunners dead	and baled out; he was later found to be a POW at
after an attack by a fighter.	Stalag LIII
	Sgt J.M. Cantor Killed
	Sgt J. McKenzie Killed
	Sgt Cantor buried Willesden Jewish Cem. Middx.
	Sgt McKenzie Havelock Cemtery, Middx.
626 Sqdn: Lanc LN 584-Y2	Pilot F/O W. Breckenbridge
Attacked by a fighter.	Sgt J. Hall Killed
	Sgt J. Schwartz Wounded
	P/O W.B. Baker Wounded
	W/O R.J. Meek Wounded
640 Sqdn: Lane LW 513-W	P/O D. Affleck Killed
Crashed near Catfoss.	F/Sgt D. Price Killed
	F/Sgt S. Kennett Killed
	Sgt W Milne Killed
	P/O R. Andrews died later
	F/Sgt C. Price Killed
	P/O J. Cutler Killed

15th/16th February 1944

Squadron and Aircraft	Crew
7 Sqdn: Lanc ND 365-L	F/Lt P.K.W. Williams DFC POW Stalag III
Crashed in the water at Vornaes, Tasinge,	F/Lt A.J. Sayer Killed
Denmark. The bodies of P/O Alexander and WO	P/O J.M. Alexander CGM Killed
Hawkins were found by Marious and Inger	F/Sgt G.S. Staniforth POW Wounded Repatriated
Erichsen but were taken over by the Germans who	6/2/1945
buried them at Skaro. The bodies of F/Lt	W/O W. Hawkins Killed
Ballantyne and F/Sgt Sefton were not found until	F/Sgt N.B. Sefton Killed
after the war. They had been buried by the	F/Lt R.R..S. Ballantyne Killed

Squadron and Aircraft

Crew

Germans at Dragonkasernen and were later reburied at Svendborg. F/Lt's Sayer and Glaus are buried at Landet, they were found on the 6th of March and 30th of June respectively. Two of the crew survived the initial crash Marius Erichsen pulled one out of the water and the other one landed by parachute in a field near the coast. Shot down by a nighfighter and exploded over the Baltic, the survivors blown clear.

F/Lt L.G. Glaus Killed

7 Sqdn: Lanc ND 445-D
Crew are buried in Berlin.
Crashed nr Griebenstrasse, Linke.

S/L R.D. Campling DSO DFC Killed
F/Lt R.J.H. Clayton DFC Killed
F/Lt D.F. Langham DFC Killed
Sgt G.E. Combe Killed
F/Sgt C.H.L. Wright DFM Killed
F/Sgt B.S. Cubbage DFM Killed
W/O C.L. Quinn DFC DFM Killed

7 Sqdn: Lanc JB 414-Y
Crew buried in Berlin.

S/L J.A. Hegman RNAF DSO DFC Killed age 40
W/C J.D. Tatnall OBE Killed
P/O W.G.K. McLaren DFC Killed
F/Sgt D.E. Harrison DFM Killed (Brother also
    killed in action)
F/Sgt A.K. Buchanan DFM Killed
F/Sgt J.K. Williams Killed
F/Sgt W.D. Nichols DFM Killed
Sgt F.L. Cook POW Stalag LI

7 Sqdn: Lanc JB 224-W
Crew are buried in Berlin.

F/Lt R.L. Barnes DFC Killed
P/O J.T.D. MeLachlan Killed
F/Lt F.C. Jones DFC Killed
P/O R.C. Bett Killed
Sgt J.R. Dalziel Killed
F/Sgt E. Marshall Killed
F/Sgt E. Campbell Killed

10 Sqdn: Halifax JN 883-S
Crew are buried in Berlin.

F/O W.G. Clarke Killed
Sgt A. Williams Killed
Sgt P.J. Ferguson Killed
Sgt R.P. Harris Killed
Sgt S.Jenkins Killed
Sgt H.J. Clarke Killed
Sgt F. Coffey Killed

12 Sqdn: Lanc ND 404-R
Hit by flak over the target causing all four engines to fail. The crew baled out but Auty's parachute got cuahft on the tial and he was drawn down with the stricken aircraft.

F/Sgt J.P.Jones POW Stalag 357
Lt L.K. Oldmixon POW
Sgt R. Smithson POW Stalag 357
Sgt T.H. Adderley POW
Sgt E. Auty Killed
F/O W.J. Maltby POW Stalag III
Sgt T. Hamilton POW Stalag IVB

15 Sqdn: Lanc ED 628-O
Harris buried in Berlin. The reaminder are on the Runneymede Memorial.
Crashed into the Baltic nr Hiddensee.

F/Lt W. M. Harris RNAF Killed age 23
F/O N.G. Totty Killed
W/O H. Entwisle Killed
F/O J.S. Ragliss Killed
F/Sgt B.W. Ralph Killed
Sgt H.C.. West Killed
Sgt E.C.. Sparkes Killed

35 Sqdn: Halifax LV 861-O
Those killed buried Diepenveen, Overijssel,

P/O C.F. Blundell RAAF Killed age 28
F/Lt PG. Ranalow Escaped

Squadron and Aircraft	*Crew*

Holland. Shot down by a fighter on the homeward journey.

W/O A.W. Bennett Evaded
F/Sgt R. Moreton Evaded
Sgt R.V. Daniels Killed
F/Sgt J. Pogonoski Killed
F/Sgt A. Hazell Killed

50 Sqdn: Lanc DV 376-F
Crew buried in Berlin.

F/O HA. Litherland DFC Killed age 22
Sgt M.E. Green Killed
F/O R.A. Chilcott Killed
Sgt P. Harris Killed
Sgt E.C. Gornall Killed
Sgt M. Hartley Killed
Sgt A.W.R. Gross Killed

57 Sqdn: Lanc JB 420-S
Crew buried Blokzijl, Overrijssel, Holland.
Crashed at Blokzyl.

F/O T.W. Briggs Killed age 29
Sgt P.J. Doyle Killed
Sgt L.S.D. Swanston Killed
Sgt A. Munday Killed
Sgt H. Lewis Killed
Sgt E. Mell Killed
Sgt L. North Killed

76 Sqdn: Halifax LL 140-A
Crashed near Schweinfurt shot down by a Ju88.
Those killed are on the Runneymede Memorial.

F/Sgt D.A. Eaton POW Stalag LVI
F/Sgt R. Neal POW Stalag LVI
F/Sgt G.K. Wilson POW Stalag LVI
Sgt J.C. Harding Killed
Sgt E.B. Upton Killed
Sgt R.S. Becker POW Stalag LVI
Sgt J.A. Watson POW StalagL6

77 Sqdn: Halifax LW 341-D
Crashed at Western Baltic. Sgt Newell is buried at
Kappel at Lolland, Denmark. F/Sgt Edmonds and
Sgt Tyler are on the Runneymede Memorial.

F/Sgt A.F. Edmonds Killed age 23 later WO
Sgt J.A. Coughlin Killed
F/O R.E. Padget Killed
F/Sgt J.J.O. Kennedy Killed
Sgt C.O. Tyler Killed
Sgt N.L. Newell RAAF Killed
F/Sgt R.W. Wheeler Killed

77 Sqdn: Halifax LK 726-O
Crew buried in Berlin.

F/O G. Bodden Killed age 25
Sgt J.L. Green Killed
F/Sgt H.F.W. Gooding Killed
Sgt W.H. Beere Killed
Sgt R.C. Hall Killed
Sgt J. Smith Killed
Sgt A.L. Fairbrother Killed

77 Sqdn: Halifax LL 244-T
Crew buried Hanover.

Sgt H. Blewett Killed age 22
Sgt B. Thorpe Killed
Sgt N.L. Holder Killed
Sgt J. Wood Killed
Sgt W. Baines Killed
Sgt G. Sullivan Killed
Sgt M. Gallagher Killed

97 Sqdn: Lanc ND 478-Q
Shot down by a nightfighter over Farborg the four
bombs exploded smashing every window in the
town. P/O McLean landed at Horne Island and
walked to Nyborg where he was taken to hospital
and operated on for a bleeding ulcer. In September
1944 he was sent to Sweden and exchanged with a
German POW's and sent back to the UK. Sgt's

P/O J.F. McLean POW Stalag Ll
Sgt W.D. French Killed
Sgt A. Pestell Killed
P/O L. Stevens POW Stalag LIII
Sgt W.E. Brown Killed
Sgt R.T. Charles Killed
F/Sgt R.D. Murdoch RAAF Killed

Squadron and Aircraft	*Crew*

Brown, Charles, French, and Pestel are buried at Faborg, as is F/Sgt Murdoch.

100 Sqdn: Lanc ED 391-H
Crew names on the Runnymede Memorial

P/O E.E. Tunstall Killed age 21
F/O G.R. Balcombe Killed
Sgt J. Duguid Killed
Sgt W.C. Sharp Killed
Sgt J.M. Garde Killed
Sgt R. Parsons Killed
Sgt D.W. Young Killed
Sgt R.F.N. Allison Killed

101 Sqdn: Lanc DV 236-G
Shot down by a nightfighter over Berlin. Crew buried in Berlin.

P/O D.W. McConnel DFC Killed
Sgt C. Thompson POW Stalag 357
Sgt D. Hall POW Stalag 357
F/Sgt R.R. Clarke POW Stalag 357
F/Sgt D.W. Hall POW Stalag VI
Sgt L. Young DFM Killed (Brother died on service also)
W/O R.W. Brown POW Stalag LVI
P/O O. Fischl POW

102 Sqdn: Halifax LW 339-F
Crew buried Berlin

F/Lt A. Hilton Killed age 23
F/Sgt R.J. Paige Killed
Sgt L.F. Can Killed
Sgt F.A. Pashell Killed
Sgt A. Dean Killed
Sgt E.A. Goslin POW Stalag LVI
W/O R.F. Sykes Killed

102 Sqdn: Halifax HX 155-Q
Crew names on the Runnymede Memorial.

P/O A. Kularatne Killed age 22
Sgt R. Whitaker Killed
F/Sgt W.F. Johnson Killed
P/O JA. Downs Killed
P/O A.J. Stapleton Killed
F/O J.M. Filmer Killed
Sgt K.W. Sherlock Killed
P/O W.M.M. Manser Killed

103 Sqdn: Lanc ND 363-A
All but Lindo and Minn buried Texel, Noord-Holland, Holland.

Crashed into the Waddensee after bing shot down by a nightfighter flown by Oblt Heinz -Wolfgang Schnaper IV/NJG1.

F/Lt K.H. Berry DFM Killed age 20
P/O K. Wilcock Killed
S/L H.L. Lindo DFC Killed
F/O K.L. Atkins Killed
F/Sgt J.J. Peacock Killed
W/O W.E. Mitton Killed
F/O J.C. Southey Killed

115 Sqdn: Lanc LL 651-A4
Crew buried in Berlin.
Crashed nr Neuruppin

F/Sgt A.C. Whyte Killed
F/Sgt J.A.K. Ellis POW
Sgt J. Landles Killed
Sgt A.M. Rogers Killed
Sgt J. Adams Killed
Sgt J.H. Jones Killed
F/O C.J. Lidhetter Killed

116 Sqdn: Lanc LL 689-P
Those killed on the Runnymede Memorial.
Shot down by a nightfighter over the Ijsselmeer flwon by Oblt Heinz -Woolfgang Schnaufer IV/NJG1

F/Sgt J.P. Ralph Killed age 20 later P/O
Sgt J. Johnston POW Stalag 357
Sgt D.J. Young Killed
Sgt J.D. Tomlin POW Stalag 357
P/O J.D. Dill-Russell Killed
Sgt B.S.J. Akehurst Killed
Sgt J. Rareliffe Killed

Squadron and Aircraft   *Crew*

156 Sqdn: Lanc ND 604   F/Lt M.C. Stimpson Killed age 22
Crew names on the Runneymede Memorial.   P/O H.N. Jackson Killed
                                                F/O J.H. Wright Killed
                                                F/Sgt W.J. Catchpole Killed
                                                F/Sgt J.L. Gurton Killed
                                                F/Sgt W.H. Smith Killed
                                                F/Sgt T.R. Dutton Killed

158 Sqdn: Halifax LV 772-H   P/O R.W. Hilton RAAF Killed age 23
Those killed buried in Berlin.   Sgt J.A.T. Griffith Killed
                                                F/O R. Runciman Killed
                                                P/O M.S. Lynch Killed
                                                Sgt J.G. Howell Killed
                                                F/Sgt H.L. Munro POW
                                                Sgt G.W. Yates Killed
                                                Sgt D.G. Whittaker Killed

158 Sqdn: Halifax HX 348-O   F/Sgt W.C.M. Hogg POW
Crash landed at Trappe.   F/Sgt B.V. Millett POW
                                                Sgt P. Chamberlain POW
                                                Sgt R. McDonald POW
                                                Sgt R.H.E. McLaren POW
                                                F/Sgt G.E. Ksendz POW
                                                Sgt G.A. Naylor POW

166 Sqdn: Lanc ME 636-E   W/O G.A. Woodcock-Stevens Killed
Crew are buried in Berlin.   F/O H.J. Miller Killed
Shot down by a nighfighter and crashed between Sgt C. Glen Killed
Hagenow and Jabel   F/O H.J. Miller Killed
                                                F/Sgt L.J. Donaldson Killed
                                                Sgt R.G. Potter Killed
                                                Sgt H. Daggett Killed
                                                Sgt R. Dent Killed

166 Sqdn: Lanc ED 841-L   F/O R.J. Robinson Killed
Those killed buried in Berlin.   Sgt H.K. Harrison POW Stalag LVI
Crashed heavily into a forest nr Freudenberg.   F/Sgt R.A. Smith Killed
                                                Sgt G.F. Clarke Killed
                                                F/Sgt D.J. Stokes Killed
                                                Sgt N.O. Jones Killed

207 Sqdn: Lanc ND 510-T   P/O F.W. Cosens DFC Killed age 28
Crew name on the Runneymede Memorial.   Sgt E. White Killed
                                                Sgt M.J. Litchfield Killed
                                                Sgt J. Taylor Killed
                                                Sgt L.H. Dunlop Killed
                                                Sgt A.G. Owen Killed
                                                Sgt L.A. Field Killed

419 Sqdn: Halifax JD 456-B   P/O J.A. Parker RCAF Killed age 23
Crashed in the Western Baltic, Kiel Bay   F/O J.A. Hartnett Killed
F/Sgt Donald was found dead in the sea on the   F/Sgt J.L. Donald RCAF Killed
17th Feb, Sgt's Fournier on the 18th June and Raine   Sgt R.N. Ross Killed
on the beach at Momark on the island of Also on Sgt H.T. Raine RCAF Killed
the 21st Feb and buried o the 25th at Aabenraa. Sgt D.A. Hopper Killed
P/O Parker on the Runneymede Memorial.   Sgt N.A.G. Fournier Killed
F/Sgt Donald buried Magleby, Langeland,
Denmark. Sgt Raine is also buried in Aabenraa,
Denmark.

424 Sqdn: Halifax HX 311-A   S/L A.V. Reilander Killed

Squadron and Aircraft	*Crew*
Crew are buried in Berlin.	F/O B.W. Foskett Killed
	P/O R.W. Fisher Killed
	P/O K.W. Janes Killed
	P/O AF. Dowding Killed
	Sgt S. Lucas Killed
	F/Sgt F.W. Bartley Killed
	F/Lt R.H. Penalagan Killed
426 Sqdn: Halifax DS 794 All but F/Sgt's Love and Labach are on the Runneymede Memorial.	F/Sgt B.W. Pattle RCAF Killed later P/O
	F/Sgt P. Labach Evaded
	Sgt L.T. Proser Killed
	F/Sgt L.W. Hicks Killed
	Sgt A.B. Chester Killed
	F/Sgt W.K. Love Evaded
	Sgt O.W. Hicks Killed
434 Sqdn: Halifax LK 971 Crew names on the Runneymede Memorial.	S/L F.E. Carter RCAF Killed age 24
	F/O W. McPherson Killed
	P/O S.D. Jenkins Killed
	W/O D.G. Goodfellow Killed
	P/O E.G. Forde Killed
	P/O W.E. Rood Killed
	P/O J.W. Wheeler Killed
	P/O J.J. Blanchard Killed
466 Sqdn: Halifax HX 336-A	F/Lt J.D. Cairns POW Stalag LIII
	F/Sgt W.N. Wiffen POW Stalag LVI
	P/O P. Shine POW Stalag LIII
	F/Sgt C. Righy POW Stalag LVI
	W/O A.C.H. Oliver POW Stalag LVI
	F/Sgt J.W. French POW Stalag LVI
	Sgt G.E.O. Haggard POW Stalag LVI
466 Sqdn: Halifax HX 293-F Buried Grootegart, Groningen, Holland.	F/Sgt J.D. Wormald Killed
	F/S C. Sheldon Killed
	F/Sgt F.K. Williams RAAF Killed
	F/Sgt H.C.L. Thomas Killed
	F/Sgt T.F. Eastcott Killed
	F/Sgt R.J. Newell Killed
550 Sqdn: Lanc JA 934-H Crew names on the Runneymede Memorial.	Sgt R.W. Woodger Killed age 20 later F/Sgt
	Sgt D.L. Jones Killed
	F/Sgt A.H. Stockton Killed
	F/Sgt J.D. McIntosh Killed
	Sgt V.H. Mate Killed
	Sgt D. Willsden Killed
579 Sqdn: Halifax LW S67-Q Shot down by a fighter. Those killed buried in Berlin.	W/O J.B. Horgan RAAF Killed age 27
	P/O Linbridge POW Stalag LIII
	P/O J.K. Kerr POW Stalag LIII
	Sgt F.W. Haytnan POW Stalag LVI
	Sgt M.K. Piper Killed
	Sgt E.B. Blair Killed
	Sgt W.J. Leiper POW Stalag LVI
619 Sqdn: Lanc DV 330-O Rumble, Coleman and Paterson buried Svino, Denmark. Having crashed in Smallandsfarvant, water between Zealand and Lolland. Sgt Cole is on the Runneymede Memorial. Crashed into the Baltic.	F/O R.M. Rumble RCAF Killed age 23
	Sgt J.P.V. Cole Killed
	F/Sgt R.H. Little Killed
	F/O W.H.C. Pateman Killed
	Sgt G.H. Carpenter Killed
	F/O R.C. Parry Killed
	F/O P.J. Coleman Killed

Squadron and Aircraft	*Crew*
622 Sqdn. Lanc W 4268-A Crew are buried in Berlin. Crashed at Neu Gaarz	F/Lt G.A. Welch Killed age 22 F/Sgt J.R. Garbutt Killed Sgt S.G. Rees Killed F/Sgt K.Mc Neilson RNAF Killed Sgt F.P. Bramley Killed Sgt J. McSpadyen Killed F/Sgt M.S. Pearson Killed Sgt A. Allsop Killed
622 Sqdn: Lanc W 4272-C Crew name son the Runneymede Memorial Shot down by a nightfighter on return leg and crashed into the Ijsslmeer.	F/Lt T.L.A. Griffiths Killed Sgt H. Morrall Killed F/O R.C. Taylor Killed Sgt J.W. Grifliths Killed Sgt B.J. Allen Killed Sgt P.W. Wright Killed Sgt C.A. Brown Killed Sgt F.E.W. Chapman Killed
625 Sqdn: Lanc R 5702-Y Crashed in flames by a nightfighter at Avne Vig. Crew buried Aabenraa. The local people have placed a memorial stone at the place of the crash.	Sgt R.W.. Ashurst Killed Sgt H.R. Reardon Killed F/O H.J. Proskurniak POW Stalag LIII W/O E.T. Edwards Killed Sgt R.A. Campbell Killed F/Sgt S.W. Downes Killed Sgt C.F. Lewis Killed
626 Sqdn: Lanc JB 595-02 Shot down by a fighter over Berlin. Shot down in the area of Ejrfort by a nightfighter.	F/Sgt S.Jacques POW/Wounded Stalag 357 Sgt G.C. Farran POW Repatriated 612/1945 Sgt J.G. Morton POW Stalag 357 Sgt A.A. Phillips POW/Wounded Sgt J.E. Holford POW Stalag 357 Sgt D.C. O'Donnell POW Repatriated 6/2/1945 Sgt Seddon Stalag 357
630 Sqdn: Lanc JB 665-B Crew are buried in Berlin. Crashed nr Gustrow.	F/Lt W. English Killed age 22 P/O J.L. Richards Killed Sgt N.H. Mitchell Killed F/O J.E. Evans Killed Sgt L.V. Fussell Killed F/Sgt L.G. Lane Killed P/O D.R. Carlile Killed P/O W.P.R. Hewitt Killed

Aircraft that crashed in the United Kingdom

Squadron and Aircraft	*Crew*
106 Sqdn: Lanc JB 534 Crashed at Tumbeland Fen, hit the ground and broke in two after trying to avoid another Lancaster.	P/O R.W. Dickerson Killed Sgt G.H. Boffey Killed F/O R.H. Lewis Killed Sgt F.O.W. Pauley Killed Sgt W.C. Hills Killed Sgt B. Krukowski Injured F/O W.H.C. Ramsay Injured P/O Dickerson buried Thetford Sgt Boffey buried Ocker Hill, Staffs Sgt Lewis buried Dagneham, Essex Sgt Pauley buried Oakington, Cambs

Squadron and Aircraft

Crew

Sgt Hills buried Greenwich, London.

420 Sqdn: Halifax LW 396
Crashed after several overshoots.

F/O Dammard
WOII L.L. Whale Killed
Sgt B. Downey Killed

40 Sqdn: Lanc LW 439-E
Crashed near Thornaby, Durham.

F/S E. Vicary pilot
Crew baled out safely.

630 Sqn: Lanc JB 655-J
Crashed nr Old Bolingbroke, Lincs.

F/O K.Roberts RAAF
Sgt J.F.J. Forrest
Sgt J. Lett
Sgt W. De Kiell
Sgt J.H. Tucker
Sgt L.E. Williams
Sgt C.F. Virgo RAAF

640 Sqdn: LW 500-H
Crashed near Scarborough.

F/O H. Barkley pilot Killed
F/O J. Sommerville Killed
Sgt W.Jackson Killed
F/S J. Smart Killed
Sgt E. Brown Killed
Sgt T. Leitch Killed
Sgt A. Elkington Killed

24th/25th March 1944

Squadron and Aircraft

Crew

7 Sqdn: Lanc ND 581-M
Crew names on the Runneymede Memorial.
Shot down by a nighfighter over Berlin wreckage
spread over a wide area.

F/O J.M. Mee RNAF DFC Killed age 25
P/O D.P. Bain DFC RNAF Killed
F/Sgt V.V. Mortlock Killed
F/Sgt G.L. Grimes Killed
F/Lt L.T. Berrigan DFC Killed
F/Sgt R.A. Webb Killed
F/Sgt D.N. Luxton RNAF

7 Sqdn: Lanc ND 457-O
Crashed at Schleswig Holstein. Those killed buried
in Hamburg.

P/O TE.B. Kyle RAAF Killed
P/O D.G W. Humpherys Killed
F/Sgt J.H.D. MacDonnell RAAF Killed
Sgt R.A. Hide POW Stalag 357
Sgt F.H. Fowler Killed
Sgt C. Butson Killed
F/Sgt C. Hughes POW Stalag LIII

12 Sqdn: Lanc ND 710-L
Shot down by a Ju99 fighter and crashed at
Magdeberg. Crew buried in Berlin.

F/O G.J.G. Mariguy Killed
F/Sgt R.G.W. Beer POW Stalag 357
Sgt S.G. Bentley Killed
Sgt P. Holland POW Stalag 357
Sgt J.S. Wright POW Stalag 357
Sgt G.W. Henson Killed
Sgt E.A. Anthony Killed

12 Sqdn: Lanc JB 359-Q
Crew buried in Berlin.
Crashed nr Harzerode on return leg.

F/Lt J.H. Bracewell DFC Killed age 23
F/O D.A. Colombo DFC Killed
F/O R.H. Stevens Killed

Squadron and Aircraft

Crew

F/O A B Hunter Killed
F/Lt F.J. King RAAF Killed
Sgt H.N. Norton Killed
Sgt C.W. Hicks Killed

12 Sqdn: Lanc ND 439-K
Shot down by a night fighter and crashed at
Dalhausen. Those killed are buried in Berlin.

F/Sgt C.J. Bates POW Stalag 357
F/Sgt J.A. Bramnsall Killed
Sgt R. Plant Killed
Sgt H.F. McPherson POW Stalag 357
Sgt P.G.W. Hendon Killed
Sgt P.C. Emms Killed
Sgt D. Brown Killed

12 Sqdn: Lanc ND 65O-X
Hit by flak over Duisberg fire in the nose.
Abandon well south of track and crashed at
Geldem-Keert.

Those killed buried in the Reichswald War
Cemetery.

F/O F.C. Hentsch Killed
F/O C. Rudyk POW
Sgt E. Birch Killed
Sgt A.J. Keveren Evaded
Sgt R.M. Cringle Killed
Sgt A.C. Summers POW
F/O D.R. Wimlett Killed

15 Sqdn: Lanc LM 490-L
Shot down by a night fighter and crashed at Tetlow.
The crew are buried in Berlin.

F/Sgt L. Wheeler Killed
Sgt R. McIntosh Killed
Sgt F.D. Wells Killed
Sgt A.E. Smith Killed
F/Sgt E.D. MeCallum Killed
Sgt J. Briggs Killed
Sgt H. Longworth Killed

15 Sqdn: Lanc LM 441-T
Aircraft shot down by flak. Crew buried in the
Rheinberg War Cemetery.

F/Lt W.G. Grove Killed age 24
Sgt A.R. Jackson Killed
P/O J.A. Sills Killed
F/Sgt F.G. Holland Killed
F/Sgt A. Thompson Killed
P/O I. Tvrdeich Killed
Sgt J.A. Johnson Killed

35 Sqdn: Lanc ND 597-A
Crashed at Schonebeck-Elbe after being hit by a
nightfighter and exploding crashing at Welsleben
survivors blown out by the blast.
Those killed buried in Berlin.

S/L R.T. Fitzgerald RAAF DFC Killed
F/O J.F. Savage Killed
F/Lt W.S. Miego Stalag 9C
W/O R.A. Brewington Killed
F/Sgt F.K. Smith Killed
F/Sgt S.H. Boulton POW Stalag 357
P/O C.J. Dineen Killed

44 Sqdn: Lanc ME 672-A
Crashed at Woensel. Crew buried in Eindhoven,
Noord – Brabant, Holland.
Hit by a nighfighter.

P/O B.M. Hayes Killed
Sgt J.M. Ella Killed
Sgt R. H.J. Wellfare Killed
Sgt M. Fedoruk POW
Sgt W.K. Walker Killed
Sgt K.L. Radcliffe Killed
Sgt W.G. Perrie Killed

44 Sqdn: Lanc ND 565-C
Hit by flak after drifting of track and crashing at
Angermund.
Crew buried in the Reichswald War Cemetery.

P/O A. Evans Killed age 22
Sgt C.J. Evans Killed
F/O G.F. Garland Killed
F/Sgt P.J. Hatton Killed
F/Sgt A.G. Terrell Killed
Sgt A.P. Myles Killed
Sgt M.E. Burnard Killed
Sgt K.V. Miller Killed

Squadron and Aircraft	*Crew*
51 Sqdn: Halifax LW 539-N2 Sgt Bowthorpe is buried in Berlin.	F/O G. Mek McPherson POW Stalag LI F/O W.B. Gillespie POW Stalag LI F/O R.J.H. Nelson POW Stalag LI Sgt D.F. Bowthorpe Killed Sgt S.D. Herbert POW Sgt T. Cloutier POW Stalag LI Sgt K. Davies POW
51 Sqdn: Halifax MZ 507-P2 Those killed buried Parchim, Mecklenburg- Vorpommem, Germany.	F/Lt R. Curtis Killed Sgt W.V. Willson Killed F/Sgt J.S. Scott Killed Sgt A. Sidebotham POW Stalag LVI Sgt R. Hepworth Killed Sgt J.L. Middleton Died while a POW Sgt A.L. Taylor Killed
57 Sqdn: Lanc JB 539-S Shot down by a night fighter and crashed at Westkirchen. Crew buried in the Reichswald War Cemetery.	P/O E.P. Cliburn Killed Sgt T.J. Evans Killed F/Sgt A. Hamilton Killed Sgt L.H. Green Killed Sgt P.R. Oxlcy Killed Sgt H.A. Spencer Killed Sgt P.J. MacInness Killed
57 Sqdn: Lanc ND 671-I Crashed at Geske. Crew buried in Hanover. Hit by flak and return trip crashed at Geseke.	P/O G.A. Hampton RAAF Killed age 22 Sgt F.S. Bodkin Killed Sgt K.E.G. Nuttall POW Sgt T.J. Adkison Killed Sgt J. Milfull POW Stalag 357 Sgt C.W. Strom Killed Sgt D.C. Youngs Killed
61 Sqdn: Lanc DV 397-W Aircraft crashed at Gehrden. Crew buried in Berlin.	P/O D. Carbutt Killed Sgt J. MeCreavy Killed Sgt A. Fulker POW F/O J. Palmer Killed Sgt A.W. Sherwood Killed Sgt H.E.. Short Killed Sgt R.N. Cunningham Killed
61 Sqdn: Lanc: JB 129-G Shot down by a night fighter and crashed at Rienbeck, near Wasburg. Crew buried in Hanover.	P/O J.G. Cox RNAF Killed age 22 Sgt G.F. Lowe Killed Sgt E.G. Grundy Killed F/O E.W.T. Mellander RCAF Killed Sgt R. Peacock Killed Sgt K. Finch Killed Sgt W. Broderick Killed
76 Sqdn: Halifax LK 790-K Crashed near Gatow, Germany. Crew buried in Berlin.	F/Sgt L. Marshall RCAF Killed later P/O F/Sgt TE. Wilkinson Killed F/Sgt F.W. Kinch POW Stalag L1 Sgt P.J.F. Cramp POW Stalag L1 Sgt W. Longhorn POW Sgt W.E. Lawton POW Sgt E.J. Albon POW Stalag LI

Squadron and Aircraft   *Crew*

78 Sqdn Halifax LV 903-H   F/Lt D.F. Constable DFC Killed* age 24
Crew buried Berlin.   Sgt C.H.A. McLeod POW
                                                  Sgt T. Rateliffe POW
                                                  F/O A. Mace POW Stalag LI
                                                  Sgt D.T. Cash Killed
                                                  F/Sgt T.L. Scholar Killed
                                                  Sgt E.T. Byford Killed
                                                  F/Sgt G.T. Lovell

* Awarded immediate DFC at the end of March 1944.

78 Sqdn: Halifax LW 507-K   Sgt B.T. Smith Killed age 21 later F/Sgt
Crashed at Proyzen. Crew buried in Berlin.   Sgt L.W. Edwards POW
                                                  Sgt H. Middleton POW
                                                  Sgt S. Johnson POW
                                                  Sgt T. Willis POW
                                                  Sgt R.J. Finn POW
                                                  Sgt L. Daniels Killed

78 Sqdn: Halifax LW 518-A   F/Sgt K. Barden Killed
Crashed at Fahlhorst after being hit by flak. Crew F/O A. Lees Killed
buried in Berlin.   F/Sgt S. Davidson Killed
                                                  F/Sgt W. Spencer Killed
                                                  Sgt F. Curtis Killed
                                                  Sgt P. Cleal Killed
                                                  Sgt J. Lincoln Killed

78 Sqdn: Halifax HX 355-D   F/Lt E.W. Everett POW Stalag L1
Hit by a fighter over Berlin, but did not crash until Sgt J.R. Stewart POW Stalag L1
the Hague area.   F/O J.K.M. Green POW
                                                  Sgt J.E. Johnson POW
                                                  Sgt K.H. Jones POW
                                                  P/O A.P. Sinden POW Stalag LI
                                                  Sgt J.P. Graham POW

78 Sqdn: Halifax LW 589-G   F/Sgt H. Jackson Killed
Crashed at Fallove. Le-Hautes, Rivires, Ardennes, Sgt J. Dear Killed
France.   Sgt J. Smith Killed
                                                  Sgt H.D. Petchett Killed
                                                  Sgt P.J.S. Crawford Killed
                                                  Sgt W.G. Baker Killed
                                                  Sgt R.W. McNeil Killed

97 Sqdn: Lanc JB 671-A   P/O W.D. Coates DFM Killed
Crashed at Woensel, Eindhoven. Crew buried   Sgt B.H. Nicolas Killed
Eindhoven, Noord Brabant, Holland.   F/Sgt S. Nuttall Killed
                                                  F/O J.M. Baldwin Killed
                                                  Sgt W. Chapman Killed
                                                  Sgt W.L. York Killed
                                                  Sgt F. Thompson Killed

97 Sqdn: Lanc ND 440-H   F/O P.H. Todd POW Stalag LI
Hit by flak over the Ruhr; signal received near   Sgt S. Robson Killed
Calais on return but nothing further. Aircraft   P/O C.T.H Fuller POW
ditched between Dover and Calais Cap Gris Nez   F/Sgt J.R. Duvall POW
Area.   F/Sgt W. Housley POW Stalag 357
Sgt Robson on the Runneymede Memorial   Sgt S. McCloskey POW Injured Stalag 357
                                                  Sgt J. Cartwright POW Stalag 357

Squadron and Aircraft	Crew

100 Sqdn: Lanc ND 642-N
Crew are buried in Berlin.
Crashed nr Gruna-Laussig shot down bya nightfigher.

P/O A.J. Jenkins Killed age 31
Sgt W.J. Moore Killed
F/Sgt G.A. Saunders Killed
Sgt G. Pearson Killed
Sgr R.Mc. Ross Killed
Sgt D.G. Harris Killed
Sgt FA.L.A. Farr Killed

103 Sqdn: Lanc ME 665-C
Crew names on the Runneymede Memorial.
Exploded and crashed nr Luckenwalde.

S/L K.G. Bickers DFC Killed
F/Sgt J. Wadsworth Killed
F/O C.J. Plummer DFC Killed
F/Sgt D. Cannon Killed
F/O P.A.C. Bell Killed
F/Sgt L.J. Coiner Killed
F/O N. Tombs Killed

115 Sqdn: Lanc DS 678-J
Shot down by night fighters at Leipzig. Those killed names on the Runneymede Memorial.

P/O L.M. McCann RCAF Killed
W/O 2 H.L. Gray RCAF POW Stalag 357
Sgt W. Bowey Killed
Sgt D.G. Geach POW Stalag 357
Sgt D. Keeley Killed
Sgt V.J. Watson Killed
Sgt J.W. Burke Killed

115 Sqdn: Lanc LL 694-W
Crashed at Epse, 4 to 5 KM SE of Deventer. Crew buried Gorssel, Gelderland, Holland.
Shot down by a nightfighter flown by Hptm Martin Drewes III/NJG1 crashed at Epse.

P/O T.E. Vipond Killed age 23
F/Sgt J.L. Duffy Killed
Sgt J.E. Hammond Killed
F/O E.J. Deemer Killed
Sgt A.J. Hull Killed
Sgt R.L. Coulter Killed
Sgt A. Diggle Killed

115 Sqdn: Lanc LL 730-G
Those killed buried in Berlin.
Boam load set on fire by a nightfighter an attempt made to head for Sweden lost height and crashed in Ostseebad Renk.
Sgt Meikle baled out just before the crash.

F/Sgt I.G. Williams Killed
Sgt M.A. Ward Killed
Sgt J.W. Kearley Killed
Sgt E.A. Meikle POW Stalag L1
Sgt T.C. Watson Killed
Sgt R. Howells Killed
Sgt J.A. Morris POW Camp 344

115 Sqdn: Lanc DS 664-A4K
Shot down by a night fighter over Oberkirchen.
Those killed buried in Hanover.
Sgt Alkemade was found without a parachute in snow.

F/Sgt J.. Newman Killed
Sgt J.P. Cleary POW Stalag LVI Repartriated 6/2/1945
Sgt G.R. Burwell POW Stalag LVI
Sgt C.A.ilder Killed
Sgt N.S. Alkemade POW Stalag III
Sgt J.J..McDonough Killed
Sgt E.A. Warren Killed

156 Sqdn: Lanc JB 667-T
Crashed at Gross Benthen. Those killed buried in Berlin.

F/Lt R. Richmond Killed
Sgt H.L. Bird POW Stalag 357
Sgt J.A. Green Killed
Sgt G.P. Rae Killed
F/O R. Kearney Killed
Sgt R.J. Faulkner Killed
Sgt K.A. Ward Killed

158 Sqdn: Halifax LW 721-S

F/Sgt A.R. Van Slyke RCAF Killed age 23

Squadron and Aircraft	*Crew*
Those killed buried in Berlin.	P/O J. McGillivray POW F/Sgt J.N.A. McDonagh POW Sgt H. Ball POW Sgt W. Grant POW Sgt M. Mowbray Killed Sgt R. Whitelaw Killed
166 Sqdn: Lanc ND 620-I Last heard broadcasting winds at 2227. Those killed buried in Berlin.	F/Lt W.R. Jackson POW Stalag LI Sgt R.V. Keen POW Stalag 357 F/O B.C. Jones Killed F/O G.C. Reed Killed Sgt F. E. Fountaine Killed Sgt K.G. Mitchell Killed Sgt P.O. Owen Killed
166 Sqdn: Lanc ND 401-D Those killed buried Berlin. Crashed at Treuenbrietzen on return leg.	F/O J.L. McGill RCAF Killed age 27 Sgt J. Mowbray Killed F/O C.M. Torget POW Stalag LI F/O E.J. Underhill Killed Sgt R. Tugrnan Killed Sgt O.S. Roberts Killed Sgt E.F. Pates Killed
166 Sqdn: Lanc ED 731-Q Those killed buried in the Reichswald War Cemetery. Crashed nr Kempen on the homewood leg.	F/O T.L.W.Teasdale RCAF Killed age 21 Sgt W. Dawson Killed F/O J.B. Auld POW Stalag LI F/Sgt F.E. Johnson Killed later WO2 Sgt L. Gammage Killed Sgt D.E. Hunt Killed W/O J. Skeel Killed
166 Sqdn: Lanc ME 635-C Crew buried in Berlin.	F/Sgt E. BrownRAAF Killed age 22 later P/O Sgt J.E. Scruton Killed Sgt R. Boyde Killed F/Sgt W. Mitchinson Killed F/Sgt J. Flavell Killed Sgt W.H. Burnell POW Stalag 357 Sgt W.C. Mason Killed
207 Sqdn: Lanc ME 680-R Shot down by a night fighter, 12 km NNW of Finsterwalde. Crew buried in Berlin.	P/O G.F. Polley Killed P/O G.C. Dunkley RCAF Killed Later F/O Sgt. G. Williams Killed F/Sgt R.J. Thompson Killed Sgt D. Smith Killed Sgt R.G. Atkinson Killed Sgt W. Orr Killed
420 Sqdn: Halifax LW 373-W	F/O H.W. Rice POW Stalag LI F/Sgt C.G. Fraser POW Stalag LVI F/O NI. Altic POW Stalag L1 WO I.G. Renwick POW 2/Lt J.H. Thomson USAAF POW Sgt J.D. Boire POW Stalag LI Sgt F.G. Busehell POW
424 Sqdn: Halifax LW 435-R Crashed at Olfen. Those killed buried in Reichswald War Cemetery.	F/O W.E. Krampe RCAF Killed age 20 F/O A.G. Fleming Killed F/Sgt W.G. Tillmann POW Sgt L.G.Jewell Killed Sgt J.L. Macintosh Killed Sgt E.G. Evans Killed Sgt R.D. Wilson Killed

Squadron and Aircraft

425 Sqdn: Halifax LW 428-C
Lost at Sea. Crew names on the Runneymede
Memorial.

425 Sqdn: Halifax LW 425-V
Shot down by a night fighter at Seydon. Crew
buried in Berlin.

427 Sqdn: Halifax LK 752-V
Those killed buried in the Rheinberg War
Cemetery.

427 Sqdn: Halifax LW 574-J
Shot down by flak.
Those killed buried in the Reichswald War
Cemetery

428 Sqdn: Halifax LW 577-K
Crew buried in the Reichswald War Cemetery.

429 Sqdn: Halifax DV 914-V
Conroy had previously baled out, evaded and
returned to the UK. Now buried in Berlin.

429 Sqdn: Halifax LK 805-H
Those killed buried in Berlin.

429 Sqdn: Halifax LW 688-J
Shot down at Kiel. Those killed buried in Kiel,
Germany.

Crew

P/O N.H.Jones RCAF Killed age 28
P/O M.C. Laternell Killed
P/O J. Laviolette Killed
P/O M.H. McLeod Killed
P/O J.G. Teacey Killed
Sgt J.E. Bouchard Killed
Sgt G.W.C. Mabbott Killed

P/O JA.L.L. Renaud RCAF Killed age 21
P/O J.R. Brazeau Killed
P/O R.A. Hanks Killed
Sgt J.J. Boyer Killed
Sgt J.J. Huotea Killed
P/O C.S. Turner Killed
Sgt J.R. Nutman Killed

W/O W.F. Magdalinski POW (on his 3rd trip)
F/O R.A. Parry POW
Sgt J.V. Roberts RCAF Killed
Sgt L.C. Glasser Killed
Sgt C.M. Fugere Killed
Sgt J.P. Papineau Killed
Sgt P. Guilder POW

W/O A.E. Yaworaski Killed (on his 7th trip)
Sgt A.J. Young Killed
Sgt J.J.L. Hamel POW Stalag LVI
W/O H.R. Armstrong POW Stalag LVI
Sgt J.L. Jette RCAF Killed
Sgt R.A. McBeath RCAF Killed later F/Sgt
Sgt T.K. Rigby Killed

F/Sgt S.G. Dwell Killed (on his 7th trip)
F/O G.I. Mackay Killed
F/O O.L. Jackson Killed
Sgt M.G. Webb Killed
Sgt E.J. Halbert Killed
Sgt L.J. Lozo POW
Sgt J. Nesom POW

S/L .W. Bell DFC POW Stalag LI Navigator and
   'B' Flight Commander
Pilot F/O R.F. Conroy RCAF Killed
WOI O.D. McLean POWStalagLI
F/Lt G.W. McIntyre POW Stalag LI
F/Lt A.P. Smith POW Stalag L1
Sgt L.C.P. Spencer POW Stalag LI
Sgt G. Wilton POW Stalag LI

P/O S.A. Wick RCAF Killed age 21
WO II R.S. Clendinneng POW
F/OJ.H. Warkentin Killed
W/O H. Hull Killed
W/O S. Boustead POW Stalag L1
Sgt R.L. Kift POW Stalag L1
Sgt U. Keely Killed
P/O E.A. Giles RAAF Killed age 25
F/Sgt H.J. Nicholls Killed
F/O F.C. Rousseau Killed
Sgt R.M. Byrne Killed
F/Sgt W.T.G. Peckham Killed
Sgt W.S. Hampton Killed
F/Sgt A.W. Larochelle POW Stalag LI

Squadron and Aircraft	*Crew*
429 Sqdn: Halifax LK 806	F/Sgt Thompson pilot Sgt R.F. Budgen Baled out over Target POW
432 Sqdn: Halifax LW 593-O Those killed buried Berlin.	P/O J. McIntosh POW Stalag LI F/O A. Small POW Stalag L1 P/O R. Elvin POW Stalag L1 P/O C. Schell POW stalag LI Sgt L. Handle Killed Sgt A. Dedauw Killed Sgt W. King Killed
433 Sqdn: Halifax LV 841-H Shot down by flak crashed 5km N of Sanders Leben. Crew buried in Berlin.	F/Sgt H.W. Lossing RCAF Killed age 24 F/O D.A. Robinson Killed Sgt U.G. Davey Killed F/Sgt G.A. Dancey Killed Sgt E. Osborne Killed Sgt O.W. Sporne Killed Sgt F.E. Simons Killed
433 Sqdn: Halifax HX 284-B Crew buried in the Reicswald War Cemetery.	F/Sgt W.F. Russell RCAF Killed later P/O F/O M. Topplin POWStalagL1 Sgt W. Walmsley Killed F/O J.T. Shea POW Stalag Ll Sgt R.C. Cossar POW Stalag LVI Sgt P. McLuskie POW Stalag LVI Sgt D.W. Howell Died while a POW
460 Sqdn: Lanc ME 640-M Crew buried in the Reichswald War Cemetery. Crashed after being hit by flak at Osterbook and Teglingen.	F/Lt A.F. MeKinnon RAAF DFC Killed age 25 Sgt G.F. White Killed W/O J.I. Goodwin Killed F/O J.P. Bird Killed F/Sgt A. Craven Killed P/O G.D. Fitzgerald POW Wounded Stalag L1 F/Sgt J.D. West RAAF Killed
460 Sqdn: Lanc ND 463-S Crashed at Wusten. Those killed buried in Hanover.	P/O M.J. Cusick RAAF Killed age 20 Sgt J. Foster Killed Sgt J.W. Clifton Killed F/Sgt J.R. Martin RCAF Killed later WO2 F/Sgt P.A. Forrest POW Stalag 357 F/Sgt G.N. Speering Killed F/Sgt A. Bumpstead Killed
466 Sqdn: Halifax LV 900-H Shot down by a night fighter near Werne. Crew buried in the Reichswald War Cemetery.	F/Sgt R.L. Robertson RAAF Killed age 20 F/Sgt V.W. Bath Killed F/Sgt H.F. Smith Killed F/O E. Iveson Killed F/Sgt R.I. Cummings Killed Sgt H. Hughes Killed Sgt J. Strathern Killed
514 Sqdn: Lanc LL 625-C Crew buried in Berlin. Crashed at Worlitz on return leg.	F/O J.R. Laing Killed Sgt A. Vickers Killed F/Sgt J. Knights Killed F/Sgt G.E. Scott Killed F/Sgt R.B. McAllister POW Stalag VII Sgt C.A. Salt Killed Sgt P.C.K. Bennett Killed

Squadron and Aircraft	*Crew*

576 Sqdn: Lanc LM 469-E2
Exploded and Crashed at Kohra. Those killed buried in Berlin.

F/O P.U. Brooke Killed
Sgt E.A. Lodge Killed
T/Sgt S.G. Chidester USAF Killed
F/O N.R.G. Pronger Killed
Sgt A.E. Evans POW Stalag LVI Repatriated
   6/2/1945
Sgt A.A.S. Daines Killed
Sgt N.V. Burgess Killed

576 Sqdn: Lanc LM 471-J2
Crew buried Reichswald War Cemetery.
Crashed at Beeck having bene blown off track and hit by flak over the Ruhr.

F/Sgt L.J. Collis Killed age 27
Sgt E. Smith Killed
F/O A.C. Harper POW Stalag L1
Sgt R.J. Roper POW Stalag L1
Sgt K. MacDougall POW Stalag L1
Sgt B. Warren POW Stalag LVI
Sgt J. Robinson POW Stalag LI

578 Sqdn: Halifax LW 472-H
Those killed buried in Berlin.

P/O J.M. Row Killed age 21
F/Sgt V.R.Glaysher Killed
F/O R.J. Hayhurst POW Stalag LI
F/Sgt W.R. Crick POW
Sgt F. Eland Killed
W/O R.V. Burch Killed
W/O F.C. Wood Killed
P/O G.A. Pope 2/Pilot Killed

578 Sqdn: Halifax NZ 512-C
Crew buried in Berlin.

Sgt R.G. Arthur Killed age 22
F/O K.J. Advant Killed
F/Sgt R.J. Middlemas Killed
Sgt L.R. Morgan Killed
Sgt N.B. Lowlett Killed
Sgt P.J. Kinsella POW Stalag LI
Sgt R.C.F. Davidson Killed

578 Sqdn: Halifax LW 508-Y
Crashed at Ederbrighausen. Crew buried in Hanover.

P/O D.A. Long DFM Killed age 28
F/Sgt R.E. Priest Killed
Sgt H. Burkitt Killed
Sgt L.K. Clack Killed
F/Sgt A.W. Snowden Killed
F/Sgt W.G. Chase Killed

619 Sqdn: LancDV328-L
Crew are buried in Berlin. Crew buried in Berlin. Crashed to the south of Teltow.

P/O P. Thompson RNAF Killed age 29
Sgt B.F. Gratwicke Killed
Sgt J.L.G. Campbell Killed
F/O J.V. Leyland Killed
SgtJ J.D. Pedley Killed
Sgt L. Minshull Killed
F/Sgt J. Hay Killed

625 Sqdn: Lanc ME 684-V
Shot down and crashed between Varsseveld and Wisch.

F/Lt N.A.W. Clark POW
Sgt D.S. Beckworth Evaded
F/O A.D. Bull POW Stalag LI
F/O G. Brand POW Stalag LI
F/O R.C.T. Armytage RAAF POW Stalag L1
Sgt J.B. Remington Evaded
Sgt J. Munro Evaded

625 Sqdn: Lanc ND 641-T

W/O J.D. Owen RCAF Killed

Squadron and Aircraft	*Crew*
Crashed at Tubbergen, Holland. Crew buried Tubbergen, Overijssel, Holland.	Sgt W.H. Broadmore Killed W/O F.B. Magee Killed Sgt J.C.A.D. Lavender Killed Sgt P.H. Simpkin Killed Sgt H.W. Nixon Killed Sgt W. Clark Killed
625 Sqdn: Lanc ED 317-W Crew are buried in Berlin. Shot down by a nightfighter leaving the target area and crashing nr Nagelstedt.	F/Sgt R.D.W.Jamieson Killed Sgt E.B. Tones Killed Sgt E.G. Waller Killed F/O B.L. Rogers Killed Sgt J.I. Scott Killed Sgt J.F. Etheridge Killed Sgt J.R. Honey Killed
626 Sqdn: Lanc HK 539-A2 Crew buried in the Reichswald War Cemetery.	W/C Q.W.A. Ross Killed W/O 2 J. Gibson Killed F/Sgt C.C. Christie Killed Sgt H. Watt Killed Sgt T.W. Bint Killed F/Sgt S.W. Jones Killed F/Sgt C Nathanson Killed
626 Sqdn: Lanc LM 393-W2 Crew buried in Berlin. Shot down by a nightfighter and crashed at Liebatz.	Sgt K.H. Margetts Killed age 21 later F/Sgt P/O H.L. Shorteliffe Killed Sgt G.T. Probert Killed Sgt D.F. Brooker Killed Sgt R.W. Chandler Killed Sgt R.C. Waters Killed Sgt C.J.G. Bateman Killed
630 Sqdn: Lanc LL 886-I White buried in the Reichswald War Cemetery.	W/O J. White Killed Sgt T. Southworth 2/Pilot POW Stalag L1 Sgt F. Elwood POW Stalag LI Sgt R.J. Brydon POW Stalag L1 F/Sgt .V.E. Moor POW Stalag L1 Sgt F.P. Settle POW Stalag LI F/Sgt F.W.C. Guy POW Stalag LI Sgt J.L.A. Jukes POW Stalag L1
630 Sqdn: Lanc ND 788-U Shot down by flak over Munster.	F/Sgt A.J. Perry POW Stalag 357 Sgt J.D.. Morrison Evaded F/Sgt G.C. Hather POW Stalag LVI F/Sgt J. Duncombe POW Stalag LVI Sgt J.E. Naisbitt POW Stalag L1 Sgt M.G.C. Todd POW Stalag 357 Sgt F.J. Giblin POW Stalag LVI
630 Sqdn: Lanc ND 657-W Crashed at Lengen-Ems. Crew buried Reichswald War Cemetery.	P/O C.L.A. Allen Killed age 22 P/O K. Peacock Killed F/Sgt AS. Leyva POW Stalag LVI F/Sgt W.J. MeMeekan Killed Sgt A.E. McCormick Killcd Sgt L.R. Ingell Killed Sgt R.S. Bourne Killed
635 Sqdn: Lanc ND 704-L Crashed at Scheveld. Crew buried at Hoogeveen, Drenthe, Holland. Shot down by a nightfigher.	P/O W. Still Killed P/O E.O. Deveson Killed W/O J.N. Holmwood Killed Sgt J.L. Tillam Killed F/Sgt A.A. Stanbridge Killed

Squadron and Aircraft	Crew
	Sgt C. Talby Killed
	Sgt W.J. Sander Killed
640 Sqdn: Halifax MZ 510-Q Crew buried in the Reichswald War Cemetery.	F/O R. Hodgson Killed F/O A.H. Bunster POW Stalag LI Sgt S.E. Rayner Killed Sgt R.C. Thorne Killed Sgt E. Ayres Killed F/Sgt R.J. Draffin Killed F/Sgt F.G. Hursey Killed
640 Sqdn: Halifax LW 430-T Shot down by a night fighter north of Torgan. Crew names on the Runneymede Memorial.	P/O W.C. McLeod Killed age 31 Sgt S.W. Wheeler Killed Sgt N.L. Cooper Killed Sgt J.C. Burdett Killed Sgt RA. Turner Killed Sgt J.N. Boston Killed Sgt A.P. Webb Killed

Aircraft that crashed in the United Kingdom

Squadron and Aircraft	Crew
78 Sqdn: Halifax LW 510 Crashed at Cranfield after returning on one engine.	F/O A. Wimberley Killed F/Sgt W. Shields Killed F/O S. Kelly Killed Sgt J. Edge Killed Sgt H. Neal Killed Sgt R. Nelson Killed Sgt A. Brignell Killed
103 Sqdn: Lanc ND 572-M Crashed on landing at Dunsfold, when the brakes failed, it swung off into a Flying Fortress. The rear gunner Sgt R. Thomas had been killed in combat. Remainder of the crew were uninjured.	F/Sgt F.G. Brownings
158 Sqdn: Halifax LW 718-T Crashed on the water's edge at Cromer in a minefield after returning on two engines.	P/O K.S. Simpson Killed F/O M. Hindley Killed P/O D.J. Heinsley Killed F/Sgt W. Suddaby Killed Sgt W.A. Buchan Killed F/Sgt M.F. McKay Killed Sgt T.J. Barnett Killed
207 Sqdn: Lanc JB 693	P/O J. Lett Bomb aimer Sgt E. McDonald killed in combat.
550 Sqdn: Lanc ME 581-D	F/Lt R.W. Picton Both gunners Sgt W.H. Keen and Sgt J.W. Porteous wounded in combat.

Attacks on Berlin

1940
34 Attacks
934 Aircraft despatched of which 573 attacked Berlin
525 Tons of bombs dropped
106 Aircraft missing

1941
21 Attacks
1,011 Aircraft despatched of which 604 attacked Berlin
860 Tons of bombs dropped
20 Aircraft missing

1943
54 Attacks
7,392 Aircraft despatched of which 6,400 attacked Berlin
21,343 Tons of bombs dropped
390 Aircraft missing

1944
76 Attacks
7,055 Aircraft despatched of which 6,353 attacked Berlin
18,262 Tons of bombs dropped
340 Aircraft missing

1945
70 Attacks
4,015 Aircraft depatched of which 3,802 attacked Berlin
4,525 Tons of bombs dropped
14 Aircraft missing

Total attacks 255

Total Aircraft Missing 870

Bomb Tonnage Nov 1943 – March 44

18/19th November 1943	–	1,593.6
22/23rd November 1943	–	2,464.5
23/24th November 1943	–	1,334.5
26/27th November 1943	–	1,575.6
2/3rd December 1943	–	1,685.6
16/17th December 1943	–	1,815.0
23/24th December 1943	–	1,287.9
29/30th December 1943	–	2,314.5
1/2nd January 1944	–	1,400.4
2/3rd January 1944	–	1,116.4
20/21st January 1944	–	2,400.6
27/28th January 1944	–	1,760.5
28/29th January 1944	–	1,954.0
30/31st January 1944	–	1,960.3
15/16th February 1944	–	2,642.6
24/25th March 1944	–	3,493.1

Sources

Public Record Office References

Air 14-905	Air 14-2791	Air 24-261
Air 50-188	Air 50-185	Air 24-269
Air 34-551	Air 14-3221	Air 20-5748
Air 27-1931	Air 27-482	Air 27-836
Air 27-1980	Air 50-300	Air 20-842
Air 24-206	Air 24-265	Air 20-4890
Air 50-232	Air 8-333	Air 24-280
Air 24-294	Air 14-2222	Air 14-3012
Prem 3/14/2	Air 27-652	Air 34-544
Air 20-5748	Air 41-43	Air 24-263
Air 22-338	Air 14-621	Air 24-262
Air 22-79	Air 27-2037	Air 14-1245
Air 24-266	Air 24-264	Air 24-263
Air 20-8148	Air 14-2476	Air 2-4645
Air 50-271	Air 14-2687	Air 50-260
Air 27-128	Air 34-543	Air 14-2800
Air 24-304	Air 27-1860	Air 14-2234
Air 22-338	Air 24-262A	Air 20-842
Air 25-157	Air 14-2226	Air 8-435
Air 27-687	Air 8-440	Air 14-1616
Air 40-1397	Air 40-1345b	
Air 10-3870	Air 40-1679	Air 40-2108

Official Sources

*(Individuals to whom I am indebted
are listed in the Aknowledgments)*

Air Historical Branch (G/Capt Probert, Eric Munday
  Les Howard, Mrs Cummins)
Imperial War Museum
RAF Museum Hendon
RAF Records, Gloucester
Commonwealth War Graves
Bomber Command Association
Aircrew Association
Air Gunners Association
RAF Prisoners of War Association
RAF Escaping Society (Elizabeth Harrison)
Humberside Aircraft Preservation Society
Lincolnshire Lancaster Committee
S/L Scott-Anderson – Battle of Britain Memorial Flight

Foreign
Landesarchiv, Berlin

Newspapers
The Times

Other Sources
Battle Over The Reich – Alf Price
Lancaster Target – Jack Currie DFC

Index